LITERARY CRITICISM AND PSYCHOLOGY

YEARBOOK OF
COMPARATIVE CRITICISM

VOLUME VII

Literary

Criticism and

Psychology

Edited by

Joseph P. Strelka

THE PENNSYLVANIA STATE
UNIVERSITY PRESS

University Park and London

Library of Congress Cataloging in Publication Data
Main entry under title:

Literary criticism and psychology.

  (Yearbook of comparative criticism; v. 7)
  Includes index.
  1. Criticism—Addresses, essays, lectures.
2. Psychology and literature—Addresses, essays, lectures.
I. Strelka, Joseph, 1927–   II. Series.
PN98.P75L5   801′.95   75–27285
ISBN 0–271–01218–8

CONTENTS

PREFACE

THE PSYCHOLOGICAL PROBLEMS WITHIN LITERARY STUDY ARE MANIFOLD. The most important areas for investigation include the writer as a psychologically complex person involved in the creative process, the literary work of art itself, and, finally, the concretization of the work by the audience. Each area generates its own psychological questions. One important perspective in the context of the creative process, the work as expression by the writer and comprehension—expression's reversed process—by the reader, has been illustrated by F.W. Bateson in a scheme which he called the "literary cycle."[1] The term itself confirms that the literary student is interested in the entire creative process not as a psychological study but as a contextual concatenation in the middle of which stands his subject matter, the literary work of art. The greatest error on the part of the literary critic would be therefore to reduce a work's literary aspects to psychological means and ends, to psychologize it totally and thus virtually abandon literary criticism as an autonomous discipline altogether. A psychologist could do this legitimately, but a literary critic cannot, though this by no means precludes the critic's bringing the knowledge of psychology to bear on his own work.

Psychology thus only assists the literary scholar by providing him with different methods and means for his own study. His main task will remain the investigation of the work of art itself, from a psychological perspective as well as, of course, from many others. With regard to the work itself, the critic could be concerned with the psychological implications of character and plot in fiction or with the psychological implications of specific types of poetic utterance like imagery or rhythm. But he would concern himself with the author as a person and the elements of the creative process only to the degree that insights into both could aid him in comprehending the work in question or broadening his understanding of it. The same limitation applies to the critic's concern with the past and the process of the comprehension of the literary work of art by different critics and audiences. The critic is not interested in the psychological aspects of this process, but rather in its aesthetic ramifications.

At the beginning of this century many poetics were founded primarily on a psychological base. The unjustified predominance of psychology in literary criticism in the past has led to an apparent antipsychologism, especially among scholars of phenomenological philosophy involved in literary studies. It is, however, fair to say that the best phenomenologists have limited their rejections of psychology to the application of pedestrian and often misunderstood psychological "solutions" and to certain extreme reductions of literary problems to psychology.[2] Of course, the phenomenologists are more concerned with the subject itself—the literary work of art—than with the process by which it came into being. And, it must be remembered, the use of psychology in criticism is, like the application of historical or sociological methods, primarily genetic.

This kind of genetic psychological approach has a venerable past— it was Plato in his *Ion* who first gave a psychological account of literary creation—and its application has repeatedly produced impressive results, especially since the work of the Romantic critics. There can be no question that the contributions of Leon Edel, Lionel Trilling, Maud Bodkin, G. Wilson Knight, Josef Körner, the young Leo Spitzer, Charles Mauron, and L.S. Wygotski to literary study using psychologically oriented methods have added invaluable insights to the body of knowledge of literary criticism and theory. Their names represent only a few arbitrarily chosen examples, and the number could easily be multiplied.

The great impact of psychology on literary criticism was intimated by René Wellek in a short and excellent overall view of the main trends of twentieth-century criticism. Of the six international movements in criticism which he listed, one is primarily influenced by psychology and a second is heavily influenced by it. The first is psychoanalytic criticism, inaugurated by Sigmund Freud, and the second is connected with myth criticism and closely related to the ideas of C.G. Jung and cultural anthropology.[3]

It was certainly not accidental that behavioristic psychology proved to have almost no influence on literary criticism, though the impact of the various psychoanalytic schools, those of so-called depth psychology, has been tremendous. To be sure, there have been psychologists other than Freud and Jung who have contributed to literary criticism and around whom schools have clustered. Theodor Spoerri is one especially worthy of mention. As a representative of phe-

nomenological psychology, Spoerri started out to create a method
which he called "anthropography" and which proved unusually
fruitful when applied to the personality and work of the Austrian
poet Georg Trakl.[4]

The application of psychoanalytical methods to literary criticism
is justified mainly on the grounds that both psychoanalysis and criticism are involved in the interpretation of symbols—the symbols of
the human subconsciousness on the one hand and those of literary
language on the other. This common ground can easily be extended if
one considers that both disciplines often draw on myth in their
analyses and interpretations. Erich Fromm has pointed out some of
the most important parallels between psychoanalysis and literary
criticism in the last chapter of his book *The Forgotten Language*.[5]

Of course, psychoanalytical methods have their possibilities as
well as their limitations for literary criticism. A most excellent and
highly critical survey of both has been provided in a condensed form
by Wladimir Weidlé.[6] He warns of some of the almost mechanical
and deterministic implications in the thoughts of Freud and considers what he calls the "humanistic perception" of C.G. Jung an exception. Close inspection reveals that Freud's interpretations of fairy
tales and myths are based on the same principles as his theory of
dreams. He considers their symbolism to be a regression to earlier
stages of human development: earlier repressed libidinous satisfaction is ultimately expressed by a "compensated satisfaction" ("Er-
satzbefriedigung"), which enables man to limit the gratification of
sexual desires to the realm of the imagination. C.G. Jung and the
ingenious young Herbert Silberer were the first to oppose this view.
Silberer[7] distinguished between "anagogic" and "analytic," Jung
between "prospective" and "retrospective" interpretations of dreams.
Many more analysts subsequently went their own ways in this respect; Ludwig Binswanger[8] and Erich Fromm became especially
important for literary criticism.

The present volume of the *Yearbook of Comparative Criticism*, in
keeping with tradition, does not show partiality to any one psychological school. Several schools are represented, though I regret that
the ideas of C.G. Jung are dealt with specifically in only one article,
that of James Baird. In general, the collection of essays in this volume
illustrates the many possibilities that exist for the application of
psychological methods to literary criticism beyond those developed
and applied by Freud and Jung and the psychoanalytical tradition.
Rudolf Arnheim and Robert Durr have presented viewpoints differ-

ent from those arrived at through psychoanalytical methods, and Jean Starobinski and Morse Peckham, E. Bond Johnson, and Paul Hernadi have made contributions that are independent and personal studies in literary criticism notwithstanding the possible influence of psychoanalytical thought on one or the other.

Also included are two behavioristic studies. The first, by Charlotte Lackner Doyle, is concerned with the psychological problems of the creative process in general rather than with the literary work as the subject matter of criticism. It is complemented by Harry Slochower's article, a psychoanalytical approach to the same topic. The second behavioristic contribution by Robert Sears is more specific, as it deals with literary problems of Mark Twain's novels. In my opinion it has interesting implications for literary criticism, but at the same time it seems unlikely that this method could be applied with the same degree of success to—let us say—a metaphysical poem by John Donne. The usefulness of different psychological schools as well as critical methods in general is obviously not something absolute, but among other things is dependent on and related to the specific subject matter. When Freud himself analyzed Ibsen's *Rosmersholm* the results were overwhelming because the incest motive represents the core of the work. But a novel like Melville's *Moby Dick* seems to ask for a more Jungian approach. "Realistic" writings like the novels of Mark Twain can certainly be elucidated to some extent through a behavioristic approach.

The scope of interdisciplinary connections between criticism and psychology is so broad, however, that it is simply impossible to give a completely representative cross section of samples within one volume of essays. The metacritical survey articles on psychological methods in literary criticism by Melvin Goldstein (Anglo-American contributions), Anne Clancier (French contributions), and Peter Dettmering (German contributions) suggest a wealth of possibilities.[9] For example, psychological implications are inherent in the two "languages of literature" which Wladimir Weidlé has distinguished in contrast to the everyday language of communication. There are the psychological implications of specific passages of fiction. And a poet's peculiar idiom has consequences for psychology in terms of its autobiographical revelations (to a limited degree), but more significantly this idiom yields for inspection its own special symbolic language.

Although critics will not be inclined to reduce the problem of literary criticism entirely to psychology, but rather will use psychological means to attain their own ends, psychologists who interpret literature react differently. From their own methodological base they do so quite rightfully, though it is puzzling to see Freud analyze literary figures as if they were his patients, even if he does it in an ingenious way.[10] Jung recognizes the problem and acknowledges the autonomy of literary studies. Only if psychology could show and prove true causalities—which it cannot—could it reduce the study of literature to a mere special area of the psychological discipline itself.[11]

Of great importance is Jung's distinction between "psychological literature" in the narrower sense and "visionary literature." "Psychological literature," or what is usually called such, is of less psychological significance than "visionary literature" according to Jung, whether viewed from the perspective of the literary critic or the psychologist.[12] The distinction and its implications, in addition to what Weidlé has called Jung's "humanistic perception," seem to make the ideas of Jungian psychology especially suited for use by literary criticism. In addition, Jung's psychology guards against the oversimplification, which René Wellek stressed in his and Austin Warren's *Theory of Literature*.[13] And above all, it is flexible and openminded both in approaching literary problems—virtually ruling out any reduction of criticism to mere psychology when its methods are correctly applied—and in realizing the impossibility of ever entirely comprehending a great literary work by means of an approximation. As Aniela Jaffé once phrased it after a remarkable interpretation of E.T.A. Hoffmann's fairy tale *The Golden Pot*: each attempt to touch upon the hidden world of the soul and its images as they are expressed in a great work, and each attempt to force the work's ineffable life inside the limitations of human understanding creates necessarily the conflict of too much and too little as well as the doubt in the expressed result and the renunciation of the inexpressible one. Such attempts will be undertaken again and again, however, because of that spiritual spark which lives as a question in the hearts of men, seeking that answer which one can find only in himself and in the world around him.[14]

It only remains for me to convey my thanks to the Awards Committee of the State University of New York at Albany and especially to Vice President Louis R. Salkever for financial assistance for the purpose of editing this volume of the *Yearbook*.

JOSEPH P. STRELKA

Notes

1. *The Scholar-Critic* (London, 1972), pp. 101–10.
2. Roman Ingarden, *Das literarische Kunstwerk* (Tübingen, 1965), pp. 9–13, 289–93; *Vom Erkennen des literarischen Kunstwerks* (Tübingen, 1968), pp. 1, 12, 22, 24, 25, 123, 160, 194, 364.
3. René Wellek, *Concepts of Criticism* (New Haven and London, 1963), pp. 344–64.
4. *Georg Trakl* (Bern, 1959), pp. 7–14.
5. New York, 1951, pp. 195–263. Cf. also Joseph Strelka, "Psychoanalyse und Mythenforschung," *Zur Kritik literaturwissenschaftlicher Methodologie*, ed. Viktor Žmegač and Zdenko Škreb (Frankfurt am Main, 1973), pp. 199–200.
6. *Die Sterblichkeit der Musen* (Stuttgart, 1958), pp. 78–83.
7. Cf. *Probleme der Mystik und ihrer Symbolik* (Darmstadt, 1961).
8. Cf. Paul de Man, *Blindness and Insight* (New York, 1971), pp. 36–50.
9. Cf. Norbert Groeben, *Literaturpsychologie* (Stuttgart, 1973).
10. Sigmund Freud, *Psychoanalytische Studien an Werken der Dichtung und Kunst* (Wien-Leipzig-Zürich, 1924).
11. C.G. Jung, *Gestaltungen des Unbewussten* (Zürich, 1950), p. 7.
12. Ibid., pp. 8–26.
13. René Wellek and Austin Warren, *Theory of Literature* (New York, 1956), p. 84.
14. C.G. Jung, *Gestaltungen des Unbewussten* (Zürich, 1950), p. 593.

BASIC THEORETICAL PROBLEMS

James Baird

JUNGIAN PSYCHOLOGY IN CRITICISM
Theoretical Problems

THE PRESENCE OF CARL GUSTAV JUNG IN CRITICISM HAS ENDURED FOR half a century. Yet this presence, however commanding or repellent to scholars, is essentially indistinct. Clinical psychology, with which I am unconcerned, has no doubt reached certain categorical assessments qualifying the admissibility of Jung to scientific method. For the scholar-critic who studies and evaluates the work of art, the perseverance of Jung is cloudy and obscure at the edges. The modern interpreter of art knows of the gulf between Jung and Freud. He may have in mind Jung's own insistence upon the *visionary* as the distinctive attribute of art: "It is essential that we give serious consideration to the basic experience that underlies it—namely, to the vision." In the same statement Jung names the Freudian opposite: "The psychologist who follows Freud will of course be inclined to take the writings in question as a problem in pathology . . . to account for the curious images of the vision by calling them cover-figures and by supposing that they represent an attempted concealment of the basic experience."[1] The critic may recognize this "basic experience" as the common inheritance of humankind, a vision rising from the mysterious depths of the unconscious and given form through the medium of the artist. He may assume his critical task to be an explicator of the symbol in art as evidence of the primary, basic experience shared by all humankind. Or he may be hostile to this basic experience because it is unnamable. He will resist the persuasions of the anagogic. He may then choose to follow a Freudian problem in pathology as he conducts his reading. Or perhaps he rebels against all psychological method and turns to the anthropological premises of Frazer. In the end, he may declare the work under study an artifact, created through the sovereign choice of the artist, a making fully open to empirical inspection of its unique character. But the problem of the anagogic in the genesis of art will continue to disturb him. He cannot totally escape Jung's insistence on the unnamable vision. The perseverance of Jung is indistinct simply because the vast stores of the unconscious cannot be defined. They can be known only through the aperture of the work of art as a symbol suggesting the vision.

Certain critics who have written handbooks of modern criticism may have disavowed concerns with the basic experience. But the unanswerable questions remain. Let us assume that such questions pertain to a multiplicity of works of art, in a variety of cultures, displaying a basic impulse toward the creating of a cosmos. What commonly held basic experience is revealed, for example, by symbols in quite disparate modes of landscape architecture? The first of these, for present illustration, may be Japanese, the classic Shugaku-in, in the vicinity of Kyoto. When the sensibility and the taste of its time and its evidence of Buddhist aesthetic have been analyzed, the power of the vision has still to be encountered. This garden in its symbols of rock, flowing water, and figuratively shaped trees manifests a deep thrust toward the creation of a man-fashioned cosmos. The same thrust necessitated the symbols of the gardens in the Alhambra—polished esplanades, fountains, beasts of stone, grand allées—all fashioned through the strict geometry of sovereigns with a passion for mathematics, and yet all realize a human vision of cosmic order. There is no name for the basic experience, Japanese and Moorish. But there is a major difference in expression: in the first, a cosmos is shaped in conformity with Japanese insistence upon occult balance; in the second, a cosmos is shaped with axial exactitude. But the unanswerable question remains: what is the nature of the material in the unconscious which impels these aspirations toward the making of cosmic symbols, gardens for the magisterial seclusion of princes, and gardens now in the public domain which elicit unnamable responses of satisfaction and reverence? The viewer's response transcends a simple sensuous delight. The problem of the anagogic is there. What is the significance of the kinship he feels with the creators of these enclosures?

The same questions arise when the viewer turns to examples of disparate temple complexes. The distance between Delphi and Isphahan is immense. Yet the temples of each are treasuries erected in praise of gods. Each is a man-made cosmos, imperiously insisting upon a human knowledge of divine order. The ruins of Delphi are a celebration of the human mind, its strength displayed in columns thrusting toward the power of Zeus. The domes of Isphahan speak of the sun; and every lunette in every mosque symbolically admits light into the shadowy vault of human existence. Beyond Delphi stands the cosmos once realized in the Acropolis. Beyond Isphahan lies Persepolis, where every remaining symbol speaks of the convergence of the known world upon Darius, master and cosmic king. What does one name in these monumental evidences of *vision*? The visitor open to the power of these disparate symbols will experience a mysterious recognition. Yet he will remain inarticulate, since his recognition is closed to discourse.

The questions posed by these examples are appropriate to the basic premises of Jung. It must be stated initially that the major theories of Jung are primarily intuitive. They are founded upon what he believed to be a human sharing, common from culture to culture, in the visionary. I propose that architecture for Jung is an art of manifesting the basic experience, the vision, through symbols, varying from culture to culture, of the human impulse to reflect, or to rival, a suprahuman cosmic order. If he is an artist and not a mere utilitarian designer, the architect functions beyond the problems relating to his willed arrangement of weight, volume, and space. Architecture acts as a medium for the "flowing through" of the basic experience. His symbol is his claim upon the vision.

Some critics will be content to live with the anagogic implications of the questions just stated. Others will dismiss them as wholly unrelated to the criticism of art. But it is probably true that both groups will reject Jung as a literary critic when he turns to a long discourse upon the basic experience common to Longfellow's *Hiawatha* and the Gilgamesh epic.[2] Jung at no point in his work intended to associate himself with the profession of literary criticism. He intended to use literature only as evidence of a commonly held vision. To the professional critic Jung's alignment of Hiawatha and Gilgamesh as manifestations of an archetypal hero-reborn-from-nature will seem preposterous; and perhaps his conjoining of Longfellow's Nokomis and Hiawatha with the mythic Hera and Hercules will seem more preposterous. Obviously, such chosen affinities seem to have no place in literary criticism. But Jung was not interested in *Hiawatha* as a *form* in poetry. He was probably indifferent to the certainty of Longfellow's minor stature. Nor could he have been much concerned with the differences between an American fabricated epic and a genuine folk epic. He was in search only of evidence of the visionary as an attribute relating two examples separated by cultural differences as vast as he could discover. The foregoing questions proposed with respect to architecture in widely separated examples are again insistent as Jung himself chooses from literature. Jung is not the critic. He wishes to be the expositor of the basic experience. By this act he becomes a presence in criticism rather amorphous than distinct. He did not found a school of criticism. He created an attribute of the climate in which criticism of the last fifty years has flourished.

The purpose of the following comment is to review that portion of Jungian theory which has exerted a force in modern criticism. The problems created by the theory may be clarified. It is not assumed that the presence of Jung can be comparably and clearly identified. A possibility cannot be dismissed: the next fifty years may judge Jung to have been more the mystic than the clinician in an age anticipating a regimen of criticism as an exact science.

JUNG AND THE UNCONSCIOUS

The frames of linkage in Western thought between new and striking theory and the name of the originator quickly become too rigid for alteration. We forget that the imagination, as it plays upon theories of the past and the present, constantly wills its own anchorages in simplistic rubrics and equations. Criticism is not a creative art; it is an art of inspection and discipline. When it assumes to encompass the history of ideas formative in given bodies of primary artistic expression, it tends always to summon what it chooses from the major thinkers, and ignore the rest of the thought. The literary critic who elects to deal with mimesis returns, of course, to Aristotle. Mimesis is then equivalent to Aristotle. This is then Aristotle shorn to fit the critic's thesis. The anchorage has been made. It would have been better had the name of Aristotle been left to the philosophers. To move quickly to modern sources, I must argue that Freud and Jung have been assimilated as the critic wills. Their names become emblems of discourse. One province of Freud's theory, infantile sexuality and the libido, is plundered by the critic; and if he was an early critic, he moved toward the establishment of the tradition. Freud becomes one with infantile sexuality; the rest of Freud's thought is ignored, even his constantly careful admonition, *it may be so.*

Similarly, the name of Jung has come to mean the collective unconscious. The theory, as vital to literary criticism or absurdly irrelevant, bestows its name on Jung. The enormous range of Jung's learning in the history of religions, West and East, is peripheral to the equation, Jung = the unconscious. The equation is a misfortune, at least in criticism. I argue that the critic serves his discipline better in shunning anchorages in theory bearing the name of the maker, past or present. He should grant the persistence of his own imagination, and yet reveal to the best of his limtied abilities the intent of the artist. Certainly there is no harm in referring to ideas, historical or contemporary. But analogies are merely analogies; and the names of original thinkers, who belong rather to philosophy where they can be dealt with in their entireties, should be honestly protected from the assignments of commentators on art.

Yet the equation in which Jung is captured stands and has become traditional. The time is appropriate for new summaries of that portion of Jung's thought inviting to criticism. In restating Jung's views of the unconscious, I shall limit the discussion to literary criticism, and suggest some problems from literary analysis to which the theory might be applied.

"We mean by collective unconscious a certain psychic disposition shaped by the forces of heredity; from it consciousness has developed."[3] The disposition named cannot be defined, but it is qualified as an inheritance. This contention is not entirely original with Jung. Nietzsche had earlier named the inheritance:

> I hold, that as man now still reasons in dreams, so men reasoned also *when awake* through thousands of years; the first *causa* which occurred to the mind to explain anything that required an explanation, was sufficient and stood for truth. . . . This ancient element in human nature still manifests itself in our dreams, for it is the foundation upon which the higher reason has developed and still develops in every individual; the dream carries us back into remote conditions of human culture, and provides a ready means of understanding them better.[4]

This suggestion points to a theory of recapitulation. In my understanding, Jung is not in full agreement with Nietzsche when he speaks of the "psychic disposition shaped by the forces of heredity." Disposition means the potentiality of a mental function in an inheritance contemporaneous with the inheritance of physical, organic function.

The collective unconscious is "all the contents of the psychic experience of mankind." These contents acquire value and position through confrontation with consciousness,[5] of which reason is a function. The most striking aspect of the theory then emerges: individual consciousness is born mysteriously of the hereditary psychic disposition, from the totality of the experience of the race. The true genesis of consciousness is not in experience, but in the inheritance of disposition. If the literary critic wishes to be faithful to Jung, he must recognize the disposition of the unconscious as it urges consciousness toward the making of images and symbols to represent its material. The content of the material will, then, inevitably refer to a large province of mind apart from the artist's individual ability to create. Reason in the conscious mind governs in the making of images and symbols. But these are empty and superficial—invalid as art—if they do not reflect the content of the unconscious.

The unnamable in the deep content engenders an absolute blockage of empirical method for the critic, whose inspection must be intuitive. He can do no more than Jung did with *Hiawatha*. Comparative readings of other material enable him to say: here and here is a likeness of content, even though image and symbol differ from consciousness to consciousness. The critic is unwilling to surrender his task as interpreter to an evidence of multifarious and singular states of consciousness as paramount in the genesis of art. At this point the presence of Jung becomes indistinct. For Jung asks the critic to believe in the content of the unconscious as *ab initio* accreting in the whole cosmic process. In *Aion* Jung writes: "Sooner or later nuclear physics and the psychology of the unconscious will draw closer together as both of them, independently of one another and from opposite directions, push forward into transcendental territory, the one with the concept of the atom, the other with that of the archetype."[6] The critic will no doubt grasp at *later*. Even so, this proposed "transcendental territory" will probably tax his imagination beyond the possibility of space probes to the edge of the solar system. Jung's prediction is arcane. How can it be that the science of nuclear physics "pushing" empirically and the psychology of the unconscious "pushing" intuitively move toward convergence?

The Libido

One must go to Jung's theory of energy from the unconscious. He assigns this energy to the concept of the *libido* (at total variance with Freud's clinical concept of sexual urgency): "Libido as an energy concept is a quantitative formula for the phenomena of life. Its laws are the laws of vital energy." Turning immediately to the mysticism of a Brahman principle, Jung continues: "The way is Rita, the '*right way*,' the flow of vital energy or libido, the determined course upon which the ever-renewing process is possible."[7] Atomic energy is the force of cosmic inception, endurance, and entropy; libidinal energy is the force of urgency in the human mind to live. What methods of the laboratory are open to psychology for a measurement of this "right" way? Since Rita is not measurable in the premises of Hindu systems of meditation, does not Jung deliberately borrow an Indian terminology to name the impenetrable mystery of libido?

How, then, can libido as a concept of energy apply to the work of the critic? Presumably he can study the waxing and the waning of the individual poet's energy, and name certain symbols and images as evidence of the life force and of its diminution in prospect of death. But he has no means of analysis. He responds intuitively. He cannot even say that the life force of the artist is greater than that of other men surrounding him. As will be noted later in the theory of Jung, the artist is the person who opens his consciousness to a free flowing of the libido from the unconscious. His work is his symbol of the pulse of life. But the critic, as we have known the critic through history and as we name him now, will scarcely abdicate his position by an entrance into that "transcendental territory" predicted by Jung. He has not, and he will not be prepared to equate libidinal energy with the primal energy in the structure of matter.

The Archetype

The nature of the unconscious, as associated with the theory of Jung, is recognized in the *archetype*. Jung employs his term in the radical Greek sense: the primal image, the original form, the model. Hence the material of the collective unconscious is a collection of archetypes. But it must be understood that the archetype cannot be named until it is represented by a symbol. The term derives from the Greek *symballein*, literally, "to throw together." I take it that Jung intends in his use of the term symbol a "throwing together" of representations in the forms of images chosen by the conscious mind to describe the authoritative archetype. Jung was keenly aware of notional misreadings of his texts. In a foreword of 1956 prepared for Jacobi's study of his theory he wrote: "My critics, with but few exceptions, usually do not take the trouble to read over what I have to say on the subject, but impute to me, among other things, the opinion that the archetype is an inherited representation. Prejudices seem to be more convenient than seeking the truth."[8] The archetype is inherited, but *not* the representation of it. We may take as statements ignored by certain of Jung's misinterpreters the following:

> The archetypes are . . . the hidden foundations of the conscious mind. . . . They are systems of readiness for action, and at the same time images and emotions. They are inherited with the brain structure —indeed, they are its psychic aspect.[9]

> I mean forms or images of a collective nature which occur practically all over the earth as constituents of myths and at the same time as autochthonous, individual products of unconscious origin.[10]

> You cannot explain one archetype by another, that is, it is impossible to say where the archetype comes from, because there is no Archimedean point outside the *a priori* conditions it represents.[11]

Thus, to return to initial proposals in this essay, it may be said that the garden-cosmos in each instance cited comes of a master system of "readiness for action," from "forms of a collective nature"; that the same is true for the origin of the temple-complex-as-cosmos in each instance; that the archetype genetic in the garden symbols will not explain the archetype genetic in the temple symbols; that the diverse *representations* of the two archetypes are in no sense inherited. The impossibility of inherited representations is perhaps best expressed in this contention of Jung:

> The archetype as such is a psychoid factor that belongs, as it were, to the invisible, ultraviolet end of the psychic spectrum. . . . We must . . . constantly bear in mind that what we mean by "archetype" is in itself irrepresentable, but it has effects which make visualizations of it possible, namely, the archetypal images.[12]

This question of "archetypal images" leads to confusion unless it is understood that Jung is speaking of a pattern from the unconscious rather than of an image figuring in the consciously designed metaphor, for example, of a poem or a painting. The image is inherited, in the Jungian sense. At one point Jung chooses a vocabulary specifying *imprints* of unknown origin upon the contents of the unconscious. He speaks of "the entire succession of engrams (imprints), which from time immemorial have determined the psychic structure as it now exists." These engrams "may be regarded as function-traces which typify, on the average, the most frequently and intensely used functions of the human soul." They "present themselves in the form of mythological themes and images, appearing most often in identical form and always with striking similarity among races; they can also be easily verified in the unconscious material of modern man."[13] In the context of these premises the archetypal image is a primary model which again and again reaches expression in the history of the race. Thus, "the God-renewal is a familiar archetypal image . . . the whole complex of the dying and rejuvenating God with all its mythological precursors, down to the re-charging of fetishes . . . with magical force." "[A] new potential of energy, a new manifestation of life, a new fruitfulness have come into being. This latter analogy explains the connection . . . between the God-renewal and seasonal and vegetational phenomena."[14] The engrams, as function-traces, prompt again and again the God-renewal. They are the determinants of archetypal images which will be given a variety of representations in a sequence of God-renewals, each with its own forms of ritual. They are not the equivalents of images made by conscious minds to embody the primary image and to signify it in ritualistic modes.

The God-Imago

At some time in the long accretion of engrams God became "a function of the unconscious, namely the manifestation of a split-off sum of libido, which has activated the God-*imago*." A conception of an absolute God existing in Himself "implies a complete severance from the unconscious, which means, psychologically, a complete unawareness of the fact that the divine effect springs from one's own inner self."[15] Immediately Jung chooses a representation of this "divine effect" springing from the inner self in the mysticism of Meister Eckhart. For Eckhart, "man is truly God, and God truly man." In the confessions of Eckhart "God is a psychological, or more accurately a *psychodynamic, state.*"[16] The critic who follows Jung will not be concerned with "passages" in the history of thought, that is, with "influences."[17] No doubt there may be "reflections" of Eckhart in Rilke, just as, by another passage, there is a "reappearance" of Plato in Shelley. And to place Jung momentarily at the center, it may be argued that Wallace Stevens, among poets in the twentieth century, most closely approximates Jung's concept of "a split-off sum of the libido, which has activated the God-*imago*."[18] But the theory of Jung cannot be applied to a critical method devoted to chronologies in literary history. *This* poetry does not grow from *that* poetry preceding it. Tradition, in the usual sense of the term, is meaningless. Affinities between writers are not incidental to "influence." They are affirmed by similar thrusts from the unconscious; the nomenclature of thinkers and of schools of thought is irrelevant; and centuries may separate the likenesses.

Jung's insistence upon God as a psycho-dynamic state proposes that the critic be concerned with Romanticism. To this premise must be added Jung's notion that this God-in-man is a function reconciling opposites. Jung is the chief Western interpreter in this century of Brahmanical doctrines propounding a union of opposites through the governance of the unconscious. He finds in the concept Brahman a realization of oneness which only the archetypes can effect. "Brahman is *sat* and *asat,* the existing and the non-existing, *satyam* and *asatyam,* reality and unreality." New studies of the phenomenon of Orientalism in Romantic poetry of the nineteenth century are overdue, for Orientalism in the Jungian sense must claim its own validity. This is not evidence of an artist's reading in Vedic literature, or of the critic's lists of the artist's references. It is the emergence of an unconscious content as the Romantic artist seeks new symbols when the symbols of his society have ceased to command him. Of special interest is the decline of Christian orthodoxy in the United States and the resultant struggle to dismiss the absolute God and to celebrate the reconciliation of opposites. In the Jungian sense, the Orientalism of Emerson and Whitman, for example, is archetypal. A reading of "Uriel" or "Brahma" or "Chanting the Square Deific" suggests affinities with Jung's explorations of archetypal material in Indian thought. Yet neither poet had a wide acquaintance with Indian metaphysics. Furthermore, to speak of them as "anticipating" Jung is idle if the critic is faithful to the principle advanced above, that archetypal "instances" are not susceptible to arrangement in sequences. Romanticism, as an epoch, seems to have been essentially a liberation of the unconscious and this liberation made American Orientalism possible.

There can be no doubt that Jung regarded Indian thought as supreme. Beside it we of the West are barbarians.

Our Western air of superiority in the presence of Indian understanding is a part of our essential barbarism, for which any true perception of the quite extraordinary depth of those ideas and their amazing psychological accuracy is still but a remote possibility. In fact, we are still so uneducated that we actually need laws from without, and a task-master or Father above, to show us what is good and the right thing to do.[19]

Presumably, the taskmaster God of Judaeo-Christian inheritance was brought into being in the West by the God-imago function of the libido. But this perseverance is barbarous, or "shallow," in contradistinction to the depth of Indian knowledge of the unconscious. To put the matter of such superior awareness in terms of a full comprehension of the libido is to say that Jung equates the *power* of the unconscious with the soul.

Jung stands very close to the Wordsworth of the immortality ode when he celebrates the age of childhood. "To be 'like unto a child' means to possess a treasury of constantly accessible libido." But by degrees the child "loses himself in the world through a gradual overvaluation of things." Jung speaks of "the drawing away of libido, the severance of ties." "This is the way by which the intuitive doctrine of the religious system attempts to re-assemble the wasted energy; indeed, this harvesting-process is actually represented in its symbols."[20] Wordsworth's image of the child who comes "trailing clouds of glory. . . . From God, who is our home" may be transposed to Jung's image, the child possessor of "a treasury of constantly accessible libido."

Wordsworth's poem was begun in 1802, in the "pagan" period culminating in *The Prelude*. The language is often close to that of Christian polemics, but there is no doubt that the God named is nonabsolute. It may be argued by the critic that the poet speaks, in affinity with Jung, of the soul obscured, impoverished by the world. To possess the soul, in Jung's terms and, I think, in Wordsworth's sense is to experience the unobstructed thrust of the libido in its power of intuition, God in man, and to know joy. " 'Childlikeness,' " Jung wrote, "is . . . a symbol for the inner condition which accompanies blessedness."[21] Jung does not celebrate a symbolism of childhood in Indian mysticism, but he does exalt this "blessedness" from a vaster knowledge, in his conviction, than the West possesses. This blessedness is an awareness of the depths of the unconscious, of archetypal continuity in human existence, and of the libido, the energy of life.

The Archetype Symbolized

Jung sees the follower of Freud as a pathologist who accounts for the images of visionary experience in dreams "by calling them cover-figures."[22] Freud proposed a "censor-band," a mental function which transforms dream impulses from the sex-driven libido into cover-figures, that is, concealing images distorting the basic content. When Jung dismisses this Freudian theory, he admits to a direct "open-ness" in dream. A content of the unconscious rises without restriction. In confronting the problem of this state, Jung appears to make his first encounter with the symbol which represents the archetype. The thrust of the libido claims the mind. Jung regards the dream as "*a series of images, which are apparently contradictory and nonsensical, but arise in reality from psychologic material which yields a clear meaning*" [emphasis mine]. He continues: "Dreams are symbols in order that they cannot be understood, in order that the wish, which is the source of the dream, may remain unknown."[23]

Since the experience named dream transpires in the subconscious, it must then be taken that the *wish*, flowing from the libido, is expressed in *raw* symbols. A distinction between the dream-symbol and the symbol taking shape in consciousness should be made, though Jung is not clear on this issue. Of the symbol associated with the conscious function he is specific. "When the archetype manifests itself in the here and now of space and time, it can be perceived in some form by the conscious mind. Then we speak of a *symbol.*" The symbol comes, through a "suitable situation of consciousness," from the "dynamic nucleus" manifesting itself as a symbol.[24] If "dreams are symbols in order that they cannot be understood," how then does the symbol arise through "a suitable situation of consciousness"? What is this "suitable situation"? It must clearly differ from the scrambled psychologic material of dream. Again, for the critic, the presence of Jung is indistinct.

The raw symbols of dream must be considered apart from the symbols formed by the conscious mind, which are beyond the non-sensical, and open to rational inspection. Both groups are reflections of archetypes, but there could be no conscious artistry if the symbol were simply automatic. The literary critic may, of course, follow the theories of the Surrealists, making his own directions by imposing a Jungian context upon his problem in exchange for the customary Freudian premises usually followed by Breton and other writers. He may study the dream content of Lautréamont and Rimbaud as evidence of archetypal material scrambled in the irrationality of sleep. The symbols of the *Chants de Maldoror* and *Les Illuminations* may then appear as transcriptions from the unconscious.

But my concern here is not with Surrealism as an offshoot of psychology. I regard the raw symbols of the dream state, in Jung's theory, as evidence of the genesis of myth. Joseph Campbell is right when he assesses Jung's interpretation of mythology: it is "a group dream, symptomatic of archetypal urges within the depths of the human psyche."[25] Mythology as the raw representation of this group dream can be an area of investigation for the Jungian critic.

The critic may investigate, for example, mythic manifestations of the sea monster: the leviathan-reincarnation of Vishnu bringing the sacred Vedas from the floor of the sea; the Teutonic *middengeardes* sea serpent; the albino leviathan in the American mariners' whaling lore. But this critic is merely the explorer of raw material. He is not the reader of the consciously wrought symbol. When he becomes the critic of the symbol in art, he may confront Melville's renowned chapter on whiteness in *Moby Dick*.[26] The raw archetypal material related to mythology is to be found in the substrata of the chapter: the mystical properties of whiteness. The symbol-making power of the conscious mind, that of the artist, is revealed in Melville's choices of illustration from various provinces of human history, his "throwing together," in the sense of the Greek *symballein*, of this chosen content into a symbol of radial significance.

The critic is scarcely the critic of art if he limits himself to the raw materials of mythology. When Jung deals with problems inherent in an assessment of the art of poetry, he speaks of "the saving factor . . . the symbol, which is able to reconcile the conscious with the unconscious and embrace them both."[27] In 1916 Jung proposed that two realities will inevitably be answered to by every person.

> Just as the unconscious world of mythological images speaks indirectly, through the experience of external things, to the man who abandons himself to the outer world, so the real world and its claims find their way indirectly to the man who has surrendered himself to the soul; for no man can escape both realities. If a man is fixed upon the outer reality, he must live his myth; if he is turned towards the inner reality, then must he dream his outer, his so-called real life.[28]

In this discussion Jung studies Spitteler's *Prometheus and Epimetheus*.[29] Prometheus as the inner world, or soul, and Epimetheus as the outer world, or doer in the realm of the conscious, are polarized. Spitteler's work proposes a middle ground; it reconciles, as symbol, the conscious with the unconscious, and embraces both. Similarly, Jung's theory about polarities may be applied to *Moby Dick*. "The whale, as a denizen of the sea, is the universal symbol of the devouring unconscious. The bird, as a citizen of the luminous kingdom of the air, is a symbol of conscious thought."[30] Ahab is then the Prometheus of Melville's total symbol, the full novel. He is the victim of the inner world, of the devouring unconscious. He surrenders the "middle ground" and denies the outer reality. The sea hawk, impaled on the masthead of the sinking *Pequod*, is the conscious mind annihilated. W.H. Auden, whose early psychological allegiances turned to Freud, appears to follow Jung as he writes of Melville's novel: "The hawk in *Moby Dick* is the messenger bird of Zeus who warns Prometheus-Ahab of his hybris when he cheats the lookout by snatching away his hat, i.e., his heroic crown, but whom in its last death-defiance the *Pequod* drags down with it."[31] Jung's principle applies: the symbol reconciles Prometheus and Epimetheus, the unconscious and the conscious.

But what is to be done with a seeming discrepancy? In Jung's reflections on childhood, the state of blessedness when the libido governs, Jung contends that there is a turning from the libido as the things of the outer world preempt the vision. How is it, then, that the conscious, the outer, should be served? It seems that the symbol of "childlikeness" presented by Wordsworth's ode is inadequate because it advances the inner world as solely to be treasured. But so to insist is to reduce the poem, as well as Jung's contention, to the level of the didactic. The poem stands as a symbol, in the simple fact of its recognizing and of its fusing two states of human existence, the inner and the outer, even as Spitteler's work is an encompassing of polarities. As a symbol of another order, the poem might have proposed the middle ground.

It is interesting that Jung turns again to Oriental scriptures, extending his citations from India to China and Japan. In his discussion of types in poetry he quotes from Lao-tzu, the first chapter of the *Tao-te-ching*: "Dwelling without desire, one perceiveth its essence; changing to desire, one seeth only its outer form."[32] Jung continues to Nakae Toju, Japanese philosopher of the seventeenth century. "Ri is the world-soul, Ki the world-matter. Ri and Ki are however one and the same, inasmuch as they are attributes of God, hence only existing in and through Him. God is their union. Similarly the *soul* embraces Ri and Ki."[33] The child-symbol of Wordsworth endures in its own strength. Yet, obviously, if Wordsworth had been of the persuasions of these Oriental philosophers, we would have a different poem, and a different symbol.

The symbol representing the archetype is interpreted by Jung with attention to the time span of the individual's life. Joseph Campbell has noted precisely the differences between Freud and Jung with respect to the time span. "Sigmund Freud stresses . . . the passages and difficulties of the first half of the human cycle of life—those of our infancy and adolescence, when our sun is mounting toward its zenith. C.G. Jung, on the other hand, has emphasized the crises of the second position—when, in order to advance, the shining sphere must submit to descend and disappear, at last, into the night-womb of the grave. The normal symbols of our desires and fears become converted, in this afternoon of the biography, into their opposites; for it is then no longer life but death that is the challenge. What is difficult to leave, then, is not the womb but the phallus."[34]

The individual's life describes a circle. Jung thinks of childhood as the beginning in the life cycle of a reenactment of the sexual habitudes preserved in the unconscious, "a period in which the impulses toward these archaic inclinations appear again and again." There is a youthful correspondence "to the thought of the centuries of antiquity and barbarism."[35] Of the shift in the function of the libido from youth to age Jung writes: "In the first half of life its will [of the libido] is for growth, in the second half of life it hints, softly at first, and then audibly, at its will for death."[36] With Freud infantile sexuality will account for the "passages" of the first half of the cycle, but Jung, advancing the libido as the primal life force, then meets the second half, left relatively unexplored by Freud, and names the passages in terms of archetypes ordering, through a shift in libidinal energy, the wish for death. The wish will be marked by the conscious mind with fears. Nonetheless, it is an archetypal inevitability; and the archetypes *symbolized* appear to Jung to be persevering in the endless transmission of the unconscious: "The serpent . . . represents the fear, the fear of death, and is thought of as the antithesis to the phallus."[37]

Whether Wallace Stevens had read intently in Jung I cannot say. The published letters and the prose provide implications but no firm evidence. Yet the range of the total poetry provides a brilliant opportunity for the critic who is fully committed to Jungian theory. The complete poetic record of Stevens describes the circle. The carefully disciplined "evidences" of spring and summer seem to be lyrical namings, symbols, of the thrust of phallic vitality in the libido.

The seasonal passages of the poetry to autumn and winter describe the shift of libidinal energy to the will toward, and the fear of death. The Jungian critic will find his evidence as Stevens opens "The Auroras of Autumn" with the arresting line: "This is where the serpent lives."[38] Jung would have found the passage to the threshold of death thereafter symbolized through the late poetry of Stevens a clear archetypal representation. A Jungian commitment to a reading of Stevens will, of course, require rigid exclusions of other qualities in this poet's art.

The Genesis of Art and the Artist

"Creative man is a riddle that we may try to answer in various ways, but always in vain."[39] Here is Jung's full admission of the mystery. The soul in its inner world (Prometheus) and in its expression of the unconscious is a mystery; the "strange something" of modern man "derives its existence from the hinterland of man's mind—[and] suggests the abyss of time separating us from pre-human ages." The "something" is "a primordial experience which surpasses man's understanding. . . . It arises from timeless depths."[40] For Jung it may be proposed that these beliefs amount to a Kierkegaardian leap into faith. Since the "strange something" must be reckoned with by the literary critic who accepts Jung, the work of that critic will be judged inadmissible as criticism by his adversaries, those who argue for a rational and total knowledge of works of art. The intrusion of Jung upon the field of full critical authority has been answered to in our time by indifference and more often by fury.

All that has thus far been said in this essay leads to the question: Who is the artist? For Jung there is little possibility of middle ground for traditional criticism and its empirical schools. Traditional criticism, in any hypothetical judgment of a purely Jungian critic, must either accept, and remake itself, or reject. Jung's contention is absolutely unyielding:

> Every creative person is a duality or a synthesis of contradictory aptitudes. On the one side he is a human being with a personal life, while on the other side he is an impersonal, creative process. . . .
> Art is a kind of innate drive that seizes a human being and makes him its instrument. The artist is not a person endowed with free will who seeks his own ends, but one who allows art to realize its purposes through him . . . he is "collective man"—one who carries and shapes the unconscious, psychic life of mankind.[41]

To this Jung adds his definition of the artist in his public function:

> The work of the poet comes to meet the spiritual need of the society in which he lives, and for this reason his work means more to him than his personal fate, whether he is aware of this or not. Being essentially the instrument for his work, he is subordinate to it, and we have no reason for expecting him to interpret it for us.[42]

And elsewhere, as Jung discusses the problem of types in poetry, one reads:

> [Poets] voice rather more clearly and resoundingly what all know. . . . The mass does not understand it although unconsciously living what it expresses; not because the poet proclaims it, but because its life issues from the collective unconscious into which he has peered.[43]

Jung concedes that the public function of the great artist is not admitted by the society. "The reading public for the most part repudiates this kind of writing—unless, indeed, it is coarsely sensational—and even the literary critic feels embarrassed by it."[44] Emerson defines the poet as the *namer* in his essay "The Poet." When he writes fully as poet, the artist names existence as of the moment he writes, not for himself alone but for all his contemporaries. And yet how many of Whitman's American contemporaries tolerated *Leaves of Grass*? (Whittier said, "This will never do!" as he threw the volume into the hearth fire.) How many Americans judged Herman Melville, after the Polynesian romances and *Redburn* and *White-Jacket*, to be other than a madman? Or, for that matter, how many French readers, apart from the academicians, were disposed to "receive" the poetry of Valéry, for example, the "Ébauche d'un Serpent"? But what is the good of art, if it is the artist's transcription of the truth of the unconscious and yet is publicly rejected? The artist does not impart knowledge of the soul to contemporaneous masses. Jungian and traditional criticism must recognize that art is received exclusively by the élite, though it might be guidance and revelation for the masses. It is better to follow the judgment of Wallace Stevens in his notebook, the "Adagia." It reads: "Poetry is the scholar's art."

Shifts in Symbolic Systems

W.H. Auden quotes the following from Dryden:

> Expression and all that belongs to words is that in a poem which coloring is in a picture. . . . Expression is, in plain English, the bawd

> of her sister, the design. . . . She clothes and dresses her. . . . She
> paints her, she makes her appear more lovely than she is.[45]

This neoclassical dictum serves Auden appropriately as the antithesis of subsequent Romantic convictions. Expression as coloring and clothing of a poem such as Pope's "Windsor Forest" is displaced in Romanticism by expression as oracle. Auden notes that "it [the 'romantic reaction'] substituted imagination for reason, and in place of the man of esprit the artist as the priest-magician."[46] In Romanticism the artist is both priest and his own hero. Auden finds Wordsworth's *The Prelude* impressive with its poetic evidence, announced in its subtitle, "Growth of a Poet's Mind."[47] In its uniqueness this mind is heroic. The subject for exaltation is not, as it is with the classic poet, the deeds of others. It is the poet's oracular power, fully demonstrated for the Romantic critic in the vision closing *The Prelude* in Book XIV. Expression does not clothe design. It is the speech of the heroic soul.

I have seen no instances of Jung illustrating his theory from literary texts of anti-Romantic writers, apart from his citations of myth and of epic poetry. I suppose his predilection for Romantic art marks him as a Romantic in the brief history of psychology. But Jung's arguments centering on Romanticism as a phenomenon in recent cultural history cannot be ignored. He gives us his psychologist's reasons for the inception and the perseverance of the Romantic. Harry Levin has proposed that the mythopoeic revival of the Romantic movement came of the German "transcendental world view." "It is no mere historic accident that this impetus originated in Germany, or that it found itself pitted against the more classicized culture of France."[48] Certainly these judgments must hold. We all know that French neoclassicism flowed from the Continent into the theory and the practice of such poets as Dryden and Pope; and we know that the Romanticism of Coleridge in the *Biographia Literaria* derived deeply from German transcendentalism. But Levin, as I understand him, did not purpose to explore the origins of these "movements." Jung asks his questions at their thresholds. He directs his major attention to the beginnings and the endurance of Romanticism with, as we should expect, primary dependence upon the reassertion of archetypes.

Jung posits a theory of "extinct symbols." He studies the waning power of traditional Christian symbolic forms. These symbols, originally representations of contents of the unconscious, exerted a sovereign power over art. With their extinction, there occurred un-

conscious thrusts toward consciousness from other achetypes which
have preserved their power throughout a long period of "blockage"
by the commanding symbols inherited by consciousness. Thus Jung
is prepared to write of the "paganism" which marks Romantic art.⁴⁹

> A general attitude corresponds with a religion, and changes of re-
> ligion belong to the most painful moments in the world's history. . . .
> The religion of the last two thousand years [the Judaeo-Christian]
> is a psychological attitude. . . . But the deeper levels of the psyche
> continue . . . to operate in the former attitude, in accordance with
> psychic inertia. In this way the unconscious has preserved paganism
> alive. . . . The readiness with which the vastly older primitive spirit
> reappears can be seen in our own time, even better perhaps than in
> any other historically known epoch.⁵⁰

It is clear that, for Jung, shifts in symbolic systems come about because of losses in libidinal vitality authorizing the perseverance of
symbols. When the system is on the threshold of inertia, on the same
threshold archetypes in the unconscious (in those "systems of readiness" earlier discussed) lead in the beginnings of new symbols. Yet
the new symbols are representative of material long preserved in the
unconscious; and in the instance of a reappearing "paganism" the
material is indeed old. Modern paganism, in Jung's view, and few
even among his adversaries will dispute him, arose at the end of the
eighteenth century in the West. Contents of the unconscious from
pre-Christian "holdings" reappeared. Expression came about "in
every possible way, in aesthetics, philosophy, morals, even politics
(philhellenism)." "It was the Paganism of antiquity, glorified as
'freedom', 'naiveté', 'beauty' . . . which responded to the yearnings of
that time."⁵¹ Thus the poet-priest, in contradistinction to the artisan,
the colorist, the clothier of design in neoclassicism, arose, a "romantic"
reincarnation of pagan archetypes. Here it must be understood that
neoclassicism and Romantic paganism are distinctly unlike. The reincarnation of the pagan priest, or sacerdos, is related to the God-imago
function of the libido, for a sacerdos, in his most primitive role, is the
sayer of the arcane. Before he becomes surrounded by complex creed
and ritual, he is the purveyor of the God-imago.
    The claims made by the early Wordsworth of the "pagan" period
as recorded in *The Prelude*, by Whitman in the 1855 Preface and in
"Song of Myself," and by Mallarmé in *Igitur* have in common a
sacerdotal mode. As three disparate exemplars of the priestly role
attendant upon Romanticism, their affinities must somewhere be
encountered by the critic, Jungian or non-Jungian. It seems to me

that the critic must confront these manifestations of the anagogic in the poet's role, or not concern himself with the Romantic. The question must be asked whether it is possible for the anti-Jungian fully to criticize Romantic literature. When it comes to poetic speech bearing the marks of sacerdotal "aspiration," this problem should be recognized. I have to conclude this review of Jung and the Unconscious with this assertion: since Jung insisted upon the superior evidence, for his own purposes, of Romanticism, and since he found the release of paganism still massive,[52] it must follow that the critic who examines the literature of the West from the end of the eighteenth century onward must at least recognize the Jungian problems. If he is serious, he will yet be unable to name the archetypes represented in the symbols before him. The presence of Jung will remain for him indistinct. But he will proceed toward explorations of genesis—how the last two centuries of expression in the forms of Western art came to be—as he turns in retrospect or confronts the present. For in this procedure he will think and work in the climate in which modern criticism flourishes. Jung was one of the makers of this climate, whether the critic is prepared to accept him or not.

MODIFICATIONS AND REJECTIONS OF JUNGIAN THEORY

It may be useful to notice a few acceptances and dismissals or, perhaps better, tolerances and intolerances of Jung by modern critics. I must begin with a firm contention: no purely Jungian criticism of literature has yet appeared. But I will note some instances of a Jungian "cast" in critical theory and some examples of total rejection.

Cassirer's theory, set forth in 1924, owes something to Jung. Cassirer's base is the "lower stratum," or "the logic of language." The conceiving and the understanding of phenomena must be preceded by the act of *naming*, whereby sense impression is transposed to a mental world.[53] With Jung the representation of phenomena in the poetic act is governed by the libido and the archetypes—when the poem as symbol is uninhibited by traditional and constricting modes of expression. For Cassirer, poetry springs from a necessity of naming in the lower stratum of the mind. Yet, with this difference between the two in focus, what is to be done with Cassirer's admission of the mythic power of insight, the feeling which informs the world of illusion and fantasy, as the province of poetry? Is there not here a meeting with the challenge of Jung?

> The greatest lyric poets, for instance Hölderlin or Keats, are men in whom the mythic power of insight breaks forth again in its full intensity and objectifying power. . . . The spirit lives in the world of language and in the mythical image without falling under the control of either. What poetry expresses is neither the mythic word-picture of gods and daemons, nor the logical truth of abstract determinations and relations. The world of poetry stands apart from both, as a world of illusion and fantasy—but it is just in this mode of illusion that the realm of pure feeling can find utterance, and can therewith attain its full and concrete actualization.[54]

In the Jungian sense, the neo-Hellenic "feeling" of Hölderlin and Keats represents a content of the unconscious, archetypes initiating the conscious acts of these poets as symbol makers. In the sense of Cassirer, the compulsion comes of "mythic power," which is controlled neither by the substratum of language nor by the image central to the myth. If this power is common to both Hölderlin and Keats, it seems to be equivalent to libidinal energy in the concepts of Jung. And the writing of myth by each in the mode of illusion is described by the vision of Greece which both expressed. The lifetime of Hölderlin passed before and after the years of Keats. Yet the affinity is not a question of "influence." If the power associated by Cassirer with "the realm of pure feeling" is evident in both bodies of poetry, then it must follow that these Romantic expressions belong to the same type, however disparate the languages and cultural settings of the authors.

Maud Bodkin's *Archetypal Patterns in Poetry* has for some years been regarded as the primary example of Jungian theory applied to literary criticism. A close examination of this work indicates that the presence of Jung did prompt its method. And there is no better proof of the indistinctness of Jung's presence. Bodkin understood Jung's idea of the unconscious. She did not, however, commit herself to a strict Jungian mode in the criticism undertaken. She found Jung's evidence "hard to evaluate; especially in view of the way in which certain surprising reproductions, in trance states, of old material, have been subsequently traced to forgotten impressions of sense in the lifetime of the individual."[55] What Bodkin means by an archetypal pattern is a discernible and recurring mode of feeling in the individual poet which evokes "old material" reproduced in "trance states," material accruing from earlier sense impressions. She proposes that the reader of the poetry is able to recognize the pattern by affinities between his own feeling and that projected by the poet.

This initial insistence of Bodkin on "forgotten impressions" of both poet and "sympathetic" reader gets in the way of an unadulterated Jungian approach. The arguments of the book are constantly punctuated with unresolved questions. Discussing "archetypal caverns" (for example, the caverns in the sixth book of the *Aeneid*, in Dante's *Inferno*, and in Coleridge's "Kubla Khan"), Bodkin writes: "Is it possible that this strong association of the cavern with the mysterious archaic depths of the mind itself . . . which poets have felt who never knew these cavern sanctuaries, is actually in some way influenced or determined by traces transmitted from the remote experience of which these caverns give evidence?"[56] The question is typical, reflecting the presence of Jung without full commitment. Bodkin concludes her work with the following: "the patterns, viewed psychologically, may be described as organizations of emotional tendencies, determined partly through the distinctive experience of the race or community within whose history the theme has arisen."[57] This conclusion is tentative. Presumably archetypal caverns are "organizations of emotional tendencies." They are not named as deriving from the collective unconscious. One notes here the close qualification, the community in which the theme has arisen. It is clear that Jung makes Bodkin's study possible. But the premises of the work are by no means firm; and often it is impossible to determine whether Bodkin is an objective critic or a subjective confessor as she explores affinities between her own "trance states" and those of a poet under discussion.

Some critics have rejected Jung, but they are still indebted to him. The currency of the term *archetype* resulted from Jung's wide use of it, in spite of the non-Jungian connotations placed on it. If the term appears in a title, many readers suppose that Jung is again expounded. But if the debt implied is not acknowledged, some virtue rests in the explicitness of recent critics in initial definitions of uses to which the term will be put. Introducing his theory in *Cosmos and History*, Mircea Eliade writes: "I nowhere touch upon the problems of depth psychology nor do I use the concept of the collective unconscious." "I use the term 'archetype' . . . as a synonym for 'exemplary model' or 'paradigm,' that is, in the last analysis, in the Augustinian sense."[58] In a second instance of such separateness from Jung, Philip Wheelwright equates symbols displaying "humanistic universality"[59] (such as the sky father, the earth mother, the serpent, the eye of the sun, the ear of grain, the vine) with archetypes. Eliade associates the paradigm with Augustinian concepts of the predestined. Wheelwright chooses an approximation of anthropological method. He intends full independence of Jung, whom he then judges to have discredited his approach by flouting empirical procedures.[60]

The New Criticism, beginning with Eliot and Pound, and extending through Tate, Ransom, Brooks, Warren, and others, has been written into literary history. Its primary legacy is its long sequence of models and handbooks. But its prolific instruction seems to far surpass in volume the accretions of theory (in special, directed modes of reading literature) through the English "humanistic" centuries since the late Renaissance. The curious aspect seems to be associated with the avowed principle of scrutiny, with the critic's claim on absolute readings of the literary forms before him. Literary history will, no doubt, judge this long aegis in our century as a criticism aspiring, in an age dominated by science, to make of itself a science.

But the aftermath of New Criticism has been marked with distinction by Northrop Frye in *Anatomy of Criticism*. This work stands, since its appearance in 1957, as the authoritative handbook for the present. In its eminent clarity it puts the work of contemporary abstruse theorists, such as Kenneth Burke, at a disadvantage. Frye speaks in the aftermath, but he nonetheless inherits the explicitness of his predecessors. Frye's use of the term *archetype* leaves us in no doubt. Jung and the collective unconscious are fully rejected.[61] "Archetypal criticism" is given its place among the several criticisms defined. But its function is limited to an inspection of literature in terms of the "relation of content to form only, not one of source to derivation."[62] The mythopoeic in the evidence of literature is an evidence of mimesis. Myth, for Frye, is "the imitation of actions near or at the conceivable limits of desire."[63] Classical mythology is regarded as "a grammar of literary archetypes."[64] Thus, in his third essay, Frye contends that archetypal criticism applied to myth produces the following categories: comedy as the mythos of spring,[65] romance as that of summer, tragedy as that of autumn, irony and satire as that of winter. The archetypes are, then, inevitable *forms* governing again and again in the histories of all literatures. The critic's task is to demonstrate the relation of chosen works to the forms. To study the archetypes is to choose one mode of critical investigation. But in so choosing, the critic is admonished. "On the archetypal level proper, where poetry is an artifact of human civilization, nature is the container of man. [Hence the relation of mythos to the seasons, I assume.] On the anagogic level, man is the container of nature, and his cities and gardens are no longer little hollowings on the surface of the earth, but the forms of a human universe."[66] If man is contained in nature, and if the artist is the maker of artifacts expressing this relationship, then the reflection of seasonal passage in the archetypes of mythos effectually denies the anagogic, and the sacerdotal role of the artist. Reference to my opening comment on the Jungian perceiver in his encounter with garden and temple architecture is here invited. He will perceive, and sense, on "the anagogic level"; he will assume humankind to be, in the context of Frye's judgment, containers of nature.

VARIABLES WITHIN CRITICAL RESPONSIBILITY

The chief value of Northrop Frye for criticism derives from his insistence upon postulates of criticism growing out of art. Frye attacks all determinisms in criticism, for example, Marxist, Thomist, liberal-humanist, neoclassical, Freudian, Jungian, or existentialist.[67] The critic's job is to allow his critical principles to be shaped by his encounter with literature. "Critical principles cannot be taken over ready-made from theology, philosophy, politics, science, or any combination of these."[68] The barriers imposed by schools of criticism have blocked and they continue to block the emergence of genuine criticism. Criticism is an act of inspection and exposition, and this act must vary in accordance with the unique set of problems posed by the work being studied. The critic who permits a determinism to direct his work will not fully comprehend the singularities of the artist studied, nor will he answer to the valid critical responsibility which is a demonstration of the intent of the maker. If the critic chooses allegiance to a school rather than to the art before him, by what sanctions is he then to be named a critic?

I argue against all claims made by criticism which deny the subjectivity of the critic. The long history of *Hamlet* criticism provides clear proof of this continuing subjectivity. The critic cannot escape his own imagination. R.G. Collingwood wrote some years ago of the unreliability of written history due to the historian's imagination. The a priori imagination does the work of historical construction and supplies the means of historical criticism. "As works of imagination, the historian's work and the novelist's do not differ."[69] Variables within

historical criticism for Collingwood tend always to invalidate interpretations of the past as proposed truth. We do not hold the novelist
to veracity. But if we take any novel dealing with the past, for example, Hawthorne's *The Scarlet Letter*, as a permissible play of the
writer's imagination upon the past, how can the critic devoted to
exposing the novelist's intent escape the play of his own imagination
upon the work? Or, with respect to poetry, how can the critic of
Paradise Lost, perhaps the supreme poem in English with respect to
ultimate ranges of the poetic imagination, countermand the presence
of his own imagination as he reads Milton?

The critic's imagination is not a deterrent, for it is the urgency of
this faculty which commands his attention to art. But a wholly objective criticism of any work or of any artist in his totality is an impossibility. Imagination drives the scientist, as well. But scientific
evidence and literary evidence from the artist's intent cannot be
equated with respect to the area of proof. Frye is correct: the best
the critic can do is to read, and to allow his critical postulates to rise
from his reading.

Thus the variables in critical responsibility endure because of the
unique set of problems exposed by each critic's reading. No purely
Jungian literary criticism has yet appeared. But why should it be
desired, or even expected? Conceivably, a critic might suppose that
he follows Jung faithfully in reading, for example, two works from
American literature. He might contend that Willa Cather's symbols
in *Death Comes for the Archbishop* are representations of archetypes:
the Southwest Indians' sacred cavern and the rock of Acoma; the
Bishop's cathedral pushing its towers heavenward in the raw settle-
ment of Santa Fe; the emergence of human greed as the new American frontier seeks the gold under Pike's Peak. He might argue that
William Carlos Williams' *Paterson*, with its symbolic patterns of
descent into the dark underworld of despair and of ascent into the
light of affirmation, is a reenactment throughout of the archetypes
represented in the classic Persephone-Kora myth. Presumably, the
critic would begin with Williams' deliberate adherence to the myth,
a Jungian openness of himself to permit passage of material from the
unconscious, as he, the poet, begins to frame the poem. But apart from
other questions posed by the poem, an answer to a Jungian mandate
will negate the act of the critic. In the same vein the Jungian critic
will fail in his reading of Cather's novel.

I return to the perseverance of questions of the anagogic, of the
visionary in the sense of Jung, with which this essay opened. If ques-

tions of the anagogic are present in the critic's final and thorough reading, why should they not be recognized along with all the other questions? And why should the critic assume, as he establishes his postulates, that he has escaped the play of his own imagination on the material? The state of criticism to be hoped for is a liberation from determinisms, which, in particular, this century has produced. The vitality of any genuine work of art comes out of the complex interplay of the artist's own variables within his intent. Until the critic admits this variety as his governance, his conclusions will inevitably miss the mark, for the density and the complexity of great art will never yield to a full critical exposition when the critic has initially yielded himself to a theory constructed apart from the work to be examined. The conclusion is that critical theory cannot be equated with the authority of art.

Notes

1. *Modern Man in Search of a Soul*, trans. W.S. Dell and Cary F. Baynes (New York, 1933), pp. 159, 160–61.
2. *The Psychology of the Unconscious*, trans. Beatrice M. Hinkle (New York, 1931), pp. 360 *et passim.*
3. *Modern Man in Search of a Soul*, p. 165.
4. Friedrich Nietzsche, *Human All Too Human*, Pt. I, trans. Helen Zimmern, vol. 6 of *Complete Works* (New York, 1964), p. 25.
5. Jolande Jacobi, *Complex Archetype Symbol in the Psychology of C.G. Jung*, trans. Ralph Manheim (New York, 1959), p. 60.
6. *Aion: Researches into the Phenomenology of the Self*, vol. 9, pt. 2 of *Collected Works*, trans. R.F.C. Hull, Bollingen Series 20 (New York, 1959), p. 261.
7. "The Problem of Types in Poetry" in *Psychological Types of The Psychology of Individuation*, trans. H. Godwin Baynes (New York, 1923), p. 262.
8. Jacobi, *Complex Archetype Symbol*, pp. x–xi.
9. "Mind and Earth" in *Civilization in Transition*, vol. 10 of *Collected Works* (1964), p. 31.
10. *Psychology and Religion: West and East*, vol. 11 of *Collected Works* (1958), p. 50.
11. "Concerning the Archetypes and the Anima Concept" in *The Archetypes and the Collective Unconscious*, vol. 9, pt. 1 of *Collected Works* (1959), n. 27, p. 69.
12. "On the Nature of the Psyche" in *The Structure and Dynamics of the Psyche*, vol. 8 of *Collected Works* (1960), pp. 213–14.

13. "The Problem of Types in Poetry," p. 211.
14. Ibid., pp. 240–41.
15. Ibid., p. 301.
16. Ibid., pp. 303, 305.
17. I refer to critical studies in vogue earlier in this century which belong to a school inspired by German literary studies of "Einflüsse."
18. In the work of Stevens see, in particular, "Chocorua to Its Neighbor" and "The Auroras of Autumn."
19. "The Problem of Types in Poetry," pp. 245, 263–64.
20. Ibid., pp. 308–9.
21. Ibid., p. 308.
22. Vide supra, n. 1.
23. Psychology of the Unconscious, pp. 9, 12.
24. Quoted by Jacobi, Complex Archetype Symbol, p. 74.
25. The Hero with a Thousand Faces, Bollingen Series 17 (Princeton, 1968), p. 382.
26. Jung's regard for Moby Dick is well known: "the greatest American novel." See Modern Man in Search of a Soul, p. 154.
27. "The Problem of Types in Poetry," p. 326.
28. Ibid., p. 210.
29. See Jung's conclusions, ibid., p. 222.
30. Ibid., p. 335.
31. The Enchafèd Flood (New York, 1950), p. 76.
32. "The Problem of Types in Poetry," p. 265.
33. Ibid., p. 268.
34. Hero with a Thousand Faces, p. 12.
35. Psychology of the Unconscious, p. 35.
36. Ibid., p. 480.
37. Ibid.
38. In my study of Stevens, The Dome and the Rock (Baltimore, 1968), I have demonstrated the seasonal passages of the poetry. After publication of the study I became aware that I should have admitted some of the premises of Jung under discussion here.
39. Modern Man in Search of a Soul, p. 167.
40. Ibid., pp. 156–57.
41. Ibid., p. 169.
42. Ibid., p. 171.
43. "The Problem of Types in Poetry," p. 238.
44. Modern Man in Search of a Soul, p. 158.
45. Op. cit., p. 60.
46. Ibid., p. 58.
47. Ibid., p. 150.
48. "Some Meanings of Myth" in Myth and Mythmaking, ed. Henry A. Murray (New York, 1960), pp. 108–9.
49. See Jacobi, Complex Archetype Symbol, p. 85.
50. "The Problem of Types in Poetry," pp. 229–30.
51. Ibid., 231.
52. Note, for instance, his observation on the return of a pagan "licentiousness ... exemplified by life in our large modern cities." Psychology of the Unconscious, p. 258.
53. Language and Myth, trans. Susanne K. Langer (New York, 1946), p. 28.
54. Ibid., p. 99.
55. Originally published in 1934. I use the edition of 1948 (London), p. 4.
56. Ibid., pp. 128–29.
57. Ibid., p. 314.

58. *Cosmos and History: The Myth of the Eternal Return*, trans. Willard R. Trask (New York, 1959), p. ix.
59. "The Archetypal Symbol" in *Perspectives in Literary Symbolism, Yearbook of Comparative Criticism*, vol. 1, ed. Joseph P. Strelka (University Park, Pa., 1968), p. 222.
60. Ibid., p. 223.
61. I use the first edition (Princeton, 1957). See pp. 111–12.
62. Ibid., p. 109.
63. Ibid., p. 136.
64. Ibid., p. 135.
65. I must note that Frye's erudite juxtapositions of disparate expression often produce relationships as strange as that proposed by Jung in his discussion of *Hiawatha* and the Gilgamesh epic. See, for instance, *The Vicar of Wakefield* and the Indian (Hindu) *Sakuntala* placed side by side in Frye's discussion of comedy (p. 171).
66. Ibid., p. 145.
67. Ibid., p. 6.
68. Ibid., p. 7.
69. "The Historical Imagination" in *The Idea of History* (New York and Oxford, 1956), pp. 231–49.

Laurence Lerner

PSYCHOANALYSIS AND ART

FOR THE PURPOSES OF THIS ESSAY, I ASSUME THE CORRECTNESS OF THE following Freudian views. First, the mind is divided into three psychic functions—id, ego, and superego. The id consists both of primal instinctual drives and of repressed material; the ego is consciousness and the exercise of reason; and the superego is the unconscious mechanisms by which the id is controlled. Second, there are various unconscious mechanisms such as projection, displacement, rationalization, and so on, which control behavior. Third, material from the unconscious slips past the censor and reveals itself in behavior such as dreams, free association, neurotic symptoms, jokes, folklore, and possibly art. Fourth, the significance of sexuality is wider than was believed in pre-Freudian psychology; there is a sexual element in much human activity traditionally considered "innocent," because sexuality often takes disguised and displaced forms. Finally, I assume that there is a language of symbols we can interpret by relating it to the unconscious material it represents.

For readers who have already decided that such assumptions betray enough gullibility to invalidate anything that follows, I hasten to add that I do not make the assumptions because I believe them to be true, but because they are sufficiently widely held to make it worth asking what theory of art can be built on them. I do not, of course, believe them to be nonsense, or the whole ensuing discussion would be a barren academic exercise; so perhaps a preliminary word is in place on the kind of assent they will necessarily command from the literary reader.

Much psychoanalytic theory restates more systematically (and, Freud himself claimed, more scientifically), ideas which, traditionally, have guided accounts of the working of the mind. To believe in reason, in any but the most naive form, is to believe that there are other mental functions contrasted with it (if man is *homo rationis copax*, he is clearly capable of other, more Yahoo-like, functions), so that the idea of the ego as separated off from, and having to control, the rest of our mental processes is nothing new—nor is the view that it is not always successful. The superego is similar to the traditional idea of conscience; it inhibits socially destructive activity not by confronting us with a clear view of its consequences, but by accompanying the activity with a feeling of guilt that arises with immediate force, and which may prevent committing the offense. Conscience and the superego are identical in their mode of operation, and differ only in the explanation of their origins; but even here there is a resemblance, since both imply the existence of a moral order outside the self, and therefore both are the internal or—to use the Freudian term—the introjected spokesmen of that order. In the one case, of course, the order is God's, in the other it is society's, conveyed mainly through parental prohibition. The often surprising strength of the inhibiting guilt is explained in the one case in theological terms, and in the other it is explained by the ingenious theory that the inhibited aggression is itself used in the service of the inhibiting superego in that it is turned against the self.[1] This can then be used to explain the startling drive toward self-punishment of which the superego is capable.

The id, which is the largest area of the mind, has a greater variety of names in traditional theories. Phrases such as the old Adam suggest that the unreflecting drives to self-gratification are somehow primary and basic, that the moral life is attained by the imposition on them of other levels of mental activity. Even what seems most distinctively characteristic of the Freudian id, the view (though this is a point sometimes glossed over by Freud himself) that it has two distinct kinds of content, the primal and instinctive, and the repressed, corresponds in a way to the distinction between sin as natural and sin as perversion. Man has risen from nature and has fallen from grace; the sinner is seen as a worm, a fox, a tiger, subject to all the natural passions and incapacities. The sinner is corrupted; sin draws upon what makes us human ("Aux objets repugnants nous trouvons des appas"[2]).

Whether or not we accept the scientific status of psychoanalysis, and whether or not we accept the more specific and elaborated elements in its theories, such as the details of dream interpretation or the amazingly complicated boundary lines drawn between preconscious and unconscious, let alone the elaborations of an actual analysis, the Freudian view of the mind is difficult for the student of literature to refuse, since he has so often met it before. This is my excuse for proceeding as if psychoanalytic theory were in some sense true. I now move on to discuss the consequent theories of art.

The classic statements by Freud himself are well-known. His discussion of fantasy in the *Introductory Lectures* concludes with the ingenious suggestion that there is one path from fantasy back to reality, and this path is art. The artist is a person of clamorous instinctual needs which cannot be satisfied; the artist therefore turns away from reality to satisfy the needs in fantasy, but because of the ability "to elaborate his day dreams so that they lose that personal note which grates upon strange ears, and become enjoyable to others," the artist avoids neurotic escapism. He possesses the "mysterious ability" to disguise his fantasies and render them acceptable to others, and he is able, too, "to attach to this reflection of his fantasy-life so strong a stream of pleasure that, for a time at least, the repressions are out-balanced and dispelled by it." The successful artist is highly esteemed, and the result of this (described no doubt with something of a malicious chuckle by Freud) is that "he has won—through his fantasy—what before he could only win in fantasy: honour, power and the love of women."[3]

This theory is further elaborated in the essay entitled "The Relation of the Poet to Day-Dreaming." Once again art is seen as wish fulfillment, as the vicarious gratification, in fantasy, of desires that are denied in reality. Do we dare, asks Freud, compare an imaginative writer with a daydreamer?

> Let us not choose for our comparison those writers who are most highly esteemed by critics. We will choose the less pretentious writers of romances, novels and stories, who are read all the same by the widest circles of men and women. There is one very marked characteristic in the productions of these writers which must strike us all: they all have a hero who is the centre of interest, for whom the author tries to win our sympathy by every possible means, and whom he places under the protection of a special providence.[4]

The reader identifies with that hero and thus experiences the pleasure of feeling invulnerable, of being the center of attraction and the chosen of women, and of being invariably successful. Kingsley Amis's poem "A Dream of Fair Women" is a succinct and witty statement of this view—a poem that could hardly, I suppose, have been written in pre-Freudian times:

> Feigning aplomb, perhaps for half an hour,
> I hover, and am shown by each princess
> 　　The entrance to her tower;
> Open, in that its tenant throws the key
> At once to anyone, but not unless
> 　　The anyone is me
>
> . . . . But honesty compels me to confess
> That this is "all a dream," which was, indeed,
> 　　Not difficult to guess.[5]

At the end of the essay, Freud returns to the question of what distinguishes the artist from other people. The ordinary daydreamer, ashamed of his fantasies, conceals them.

> But when a man of literary talent presents his plays, or relates what we take to be his personal day-dreams, we experience great pleasure arising probably from many sources. How the writer accomplishes this is his innermost secret; the essential *ars poetica* lies in the technique by which our feeling of repulsion is overcome, and this has certainly to do with those barriers erected between every individual being and all others. We can guess at two methods used in this technique. The writer softens the egotistical character of the day-dream by changes and disguises, and he bribes us by the offer of a purely formal, that is, aesthetic, pleasure in the presentation of his phantasies. The increment of pleasure which is offered us in order to release yet greater pleasure arising from deeper sources in the mind is called an "incitement premium" or technically, "fore-pleasure". I am of [the] opinion that all the aesthetic pleasure we gain from the works of imaginative writers is of the same type as this "fore-pleasure", and that the true enjoyment of literature proceeds from the release of tensions in our minds. Perhaps much that brings about this result consists in the writer's putting us into a position in which we can enjoy our own day-dreams without reproach or shame.[6]

This then is the famous theory of art as secondary gratification, or wish fulfillment. Let us look for a simple example. Everyone who admires the work of Toulouse-Lautrec values it for its easy, nervous line, its effortless but vigorous elegance, its ability to render energy and graceful movement. Turn from his pictures to a picture of the man himself; we see a stunted dwarf, grotesque and clumsy; but he was descended from an aristocratic line of warriors and horsemen, his father in particular was a colorful anachronistic character who lived with panache and self-assertion. The longing to be able to ride, dance, and fulfill himself physically must have been peculiarly intense, and it must have been responsible for the nervous intensity of

Toulouse-Lautrec's drawing and the obsessive interest he showed in cyclists, dancers, and circus performers. Few artists offer so clear an illustration of art as wish fulfillment.

But this is a limited illustration, because it takes place at the conscious level. Toulouse-Lautrec must have been well aware of his own frustration, and in his painting he is symbolizing what he could—and doubtless often did—give direct verbal expression to. There was no need for the material of his art to evade the censor, and it is therefore not possible to explain its intense power by claiming that it is expressed with the violent force of what was, otherwise, unable to find expression. It is not, however, possible to give a simple example of art as the secondary gratification of *unconscious* wishes. A theory of the various defense mechanisms at work and the displacements and condensations that conceal the forbidden material and thus allow it to be expressed would have to be incorporated into our example. And, above all, a theory of symbolism would have to be formulated. In any example chosen, it is necessary to steer a course between implausibility and obviousness. If the work is interpreted as being "about" unconscious material utterly unlike the manifest content (and there is no shortage of Freudian criticism that does just this), the interpretation appears arbitrary, but if plausible interpretations are offered, the natural corollary seems to be that the author was himself aware of them, so that his symbols do not disguise, and therefore contain none of the psychic power associated, in psychoanalysis, with displacement mechanisms.

The example I have chosen is not altogether orthodox, but is perhaps more interesting because of that; it is the interpretation of Baudelaire offered by Michel Butor under the title *Histoire extraordinaire*. Butor begins from an extraordinary letter by Baudelaire to Charles Asselineau,[7] describing a dream in which he visited a brothel, in order to present to the madam a copy of a book he had just published, which he observes to be an obscene book. The usual embarrassing experiences of dreams happen to him, including discovering that his trousers are indecently torn, and that he has no shoes on; and he has a conversation with a monster who has a long black rubbery projection attached to his head. Butor offers an ingenious interpretation of this dream, involving Baudelaire's relationship with his mother (who is identified with the madam) and his stepfather, General Aupick, on whom he felt humiliatingly dependent and who had reproached him for wearing indecent clothes. From this he moves to a discussion of Baudelaire's ideas on art and on sex, and the relationship between the two ("le jour où le jeune écrivain corrige sa première épreuve il est fier comme un écolier qui vient de gagner sa première vérole"). Since the dream took place on the very day on which Baudelaire's translation of Poe's *Tales* was published, it is related to his ideas on Poe, and by means of the process of substitution so common in dream interpretation Butor recognizes (his word) without difficulty elements from Poe's life and stories in the details of the dream. A certain amount of punning too is used in the interpretation, and in his conclusion Butor observes: "la plaque tournant du rêve donne sur tant de voies."[8]

A few brief comments on this study may help our ensuing discussion. First, the distinction between what is and what is not a work of art is more or less ignored: Butor moves from Baudelaire's poems and essays into the details of his emotional life in much the same way as he moves from the actual dream. In one way, the distinction is unimportant here, for the dream is described at such length, and with such vivid elaboration, that it could easily pass for one of the prose poems of *Le Spleen de Paris*. Yet this is no answer: the offense, if offense it is, consists not in treating the actual dream as a work of literature, but in treating works of literature like biographical material, and its most questionable result consists in a trick of vocabulary that one soon learns to recognize in Freudian criticism. I have already singled out the way Butor "recognizes" elements from Poe's life in the details of the dream; later in the essay he claims that the rope which figures in the "Balloon Hoax" "becomes" the murderous rope of "The Black Cat." Verbs like "becomes," "is," or "really is" have a single real meaning, taken from the unconscious of the author, which underlies the apparent meaning of his work. I shall return to the point, and will simply remark now that they are clearly reductivist in their effect.

Second, we can notice that although Butor's method is Freudian, his interpretation is not. He detects substitution, overdetermination, and displacement in orthodox psychoanalytic fashion, but the material is not necessarily sexual. He does sometimes find that a sexual element symbolizes a literary concern, but he seems to believe that Baudelaire's writing is at least as important to Baudelaire as his relationship with his mother. The complete independence of a theory and a method that were developed in conjunction could hardly be better illustrated.

In developing the example I have moved to the edge of criticizing Freud's theory of art, but before doing this I want to ask what kind of theory it is. I suggest that it is a theory of content, not of form.

A vivid and apt example of the theory can be found in Dostoievski. The frustrated narrator of *Notes from Underground*, living alone in his cellar, consumed with envy and bitterness, is nursing elaborate plans to humiliate an officer whose name he does not even know, but whom he hates for being handsome, confident, at ease in the world. He follows the officer about, trying—with indifferent success—to learn something about him.

> One morning, though I had never tried my hand with the pen, it suddenly occurred to me to write a satire on this officer in the form of a novel which would unmask his villainy. I wrote the novel with relish. I did unmask his villainy, I even exaggerated it; at first I so altered his surname that it could easily be recognized, but on second thought I changed it, and sent the story to the *Otetchestvenniya Zapiski*. But at that time such attacks were not the fashion and my story was not printed. That was a great vexation to me.[9]

A few pages later he describes his dreams. At the lowest point of frustration and dissipation, he is visited by dreams of the good and the beautiful, in which he is "triumphant over every one."

> Every one, of course, was in dust and ashes, and was forced spontaneously to recognize my superiority, and I forgave them all. I was a poet and a grand gentleman, I fell in love; I came in for countless millions and immediately devoted them to humanity. . . . Every one would kiss me and weep (what idiots they would be if they did not), while I should go barefoot and hungry preaching new ideas and fighting a victorious Austerlitz against the obscurantists. Then the band would play a march, an amnesty would be declared, the Pope would agree to retire from Rome to Brazil; then there would be a ball for the whole of Italy at the Villa Borghese on the shores of Lake Como, Lake Como being for that purpose transferred to the neighbourhood of Rome.[10]

Neither Dostoievski nor his narrator would have had much time for Freud. Since the main point of *Notes from Underground* is to use human perversity and irrationality as a refutation of scientific theories of man, the most infuriating response possible must surely be an attempt to offer scientific explanations of irrationality and perversity. Yet this radical rejection of Freud's basic enterprise is combined, in Dostoievski, with considerable anticipations of Freudian theory—as can be seen here. For these passages clearly state the view that art, like dreaming, is wish fulfillment.

The dreams of the good and the beautiful are obviously wish fulfillment: they offer the dreamer exactly those roles of which life deprives him, and his fantasies of being a grand gentleman and fighting a victorious Austerlitz have the same function as Toulouse-Lautrec's displaced fantasies of horse riding and dancing. There is even a quite explicit admission that the function of these fantasies in waking life is to enable him to endure the lack of such achievement: "Anything but the foremost place I could not conceive for myself, and for that very reason I quite contentedly occupied the lowest in reality." The connection of these dreams with art is also quite explicit: "and I can assure you that some of these fancies were by no means badly composed," and the parallelism between the account of his dreams and the satire he wrote on the officer is quite clear. He does not appear to have figured as a character in that satire, but this need not invalidate its function as gratification, since the work as a whole fulfilled his longing to put down the officer, so that the implied narrator fulfills the role that the hero of his dreams played explicitly.

Now it is clear that what his own personal involvement contributed to the story he wrote is the emotional content: the events insofar as they express the needs of the writer, or offer a parallel emotional satisfaction to the reader. The same is true of Freud's own example: the elements of a story which are relevant to his theory are those which can be reproduced in paraphrase. He admits this quite openly by his confessed inability to deal with form. When he asks how a work of art *differs* from other forms of fantasy, he has no answer: Freud calls how the writer achieves these differences an "innermost secret" in the daydreaming essay, and a "mysterious ability" in the *Introductory Lectures*. This does not in itself make the theory valueless: if there are significant resemblances between art and daydreaming, then to point these out without being able to explain the differences is to offer not a false but a partial theory.

The next question then is obvious. Is there a Freudian theory of form? I believe there is, and to find it we must turn to the book on jokes. The main distinction made in this book is that between innocent and tendentious jokes. An innocent joke is an aim in itself, but a tendentious joke serves one of two purposes: "it is either a hostile joke (serving the purpose of aggressiveness, satire or defense) or an obscene joke (serving the purpose of exposure)." The discussion of tendentious jokes is a clear parallel to the discussion of art.

> We can see that the case of tendentious jokes is a special case of the "principle of assistance". A possibility of generating pleasure supervenes in a situation in which another possibility of pleasure is obstructed so that, as far as the latter alone is concerned, no pleasure would arise. The result is a generation of pleasure far greater than that offered by the supervening possibility. This has acted, as it were, as an *incentive bonus*; with the assistance of the offer of a small amount of pleasure, a much greater one, which would otherwise have been hard to achieve, has been gained. I have good reason to suspect that this principle corresponds with an arrangement that holds good in many widely separated departments of mental life and it will, I think, be expedient to describe the pleasure that serves to initiate the large release of pleasure as "fore-pleasure", and the principle as the "fore-pleasure principle".[11]

The "greater pleasure" which is thus rendered possible consists in the release of repressed material (hostile or obscene urges, as we have seen), in a way closely analogous to the vicarious indulgence provided by the fantasy element in art. But in this book Freud does what he does not attempt in the essay; he discusses the nature of the "fore-pleasure." Innocent and tendentious jokes both offer this, but the innocent joke offers nothing else: it is, we may say, pure form. And though Freud considers its psychological role to be less profound than that of tendentious jokes, he does not dismiss it as unimportant. The pleasure offered by the act of joking itself consists in "an economy of psychical expenditure or a relief from the compulsion of criticism,"[12] and the basic activity which the act licenses is that of regression. As the infant grows up, it has to forgo the pleasure of playing freely with words and thoughts, for it learns that this produces nonsense; a joke is an opportunity to go on with such play, and the meaning of the joke is a license to indulge in its true attraction, the word play and free play of ideas: it is an opportunity to escape the tyranny of having to make sense—the tyranny of the ego. Freud points out that the techniques of jokes are not proper to jokes only, but so far from finding this an objection to his theory, he claims "there is nothing strange in other procedures drawing from the same sources for the same end."[13]

Although poets in the 1970s seem to have largely given up rhyme, there is no doubt that rhyme has traditionally provided one of the main sources of formal pleasure in poetry; unless a really radical

change in the nature of poetry is setting in, the poets may well come
back to it. I choose rhyme as a conveniently limited example of fore-
pleasure, and the suggestion that its attraction is really an occasion
for regression is startling but interesting. There is no doubt of the
infant's delight—and our own in certain uninhibited moods—in the
arranging of echoing sounds, the grouping of words purely by sound
and not by meaning; and a nursery rhyme without sound patterns is
inconceivable. The obvious objection—that rhyme in poetry is not
usually random but arranged in strict patterns—is no objection at
all: the tension between the (adult) imposition of order and the (regressive) grouping of words that have nothing in common except
their sound is a tension on which art thrives; it thwarts and indulges
a not altogether permissible impulse in a rhythm of alternation.

I turn now to the criticisms of the theory I have tried to set forth and
illustrate. It is clear that Freud treats art as a function of the pleasure
principle; but there is at least one literary movement that has insisted
on relating it to the reality principle.

> I had read of thieves by scores; seductive fellows (amiable for the
> most part), faultless in dress, plump in pocket, choice in horseflesh,
> bold in bearing, fortunate on gallantry, great at a song, a bottle, pack
> of cards or dice-box, and fit companions for the bravest; but I had
> never met (except in Hogarth) with the miserable reality. It appeared
> to me that to draw a knot of such associates in crime as really did
> exist; to paint them in all their deformity, in all their wretchedness,
> in all the squalid misery of their lives . . . would be to attempt a
> something which was needed, and which would be a service to
> society.[14]

Freud's theory compels us to say that Dickens is here renouncing art
for science, giving up the kind of book in which identification with
the thief offers vicarious adventure, in order to write an objective
study that will provide the basis for social action. But Dickens
thought he was giving up false art for true, and he is certainly maintaining that Hogarth is a better artist than those who paint thieves
as fit companions for the bravest.

This is the orthodoxy of realism. The fact that Dickens is not nearly
such a good realist as he believed need not detain us here. There is
a rich irony in the fact that the description of the gallant thieves of
tradition (derived no doubt in part from *The Beggars Opera*) re-

sembles in spirit, though not in detail, the Artful Dodger, in whom hostility and identification are held in ironic tension. It would have been possible to quote from Stendhal or Zola, George Eliot or Lewes, similar statements of the realist creed that see the rejection of the stereotypes of gratification (invulnerable heroes, poetic justice) as a *literary* movement. Nor is realism an isolated or eccentric movement in the history of literature: it is rather the making explicit of elements that had always been present in the enterprise of literature, whether they described it as the imitation of an action or as holding the mirror up to nature.

We can bring together two points in Freud's theory that he does not himself connect. The first is his selection of inferior and popular writers. He is unblushing about this, and after admitting that "many imaginative productions have travelled far from the original naive day-dream," he adds, "but I cannot suppress the surmise that even the most extreme variations could be brought into relationship with this model by an uninterrupted series of transitions."[15] Could they? There is just such a series of transitions in *Notes from Underground*. I have already quoted the narrator's remark that some of his fancies were by no means badly composed; if we read it as part of its paragraph we find ourselves confronted with an ironic and brilliant discussion:

> You will say that it is vulgar and contemptible to drag all this into public after all the tears and transports which I have myself confessed. But why is it contemptible? Can you imagine that I am ashamed of it all, and that it was stupider than anything in your life, gentlemen? And I can assure you that some of these fancies were by no means badly composed. . . . It did not all happen on the shores of Lake Como. And yet you are right—it really is vulgar and contemptible.[16]

Freud was of course told that it was vulgar and contemptible to drag into public the underlying psychic mechanisms of apparently normal behavior. The underground man's reply to the charge is very like Freud's: neurotic mechanisms are not distinct and unusual states, to be contrasted with healthy mental life, but simply intensified forms of the patterns of all psychic life. We are all ill, says Freud; it was no stupider than anything in anyone's life, says Dostoievski's narrator. And so it is natural to go on to assert a continuity between such mechanisms and the creation of art, which Dostoievski then does. But he does not stop there. There is good art, and there is less good— and what is the difference? "It did not all happen on the shores of

Lake Como." Lake Como is the happy refuge where all dreams are fulfilled (perhaps the idyllic scenes in *La Chartreuse de Parme* which are set on the lake play a part in the choice of this image); it is the symbol of wish fulfillment, and the artistic success of the day-dream ("by no means badly composed") consists in the reduction of this element. Since Lake Como was transferred to the neighborhood of Rome in the service of the fantasy, it is no doubt the reality principle too which is glad to see that it is not always the setting. The doubt expressed in the last sentence is not, I take it, a doubt whether such wish fulfillment is the basis of literary composition, but a revulsion from self-display, literary or not, well-composed or not. Poetry is full of such revulsions, of such surges of distaste for even the most beautiful compositions because of their basis in ostentatious egoism. Yet how little the emphasis needs to be changed for revulsion to turn into boasting, for the underlying egoism of art to be, paradoxically a source of its glory:

> I must lie down where all the ladders start
> In the foul rag and bone shop of the heart.[17]

The other point in Freud's theory is the central one: the relationship between the work of art and the wish is simply one of gratification. To identify the presence of wishes in the artistic impulse was an invaluable insight; but if we consider the complexity of our emotional life, and the complexity of a great work of art, it seems a ridiculous oversimplification to say that the function of art is merely to allow us to yield to the wish. The next point is obvious: it is clearly the inferior work of art that simply gratifies the wish. Freud's pious hope that he could reduce even the finest works to the same pattern is nothing more than a hope; it is a cavalier assertion impossible to demonstrate.

When Freud is concentrating on patterns of human development he often turns to literature for examples. Unable to go into details of actual case histories, because of the confidentiality of the material, he never hesitates to take his examples from Shakespeare, Schiller, or Ibsen, often adding a remark on the intuitive understanding shown by the dramatist, which psychoanalysis has now confirmed.[18] This is not a theory of literature as substitute gratification; literature is a kind of knowledge offering insights that are less systematic and less explicitly discussed than psychology. But it is just as possible to ask if the insights are true. The reality principle plays its part in literature after all.

There is no reason for psychoanalytic theory to yield a reductivist account of art, or to deny complexity to the way in which art is related to emotional needs. I will therefore look briefly at another psychoanalytic theory of art, which involves a richer awareness of art nature, that of Simon O. Lesser.

The culmination of Lesser's study *Fiction and the Unconscious* is found in his theory of tragedy. Tragedy offers the supreme example of an aesthetic experience, which he describes in a way similar to Dewey's. In *Art as Experience*, Dewey sees actual living as a more or less indeterminate succession of what can in general be called experience. Only rarely do elements in it sufficiently cohere to form the shaped and satisfying whole Dewey calls "an experience." When this does happen, we are on the road to art, for a work of art, though built of the same materials as actual living, differs by structuring them into a coherent whole. In the same way, Lesser maintains that everyday experience may very occasionally offer us the consummate satisfaction of an aesthetic experience, but that on the whole we need art for this. To describe the aesthetic experience in its highest form, he turns to tragedy. The first striking characteristic of tragedy is its seriousness: by this Lesser appears to mean something very like an awareness of the reality principle. Tragic seriousness shows the most intense and painful experiences as they truly are: tragedy's realism is faithful not to the external world but to the internal enacting of crisis. Turning then to the nature of the tragic hero and of tragic action, Lesser develops many traditional points with great insight. He does not really introduce psychoanalytic concepts until he turns to his central point, which is that tragedy satisfies all three areas of mental life—id, ego, and superego.

> It is obvious that tragedy richly gratifies the instincts. It not only permits the vicarious fulfillment of some of our most urgent and stubborn —and *therefore* most strongly resisted—desires; it permits the satisfaction of those desires under conditions which momentarily re-establish their authority and invest them with a grandeur commensurate with their outrageousness. The satisfaction the events of tragedy offer the superego is equally obvious and equally prodigal. Tragedy is as relentless as the superego itself in punishing wrongdoing and in discovering appropriate punishments. . . . Though it is less apparent, I believe that the events of tragedy are also richly satisfying to the ego. It benefits from having the claims of the instincts specified and brought into the open. It benefits from having them symbolically gratified and made more amenable to its control. Above all, it benefits from letting desire and inhibition, id and superego, engage in a mock but violent battle under the strict terms which tragedy proposes.[19]

What is satisfying about this view is that it does full justice to the complexity of artistic experience. We need not feel that in its eagerness to use art in order to exemplify a view of the functioning of the psyche it is brushing aside some of the elements of the poem, as Freud so clearly was doing. Indeed, our suspicion is more likely to be the opposite: that in respecting the work of art, it is not doing a great deal to turn the account of it from the terms of literary criticism into those of psychology. This is not true of Lesser's book as a whole, which elsewhere uses quite specifically Freudian interpretations; but what really matters is the terminology and concepts he uses when developing his final and most general insight. I have of course given a misleading picture on this point by quoting the very passage in which Lesser does use psychoanalytical terminology, but to balance this I deliberately began by comparing his theory with that of Dewey.

Two things distinguish this view of tragedy from traditional views. The first is that it is completely internalized. Tragedy is no longer concerned with Eternal Justice, Providence, or man's relationship with the universe, but is seen entirely in terms of an inner psychic harmony in the spectator or reader. The second is that this inner harmony is stated in Freudian terms. Now the first is not new to Lesser; as he himself admits it is anticipated, in similar terms, by I.A. Richards. Richards sees tragedy as an experience in which the mind does not shy away from anything, but contemplates reality, even at its most painful, without any of the usual suppressions and sublimations. "When we succeed we find, as usual, that there is no difficulty: the difficulty came from the suppressions and sublimations. The joy which is so strangely the heart of the experience is not an indication that 'all's right with the world,' or that 'somewhere, somehow, there is Justice'; it is an indication that all is right here and now in the nervous system."[20] There is a striking parallel here to the process of being psychoanalyzed, but it is presented by Richards in wholly general terms. His concept of inner psychic harmony is compatible with almost any theory of mental dynamics, since he does not closely specify the nature of the conflict that is transcended or the forces that maintain the harmony. Has Lesser, by spelling out the nature of that harmony as one between id, ego, and superego, made it a more valuable critical tool than it was in the more general formulation of Richards?

I have space for only one example, and I choose *Antony and Cleopatra*.

His legs bestrid the ocean, his rear'd arm
Crested the world: his voice was propertied
As all the tuned spheres, and that to friends:
But when he meant to quail, and shake the orb,
He was as rattling thunder. For his bounty,
There was no winter in 't: an autumn 'twas
That grew the more by reaping: his delights
Were dolphin-like, they show'd his back above
The element they lived in: in his livery
Walk'd crowns and crownets: realms and islands were
As plates dropp'd from his pocket.

(V.ii.82–92)

This is the apotheosis of Antony, as delivered by Cleopatra after his death. It is undoubtedly the finest and most eloquent account of what so irresistibly appeals to us in that magnificent but unreliable leader. The fact that it can be delivered only after his death can be attributed to the superego without difficulty. Antony's irresponsibility has been so palpable that while he is alive we can identify with him only if we feel guilt at the same time; the need to punish him having now been fulfilled, we can at last indulge in the magnificence of this description without qualifications. The fact that the description is introduced as a dream and defended as reality fits very neatly into the theory. Cleopatra is indulging in her wish (and ours) to believe in a perfect Antony who does not cause the suffering that, as we have seen, too often follows after the exhilarations of the real Antony. Such wishes are indulged as dream, as she tells Dolabella, projecting onto him the cold role of ego ("you laugh when boys and women tell their dreams"); but she is playing a trick on Dolabella so that she can triumph over the ego by asserting that there *was* such a man. What she could never say, however, is that there *is* such a man. Ego can only be persuaded the wish is true when there is no reality to disprove it.

But are we justified in describing the wish as the id? What Antony stands for in this play is certainly not the direct gratification of instinctual drives. The fact that he is a middle-aged man introduces a great deal of secondary elaboration, and less urgent clamor of instinct, into his sexual life. The magic of Antony is not the appeal of uninhibited aggression or sheer sexual drive, but a more complex human attraction that wins the devoted loyalty of his followers and makes it impossible for Enobarbus to reject him without destroying himself. We do not need to describe that magic, since Shakespeare has done it in this very passage. What we are shown there is an alternation of impulses: first he has a God-like benevolence, then aggression that is once again underwritten by being identified with natural processes. Bounty, similarly, is followed by delight, and then again by bounty.

There is a strong element of instinctual gratification in all this. The image of the dolphin clearly has sexual overtones, and we are tantalized into thinking for a moment that Antony is himself the dolphin, that it threshes about in the waves as a simile for sexual activity, only to realize on rereading that the dolphins show *his* back not their own. The image has something of that incoherent confusion so marvelously used in this play, and it plays the sexual suggestion against a suggestion that Antony somehow emerges from, even transcends, his delights. It would be a travesty of the richness of this poetry to say that the gratification of our wish to see Antony triumphant is a gratification of the instincts.

The only way to do this would be to regard the poetry as a disguise, and to address ourselves to the task of stripping it away in order to reveal its latent meaning exactly as one does in dream interpretation. I do not suggest that Lesser wishes to do this; he is too scrupulous and sensitive a critic. But unless it is done, I do not see what is gained by speaking of the id. To allow to the impulse of assertion in the play the kind of complexity that this poetry holds, is to refrain from making any real use of the splendid simplifications of the psychoanalytic vocabulary, and to say no more than Richards had already said so well in his more general terminology.

I conclude this essay with two observations. One simply sums up where it has been leading; the second is more far reaching and perhaps incompatible with the first. First, there are better Freudian theories of art than Freud's. I have space only for Lesser's, but would have liked to discuss Kubie and Kris as well.[21] Second, the value of a psychoanalytically oriented theory of art may diminish as it begins to occupy itself with the specifics of psychoanalytic theory, looking in the literary work for examples of the various defense mechanisms that analysis and dream interpretation strip away. If that is so, we must wonder about the dream interpretation too, but to pursue that line of thought would lead to questioning the assumption with which this essay began.

Notes

1. See *Civilisation and its Discontents*, ch. 7.
2. Baudelaire, "Au Lecteur" (proem to *Les Fleurs du Mal*).
3. *Introductory Lectures*, 23, "The Paths of Symptom-Formation."
4. "The Relation of the Poet to Day-Dreaming," *Collected Papers*, vol. 4, no. 9.
5. Amis, "A Dream of Fair Women": conveniently available in A. Alvarez's anthology, *The New Poetry* (Penguin).
6. "The Relation of the Poet to Day-Dreaming."
7. 13 March 1856, *Corréspondence Générale*, vol. 1, no. 230.
8. *Une histoire extraordinaire: essai sur un rêve de Baudelaire*, 1961.
9. Trans. Constance Garnett, pt. 2, ch. 1.
10. Ibid., ch. 2.
11. *Jokes and their Relation to the Unconscious*, vol. 4, ch. 2.
12. Ibid., ch. 1.
13. Ibid., ch. 2.
14. Dickens, Preface to *Oliver Twist*.
15. "The Relation of the Poet to Day-Dreaming."
16. Pt. 2, ch. 2.
17. William Butler Yeats, "The Circus Animals' Desertion."
18. See, for example, *The Interpretation of Dreams*, ch. 2 (Schiller on Poetic Creation) or ch. 5, section D (Sophocles and Shakespeare on Oedipus); or "Some Character-Types met with in Psycho-Analytic Work," *Collected Papers*, vol. 4, no. 18 (Shakespeare and Ibsen).
19. Ch. 9, para. 2.
20. Richards, *Principles of Literary Criticism*, ch. 32.
21. Lawrence S. Kubie, *Neurotic Distortion of the Creative Process*, 1958; Ernst Kris, *Psychoanalytic Explorations in Art*, 1952.

Morse Peckham

PSYCHOLOGY AND LITERATURE

DISTRUST, SUSPICION, AND EVEN CONTEMPT ARE COMMON ENOUGH BE-
tween members of both the humanistic disciplines and behavioral
sciences. There is justification enough on both sides for such hostility,
but it may be that both sides pay too high a price for their com-
placency. Some years ago I was a member of what was supposed to
be an important committee of the Modern Language Association,
though events proved otherwise. During nearly three days of meet-
ings the committee members, all English professors, frequently punctuated the discussion with sneers at the behavioral scientists. Ignorant
of what psychologists and sociologists have learned about small-
group behavior, they were trapped into determining to do something
which could not in fact be done and which, in a different form, they
had initially rejected, although the first form of the proposal was at
least feasible, though probably of no great value. A suggestion that
a technique common among behavioral scientists be employed was
roundly and contemptuously rejected, although six months later, at
a second meeting of the committee, it was again proposed by a member who had initially been the most vociferous in attacking it. As was
to be expected, once again it was rejected, and the committee was dismissed, since it had failed to achieve anything.

Behavioral convergence is a common characteristic of small-group
behavior, whether or not the convergent behavior is rational or appropriate to the problem being considered. It is one of the reasons
why committees and seminars so frequently produce nothing of
value and make decisions and arrive at conclusions on inadequate
evidence and irrational grounds. If small groups of this sort do arrive
at reasonable and appropriate decisions, the explanation is probably
that of random effect. That is, the small group in itself does not con-

duce to rational and appropriate behavior; only the randomly controlled presence of a personality both rational and intelligent can make a group productive. The intimate group of William and Dorothy Wordsworth and Coleridge, with such temporarily attached and distantly associated members as Southey and Lamb, is a good instance. It has been suggested recently that Coleridge did first-class and original work only during the existence of that small group. Otherwise his work was characterized by confusion, obfuscation, and plagiarism.

If this is the case it is not surprising. The Wordsworth-Coleridge small group was an early instance of how the alienated Romantic resolved the problem of alienation: he became a member of a small group of like-minded artists and their hangers-on. To be sure, many of these groups have produced work of value, that is, work subsequently socioculturally validated; but as Murger shows so well, the overwhelming majority of them have produced, and continue to produce, little but the gratification of social support in the form of the convergent behavior of small groups.

This is an example of how students of literature might make profitable use of the conclusions of the behavioral sciences and particularly psychology. There is yet another reason why the hostility of students of literature is proving costly to them. One of the most common rhetorical phenomena of criticism is to justify an interpretation by an explanatory regress to a general statement about human behavior. These are at best intuitively arrived at—that is, like all intuitions, we do not know how we arrive at them—but are more frequently truisms, platitudes, old wives' tales. I have rarely observed any effort to support the probability of such statements by an appeal to the literature of psychology, except to psychoanalysis, a matter to which I shall return.

As an example, probably few words recur more frequently in the rhetoric of criticism than does "creative." Yet how many literary students are familiar with the extensive work done on creativity by psychologists? On the other hand, to turn our attack in the opposite direction, it must be admitted that much of that work is rather dubious. The general way of procedure is to study some particular kind of creativity, such as that of architects. A large and carefully sampled group of architects is asked to identify the creative architects of the country working at the time of the study. These architects now designated by their colleagues as "creative" are then studied, and much of interest is learned. For example, one of the childhood factors often characteristic of the architects so designated was "the experience of frequent moving within single communities, or from community to community, or from country to country, which provided an enrichment of experience, both cultural and personal, but which at the same time contributed to experiences of aloneness, shyness, isolation, and solitariness during childhood and adolescence."[1] But the question that arises here is whether or not McKinnon and his research associates were influenced by the Romantic tradition maintaining that isolation and solitariness, that is, social alienation, are conducive to creativity. Would they have made the observation were it not for that tradition? Is the frequency of such experiences among creative architects of a high or low statistical significance? That is, were it not for that tradition would McKinnon have given that observation an importance ranking with the other childhood-adolescence phenomena he mentions? To put it more bluntly, does a general ignorance of cultural history distort the findings of psychologists? They are aware, of course, of cultural differences among societies, for such information has been made widely available by the closely associated anthropologists, but I find little awareness of cultural history. Further, it will be observed that the creative architects studied are those so designated by other architects. This appears to give the students of creativity their desired objectivity. But does it? Are they not in fact studying those innovative and productive architects who have been labeled by other architects with the honorific term "creative"? Are they not, then, studying the current fashions in the architectural profession of using the word "creative"?

To spell this out, "innovation" is a constant of behavior, but it must be socially validated to be called "creative." I do not deny that McKinnon and Barron have made valid generalizations about creativity, or at least interesting and perhaps useful ones, but at the same time I find that their conclusions are distorted and deprived of some substance because while they were studying creativity among their designated architects they were also studying, though apparently without knowing it, the current mode of creativity-validation among architects at the time of the study. One meaning, though not the only meaning, of "deviant" is innovation that is socioculturally invalidated. Al Capone and others in the 1920s, under the cultural stimulation of prohibition, applied the methods of American nationally organized business to crime, thus innovating what is probably best understood as the criminal counterbusiness. Another meaning of "deviant" is behavior designated as socially invalid. Such a usage conceals the creativity of social "deviants" like Al Capone, who generated what was probably one of the most creative acts of recent American history. Nor can that innovation even be said to be socially invalidated. On the contrary it has been enthusiastically validated by a subculture of respectable size, considerably larger, one would guess, than the subculture of American architects.

As for productivity, in my readings in this field of psychology, I believe I discern a confusion between "creativity" and "productivity." High productivity of an individual member of an occupation, whether poetry or chemistry, is often considered a mark of creativity. But high productivity is frequently productivity within the subculturally recognized paradigms of that occupation. But if "creativity" is used to refer to innovation or, preferably, deviancy from norms, high productivity within the limits of the paradigmatic tradition is mistakenly identified with creativity. (I am using "norm" here in the popular and imprecise sense. A "norm" is a fairly high-level regressive construct, quite complex in character. The imprecise sense seems to be the one most used by behavioral scientists.) It is as if one were to say that Robert Montgomery was as creative as Tennyson. Yet there is little question that psychologists have taken over "creativity" from humanists, particularly literary critics, and have scarcely attempted to remove from it the confusions which have steadily been introduced into the usage of the term for the past several hundred years. Thus it is used to validate literary deviancy but also to validate paradigmatic productivity. This latter usage sheds some light on the individual writer. Since any individual knows about himself in the same way that he knows about others, and since he generates instructions for himself in the same way that he generates instructions for others, he is most usefully regarded as a social dyad, that is, as a small group. He is thus subject to the behavioral convergence of all small groups. Thus arises a puzzle of validation. Should a writer be called creative who continues to write with equal value in a literary paradigm he himself has innovated, or should a writer be called creative if and only if he deviates from the paradigms he himself has innovated? Roughly speaking, the first is the test for creativity which obtained before 1800, the second has obtained since. Finally, "creativity" is most commonly used in neither of these senses but merely as a eulogistic term without attributes other than mere approbation.

"Creativity" is but one of several terms which are common both to students of literature and to psychologists, but I think what is true of this term is probably true of others: a word with multiple meanings in literary rhetoric is taken over into the rhetoric of psychology without having been subjected to semantic analysis. It also works in the other direction. The term "reinforcement" has gradually emanated from psychology and penetrated the general culture. Although I rarely see it in literary criticism, I hear it with increasing frequency from my literary colleagues, and I know that they use it in teaching. This is no doubt laudable, an instance of the serious effort to make use of psychology in the study of literature, just as the psychological study of creativity is a serious effort to use what was believed to have been an important discovery in the criticism of literature and the other arts. Unfortunately, "reinforcement" in psychology itself is as vaguely and imprecisely used as "creativity" is in the rhetoric of discourse that purports to be an appropriate response to works of literature.

Nevertheless the two words have an important function in common. Both are terms of a high-level explanatory regress; that is, both are theoretical terms; both are constructs. Now just as the rhetoric of criticism frequently regresses to general statements about human behavior, sometimes taking its vocabulary from psychology itself, though rarely, so psychology can find exemplifications of its explanatory propositions in literature. I have been fortunate in being able to examine a manuscript, regrettably unpublished, prepared by a psychologist friend of mine—it is possible for humanists and behavioral scientists not only to be friends but even to be intellectual companions —which consisted of a series of propositions of behavioral psychology exemplified by poems. In his *Verbal Behavior*, B.F. Skinner uses poems both to exemplify his propositions and to provide material for analysis. This does not mean much to me, because I do not think that he is a very good scientist, and I am sure that he is a very bad philosopher and moralist. Perhaps the explanation for both of these limitations is that he started out in life to be a writer.

A better example comes again from my own experience. Some twenty-five years ago a nonpsychoanalytically oriented clinical psychiatrist told me that his teacher, a man for whom he had the greatest respect, had instructed him that one could not be a good psychiatrist unless one were thoroughly and richly familiar with the great fiction of nineteenth-century Europe, England, and America. As a still rather naive student of literature I was immensely exhilarated by this splendid validation for my profession—or so I thought. But I was also puzzled. Granted that this was so, why should it be so? I believe that now I can offer an explanation for what still seems to me an interesting proposition, though I am not so naive as I was and certainly far less exhilarated by the study of literature; the notion seems now an insufficient validation.

To use a starting point familiar to students of literature, if one accepts Sir Philip Sidney's justification for poetry as the beginning of a comprehension of what happens in literature, one can say that poetry exemplifies what Sidney called a "truth," but what I would call an explanation, or more precisely an explanatory regress, without worrying, for the present purposes, about whether the explanatory proposition which the work of literature exemplifies is or is not true. (For my own part I do not believe that any explanations are true; or, more precisely, a "true" explanatory proposition is one that has heuristic value only.) Sidney's is also the position of Hegel in his *Philosophy of the Fine Arts*. But I do not believe that either Sidney or Hegel has given an adequate account of the matter, which is considerably more complex. Let us postulate, however, on their models an explanatory-exemplary axis to language. This theory asserts that explanatory statements explain exemplary statements, that exemplary statements exemplify explanatory statements, that in any rhetoric the number of levels between the most exemplary statement and the most explanatory statement is indeterminable, and that movement from exemplification to explanation is an explanatory regress. (I do not believe that an ultimate explanatory proposition or term can do more than terminate an explanatory regress; and I do not believe that exemplary statements can transcend the gap between language and the nonverbal; that is, I do not believe that any statements can be rightfully called empirical, or concrete, or descriptive. But these restrictions are not necessary to the comprehension of the theory of explanatory-exemplary axis.)

Now the Hegel-Sidney theory asserts that art is always under the control of explanation, that it always exemplifies an explanation or set of interrelated explanations. But the Romantics discovered what Spenser's allegorical thinking had already shown, as one example among many. Just as it is possible to generate new theoretical, that is, explanatory propositions from a meditation upon such propositions, so it is possible in response to exemplary propositions to generate innovative propositions of the same sort which are not under the control of any existent explanatory propositions. Indeed, under the press of the failure of explanation it frequently happens, and perhaps very commonly with artists, that thinking moves out of the verbal into the nonverbal, that is, into thinking, even problem solving, by generating subjective verbal imagery. That seems to be one of the many possible functions of dreaming. Considerable confusion is caused in literary discourse by the failure to distinguish true imagistic thinking from sentences which are not imagistic (though they are called that), but rather highly exemplary. Imagistic and exemplary innovation generated by response to verbal exemplifications was, for complex cultural reasons, not only a discovery of Romanticism but even central to it, the imagistic being translated into exemplary rhetoric. It is the tradition vaguely and inadequately called Symbolism. Before Romanticism a symbol was an exemplification of an existent explanation. With Romanticism literature began to be marked by exemplifications for which there was no existent explanation. One of the central themes of Romanticism, to the present day, in all the arts has been what might be called "free exemplification." Actually, my statement that Hegel asserts that art is always under the control of explanation is not strictly true. He does make such assertions, but it is clear that in his speculations about the origins of art he conceives of it in precisely this way, free exemplification, or nonexplanatory thinking, which generated explanation. Indeed, the principles of his *Phenomenology of Mind* and his position as a fundamental Romantic thinker almost demanded that art be so conceived.

This discovery of the Romantics provides a partial explanation also for the enormous expansion of fiction writing in the nineteenth century and particularly the movement of fiction to a much higher cultural level. It further serves to provide a partial explanation for the increasing self-conscious "realism" of fiction, a fictional technique whereby the massive use of exemplary sentences provides a matrix for the generation of free exemplification. This tradition culminates in such works as *Billy Budd*, which defies explanation, and *Ulysses*, which ignores it, governing its generation of exemplary statements by a completely arbitrary schema derived from another work of fiction. Hence to the student and therapist of the psyche, the psychologist and the psychiatrist, nineteenth-century fiction offers both training in free exemplary thinking and massive amounts of material which can be used to generate innovative explanations of behavior. The psychologist can benefit by adequate use of nineteenth-century fiction and Romantic-Symbolist poetry, and by earlier fiction and memoirs. (One of the models of much early nineteenth-century fiction is pre-1800 memoirs.) This use would provide a learning experience that could break down the paradigmatic experimentation characteristic of academic and professional psychology which is so noninnovative.

Material with which to extend and supplement both his experimentation and his theoretical constructions would also be provided. Probably my friend's teacher could not explain his interest in nineteenth-century fiction this way, or perhaps any way, but experienced in reading that fiction a fruitful disorientation.

Thus it can, I believe, be reasonably said that literary criticism ought to be able to find in psychology explanatory propositions for its justifications and interpretations; it ought to be able to find exemplifications for such propositions both in psychological experimentation and in literature; and it ought to be able from a knowledge of psychology to generate innovative explanations which will reveal hitherto unobserved aspects of literature and its origins in the individuals who produce it. And psychology ought to be able to use the theoretical explanations of literary criticism as directions for innovating scientific investigation; it ought to be able to find exemplifications for its explanatory propositions in literature as well as psychological experimentation; and it ought to be able to generate theory with the aid of the theoretical propositions of criticism. Psychologist and literary critic, then, each ought to be able to incorporate into his own rhetoric segments of the other's, both to generate and control high-level explanatory regress, or theory, and to generate and control specific investigations into categories of units of study in their respective fields. This kind of disciplinary interaction ought to be happening, but except for a very limited number of studies in both fields, it is not.

The explanation for this is not merely the hostility between humanists and behavioral scientists. That in itself is absurd and unnecessary. Both, after all, are concerned with studying human behavior and the consequences of human behavior. The reason for the hostility may, after all, be mere academic jealousy, a social phenomenon, not an intellectual one, and further evidence that being a humanist does not make a man either morally or intellectually better, and that the scientific study of the psyche does not make a man more objective, propositions for which there is abundant evidence to be found elsewhere and in both disciplines. There is no intellectual reason why psychology and literary criticism (to use the term in its widest sense as the study of literature, from inspirational evaluation to bibliographic analysis) should not fruitfully interact. The reason that they do not, except for an occasional isolated study, is the theoretical weaknesses of both.

It is hardly necessary to adumbrate at length about the weaknesses of literary theory. Literary criticism engages in evaluation without a theory of evaluation. It does have modes of evaluation, but they are endless and all equally valid, as far as I can determine. It is possible to conclude, as I have, that the least interesting thing possible to say about a literary work is that it is good or bad. Rather, there is no theory of what the literary critic is doing when he engages in evaluation. The critic rarely sees evaluation as a social process which has little to do with the work he is evaluating, but has a great deal to do with the generation of literature subsequent to his evaluation. What happens as the consequence of literary evaluation? This question may belong to sociology, but it seems to me a puzzle that the literary critic should wrestle with, though he rarely does so. Explanation of literary evaluation is ordinarily justification, a rhetorical demonstration that the kind of evaluation that particular critic is doing is the kind he ought to be doing.

Literary criticism engages in hermeneutics, though it does so without a theory of interpretation. The most sophisticated literary criticism is founded on a naive use of such terms as "meaning," "intention," and "mind." Not one of these terms is subjected to analysis, although they are among the most scandalous terms in modern philosophy and psychology. There are, to be sure, various controls over literary hermeneutics, but, like evaluative controls, they are modes, not theories. A general theory of literary interpretation based on what there is useful in psychology and philosophy—and there is less in both than there should be—has yet to make an appearance.

Literary criticism engages in an explanation of the situations from which a work emerged and into which it enters, that is, the consequences of its emergence. This is traditionally known as "historical criticism." Of the three kinds of literary criticism it is the most mature. It is soundly based, in the sense that the distribution in space and time of the emergence of literary works is structured, not random. On the other hand, that distribution is not yet understood or explained by what scientists and some philosophers of science like to call "laws," though a scientific law is merely a termination of an explanatory regress, a termination which has not yet been overthrown. Thus explanatory criticism has an enormous wealth of information about the emergence of individual works, but very few general explanations that can subsume exemplary statements the content of which is the identification of factors of emergence and its consequences. Thus, in another sense, the emergence of literary works is random, in that explanations for such emergence are either feeble or nonexistent.

Finally, literary criticism is further limited by fashion. It turns its attention to and defines as literature, or sometimes with a little more sophistication as "serious literature" or "literature worth studying" or "great literature," those works which are currently validated at a high cultural level.[2] Consequently in all three kinds, literary criticism ascribes universality to attributes of literary works which are culturally localized in time and place. As a further result of this situation "literature" is a field which has no boundaries. Hence the study of literature is even more paradigmatic than are the scientific disciplines —and that is saying a good deal. As a further consequence it is, except for "historical criticism" within its limitations, nonaccumulative and astoundingly repetitious.

It is hardly surprising, therefore, that though an occasional psychologist is ingenious enough to use literature, psychology can find little to use in literary criticism. When the psychologist does attempt to use a bit of critical rhetoric, such as "creativity," he gets into a terrible mess. However, there is no reason for a psychologist to assume a position of intellectual and moral superiority vis-à-vis the literary critic. The weakness of psychology, however, does not at first glance lie in its weakness of theory. Psychology has lots of theories, often elaborately structured, and its field of inquiry is on the whole well-bounded, though my own opinion is that the distinctions between psychology, sociology, and anthropology rightfully cause great discomfort. I think August Comte was correct when he defined sociology to include all three, that is, made "sociology" identical with the modern term "behavioral sciences." (I also believe he was right in asserting that even mathematics, astronomy, physics, chemistry, and biology are properly subsumed by "sociology"—a proposition that one finds an occasional psychologist in agreement with.) This uneasiness is reflected in the introduction to *Human Behavior: An Inventory of Scientific Findings* by Bernard Berelson and Gary A. Steiner,[3] a work that lists and discusses 1,045 reasonably reliable generalizations at which behavioral psychology has arrived, plus a group of unnumbered Freudian generalizations, which the authors think should be included for completeness but which they do not consider even reasonably reliable. Nevertheless they think that though their field may be fuzzy at the edges, a characteristic, to be sure, of all disciplines, it is reasonably clear toward the center, though the location of the center is possibly a little unclear. The chapters have the titles of the more or less current areas of psychology: development, perceiving, learning, and so on. But there are also chapters on the family, organizations, the society, and even one on culture; thus the uncertainty of the boundary of psychology is manifest. At any rate it is unquestionably a fascinating book, though somewhat miscellaneous in character. The most notable lacuna in the book is discussion of theory, but that is what the authors designed and what their title indicates.

Quite a different work is *Handbook of General Psychology*.[4] This consists of forty-five chapters by sixty behavioral scientists, and the emphasis is on metatheory and theory and the history of each area of psychological study. Together these two books give a sweeping picture of the current state of psychology; and the *Handbook*, with little that could be said to belong to sociology and anthropology, is more representative of the organization and activity of academic psychology, though there is a paper on humanistic psychology and some serious attention to Freud, particularly in the chapter on psychosomatic medicine. (An interesting aspect of the book is that though there has been for at least a decade a considerable rebellion [usually now known as neobehaviorism] against classical academic psychology from within the ranks of academic psychology, and a seeking of new possibilities in phenomenalism, for example, and fieldwork, rather than laboratory work, it would be almost impossible to guess that from the *Handbook*.)

One rises from these two books with certain distinct impressions. First the amount of work and money poured into psychology in the last fifty years has been staggering. Equally impressive is the ingenuity in designing experiments and the intellectual and scientific rigor which if not always achieved is always attempted. But second, one is equally impressed by the fact that so little has been accomplished in the fulfillment of psychology's program of arriving at solid, verified propositions about human behavior. And equally impressive is the absence of large-scale theory. There are frequent references to the fact that psychology has as yet very little to say about higher-level cognitive activities. Here, then, is one reason why literary criticism can find little in psychology to help it. Psychology has not yet reached those higher-level modes of behavior which are responsible, it would seem, for the production of literature, even literature at a low cultural level.

The recognition that psychology has not yet reached higher-level cognitive activities is usually accompanied by the implication and often the statement that it is, after all, on the way, and that it is only a matter of time before it gets there. I do not think that it will. The belief is that psychology will build from what one author calls mini-theories to a large, inclusive, and solid general theory. These miniature theories are generalizations based upon carefully controlled laboratory experiments. The assumption is that a stimulus may be isolated from a real-life stimulus field and responses to it observed in animal and human behavior under laboratory conditions, conditions in which the stimulus factors may be controlled, in short, a psychologically neutral situation. That a stimulus is the same stimulus when it is isolated from a real-life stimulus field is itself questionable. The nature of the human brain certainly appears to be such that in real-life situations a particular stimulus cannot be identified, since the interpretative response is affected not merely by the (hypothetical) stimulus but by all the stimuli in the perceptual field. Further, the life experiences of the experimental organism affect, as in psychologists themselves, the interpretation of the response. This appears to be true in animals as well as in humans, for in reinforcement experiments on animals, those animals that do not get reinforced are ordinarily removed from the experimental situation as not being good experimental subjects. There is an intellectual charm in this methodology which I find unable to resist, partly because it is so much like the studies of humanists.

A California psychologist named Brunswik has objected that experimental situations are not isomorphic with real-life situations and that on these grounds much psychological experimentation must necessarily produce invalid results.[5] However, experimental situations, whether involving animals (including that strange strain, the laboratory rat, of which the less said the better) or humans are in fact real-life situations. In experiments involving humans, for example, the psychologist is actually channeling their behavior, policing them, exercising social control. The social control cannot be objected to, since social control is the ineluctable condition of all human interaction, including interaction with oneself. Rather the psychologist does not know he is doing this. His objectivity is thus spurious, and he is as much a "humanist psychologist" as the psychoanalyst.[6]

Another "humanistic" aspect of psychology can be discerned in a different kind of study. Berelson and Steiner (p. 269) present an example of "long-lasting aggressive consequences of extended frustration in childhood." A table is headed "Differences in aggressive behavior in persons having different degrees of childhood frustration." The behavior traits listed are "Rude answering to parents," "Irritated by parents," "Feeling that teachers are unfair," "Carrying grudges,"

"Frequent quarreling with friends," "Broken engagements." Group 1, the most frustrated, showed an average of 64.0% of these behavior traits, while Group 4, the least frustrated, showed an average of 36.2%. This difference is impressive, perhaps; it suggests that childhood frustration has a high probability of producing long-lasting adult aggression. The trouble with this is that there is no explanation of why Group 1 had *only* an average of 64.0% or why Group 4 emerged with an average *as high as* 36.2%. More important, however, is the fact that "aggression" itself is used only in reference to socially invalidated acts. To be successful does not an individual have to manifest "normal aggression"? But that merely means that the aggression is channeled in socially approved ways, not that socially approved aggression is not aggression. Indeed, there are good reasons for believing that *all* behavior is aggressive, since a nonnormative definition of aggression is "manipulation of the environment to the organism's benefit." If human beings misjudge what is beneficial, that is neither here nor there. Clearly, much socially disapproved aggression is highly beneficial to the individual who manifests it. The lesson, if any, of this investigation seems to be that if you want your child to be able to take care of himself, frustrate him when he is young, as indeed all parents have always done. In short, we have here an instance of what is so common in psychology—an explanatory term is taken from ordinary language and used without being subjected to semantic analysis. The result is that what was really happening in this investigation was an exemplification of the transmission of normative judgments of aggression. Once again, the objectivity claimed turns out to be an example of "humanistic" psychology.

This particular investigation, however, is both quite old and obviously naive. A much more sophisticated method of personality study has emerged in multivariate experimental personality study, in which the statistics are far more complex, particularly in the use of factor analysis. Even the definition of personality is reasonably acceptable: "Personality is that which enables us to predict what a person will do in a given, defined situation."[7] The upshot of this kind of study is that personality factors tend to cluster, as in "university professors are highly intelligent, low on dominance, and outgoingness, low on superego strength, high on radicalism, and self-sufficiency" (p. 806). But it is so easy to think of university professors in whom none of these factors seems to be present. Can this be true, possibly, of professors at the University of Illinois, where Cattell is located and

Howarth has worked? Such a statement might be useful to a college president in handling his faculty, but only if he recognizes that in any situation involving large numbers of his faculty he will find these traits more frequent than the opposite traits, but like all statistically-based information what is really offered is a set of numbers to which certain terms and phrases are attached. The predictive quality is applicable, perhaps, to a large population of professors in a major university, but does it apply to Okefenokee A & M? And does it apply even in a major university in all situations? My own experience is that what one encounters in a large faculty meeting is low intelligence, high dominance and outgoingness, high superego strength, low radicalism, and low self-sufficiency. Possibly the explanation is that in such situations only a minority is ever heard from, but there seems to be nothing in multivariate personality assessment that tells one that in some situations the traits of a particular group either are unreliable or must be reversed. Since, moreover, this is a statistically-based statement, it cannot be used to predict the behavior of an individual. Furthermore, in all the examples of occupations or such groups as alcoholics the cluster of personality traits resembles to an astonishing degree the popular stereotype or caricature of such professions or behavior groups. This suggests that those stereotypes help determine the traits, and that in turn leads one to wonder if the clustering might not be a statistically trivial phenomenon and that Cattell has been governed in his response by normative factors not present in the data.

What appears to be going on in multivariate personality study is quite interesting. The naive approach to personality is marked by an effort to create a coherent concept of any individual's personality, including one's own, an effort necessarily made possible only by ignoring incoherent factors. This naive approach remains unquestioned in literary study. The multivariate approach, which attempts to get away from the naive approach, tries to see the personality as an incoherent package, or as it is called, profile, and most interestingly to identify personality traits which are not recognized and categorized in naive personality rhetoric. So far so good. But then to attempt to arrive at generalizations about such categorically disparate groups as airmen, Olympic athletes, farmers, university professors, neurotics, alcoholics, and homosexuals seems to be little more than the effort to make spurious sense out of the data of personality profiles on the model of the unanalyzed naive approach. Would a different shuffling of the profile cards show farmers and professors to be alcoholic homosexuals? Here is an instance of what often happens: psychology appears to offer the student an innovative notion corrective to his theoretical inadequacies, and then withdraws it.

This failure to analyze naively used terms from ordinary language happens with technical psychological terms as well. I can do no better than to quote from one of the two of these sixty psychologists who seem to have some genuine awareness of what psychologists are in fact doing. Professor Benbow F. Ritchie, after analyzing what he calls the "pop-op" definitions of reinforcement of Skinner and others, has the following to say:

> The ideas of reinforcement, of stimulus, of response, of habit, and of drive were never given the kind of careful analysis they require. . . . As a result, all the most interesting and important questions about behavior and learning remained unanswered. The failure to provide these distinctions is, I think, the reason for the distrust of learning theory that in recent years has swept through academic psychology.[8]

We have here the same failure to subject terms to analysis that we have encountered in the discussion of "creativity."

In short, there are a number of dubious matters about experimental psychology, the foundation of psychological theory, or so it is affirmed, and apparently not a few psychologists are deviant enough to question these paradigms. But this dubious foundation of psychological theory is by no means the only trouble. Possibly a symptom, however, of that basic trouble is the increasing popularity of psychometrics and of statistical analysis. Little understanding of the nature of statistics is to be gained from the *Handbook*, but I found an illuminating discussion in *Randomness, Statistics and Emergence*, by Philip McShane, S.J.[9] It is Father McShane's contention that science has two kinds of data, the lawful and the random. By lawful he means, in my terms, that theoretical statements successfully subsume exemplary statements and are themselves subsumed and validated by such terms as "law" and "cause." His theory is that randomness is the subject of statistical investigation, and that an interaction between the random and the lawful is the source of scientific development. Statistics is the means of investigating what the lawful cannot take care of: the random is the residual of the lawful. I find Father McShane singularly convincing in this, though not in everything, and its importance here is that the increasing use of statistics in psychology indicates the lack of success in constructing the lawful, that is, verified theory, and indeed suggests the disintegration of psychological theory, instead of its integration. The increasing importance of statistics in psychology hints, therefore, that there is an increasing flow of the residual. Moreover, the increasing mathematicization of all branches of psychology, made so much easier by the ravishing joys of the computer, has had the effect, I strongly suspect, of deflecting psychologists from the study of human behavior to the study of mathematics. It would be an odd and amusing result if the computer, instead of freeing the psychologist—and members of every discipline susceptible to computer use—limits him to looking for data which can be successfully subjected to computer analysis. I would not question for a moment that the computer is a magnificent invention, but it may, like the excessively rich diet of Americans, lead to obesity.

The questionable aspects of psychological experimentation may be one reason for the increasing flow of the residual. Another is, I believe, the assumption that psychology will build from mini-theories to large-scale theory. This involves the assumption that in the various levels of theory construction—and psychological metatheorists appear to anticipate a good many levels—there is a necessary or immanent or logical relation between levels. Going up is induction; going down is deduction. It is hardly necessary to remind the reader of the terrible beating these terms have taken in the past seventy years. (Indeed, one is a bit startled by the frequency with which these terms are encountered in the *Handbook*.) But if the connections between sentence-as-stimulus and sentence-as-response is a conventional connection—and it can hardly be otherwise without postulating a metaphysic of immanence, which, to be sure, a great many philosophers now do, though they do not seem to know it—then the connection between levels of an explanatory regress is a conventional level. This means that every level of an explanatory regress has an emergent relation to the level below. And if so, the proposed Walhalla of psychology is threatened with a Götterdämmerung before it is even built. And that, I suspect, is the significance of the increasing popularity of statistics and the increasing refinement of statistics over the past seventy years. Psychologists in general and even Father McShane, I am sorry to say, appear to believe that emergence is an attribute of the natural world. But I do not think that that is the case. Emergence is an attribute of the levels of explanatory regress. We do not move from one level to a higher one by induction or by an immanent logic. We often move by the paradigms of convention to higher levels, but "creative" motion upward is by innovative deviance. Paradigmatic explanatory regression follows a rule of computer technology: "Garbage in; garbage out."

By building up from basic units of behavior, psychology will never construct a theory of human behavior which literature can use. It must begin with a level of explanatory regress that deals with what it calls higher cognitive activity, including its own. And that means it must begin with language, which is not the instrument of higher cognitive activity but is higher cognitive behavior itself. Nor can a theory of language be built up from linguistic units, as Noam Chomsky has already unwittingly demonstrated, having by now proved that what he set out to do cannot be done.[10] The Chomsky approach can never reach the crucial problem in language, the connection between two separable utterances. Since psychology builds its theory on the connection between statements, it must begin by understanding that connection. It is not easy.

Thus psychology can do something with literature itself, but almost nothing with literary theory. Literary criticism, on the other hand, can reach into psychology, into learning theory, into perception theory, into information theory, into interference theory, and so on, and find isolated low-level generalizations which it can use. In fact, the serious study of literature can ignore such isolated generalizations only at its peril, only by complacently maintaining its present theoretical impoverishment. Thus psychology is more useful to literary study than, for the most part, literary criticism is to itself. The ultimate lesson is this: if psychology should succeed in creating a general theory of human behavior, such a theory will subsume the study of literature. Currently, however, literary critics need not feel themselves seriously threatened.

A note on psychoanalysis. Freud was one of the greatest observers, but not, I think, a great theorist. The reason is that he was not observing the unconscious, but rather was interpreting the verbal behavior of disturbed individuals placed in a highly protected situation and encouraged to talk about what in their culture was socially invalid to talk about. His was a single-minded hermeneutic enterprise governed by a metaphysic of instinct which was, historically, an inversion of Romantic Transcendentalism. Since Freud used a term magical in its power to attract early twentieth-century literary critics—symbol—Freudian literary interpretation achieved considerable popularity. Every now and then it experiences a revival if some literary critic or other happens to go through, or at least into, psychoanalysis.

The contention that the psychoanalytic interpretation of literature must be invalid, since one cannot psychoanalyze a dead person, has always caused considerable embarrassment and highly defensive responses among Freudians. The answers offered have never been successful because it was not realized that the structure of the Freudian Unconscious was like Chomsky's Deep Structure of language, not a revelation of underlying structure but an explanatory regress from verbal behavior. Thus the proper answer to this particular claim of the invalidity of Freudian literary interpretation is that one can make a hermeneutic response to utterances whether the utterer is living or dead, or present or absent. Freudianism is a hermeneutics of one aspect of human behavior, uncoordinated with other aspects, except for the nonverbal thinking of dreams. Since it is not a response to the full range of behavior, it cannot be called a theory of human behavior. The pragmatic defense of psychoanalysis that it effects cures of cognitively disturbed individuals through psychotherapy is neither here nor there. What psychotherapeutic technique is not effective for some members of the population of the disturbed? It has always been admitted that psychoanalytic therapy is ineffective with some individuals. One is reminded of animals discarded from experimental psychology because they are poor experimental subjects. It also appears to be the case that cognitive disturbance is usually resolved in about two years whether the disturbed individual experiences therapy or not.

On the other hand Freud was undoubtedly a man of enormous intelligence, astounding powers of grasping personality factors, and remarkably gifted in myth construction, myth being a form of discourse that is not fully disengaged from a purely exemplary level of explanation but has not yet reached a coherent explanatory level. His was a kind of intuitive multivariate personality assessment. He thus could grasp the theme or clustering of personality factors which experimental multivariate study, using factor analysis, has likewise arrived at. Recent psychoanalytic theory, following the later Freud's interest in ego psychology, has separated out this element from Freud's writings.

All this is evident in the publications of the most intelligent and certainly the best-informed Freudian critic now writing, Professor Norman N. Holland. His recent book, *Poems in Persons*,[11] contains the following assertion in what he calls, too fiercely, "A Polemical Epilogue." Professor Holland is too kind and generous a man to be very polemical. "Psychoanalytic theory . . . has advanced to become the only psychology capable of a comprehensive view of man that spans the largest social and philosophical issues and the most precise clinical questions, especially people's choices of particular words." The last phase is the giveaway. Thus his own experimentation with responses to poems follows the Freudian model and the Thematic Apperception Test, itself derived from Freudian theory. He offers his subjects a poem by H.D., the only poet to leave a fairly complete record of her own psychoanalysis, to which he has previously given, with this aid, his own psychoanalytic interpretation. He then instructs his subjects to give any reactions to the poem that happen to occur to them. Not surprisingly, in their responses he discerns a personality theme.

There are two reasons why he should do so. As I have suggested, the construction of a coherent personality theme is the naive, unanalyzed approach to personality. What one does is to make analogical categorizations of apparently dissimilar and unrelated statements by observing the pattern of those statements. A reading of Freud's case histories shows that that is how he proceeded. There is, of course, nothing wrong with this; that is how we always proceed with any set of apparently unrelated stimuli. Freud was merely a genius who did it in a new field and with a new explanatory regress to govern his analogies. But there is a second reason why Professor Holland should have seen what he did. If you place a small group in a closed room, such as a committee room, and let them interact verbally, a group theme will emerge. I have already referred to this as the typical behavior of small groups. An individual as a social dyad is a small group. If as Freud discovered, if as the Rohrschachs and the TAT's discovered, you face any individual with a not evidently structured stimulus field, one for which validated conventions do not already provide instructions for responding, and deprive him of instructions for verbal or other performance, but also demand that he respond verbally, the result will be like that of the small group in the socially isolated committee room. There will be a convergence of behavior. Further, if you place the individual in a series of such situations, the identical theme, to be perceived analogically, will emerge. The explanation is that at an indeterminably early age any individual begins to limit the range of his behavior and to increase the limitation of that range by the redundancies of his own repeated limitations, redundancies which he responds to by observing his own behavior as a stimulus field. We need not worry about whether this process is "conscious" or "unconscious." The redundancies of his behavior are instructions for further behavior. Repeating the pattern of what Freud did, Professor Holland, not surprisingly, discovered what Freud discovered. Granted, provisionally, that there are personality themes and granted, provisionally, that they are not trivial, the interesting question would be how they are adapted to differing situations and modified and maintained and disintegrated over long periods of time.

However, Professor Holland's claim that this explains the bond between poem and reader cannot be maintained. At best it explains why there is a relation between personality clustering and modes of evaluating poetry, or, for that matter, anything else. I cannot see that Professor Holland has contributed to our comprehension of literary hermeneutics by conducting experiments in which hermeneutic restraints are cast aside.

Finally Professor Holland has insisted that in moving into ego psychology psychoanalysis has matured and has completed the work of Freud. This may be, but I cannot see that the kind of statements that Freudian ego psychologists make about personality differ very strikingly, if at all, from either naive or sophisticated statements about personality made by non-Freudians.

Notes

1. Donald W. McKinnon, quoted in Irvin L. Child, *Humanistic Psychology and the Research Tradition: Their Several Virtues* (New York: Wiley, 1973), p. 54.
2. For a nonnormative definition of "high culture" see my "The Arts and the Centers of Power," *Critiques 1971/72*, The Cooper Union School of Art and Architecture, 1972. This essay has also been published in *1972 Proceedings of Conference of College Teachers of English of Texas* 37 (September 1972): 7–18. It will be reprinted in my forthcoming *Romanticism and Behavior*, scheduled by the University of South Carolina Press for 1976.
3. New York: Harcourt, Brace & World, 1964, p. 712.
4. Edited by Benjamin B. Wolman (Englewood Cliffs, N.J.: Prentice-Hall, 1973), p. 1006.
5. Egon Brunswik, *The Conceptual Framework of Psychology* (Chicago: University of Chicago Press, 1952).
6. I owe this point to Dr. Robert L. Stewart, Professor of Sociology, University of South Carolina.

7. E. Howarth and R.B. Cattell, "The Multivariate Experimental Contribution to Personality Research," *Handbook*, p. 799.
8. Benbow F. Ritchie, "Theories of Learning: A Consumer Report," *Handbook*, p. 458.
9. Dublin: Gill and Macmillan, 1970, p. 268.
10. Considerable help in understanding this has been given me by Dr. Richard Gunter, Professor of Linguistics, University of South Carolina.
11. New York: Norton, 1973, p. 183.

Jean Starobinski

THE AUTHORITY OF FEELING AND THE ORIGINS OF PSYCHOLOGICAL CRITICISM
Rousseau and Madame de Staël

FOR THE PREACHERS OF THE SEVENTEENTH CENTURY, NOTHING WAS MORE suspect than the emotion by means of which a spectator or reader could identify with the characters of a tragedy or a novel. From the time it began to exercise its seductive powers to deliver souls to the tyranny of passion, literature ceased to be a diversion without consequence. By tempting individuals to blend with imaginary creatures and experience their desires and torments, literature became guilty not only of favoring the sins of concupiscence and pride, but also became the competitor of religion. Literature propounded a worldly forgery of the devotional act and substituted specious lures for the only legitimate object—God, Christ crucified. The enraptured spectator or reader lost himself in the passions of fictitious heroes, whereas by participating in Christ's passion he would have been in sure hands. It was necessary to divert him from pursuing the simulacrum of a happiness that only Heaven could ensure. In criticizing drama and the novel, Bossuet, Nicole, and Bourdaloue were denouncing a form of idolatry, an infidelity to the only *authority* worthy of recognition. In their eyes, the danger of literature—far from residing in mere frivolity—was to be found in the intense fascination of its audience, and in the seduction of people away from daily duties to the point of parodying the contempt of the world which the mystics experience.[1]

Literature engenders a tendency to false identification, and it is against this tendency that the censure of the preachers is directed.

This judgment is a *critical* act (in the sense of reprobation or condemnation). What makes such a criticism possible and necessary is the absolute *authority* attributed to a different form of identification—the only desirable form. Moral judgment is thus based on a thoroughly defined criterion; whatever does not agree with it is rejected. In the face of an accusation on this order, all defense and all apology have for their primordial task the demonstration of the compatibility of the work of pure fiction with the unquestioned norm, the recognized dogma.

But the norm can change. It can be displaced. The eighteenth century is considered to be the age in which the rehabilitation of passion was achieved. It is not enough to see in this the abolition of something disreputable. It is necessary, in addition, to distinguish the following essential fact: passion and feeling—as soon as they became rehabilitated—began to demand for themselves, and soon for themselves only, that authority which the preachers had wanted to recognize only in the revealed Word and in the Cross. This transferral of authority is of considerable importance, since the new authority tends to assert itself as the source and end of all moral judgments, of all critical accusations.

To rehabilitate passion is to rehabilitate the passional identification instigated by the various arts. That the spectator or the reader feels drawn into the universe of the work, that he experiences its upsetting situations, that the illusion makes him feel all of the motions of the characters is proof of the work's excellence and of the reader's sensitivity. The result is a somewhat ambiguous certainty which must come to terms with aesthetic considerations and moral motivations. This certainty is no less of an authority and the conquered reader can henceforward avail himself of it for making judgments about the reality surrounding him, for condemning the ways of the world, prejudices, injustice. . . . In his heart of hearts, he has at his disposal a universal criterion.

We must be satisfied here with one example: Diderot's *Éloge de Richardson*. No religious scruples (we may surmise) prevent Diderot from identifying with the characters of the novel, of penetrating the infinitely varied universe of the novelist not only as a witness, but as a "hidden hero." Here is a universe that resembles reality so closely that Diderot thinks himself justified in demanding that the real world be faithful to the great verities of feeling revealed by fiction. To praise Richardson would thus be not so much to speak of his literary qualities or his art of composition as it would be to speak of the moral effect felt by the reader and of the aptness of spirit with which he will henceforward confront the existing society and his fellowmen. And this aptness—warm, enthusiastic, compassionate—will find in each of the disappointments that life holds in store (and these will not be lacking) the pretext for a sharp criticism, for a condemnation made in the name of the law of the heart. The admiring examination of Richardson's work leads Diderot beyond the literary theory of sentimental "realism" to the possibility of a *criticism* directed not at literature but at the abuses and the insufficiencies of the real world.

Is it not the same with Rousseau? Does he not admit, in the *Confessions*, to the ardor with which, in his youthful years, he was carried away by the characters of history or fiction? "I became the character about whose life I was reading."[2] And if there remain in Rousseau any of the guilt feelings that Christian preaching tries to inspire in him who turns away from "the only necessary thing," then the exoneration is prompt. Rousseau summons the highest moral authority for the objects of his identification. On the one hand, he chooses virtuous models, this being the case in particular with the great figures of Roman history. On the other hand, the impulse of identification carries a kind of grace; it is innocent, and it communicates its innocence to the objects, whatever they be. This impulse transfigures the objects and invests them with a sacred value. The resulting plenitude, because it is "without intermixture," can assert itself as *pure*. And this experience soon becomes the term of comparison in regard to which the imperfections, the meanness, and the servitude of the age will incur condemnation. We must be careful here—criticism directed against society always finds its support in the image of a plenitude that Rousseau sets against it, and this plenitude is almost always felt at the end of a process of identification. One example will suffice: If we are to believe the *Confessions*, then the illumination of the road to Vincennes left its immediate trace in the prosopopeia of Fabricius. We are dealing, of course, with a rhetorical procedure, but it is passionately relived. Rousseau made himself into Fabricius, identified himself with Plutarch's hero, in order to apostrophize a corrupt world, a world unfaithful to the ancient ideals of virtue and frugality.

We can thus see the evidence: Rousseau is not content to disarm that religious accusation whose targets are all "profane" identifications; so well does he make sacred and sanctify the fictional beings with which he tends to blend, that he receives from them the power to accuse and judge in the place of the defenders of religious morals. The authority he invokes—explicitly or implicitly—is that expansive principle which ensures the unity of consciences, the transparency of hearts; everything that eludes this principle in the lives of men and nations deserves censure.

The new authority, in Rousseau, is more profoundly bound with the ego than it is in his contemporaries. This means that the authority is opposed to the world in a more radical way by claiming for its source a more purely subjective freedom. For a Diderot, the heart and the *sensibilité* are the "organs" of a relation which is never broken with surrounding reality; the good and evil which present themselves to us, always affronted, demand a perpetual vigilance, an unflagging discrimination, and solicit from us an active response. Our subjectivity, scarcely distinct from the material energy of the world, has constant access here. Rousseau takes a decisive step by casting upon the surrounding world an anathema for which there is no remedy and which exempts him from remaining compromised in that world. He renounces action, he has nothing more to do in the outside world where only insults and wounds await him. From this time we witness a vehement falling back of the subjectivity toward that fortress where it thinks itself out of reach; this is an impregnable position of withdrawal. The subjectivity does not venture out except to observe innocent plants and it will have dealings only with fanciful beings— "people from the other world"—beings called forth by its own desire and alone worthy of its love.[3] The defiance and rupture are so complete that Rousseau himself produces the objects of his identifications instead of finding them on the outside in the books of others. He summons them out of the memory and the imagination in order to create a fictional space in which to bound forward, in order to invent distances that could serve as a scene for love, satisfaction, absence, return. Thus, the consciousness reaches the point of frequenting only those images and words that express the *lack* which torments it. A new mode of creation: it is an infinite and unhappy reflection that is at work in order to put forward a substitutive universe, to try and reinvent a lost immediacy and to *represent itself* in those images that are at its sovereign disposal.

This new mode of creation calls for a new kind of criticism. Illuminated by its two prefaces, plus subsequent autobiographical commentary, *La Nouvelle Héloïse* is justified not only by its moral intentions and the social utility that its author assigns to it (in which respect it hardly differs from so many other books that would interest and edify at the same time); we are further asked to understand the work beginning from its origin and source. And Rousseau notes carefully in his various justificative texts the lines of withdrawal that allow him to place himself out of the reach of a criticism concerned with literary qualities or verisimilitude. The prefaces warn us not to complain about the grandiloquence, the *gaucheries*, the preachy tone, the provincialism of these letters; *we are not dealing with worldly people*, but with passionate young folk, whom the influence of the capital has not rendered glib.

Grammarian criticism and the objections of good taste would be out of place here; Rousseau in his prefaces is careful to warn these grammarians and thus to disarm them. And, in the notes in which he assumes the role of editor of the letters, he wants to be the first to denounce an improper term, an awkward or unreasonable development. He neutralizes critical aggression by straight off taking the responsibility himself. We are also not to accuse these characters of not being a part of nature, of not resembling anyone, of being veritable "monsters." Having thus done what he could in a sort of rearguard combat to have it admitted that it is possible to live, feel, and love far from Paris at the foot of the Alps, in the manner of his heroes, Rousseau goes on to admit that *it is not a question of imitation* but, rather, of expression. His characters are the creatures of his desire; they have no models in the external world. We therefore cannot hold against them their lack of verisimilitude, nor can we reproach the novel for showing only good creatures. The other world, to which they belong, is the heart of Jean-Jacques, which brings a sufficient guarantee to their existence. Any judgment that would not refer beyond the characters to the profound feelings of Jean-Jacques would be missing its object. Thus feeling is affirmed as an indomitable force which, though it takes the world to witness, does not wish to be amenable to the "judgment of men." It therefore appeals to an act of love, to a passional fusion analogous to that fusion that pledges Jean-Jacques to his fanciful creatures. The reader (or rather the feminine reader) for whom Rousseau prays will know how to identify emotionally with the voices of the novel and will know also immediately not to consider these except as a step toward the source which gives them their life, their warmth, their seductive force, their love of virtue. The reader will thus feel himself captured within the gravitational field of a creative desire. He will recognize that absolute authority which will subsequently make possible the moral and social *action* of the book.

If the reading of *La Nouvelle Héloïse* is to change the internal inclinations of the reader, his external conduct, his social opinions; if it is to have any outside critical function, it would have to be by means of the fascination which would carry these inclinations through the interior space of the novel to the level of the feelings that produce it. We can see the "utility" of the book, the possibility of moral change, even the possibility of a criticism directed against contemporary society (the society of false Christians and bad philosophers); all of these have their foundation in the entirely positive approval given to the authority of feeling. For having roused the fanciful image (but an image esteemed as more truthful than any real compulsion) of a reconciled universe, Rousseau offers up his person (his soul) for the fervent approval of the reader, an approval the no less global *obverse* of which would be a rejection of the injustices of the world. We should not be surprised that at the same time Rousseau gives the signal for a social criticism that goes beyond the traditional framework of satire and its commonplaces, he also gives the signal (though in a more hidden way) for the approach of a literature in which traditional criticism, a judgment aimed at the beauties and faults of a text, at the virtues and shortcomings of the characters, is transcended by the élan of a sympathy which, no longer limited to the characters of the play or novel, seeks to rejoin the subjectivity of the creator.

These two new meanings of "criticism" are born conjointly; it is the stipulated norm, within the realm of the imaginary, of that "law of the heart" whereby we define as "unjust," "unacceptable," or "scandalous" those aspects which are denied to surrounding reality. There would not be, here, any "radical criticism" of the real world if there were not also a moral absolute, heir of the divine absolute, appealing to submission or identification. Conversely, we might conjecture that the interest of an author for subjectivity would not have assumed such an importance if the givens of the objective world did not seem to have a lesser value, to be weakened by the stain of inauthenticity. The cult of inwardness and the revolt against the scandals of the world are on equal footing here.

The *Letters on the Writings and Character of Jean-Jacques Rousseau,* published by Madame de Staël in 1788 (six years after the publication of Rousseau's *Confessions*) belong, by their own admission, to the academic tradition of the eulogy or panegyric [*éloge*]. Thomas, a regular at the Necker salon, had excelled in the theory and practice of this "demonstrative genre." Germaine Necker, for her first piece of writing, could seize here a pretext for emulation, on the condition that she find a new and original subject for her praise: "There is as yet no panegyric of Rousseau. I felt the need to see my admiration expressed."[4] This literary genre, to which the newer criticism ties her work, has never attracted the attention of the historians. It has perhaps been wrongly neglected. In Fontenelle, D'Alembert, and others, the *éloge* takes the form of a true essay and is organized according to the subdivisions that would be taken up later by historians of literature—the life, the works, the influence. In the eighteenth century, the laudatory literature prefigures (often, it is true, from a distance) the most recent criticism which aims at grasping the essence of a work or thought; at any rate, it comes much closer to this at the time than does the "criticism" of the erudites (concerned with reading documents, establishing dates, and so on) or the criticism of the journalists, which scatters its traits in ambushes and skirmishes.

But the *éloge*, as Madame de Staël conceives it, is no longer an exercise. Nothing ties it to the ceremony of an event or an assembly. Here we have "letters" with no definite addressee from which the apostrophe, the exclamations, the emotional rhetoric of the age are not absent. It is nevertheless not without reason that Georges Poulet, in a study which he places at the beginning of *La Conscience critique,* cites the opening of the *Letters on Rousseau* for the purpose of signaling the inaugural act of modern criticism. Rousseau, we have seen, calls for a new type of critical commentary, and everything goes on as if the young and enthusiastic female reader brought the expected response to the admired author, outside of any antecedent literary traditions. A new criticism for a new literature.

What reverses from the very beginning the traditional moments of examination and judgment is the *primary* fact of passional admiration (which goes so far as to constitute the initial *cogito* Poulet discerns). Normally, the judgment and the decision followed the scrupulous presentation of the reasoning, once the qualities and faults had been carefully weighed. Here, the admiring outburst of feeling comes first. In a single stroke, Rousseau had established the acceptance of feeling.

The critical activity will consist in "expression," in making reflexively explicit that which had been lived at the highest degree of intensity: "I felt the need to see my feelings expressed. . . . I experienced a certain amount of pleasure in retracing for myself the memory and impression of my enthusiasm. . . . How can we relegate to some uncertain future age the feeling which presses upon us?"[5]

Critical discourse is elaborated not quite in the enthusiasm of the encounter, which is too scorching to find the adequate word, but rather in the memory; it is nevertheless important that the memory be recent, that the analysis of it be deferred as little as possible, and that the reflexive moving back should not accrue too much through temporal distance. The reflection must appear as a difficult conquest and as a yoke imposed on a feeling that yet keeps all of its impulsiveness. The critical statement will then imply a displacement obtained at will. Nothing is more revelatory than the preamble to the letter devoted to *La Nouvelle Héloïse*:

> It is with pleasure that I indulge in recalling the effect this work has on me; I will try above all to refrain from the enthusiasm that could be attributed more to the inclinations of my soul than to the gifts of the author. True admiration inspires the desire to share that which we experience; we control ourselves in order to persuade, we slow down in order to be followed. Therefore I will transport myself some distance from the impressions I have received and I will write on *Héloïse* the way I would, I think, if time had aged my heart.[6]

In order that critical discourse might arise, it is necessary that, by means of a kind of intellectual artifice, the consciousness of the reader tear itself away from any immediate communion—dazzling and mute —the immoderate excess of which is incompatible with persuasive communication. It is necessary to take the attitude of a "reflecting passion." Certainly, one has to account for this initial communion, and it is the initial *impression* which we must try to reconstitute by means of discursively articulated proofs. But, between the bewildering moment of reading and the second moment of the writing which attempts to transmit the substance of the first, a distance is imposed both by the law of time and by the necessities of intelligible articulation. "Finally to know," writes Georges Poulet, "depends as much on a disunion as on a union."[7]

Let us listen again to Madame de Staël speaking to us about her reading of *La Nouvelle Héloïse*: "Ah! How sorry we are to see the end of a reading that has affected us as an event in our life and that, without disturbing our heart, has put into motion all of our feelings and thoughts."[8] The reading has taken on the value of a lived experience; whether the novel had enticed the young, feminine reader into itself or whether the reader had appropriated for herself the characters and situations, the world of fiction and the world of life are no longer radically separated. Yet there is a limit imposed upon this identification: If the feelings and thoughts are put "in motion," the "heart," on the other hand, is not disturbed. The sympathy of the reader does not seem to go beyond the point recognized by Aristotle or Burke. The peril of literary heroes upsets us, but it also delights us by means of the consciousness that we keep of our security. We are not in danger.

But, as we have seen, Rousseau insists less on the verisimilitude of his characters than on their expressive functions. Although their destiny concerns and moves us, we should not dwell on this; their feelings all refer to the heart of Jean-Jacques. To identify with Julie or Saint-Preux is to stop at the halfway point. It is necessary to rejoin the source, the creative reverie. This is what Rousseau demands; and the attitude of Madame de Staël, participating and detached at the same time, the serene heart that she keeps, all tell us that she does not let herself be entirely taken by the simulacrum that the literary object deploys: she thus obeys Rousseau's injunction and pledges all her passion to the subjectivity that underlies the novel.

Georges Poulet has pointed out the movement to identification precisely: "The admiration will not rest until it has attained an identification, not, to be sure, with the admirable object, but with the very spirit [génie] which, by means of an *internal* act, *sui generis*, causes the object to exist."[9] The most profound participation will not intervene at the level of the fictional world, which is, after all, nothing but a figurative world, but rather, at the level of what Madame de Staël calls "the verities of feeling," where the consciousness of the reader feels itself burning in the same fire as the consciousness of the admired author: "The verities of feeling, these verities which the soul must grasp, woe unto him who is not kindled by them at the instant of their presentation."[10] The metaphor of the flame, the (somewhat theatrical) recourse to the formula of imprecation, signal, no doubt, the presence of the sacred. Georges Poulet has shown in a remarkable way how, in the expression of nostalgia and the happiness of reminiscence, the voice of Madame de Staël blends with Rousseau's voice and prolongs the latter in an independent fashion, in fascinated submission.

Another "verity of feeling"—this one oriented not toward the past but toward the future—gives rise to the same coincidence: this verity or truth, profoundly tied to the consciousness of the self, is also the verity of freedom. In the fourth of the *Letters on Rousseau*, we see the admiring participation culminate at the point where the presence of the sacred demands the abdication of reasoning in favor of an intuitive act that is religious in nature:

> This freedom which makes no other distinctions between men than those indicated by nature, I love it too, with all the force and vivacity of my first feelings; and in my exaltation with the author of *Letters from the Mountain*, I would like this freedom the way it is conceived at the summit of the Alps or in their inaccessible valleys. Now a stronger feeling, without being contrary, suspends all of my ideas: I believe instead of thinking; I adopt instead of reflecting.[11]

This is the language of faith, almost the language of mysticism. The act of faith, under the circumstances, is a continuation of the critical examination. It is the consequence of attentive judgment and constitutes the final state and completion of it. Our text states this explicitly:

> However, I did not sacrifice my judgment until after I had made noble use of it: I saw that the most astonishing spirit [*génie*] was tied to the purest heart and the strongest soul; I saw that neither the passions nor the character could ever lead astray the most sublime faculties with which a man was endowed; and having dared to perform this examination, I delivered myself up to faith in order to spare myself the trouble of a reasoning which would still justify it.

We notice, first of all, that Madame de Staël's argumentation follows closely the one that Rousseau repeatedly develops,[12] in order to justify the abandonment of philosophy and docility to the dictates of immediate feeling. An undeniable mimetism must be taken into account here. But there is more: In this motion at the end of which criticism "delivers itself up to faith," we perceive a circle closing up. Critical discourse, we have seen, had sprung from the remembrance of a first moment of enthusiastic approval or adherence. And now—once the acts of "judgment" and "reasoning" and "examination" are over—everything takes place as if it had become possible to retrieve this first intuition, the state of enthusiasm and its undivided plenitude. The truth which the critical glance, thanks to its detachment, could *see*, leads to a certainty without distance that can henceforth dispense with rational proofs—vigilant reason has fully accomplished its mediating task; it can now take a back seat, abdicate, reabsorb itself, and give its place up to a final intuition—an intuition which, because it renounces an external view, can call itself "blind feeling" [*sentiment aveugle*]. Thus, critical lucidity is transmuted into blindness or infatuation, but this blindness claims to possess an inalterable sense. Madame de Staël resorts to oxymoron and does not hesitate to suggest a singular coincidence of opposites: "The blind feeling of which I have made my light."

To attain the "verity of feeling" is to rejoin Rousseau at the fiery center of his subjectivity. It also means, because the same center can be found in oneself, to coincide with the admired author. Thus, the critical path arrives at an end which appears at once as the source of the work under investigation and as the most intimate being of the critic, revealed to himself by the attention he devotes to another. Feeling having appropriated the character of universality which until then had been the privilege only of reason, every "verity of feeling" can now become a meeting-point, a locus of coincidence.

This point or locus, once attained, could be the definitive end of critical activity if the goal of this activity were the repose in contemplative knowledge or in purely savored intimacy. But is it really so for Madame de Staël? The "verity of feeling" is the highest authority. But authority is not there just to be contemplated. It tends to impose itself, to propagate itself, and to reign. To rejoin authority is to rejoin a value which seeks to spread universally, it is to seize a norm which demands that all contingent facts be referred to it in order for one to be able to evaluate their conformity or divergence. Under the circumstances, authority is the feeling of freedom, and freedom demands to be communicated.

Having confronted internal authority and the present reality of the world, Rousseau had withdrawn within himself; the world had appeared to him rebellious to the norm and thus uninhabitable. The reader who shares the same "verity of feeling" can certainly repeat Rousseau's denial; this would be to mime him perfectly, in too servile a fashion, no doubt. The reader could, nevertheless, reiterate in another present the confrontation of the world and the "sentimental" norm. He could wish, in a way, to avenge the persecuted prophet of the norm, pray for a transformation of external reality which would make it subject to the authority that had been, until then, confined in the innermost depths of the "beautiful souls" [*belles âmes*]. All of this is to make oneself the apostle of the master and to take the risk of being unfaithful to the solitude in which he had taken refuge. Thus, this reading demonstrates amply that it recognizes the feeling of

freedom, and not the solitude of a separated subjectivity, as the pre-
dominant authority. Freedom [*liberté*], having conquered the enthusiasm of a first reader, would administer the proof of an expansive
power which will have no limit except for the hostility and opacity of
the world; it is, potentially, a universal liberating force, and the
reader who has experienced it considers himself only as a first stage
in a flight which must become general. He knows that the eloquence
of freedom can "kindle" souls and he asks only to propagate the fire.

Once in possession of the "verity of feeling" communicated by the
writings of Jean-Jacques, Madame de Staël occupies herself in spreading it about her, in broadcasting it into a favorable milieu. In 1788,
the convocation of the States-General opens the perspective for a
"regeneration" of French society. It is the thought of Rousseau which
makes for the commitment to interpret the moment as the moment
of a new birth, and Madame de Staël apostrophizes the French:
"You, great nation, assembled to consult on your rights."[13]

We now see better the course of Madame de Staël's criticism. Having removed herself to "a distance from the impressions [that she]
received," she examined and judged the writings of Rousseau. In a
recapitulative sentence (which we have already quoted) we have at
first the transitive act of seeing, directed at Rousseau: "I *saw* that
neither the passions nor the character could lead astray the most
sublime faculties with which a man was endowed." After that, we
have a reflexive motion in which, drawing the consequences of the
critical act, she finds herself again facing herself and making by
herself a capital *decision*: "And having dared to perform this examination, I delivered myself up to faith in order to spare myself the
trouble of a reasoning which would still justify it." This brief moment when Madame de Staël appears to be attentive only to her own
internal life constitutes the dialectical base of operations for the
appeal to the universality of consciousnesses. Faith is generalized,
as the apostrophe to the French follows immediately: "You, great
nation . . ." Such is the novelty of this critical thinking; instead of
subjecting literature to a religious or aesthetic criterion which would
be external to it, it is at the level of the very origin of the literary
work that she discovers an authority ("freedom") which will be
the criterion applied to the historical reality of the world.

Will the French be capable of the "blind feeling" out of which
Madame de Staël made her "light"? She does not go so far as to ask
it of them and thus demarcates a persistent margin between the ideal
exigency and the reality of facts. However, she does not think it im-

possible that reason would assure a "unanimous accord" among men. This hoped for accord and unanimity—even if it were not to be based on a full communion in the "verity of feeling"—opens up the perspective for a radical change, for a true "revolution." Asymptomatically, a conciliation is heralded between the "external" world (until now devoted to a reprobating criticism) and "internal" conviction, in which Rousseau sought a protective asylum. Madame de Staël, in a tone of prayer (a prayer addressed to men, since everything depends on them) ventures to predict a moment when "internal" feelings will be recognized in the reality of the world—a moment when action and social life, overtaken by freedom, would no longer be a betrayal of subjective certainty. Madame de Staël dreams of bringing Rousseau back to life in order to offer him what he lacked—a human world, docile to his voice; a society he could accept.

Having evoked the possibility of a unanimous future, Madame de Staël, in the next sentence, turns back to the past in order this time to apostrophize Rousseau and to formulate the impossible wish for a *presence*, in which the resurrected writer achieves in the broad daylight of collective history that transparency of hearts out of which he had made his solitary passion. Rousseau come back to the milieu of men who put "in common that which they have of the celestial": [14] this is the image of a being-source brought into the presence of his desire realized on a universal scale. The "enthusiasm" of Madame de Staël invents a future that completes what destiny had left imperfect —a future where the virtual universality contained in Rousseau's eloquence is gloriously realized; the listening post of the admiring critic is enlarged to the dimensions of an immense audience:

> And you, Rousseau, great and unhappy man whom one scarcely dares to miss on this earth . . . why are you not the witness of the imposing spectacle which France will give! . . . Ah! Rousseau, what happiness for you if your eloquence made itself heard in this august assembly! What an inspiration for the talent is the hope of being useful! What a different emotion when thought, ceasing to fall upon itself, can see before itself a goal it can reach, an action that it will produce! . . . Be reborn, Rousseau, be reborn out of your ashes, and may your efficacious wishes encourage in his career him who starts out from the extremity of evil having for his goal the perfection of the good. [15]

This necromatic appeal (with its demonstrative gesticulation) makes of Rousseau the absent master of the imminent historical moment; the event in progress is interpreted as the result of Rousseau's expansive eloquence. Madame de Staël sees the desire for freedom (which, in Rousseau's lifetime, was obliged to feed upon its own substance, to "fall" upon itself) transform itself into transitive action, into a tension oriented toward a "goal."

But Rousseau is no longer concretely there to designate the goal and guide the action. The evoked image of him erects a quasi-presence which only makes the lack more cruelly felt. It is in vain that the "verity of feeling" is capable of being universalized; it only has all of its persuasive force when communicated by an admired person, in the oratorical situation in which the assembled crowd receives the decisive exhortation and injunction. Everything happens as if the presence of an incarnate authority was required in order that the collective action receive its orientation and direction, in terms of a knowledge, of a certitude, and also in terms of a goal articulated by a singular being. Madame de Staël does not formally take exception to the concept of "general will" proposed by Rousseau; but she does seem to be more attached to the image of the legislator, which she also could have found in Rousseau. The legislator, because he is a living person, can be the object of love, and Madame de Staël needs to mix the amorous attraction and the élan of action. Now if Rousseau, dead for ten years, is not accessible to her desire, if he can only be the event's witness and guide in the form of a great shadow, then Madame de Staël hastens to find an heir and substitute for him: her own father, Necker. In fact, and without it being necessary to resort to an appeal to the unconscious, the father represents the origin, the "sacred" anteriority on a rather fundamental symbolic level. In the historic role with which he is now entrusted, he holds in his hands the keys of the future. From the origin to the future, there is a directional movement. The triumphant projection of the "verity of feeling," felt at first in close communion with Rousseau, goes through a series of displacements, is carried forward, transferred, finally to end up in a filial appropriation that is at once touching and abusive.

Many important things are thus revealed to us; in its fervor and even in its naivete, this page of Madame de Staël is a perfectly illustrative example of the prerevolutionary state of mind. It appears clearly that the communion experienced by virtue of an exalted reading takes on the value of a prototype of a universal fusion—the subjective experience of a shared freedom asks to be renewed on the scale of collective history; the voice of the heart wants to be amplified to the point of becoming a general sermon. But, in order not to lose the personified presence of authority, an appeal is made to a providential man (in this instance the "paternal figure"), who fulfills the function of the absent (deceased) "master." "From the extremity of evil" to the "perfection of the good" he carries the nation to the conquest of happiness, gives history its direction, for he can only want the True and the Good. In him we begin to see the figure of the leader or "chief" to whom the revolutionary group confers the responsibility of defending the new rights and organizing the new social reality. And already, beneath the filial pen of Madame de Staël, the language of the "personality cult" arises. Necker is the one "whom France has named her guardian angel, and who, in his rapture for France has seen only his duties toward her."[16] Napoleon will come, better suited for carrying out this role and for receiving this flattery; but, we know, he will prefer to have Madame de Staël as an enemy. She thus became less of a burden to him.

This is the expansive form which a criticism that is attentive to the hidden treasures of the admired author's subjectivity takes in Madame de Staël. There is nothing paradoxical in this "propagandism" if the essence of subjectivity can be grasped as a value that can be universalized—moral consciousness, natural goodness, or freedom. The characteristic property of authority is to spread out, to solicit the broadest application. This had been the case for theological authority. Now, there is still a revelation, but its place is different—it now occurs in the "heart" of man, the subjectivity of spirit [génie]. And whereas theological revelation had for its interpreter the entire sacerdotal institution, the revelation of the "verity of feeling" obliges the critic and the reader to assume the sacerdotal role. Hence the messianic tone adopted by Madame de Staël as if in response to the religious values which in Rousseau's discourse are transplanted to personal experience and assumption.

But, as I have already indicated, nothing is less sure and less stable than the coincidence of the subjectivity with universal values. At best, the turning of consciousness upon itself will mark a desire for divergence, for difference, for irreducibility. Freedom thus exercised will consist, above all, in shielding itself from contamination through external contact; instead of being a principle of collective solidarization, it will be affirmed as the infinite power to refuse the outside, to push aside any determination imposed by others or by circumstances. Holding any meeting or sharing to be impossible, it works on putting itself out of reach. Consciousness does not, however, relinquish its claim to authority; but it is henceforward a walled-in authority, which despairs

of spreading out into the world and which, in spite of the limpid
evidence it is for itself, no longer counts on the recognition that would
come to it from other consciousnesses.

It is a challenge on this order that certain "frenzied" pages of the
Confessions, the *Dialogues,* and the *Reveries* seem to hurl at the
reader. Under the circumstances what happens to critical commentary? It may abdicate prudently and stop short of that which remains
hidden—it will not claim to seize what cannot be seized, it will only
designate it from afar. But every invitation to abdicate provokes an
aggressive leap—it is more comfortable to oppose an end of non-
acceptance to the madness of Rousseau, and, if not to condemn it
irremediably, to have pity on it in view of extenuating circumstances
which are not lacking. And what if criticism does not resign itself to
either abdication or opposition? It will attempt to reconcile with the
universal that which exposes itself under the cloak of obstinate par-
ticularity. It will seek not only to recognize the divergence, the
strangeness, the madness, but to reduce them—at the end of a patient
effort of explanation and comprehension.

Sympathy is no longer an immediately realized act of fusion which
can instantly turn itself into warm expansiveness or effusiveness. One
must start out from the scandal, the feeling of malaise and provoca-
tion; from now on, one can no longer dispense with the dangerous
work of interpretation, even if the interpretative tool be limited, in a
primitive fashion, to the most current psychological notions.

This is how a literature governed by the withdrawal of the consciousness to fortified positions gives rise to a new hermeneutics, a
new exegesis, oriented toward the hidden psychic reality. The exegetical attitude is required here just as it was when the literal meaning of
the Homeric poems or of the Bible were no longer fit for acceptance,
either because of a lack of intelligibility, because of the moral scandal
they provoked, or because they seemed to hint at a second meaning,
richer than the one gotten at first glance. At this point we persuade
ourselves that the stronger meaning, the one in which the precious
truth is announced to us, does not reside in the signification which lets
itself to read at first glance—the strong meaning is a hidden meaning,
or at least a meaning protected by him who gives himself up to an
immediate reading. In the face of the Scriptures, the exegetist seeks to
discern different levels of the text. In the face of a subjectivity that has
substituted itself for written revelation, the exegetist will similarly
seek to rejoin the most "profound" secrets—if, on the palpable level,
the message has become enigmatic or scandalous. This is the only way

to preserve the authority conferred on subjectivity; it is necessary to discern, beneath the apparent madness, a more profound reason, for one cannot remain subject to a force of aberration.

The psychological exegesis applied to Rousseau by Madame de Staël is of a rather rudimentary kind. She will disappoint; she will elicit smiles. Yet she does have some of the distinctive traits of exegetical procedure and, in spite of her naivete—or rather because of it— she becomes remarkably instructive.

For Madame de Staël, Rousseau's frenzy reaches its climax in voluntary death—Madame de Staël accepts the thesis of suicide. The subjective difference, the challenge to common rationality, find here their ultimate expression. It is in vain that this act appears incomprehensible. The task of interpretation consists in finding for it an acceptable motive, a psychological cause that each generous reader can relive in his own heart of hearts. The consciousness which flees from life is inexplicable, but Madame de Staël does not stop until she renders it explicable, reduces it to a common "meaning," to a feeling henceforward accessible to any one. In the page where Madame de Staël conjectures that Rousseau, betrayed by Thérèse, could not tolerate complete solitude, we see a certain type of critical reasoning, crudely formulated but remarkably revealing, defining itself as an effort to reduce radical strangeness to our most convincing psychic motivations.

But the interpreter, in this string of conjectures, exposes herself openly. Having accepted, without "critical spirit," the hypothesis of suicide, she invents an admissible cause for it. Thus in imagining a sort of drama of amorous jealousy, she furnishes some of her own substance—she places, in advance, Rousseau into the role of a *Zulma*. The interpreter, fictionalizing the death of the admired author, seems moved by a kind of horror of emptiness—the existence of Rousseau must be, to the last moment, saturated with sentimental significance; the heartbreak of death must be a last pathetic gesture:

> He was afraid of being alone, of not having a heart close to his, of constantly falling back upon himself, of neither inspiring nor feeling any interest, of being indifferent to his glory, tired of his genius [*génie*], tormented by the need to love and by not being loved. . . . To be two in the world calms so many fears! . . . Rousseau perhaps allowed himself suicide without remorse because he found himself alone in the immensity of the universe. When we do not occupy a place in a heart that survives us, there is such emptiness in our own eyes that it is possible to count our life as nothing.[17]

It is not enough to say that Madame de Staël *projects* herself into Rousseau and attributes to him her own phobia of solitude. Let us note, more precisely, that she tries to solve the mystery of a subjectivity (incomprehensible at first) by defining that which was missing, the object that was denied. Madame de Staël invents this object in the image of her own need to love, to the extent of that which she at once claims for herself and would like to give—the consoling presence, the transfiguration of the world by the fact of *being two*. In its very substance, interpretation appears here as the desire of the reader offered to fill the lack from which the author—he who waits to be "rejoined"—suffers in the depth of his words and his destiny.

All interpretation refers to the interpreter and at the same time attaches itself to the interpreted object. Here, we largely have the impression of seeing the predominance of the designation of the self, the autoreference in which the *ego* of the critic is put into the light; Madame de Staël defines herself as the one who would have protected Rousseau from despair, who would have returned to him the taste for life. Finally, she is the one who, not capable of bringing him back to life, at least experiences his absence with such intensity that she makes of it a spectral quasi-presence: "One steals from death all that memory can tear from it, but the impression of the loss of such a man is the more terrible for it; one almost sees him, one calls him and the abyss answers."[18] The task of exegesis is to keep as close as possible to us, the one who moved to distance himself, to leave us. The vain image which haunts a mourning memory represents the highest degree of possible proximity, once separation intervenes.

The soaring of a criticism which desires to bring the complement of interpretation necessary for the plenitude of a presence responds to the autobiographical writings of Rousseau—a literature that develops as the perpetual incomplete interpretation of an enigmatic drama. It is in vain that the sentimental effusion of the young Madame de Staël appears naive to us—her aspiration to being "two in the world" defines an ideal of complementariness which she would like to experience even in the relation that attaches her to the admired author. Perhaps she thus restores to Rousseau the effusion whose language and fascination she found in *La Nouvelle Héloïse*. Perhaps the six "critical" letters are for the totality of the writings of Rousseau what so many of Julie's letters are for the missives of Saint-Preux—acts of love, reinforced by precise observations, by moral developments and some refutations (to avoid a perpetual unison). But, in doing this, Madame de Staël calls for the same loving response to herself. If she imitates what fascinates her, she causes the propagation of this fascination, and makes people's glances attach themselves to her also, the inspired interpreter. When she speaks of Rousseau, her efforts "almost to see him" against the background of the abyss, show her to us at grips with the darkness, fighting for the *restitution* of a being, for a recaptured vision of the absence. Soon it will be her turn to wish to disappear, to toy with the idea of suicide, and to await from others the *words* which would keep her among the living. The function of criticism (of the exegesis of the "heart") is revealed here in all of its importance—it is made to bring something or some one back to life or at least to try to avert the evil spell of separation. The authority she wishes to serve is that of presence, and thus, she is condemned to encounter everywhere lack and absence.

Notes

1. Nicole writes, to blame the partisans of the theater: "One does not consider that Christian life ought to be not only an imitation, but a continuation of the life of Jesus Christ, because it is his spirit that must act in them, and inspire in their works the same feelings inspired in the work of Jesus Christ. If one saw Christian life from this point of view, one would recognize immediately how much the theater is opposed to it." *Oeuvres Philosophiques et Morales de Nicole* (Paris, 1845), p. 451.
2. *Confessions*, bk. I, *Oeuvres complètes*, vol. I (Paris, 1959), p. 9.
3. Second preface of *La Nouvelle Héloïse. Oeuvres complètes*, vol. II (Paris, 1964), p. 16.
4. *Oeuvres complètes de Madame la barone de Staël-Holstein* (Paris, 1871), vol. I, p. 1.
5. Ibid.
6. *La Nouvelle Héloïse*, p. 5.
7. Georges Poulet, *La Conscience critique* (Paris, 1971), pp. 18–19.
8. *Oeuvres complètes de Madame de Staël-Holstein*, vol. I, p. 10.
9. Georges Poulet, "La pensée critique de Mme de Staël," *Preuves*, 19 December 1966, p. 28.
10. *Oeuvres complètes de Madame de Staël-Holstein*, vol. I, p. 16.
11. Ibid.
12. Notably in the *Profession de Foi* and the third *Reverie*.
13. *Oeuvres complètes de Madame de Staël-Holstein*, vol. I, p. 16.
14. Ibid., p. 17.
15. Ibid.
16. Ibid.
17. Ibid., p. 23.
18. Ibid., p. 24.

SPECIAL PROBLEMS

Rudolf Arnheim

VISUAL ASPECTS OF CONCRETE POETRY

OURS IS AN AGE IN WHICH THEORISTS AND CRITICS ARE OFFERED FEW occasions to comment on great masterworks of their own time. Rather, there is much fluctuation of the media that supply the artists with their forms—a situation not propitious for peak performances, but attractive to the experimenter and of great interest to the analyst. All media of sensory expression border on each other, and although every one of them tends to do best when it relies on its own most characteristic properties, they all are rejuvenated by cohabitation with their neighbors. For example, a confrontation of immobile with mobile art, three-dimensional with two-dimensional, polychrome with monochrome, audible with visible, alerts the observer to qualities taken for granted as long as they rule unchallenged in the precinct of one particular form of expression. Concrete poetry offers an illuminating meeting between printed language and the pictorial image.[1]

Although imagemaking and writing grew indivisibly out of each other and have never been wholly separate, their recent mutual attraction has come like the healing of a wound that had torn them unhealthily apart. The avalanche of writing and printing brought about by the industrial revolution of the eighteenth and nineteenth centuries, the skill of speedy writing made available to everyone by the public schools, the development of shorthand and typing, together with the corresponding need for rapid reading, skipping, and digesting has led to an unprecedented cheapening of language as a visual, aural, and syntactic form of expression. "Never have we possessed so much written material," noted the poet and critic Franz Mon in an introduction to a 1963 exhibition, *Art and Writing*, at the Stedelijk Museum in Amsterdam, "and never has written language itself given us so little. It covers everything like a scab."[2]

Such diagnoses refer to prevailing cultural trends, not to the divergent efforts of individuals. If we look from the same bird's-eye perspective at what happened to the pictorial image during recent centuries we find that a development toward increasing lifelikeness in painting made the formal factors of shape and color less conspicuous. The viewer's attention was monopolized by the subject matter—an attitude strongly enhanced by photography and its employment in the news services of the press. Along with this depreciation of form went, since the Renaissance, a gradual shift from subject matter embodying ideas to the portrayal of factually attractive landscapes, still lifes, animals, and human types. The symbolization of religious, monarchic, or humanistic ideas flattened out into mere illustrations of history or genre scenes.

In sum, both language and the pictorial image needed rejuvenation as media of formal expression. The stylistic developments which we think of as modern art and modern poetry can be said to have aimed at just such a rejuvenation. In addition, the visual media needed to be enriched by a return to thought. Perhaps concrete poetry serves these purposes; it refreshes the awareness of language as a vehicle of expression, and it injects abstract visual patterns with the thought element of meaningful words.

At the simplest level it is difficult to distinguish sign from image. Georg Christoph Lichtenberg tells of a gatekeeper of Frederick the Great, who had to record the comings and goings of the young princes and princesses; he indicated each exit and entrance by an *I* for a boy, an *O* for a girl.[3] Were these marks signs or images? Prehistorically, however, explicit images must have developed soon enough. Such images stand for kinds of things more often than signifying individuals. They portray *the* boar, *the* deer, superhuman powers, man and woman. This generality of meaning makes them useful when they develop into ideographs, markers of concepts.

The history of writing tells us how the need to standardize and abbreviate the images transforms them gradually into patterns simple and distinct in visual appearance and easy on the brush or the chisel. However, their iconic meaning reverberates even after thousands of years so that the modern Japanese in a thoughtful moment can still see the sun rise behind the tree when he looks at the kanji sign for east in the word Tokyo, signifying the eastern capital. And even when the visual etymology has vanished there remains at least the correspondence between a particular concept and a particular sign.

This valuable one-to-one relation between the signifier and the signified seems to be forever destroyed when syllabic or alphabetic writing replaces ideographs. The direct connection between the object and the visual sign is detoured via the speech sounds. What is worse, writing is instrumental in dissecting the unique sound pattern of each word into a small number of phonemic components, so that we are left with a set of signs whose units and combinations reflect nothing of the objects for which they stand. It is also true, however, that we profit from the complicated system of similarities and differences set up by the alphabet among the components of words and therefore of concepts. This creates a world of relations, almost totally alien to the world of things—a fabulous dream world in which the punster and the poet roam with delight.

Language describes objects as self-contained things. It grants this same autonomy also to the parts of objects, so that hand and skin and blood come to look like independent entities, just like the whole body. Language even transforms attributes and actions into things and separates them from their owners and performers. A strawberry is one verbal thing, its redness is another; and when we hear about "the slaying of Abel" the slaying is presented as an object coordinated with, and separated from, the victim. Temporal and spatial connections and logical links are equally reified. This means that to speak is to dismember a unified image for the purpose of communication, the way one dismembers a machine for shipping. To understand speech is to reconstruct the image from the disassembled pieces.

A principal device by which language aids the reconstruction of the image is spatial relation between words; and the principal spatial relation for this purpose is linearity. By no means is linearity inherent in the nature of language. If it had been necessary to remind us of this, concrete poetry would have done so. Language becomes linear only when it is used to code linear events, whether it reports on happenings of the outer world, as when it tells a story, or on an occurrence in the world of thought, as when an argument unfolds logically. Visual imagery is even less dependent on linearity. It surveys and organizes things perceived in three-dimensional space; it can also synthesize actions gathered from the time dimension, as when paintings depict stories. However, to understand relations by reasoning, we must trace linear connections through the sensory universe of simultaneity. This is what happens when we call one thing larger than, or parallel to, another, or when we observe and say that the moon rose and lit up the sea.

When language serves such narrations or arguments it must become linear. To the eyes this is expressed most adequately by a line of words, a line as long as the story itself. For convenience we chop up this line into units of standard length, and we also chop up the scroll into pages. The visual aspects of such packaging are alien to the structure of the discourse; that is, a break in the line or an end to the page indicates no corresponding break in the story.

Commonly, however, written and printed prose does contain subdivisions reflecting structural properties of the discourse. Words are separated by empty space, and so are sentences. Paragraphs mark the ends of episodes or thoughts. By carrying such visual depiction of content structure farther, poetry distinguishes itself for the eye from prose. This visual distinction is not a superficial one. The breaking up of the body of discourse into smaller units takes us back to the earliest forms of language, the one-word statements, the short phrases. If we compare the typical piece of prose with the typical poem—thereby neglecting the whole range of literary forms that combine characteristics of prose and poetry—we may venture to say that these two shapes of discourse correspond to two basic components of human cognition, namely, the tracing of causal sequences through the perceived world and the apprehension of given unitary situations, relatively self-contained and outside of the course of time. Of these two the second is obviously the psychologically earlier one.

Accessible to the early mind is the relatively limited situation, the episode, the striking appearance, the desire or fear, the confined event. These stationary units of experience, which correspond to the limited range of the young mind's organizing power, are reflected in the elementary language of, say, the child. But even at the highest level of human awareness, the conception of confined, synoptic situations remains one of the basic constituents of mental functioning. It expresses itself visually in the timeless images of painting, sculpture, architecture, and the like, and verbally in the lyrical poem.

The poem, in its prototypic shape, is short because it is synoptic like the picture, and its content is to be apprehended as a single state of affairs. Traditionally this does not deprive the poem's content of change, event, and development, but all this fits into one surveyable situation. A poem is basically timeless like a picture; and just as a picture must not be broken into two pieces, we resent it when a poem runs over to a second page.

What is true for the poem as a whole is true for its parts. The visual autonomy of each line detaches it somewhat from the continuity of the total sequence and presents it as a situation within a situation.

The progression in time, which runs from the beginning to the end of the poem like the argument of a piece of prose, is overlaid by an equally important second structural pattern, a coordination rather than a sequence of elements. The attentive reading of a poem requires much going back and forth, not unlike the scrutinizing of a painting, because the poem reveals itself only in the simultaneous presence of all of its parts.

This atemporal coordination of the parts is strengthened by repetition and alternation—two devices favored by concrete poetry, which carries atemporality to an extreme. Repetition violates the Heraclitean criterion of flux. The Same does return; and there is no before and after in the relation between identical things. As in music, poetic repetition in assonance, rhyme, or refrain knits things together outside the succession of time and stresses the simultaneity of the whole work. Alternation, which presupposes repetition, also counteracts the poem's overall sequence by presenting rivaling sequences of the same passages as equally required. The systematic permutation of lines or words, practiced by some writers of concrete poetry, serves this purpose most radically.

On the threshold between more traditional and concrete poetry there is an often cited poem by Eugen Gomringer:

> avenidas
> avenidas y flores
>
> flores
> flores y mujeres
>
> avenidas
> avenidas y mujeres
>
> avenidas y flores y mujeres y
> un admirador[4]

Simple and pleasant, the poem is traditional in its linear sequence of form and content. The poet uses the time dimension to carry his three basic components onto the stage of the image to be built for the reader. He starts with the setting of streets, decorates them with flowers, populates them with women, and even springs an old-fashioned coup de théâtre by introducing the admirer as the last touch. Verbally, there is a crescendo of growing sizes, which stops with dramatic abruptness before the punch line.

On the other hand, however, the poem as a whole is one image—a Goya painting might come to mind. The four nouns, with nothing but a linguistic plus sign to connect them, are self-sufficient bricks of experience, and the successive presentation of all the possible couplings of three of them counteracts the progression of the poem. Equal weight is given to all relations. We are shown a state of being, while the becoming is confined to the poet acting as the presenter.

In its more radical form, the concrete poem abolishes the defined relationship between elements by two principal devices. It reduces or eliminates connectives, leaving the poet with "words as hard and as scintillating as diamonds. The word is an element. The word is a material. The word is an object."[5] Second, the poem either excludes the overall sequence entirely or counteracts it so effectively by other sequences that none dominates the other.

Think of a few key words pointing to a landscape—sky, lake, boat, tree—sprinkled over a page. The reader's mind, trying to organize the material, may create a unified picture that possesses the principal property of any visual percept: all elements are fused in one organized whole, and all relations are integrated in a unified pattern. There are a few concrete poems that aim at such a pictorial response, but most of them produce networks of relations. Networks of relations are what the mind uses in reasoning. These relations do not fuse as they do in a percept, but in order to be readable they must organize hierarchically or sequentially. The diagram of a business organization is such a network; the steps of a mathematical proof are another. In order to serve the purposes of reasoning the totality of the relations must add up to an unambiguous statement. If there are contradictions, the thinker is called upon to eliminate them by doing more work.

The concrete poem uses networks but does not adopt the logician's criteria of validity. It thrives on the unresolved multiplicity of relations. An illuminating example is given by Max Bense, who derives a concrete poem from a philosophical proposition (Figure 1).[6] Descartes' *Cogito ergo sum* presents an unambiguous logical conclusion. Bense arranges the four words *ich* [I], *denke* [think], *ist* [is], and *etwas* [something] in such a way that none of the possible combinations of two, three, or four words dominates any other. If the reader takes the liberty of not limiting the meaning of the two verbs to the first and the third person singular respectively, and if he admits the concept *to be* in its double meaning of existence and of belonging in a category, he is presented with a slew of statements: I think; I am; something exists; I think something; something thinks I am; thinking is something; and so on.

ich

denke   ist

etwas

Figure 1.

Here is a challenge that can be met in two ways. As a reasoner the reader can attempt to sort out all this material and come up with an organized argument that might read like Descartes' *Meditations*. To him, in fact, Bense's display is something like the raw material that must have faced Descartes when he started thinking. But the reader can also take those four words as a poem. Then the statement on the page is final, and the multiplicity of unresolved propositions conveys a sense of the complexity of conscious experience, the wealth of human thought, and perhaps the hopelessness of making sense of it all. What is going on here is not thinking in the intellectual sense of the word, but rather the suspension of reasoning. Reasoning is contemplated as a perceptual phenomenon—like a play of storm clouds or a roused flock of birds.

If we think of language as raw material of the intellect we can attempt a guess at why concrete poetry has become so attractive. It is not simply a disenchantment with language, a shift from the verbal to the visual. In that case, words could be discarded altogether; the media of the visual arts are available for the asking. A special lure of concrete poetry is the opportunity to disavow sequential reasoning by using and dismembering its verbal devices.

An aversion to sequential reasoning cannot be expressed in a medium like painting and sculpture because even though the visual artist as a person may reason as much and as well as anybody else, the devices of sequential reasoning are not parts of his medium. Pictorial reasoning is concerned with facts and events in simultaneity. In a pictorial image all particular relations fuse in a unified pattern.

This means that all the influences impinging upon any one element balance out to establish an unambiguous visual definition of that element. If shape A is pushed to the left by factor B and to the right by factor C, it will find its particular dynamic character through the resultant of those vectors. In a completed work of visual art, there is no unresolved ambiguity of compositional vectors; they are absorbed in the interaction of their efforts.

This is different when the image is composed of verbal material. Even though the overall sequence may be weakened or entirely absent, the words come in small sequences or suggest such sequences by their juxtaposition. *Ich etwas* is processed inevitably into I am something, or I have or I want something, or there am I and there is something. As the Bense poem showed, such verbal clusters retain their individual autonomy while entering freely into simultaneously possible, varying combinations.

Perhaps one may speculate that concrete poetry is one of the antagonistic reactions of recent generations to the kind of reasoning that operates with linear links in chains of concepts, especially causal sequences. By its very nature, a causal chain has no beginning and no end. It reaches back to before the beginnings of any story and it searches beyond the end to forecast the future. Calling for anamnesis and prognosis, it asks: How did this come about? What could have happened instead? What can be done about the future? It suits an activist's approach, and it implies trust in the ability to understand and to tackle problems by intervention. Such an attitude underlies the literary novel, the drama, the narrative film, but also the clinical case study and scientific descriptions of processes. It is resisted by those who distrust psychoanalysis, which is a linear procedure par excellence, and by those who shun political doctrines that explain the mechanics of history and advocate change.

Immobile images, too, can represent connections and causal relations; but these images do not suggest links that reach beyond the confines of the situation presented. The artist shows Judith beheading Holofernes, but he does not encourage the viewer to ask what made her do it and what will come of the deed. The linearity of sequence is not in the nature of the pictorial medium, which deals with states of being, not with becoming.

By arranging words and phrases in nonsequential patterns, concrete poetry points polemically to the inconclusiveness of reasoning. It suggests that there is no beginning and no end, and that there is no way out of contradictions. In a positive mood, it displays tolerance for the multiplicity of relations and it recommends ambiguities and contradictions as resources of experience to be appreciated by the contemplating mind.

At the same time it must be admitted that to resist the challenges of the analytical mind limits the validity and also the depth of a work of art. In order to be a reflection of man, a work must engage all the powers of the human mind. This requirement is fulfilled in any good pictorial image. Perhaps, coming to the visual arts from Shakespeare or the *Divine Comedy*, one might be struck momentarily by the dumbness of Delacroix's Hamlet illustrations or the lack of verbal argument between his Dante and Virgil in Charon's bark. But once the absurd demand that the picture should speak is abandoned, it becomes evident that the image articulates characters and their interrelations with the same kind of acute intelligence that is found in literary speech.

A similar total engagement of the mind is found in traditional poetry. Beyond the conveying of moods, there is an impressive supply of thought in a poem by Leopardi or Dickinson or Yeats. By contrast, there is a temptation to complain about the simplicity of the typical concrete poem. It may be likened to the "minimal art" seen in recent years in painting and sculpture, and we may assert that although a return to the elements can be therapeutic in certain historical situations, we must guard against granting full status to such diminished products. This objection should not be dismissed too lightly. Yet it may blind us to certain stylistic trends, barely discernible now but perhaps important for the future. What I have in mind involves the fundamental difference between what I shall call *memento* and *message*.

Nicholas Poussin has given us the image of the shepherds who in the carefree setting of their fields come across a gravestone with the inscription *Et in Arcadia ego*. As a piece of information, the fact that death dwells everywhere is commonplace. As a poem the four words would not amount to much. But the inscription is no news item; it is no message but rather a memento. Instead of seeking us out for the purpose of delivering a communication, it is discovered by us, tied to a place and inseparable from that setting. If we are thoughtful it will make us meditate, as we may meditate on the intricate body of a fruit fly explored under magnification.

At the early stages of many cultures, works of visual art tend to act as mementos. They are monuments providing for a presence that is meaningful to the place where they stand. Statues are an obvious example. Murals, reliefs, or tapestries are integral properties of the caves, the tombs, the castles and churches for which they were made. As mementos such artifacts have certain characteristics. They are limited in the range of their substance; they often have the simplicity of an obelisk or pyramid, and this for several reasons. Being parts of an environment, their function is limited to a partial statement. They merely add an element to whatever else is being conveyed by the setting. Furthermore, as they are among the facilities for the activities of work and rest, traveling, visiting, delivering, providing, worshiping, they are geared to people in action. They must be relatively concise, adapted to the coming and going of the consumer.

Between the colossal heads on Easter Island and Bernini's marble figure of David there is a difference not only of historical style but of function. The gigantic stone heads are mementos, presumably objects of worship, goals of pilgrimage, tokens of divinity. Bernini's statue, displayed in a museum, is a message. Tied to no place or civic function, it comes to us as a statement on the nature of man. As such it must do the talking, it must deserve our attention, and being independent in time and space, it must tell the complete story. It is a deliverer of thought, whereas the ceremonial stone heads are occasions for thought.

The same distinction holds for works of language. The inscription on the tomb is a memento. It is in the company of signs saying *Exit* or *Silence* or *Peace*. Depending on its particular function, the memento gives directions, prescribes behavior, facilitates orientation. The verbal memento also must be concise, and it may invite thought. Just as the bronze cross on the altar is not required to vie in complexity with a crucifixion by Rubens but rather acts as a focus and stimulus for religious ideas in the churchgoer, so the ornamental quotations from the Koran on the walls of the mosques are mementos, different in principle from the disquisitions of a philosophical treatise. In the sanctuary of a Zen temple we may see a scroll displaying a single large ideograph, with perhaps a flower in a vase before it. The word and the flower invite our thought.

Such mementos are clearly different from what I call messages. The prototype of a verbal message is the letter sent by mail. It arrives and asks for the recipient's attention. It does the talking and can be expected to deserve the time spent on reading it. The letter informs and conveys thought. The development of the book from the ancient stone tablets to our modern paperbacks is one from memento to message. The tablets are not approached with the request: "Astonish me!" as may be done legitimately with a bestselling novel.

One of the intentions of concrete poetry is to lead poetry from message to memento by delivering it from the book. A book of poetry, although less recognizably so, behaves as a message, just like the letter, the novel, or the treatise. It approaches the reader from nowhere, intent on supplying him with thought and feelings at a place of his own choosing. It promises to be worth his while and invites the attitude of the judging consumer, who, according to the recommendation of Bert Brecht, leans back and smokes a cigar. Judged by the standards of the message, the typical concrete poem does not meet qualifications. We must realize that it aims at being a memento.

As an extreme example, Ronald Johnson's poem (Figure 2) will

eyeleveleye

Figure 2.

make the point.[7] It looks like one word, but when read in the conventional manner it is revealed as three words run together, the first identical with the third. *Eye level* reminds the reader of the way he is facing the row of letters, and *level eye* may set off some vague association. The repetition of *eye* suggests that we give up the left-to-right sequence and perceive the pattern in its symmetry. This restructuring is immediately rewarded by the two eyes now looking at us like those of a face. Once geared to the visual pattern, we discover the regular weave of six *e*'s, which knit the line together, and the two rooted poles of the *y*'s counterbalancing the two rising poles of the *l*'s. Fenced off by the *l*'s there appears an *eve* and an *Eve*, whose shapely symmetry is underscored by the total pattern, and we are led to ponder the relations between *eye* and *Eve*. All this works best when the mind is but half awake, willing to let come whatever will. Reasoning is caught napping, or at least it is permissive enough not to spoil the drifting images.

Clearly, the attitude called for by the example is not the heightened alertness to which the reading of good poetry arouses us traditionally. It is more like watching the gliding transformations of summer clouds, with the mind on vacation. And in fact, the place most propitious to the concrete poem is outside the book, somewhere in the practical environment. There it may catch the eye of a partially engaged passer-by, who will briefly stop and ponder the curious apparition, and then walk away musing, his thoughts slightly or profoundly stirred. Mary Ellen Solt quotes Ferdinand Kriwet as saying of his poems that they have, at least at first glance, "sign character, as have all public texts on notice-boards, house fronts, hoardings, signs, lorries, on roads and runways, etc."[8]

The maker of concrete poetry joins his fellow artists in their desire to escape from the social isolation that has haunted the arts since they tore loose from their moorings during the Renaissance and became ambulant products, made for no one in particular, belonging nowhere, and willing to bed down with anybody for a price. As the artist shies away from the blank walls of gallery and museum, the poet is disenchanted by the neutrality of the blank paper and dreams of seeing his work as a sign or placard or icon in the daily traffic of market, pilgrimage, and recreation. And just as sculptors plough furrows in a desert or decorate the mouth of a volcano with shapes that are childish when considered by themselves, the hope of the poets is that in a restored context their verbal images will reveal an eloquence suitable to their purpose.

At the beginning of this essay I noted that the encounter of poetry and the visual arts in a new typographic imagery might not only act as a refreshment to both media but also provide aesthetic theory with new insight. To the student of visual perception concrete poetry offers a quarry of striking examples for the rules of organization worked out by gestalt psychologists. I cannot make use of this attractive material now; instead I will illustrate a few more general theoretical considerations.

All representational images involve the relation between what linguists call the signifier and the signified. For our purpose we speak of the relation between two images, the percept directly apprehended by the eyes and the mental image conjured up by the percept. Although both images always participate, the weight of the viewer's or reader's experience may be located more toward the one or the other pole, and this difference matters for our investigation.

When we look at a realistic picture, perhaps a view of the Canale Grande by Guardi, the experience is all gathered in the image in front of us. Venice is right there, and it is almost impossible to conjure up our memory of the city for comparison. Even in more abstract images the weight of the experience is clearly in what the eyes see directly. Compare this with the reading of a novel or a memorandum. There the attention of the absorbed reader is focused entirely upon the mental images conjured up by the words. Nothing is actually received but the percepts of the typographic shapes on paper, but the mind looks right through the words at their referents.

The prose text acknowledges this situation by the neutrality of its appearance. As the poem abandons this neutrality of the typographic image and equips it with more and more visual characteristics of its own, it also shifts the weight of attention toward the immediate percept on the page. Not only is there now more to look at, but the visual traits of the printed matter are also more relevant to the verbal statement and therefore in competition with the mental image called up by the words.

The classic example of this liberation is Mallarmé's poem *Un Coup de Dés*, in which the standard length of lines and the standard quantity of print on the page are abandoned and phrases of varying length spread over the paper, creating totally different patterns on every page (Figure 3).[9] The result attracts the eye by its variety of shapes, but it is by no means a set of pictures. The poet uses different type faces and sizes to overlay the linear sequence of the poem with cross connections between segregated passages; but these spatial bridges are purely verbal. Similarly, the breaking up of the lines into short phrases merely reflects the syntactic structure and the rhythm of the text, as it does in the poetry of E.E. Cummings. Apart from a decently balanced typographic spacing of the phrases, the patterns of words have no pictorial autonomy as "abstract" compositions. They are entirely at the service of the poetic text.

The phenomenon becomes more acute when the words begin to form visual shapes which display a pictorial autonomy of their own. This property distinguishes concrete poetry as a category from earlier attempts. In the following Japanese scene by John Tagliabue[10] the shape of the poem echoes the slight and irregular swing of the lantern carried by the boy through the narrow street.

```
            a
         lantern
            swings
            slightly
            in
            the
                 kanji
                 of
                 the
                 alley
                 of
                 cats
               fruit
            vegetables
            fish
           and
         holding
        it
        a
        boy
          on
             geta
             is
       carrying
          the
             moon
```

In this example the typographic pattern holds its own as a visual image. Thereby an artful balance is obtained between the percept on paper and the Japanese street scene brought to mind by the words. The immediate presence of the wavy ribbon of words and the coincidence of its movement with that described in the text prevent the reader from immersing himself wholly in the exotic mental image; they keep that scene somewhat remote and affect it with the abstractness of the words and their motion—an impression strengthened perhaps by the word *kanji*, which seems to suggest that the alley of cats, fruit, vegetables, and fish is like a pageant of ideographs.

Note here that the pattern of Tagliabue's poem does not do violence to the verbal structure but causes an appropriate atomization of the grammatical sequence, a staccato rhythm, which lets each word act as an image of its own in an agglomeration of facets. Concrete poetry seems to be most successful when it preserves the structural patterns of both media, the verbal and the pictorial, and forces them into a significant union.

In the Tagliabue poem, the visible form offered a highly abstract

LE NOMBRE

EXISTÂT-IL
autrement qu'hallucination éparse d'agonie

COMMENÇÂT-IL ET CESSÂT-IL
sourdant que nié et clos quand apparu
enfin
par quelque profusion répandue en rareté

SE CHIFFRÂT-IL

évidence de la somme pour peu qu'une

ILLUMINÂT-IL

LE HASARD

Choit
la plume
rythmique suspens du sinistre
s'ensevelir
aux écumes originelles
naguères d'où sursauta son délire jusqu'à une cime
flétrie
par la neutralité identique du gouffre

Figure 3.

illustration of a movement derived from the narrative scene. Quite often, however, the typographic picture symbolizes not the subject matter but the structural relations between the concepts. It spatially interprets connections and separations, like a poetical version of diagrams, flow charts, and so on. Assonances, similarity of letters, syllables, or whole words are skillfully used to make these relations of meaning perceptually compelling.

It would be awkward for such symbolization of conceptual relations to take place in realistic space. In fact, concrete poetry, for all its objections to the asocial remoteness of the printed page, has good reasons to choose emptiness as the most suitable foil for its presentations. Ordinary print on paper is an example of what the psychologist calls the relationship of figure and ground. The homogeneous background, seen as extending behind the figures, is not clearly characterized as either solid surface or indefinite depth. In pictures it stands for nothingness or for an environment of unspecified properties.

The concrete poem tends to reject any frame, just as printing does. The rectangular edge of the paper is not a frame but simply a nondescript ending. It "bleeds" the empty ground behind the printed material, rather than framing it. A frame would create an inappropriate pictorial space. The concrete poem is not limited, however, to two-dimensional patterns in the frontal plane. It can easily extend its skeleton of abstract relations into depth by means of a stereoscope. But guided by a sure instinct, poet-designers have avoided creating illusory space by overlaps, perspective, or tilted planes. This would suggest an image of physical space, potentially inhabitable by the viewer.

Visually, concrete poetry defines its position by inventing its shapes within the limits of printed language: the line, straight or simply curved, the word, the letter. Parallels and right angles are preferred. Imitative shapes deviating from these standard elements are on dangerous territory and generate unattractive or purely humorous hybrids. Handwriting lacks the standardized perfection of designed type, which has the advantage of showing up repetitions, similarities, and geometrical relations with desirable precision. Even when conventional verbal signs are entirely abandoned, the arrangement of nonverbal shapes can maintain the appearance of print by preserving its typical properties. This leads to interpretations of the visual aspects of writing, as in the recent *Perzeptionen* of Warja Lavater,[11] or to whimsical takeoffs, such as Christian Morgenstern's ingenious *Evensong of the Fishes* of 1905 (Figure 4).[12] This poem of pure shapes plays back and forth between the rhythmical opening and closing of fish mouths, the scanning of poetical meters, the shape of poems and the shape of fishes, and the analogy between rows of print on paper and rows of scales in the fish skin.

We reach the point at which the printed word takes its place among the objects portrayed by the painter. A few observations on this aspect of the meeting between picture and written word may conclude our investigation. The particular role played by words and letters in modern painting derives from their twofold, antagonistic

Fisches
Nachtgesang.

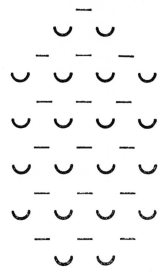

Figure 4.

nature as the prototypes of readability and as the only truly meaning-less shapes in the world of man. Let us imagine a photograph of a worm-eaten apple and compare it with Reinhard Döhl's shape made up of the German word for apple plus that for worm (Figure 5).[13] The viewer's experience of the verbal picture, hardly a poem, focuses on the directly given percept, as does the photograph. But though the fruit is bodily present in the photograph, it is coded in the verbal picture. The photograph supplies no names; the verbal picture files the object under the appropriate cognitive category even before its shape is truly perceived. With the same chilly detachment the little drama of the worm is recorded. What is symbolized here is literate man's removal from his most vital sights and their replacement by minimal signals for identification only. The eyes can no longer read anything but what has been conceptually predigested for them.

At the same time, from the point of view of the nonverbal world of our senses, the human environment has been invaded by mysteri-

Figure 5.

ous shapes, which are neither organic nor inorganic, do not reveal their nature by their appearance, and have no physical function. In this sense I called them meaningless. However, letters share with other abstract shapes those physiognomic qualities that derive directly from their perceptual character. To give just one example: Balzac, in his story Z. *Marcas,* points to the resemblance between the initial Z of his hero's first name and the man's nonconformist, erratic personality. "Ne voyez-vous pas dans la construction du Z une allure contrariée? ne figure-t-elle pas le zigzag aléatoire et fantasque d'une vie tourmentée? Quel vent a soufflé sur cette lettre qui, dans chaque langue où elle est admise, commande à peine à cinquante mots?"

These expressive but meaningless shapes have joined our world of objects as signs and inscriptions. In the collages and paintings of the cubists, bits of print are torn out of context, mutilated, and reduced to mere shapes among shapes. And whereas Döhl's apple pointed to a world that can be read but no longer seen, the printed words in modern still lifes seem to warn of a world that can be seen but no longer read.

The term *reading* stands here for two totally different mental operations: meaning revealed to the unaided eye by the mere look of things; and meaning ascribed to meaningless shapes by blind convention. It is the double existence of words as a species of pure shapes and as a non-sensory carrier of sense that has made language the most telling symbol of modern civilized life. This symbolic role of language is displayed in the images and verbal weaves of concrete poetry.

Notes

1. This paper could not have been written without the help of Mary Ellen Solt and her comprehensive and admirably perceptive work, *Concrete Poetry: A World View* (Bloomington: Indiana University Press, 1971). I am indebted also to Merald E. Wrolstad for guiding me to the pertinent literature published in his periodical, *Visible Language*, the former *Journal of Typographic Research*.
2. *Schrift und Bild*, Staatliche Kunsthalle, Baden-Baden, 1963.
3. Sudelbücher, J. 298. In *Schriften und Briefe*, ed. Wolfgang Promies, vol. 1 (Munich: Hansen, 1968).
4. Gomringer's "Avenidas" was written in 1952. Cf. Solt, pp. 90 and 253. Quoted by permission of the author.
5. Pierre Garnier quoted in Solt, p. 32.
6. Reproduced in Emmett Williams, ed., *An Anthology of Concrete Poetry* (New York: Something Else Press, 1967). By permission of Professor Max Bense.
7. Johnson's poem, from Solt, p. 250, is reproduced by permission of the author.
8. Solt, p. 20.
9. Gerald L. Bruns, "Mallarmé—The Transcendence of Language and the Aesthetics of the Book," *Journal of Typographic Research*, vol. 3, no. 3 (1969): 219–40. Contains a facsimile of *Un Coup de Dés*.
10. Quoted from the manuscript by permission of John Tagliabue.
11. Zurich: Hürlimann, 1973.
12. *Galgenlieder*, first published in 1905. Berlin: Cassirer.
13. Reproduced in Williams and used here by permission of the author.

Charlotte Lackner Doyle

THE CREATIVE PROCESS
A Study in Paradox*

IT OFTEN SEEMS THAT OPPOSITE GENERALIZATIONS ABOUT THE CREATIVE
process are true. To say, for example, that the creative process requires freedom and spontaneity runs counter to Ezra Pound's aphor-
ism, "Any damned fool can be spontaneous." It is not necessary to
agree with Mr. Pound entirely in order to say that the creative process demands discipline, concentration, and a commitment to work.
According to Freud the creative process taps the primitive and the
emotional; Shakespeare and Rembrandt would probably have said
that it requires insight, intelligence, and maturity; the psychologist
Guilford might say that the creative process involves fantasy, inventiveness, and ability for thought to diverge from what is. I remember my own interviews with artists and in my view the creative
process demands honesty and a commitment to truth. The statements
can easily crowd in: the creative process is self-expression; the creative process cannot take place unless the creator forgets about
himself; the creative process is a joy; the creative process is fraught
with fear, terror, and frustration; the creative process is its own reward; the creative process needs support and encouragement. As
contradictory statements floated around in my head, the title for this
paper came to me: "The Creative Process: A Study in Paradox." An
old trick psychologists have learned is to name what is not under-

*This paper is a slightly modified version of the keynote address entitled "The
Creative Experience: Aspects and Interplay," delivered by me at the Lucy
Sprague Mitchell Memorial Conference held at the Bank Street College of
Education, 18 May 1974.

stood. Naming presents a phenomenon for study and everyone feels better.

Having named my problem, I looked for resources to help me gain insight into it. For several years, I have been teaching a course called "The Psychology of Creativity" in which my students and I investigate what the great thinkers in psychology have to say about the creative process. We begin with Freud and Jung. In their writings about the creative person, these great clinicians dealt primarily with fine artists—writers, painters, sculptors. Artists have a unique and special talent; they delve into the depths of their personalities and give coherent form to ideas and impulses that remain buried and incoherent in nonartists. For Freud, it is the repressed wishes of infancy that the artist has the power to transform. "The writer," said Freud, "is a person with a certain flexibility of repression and the courage to let his unconscious speak."[1] Why has the Mona Lisa smile tantalized people for centuries? Because it is the tantalizing smile that every infant sees; it represents the tender, seductive, yet unavailable mother whose love each baby yearns for but ultimately cannot fully consummate. Plays like *Oedipus Rex* and *Hamlet* continue to move us, because they tell of the death of a father and the infidelity of a mother, which Freud felt was a disguised retelling of every boy's early wishes and fears. The artist tells these stories in a disguised way so that neither he nor his audience knows the true source. The disguise is like the primitive language of our dreams. Using this hidden code, we can be deeply moved and not know why.

Jung, too, sees the artist as descending into the depths of personality but for him the great artist is not simply dealing with the impulses and ideas of the personal unconscious, but with the universal images with which Jung believed everyone was born. There is a collective unconscious peopled by characters and themes which have held significance in myth, ritual, and religion throughout the ages. This collective unconscious is the source and the significance of creative work. For example, the story of death, a descent into the underworld, a resurrection and a rebirth is a universal theme that symbolizes the many deaths, hells, and rebirths encountered in life. For Jung, the artist articulates these collective themes which can then serve as a guide for the journey through life. In providing a tangible form for them, the artist fulfills a deep and little understood human necessity.

Abraham Maslow sees the creative process quite differently; it is not the making of a work of art but a way of approaching life. It is the approach to life of every healthy child. By healthy, Maslow means that the child does not want for any of his basic needs such as food, warmth, safety, and love. Infantile psychic conflict, or repressed anxiety, is not inevitable to Maslow as it is to Freud. A child, unfettered by repressed anxiety and unconstrained by fears of cultural demand, will be free, spontaneous, curious, learning by her own discoveries, constantly growing and changing. Such creativity need have no product; it may be expressed in the way food is eaten, in the way friends are made, in the decoration of a house, or in a walk in the park. Many artists may have a special talent for art, but if they are unhappy and compulsive, driven by infantile need, they are in one sense not creative. Psychologists and educators interested in creativity, says Maslow, should not focus on talented neurotics but on the conditions for a life of healthy growth.

Maslow thinks of the creative process in terms of a total life;[2] some psychologists think of it in terms of a moment, a kernel act. The essence of the creative process according to this view is the generation of new and original ideas. The same ability, the same basic psychic operations are involved whether the task is to generate ideas for a new style in painting, a new approach to cancer research, a new way to make soup, or a new wrinkle in income tax returns. The ability to produce many diverse ideas is central.

This approach has been taken by some experimental psychologists who, in order to do their research, need a concrete act to observe. The most active have been researchers who think about, develop, and validate psychological tests. Psychologists like Guilford, Getzels and Jackson, and Wallach and Kagan were dissatisfied with using the standard intelligence test as the sole indicator of a child's potential. Intelligence tests ask questions to which there are correct answers; they do not capture the ability to come up with a new idea, to be original, to create. So they designed new questions, divergent thinking questions, questions for which there are no single correct answers, questions which make observable a flow of thought rather than the ability to find a correct answer to a task. Rather than asking how a fly and a tree are alike, scoring an answer mentioning life as correct, they designed questions like: what are the different ways that a mouse and a lion are alike? Being an animal, having fleas, scaring the timid, or being movie stars in some form or other are answers. Instead of asking children to copy a drawing, a child might be asked what different things a drawing could be. "How many uses can you think of for a brick?" is one of the most famous items. These divergent thinking tasks—some people call them creativity tests—look for evidence of an ability to produce many different and original ideas. "Divergent thinking" is the ability for thought to flow from one idea to the other—the more far out, the zanier, the better. The ability to come up with wide-ranging associations is seen as the primary condition of the creative process. Once the testers defined the creative act in this observable way, psychologists from the behaviorist tradition became interested in the creative process. The behaviorists jumped in and said: if the creative process consists of giving different and divergent answers to a problem, then the way to induce creativity is to put people in situations where they do come up with a variety of answers and then reward them for it. So behaviorists have rewarded college students for unusual associations to words, porpoises for creating unusual sequences of movement, and children for building many different kinds of structures with blocks; thus they hoped to advance the creative process.

As my students and I read through each of these theories,[3] we are victims of something like the medical student syndrome. It happens to me every year. Each account, as we read it, seems right. As we read Freud, the idea of every artist reaching into and expressing in disguised form his own early infantile conflicts, which constitute everyman's early history, seems persuasive. We read Jung and are moved by the idea that at the deepest levels of our psyche are the primitive forms of the collective unconscious. We read Maslow and delight in the idea that life itself can be a creative process. We applaud Guilford and those who followed his lead for broadening the view of what talent is, for augmenting the intelligence test with items for which there is no one right answer, but which call for flexible and original thought. And we look on in wonder as the behaviorists, whose earlier work emphasized behavior as a bundle of habits, march in and try to make divergent thinking itself a habit. Psychological theory is a rich resource, but unless you are a true believer, it alone does not resolve paradox.

There is another resource: the reports and insights of creative people. My students and I also read interviews, letters, prefaces, and autobiographies of people recognized as creative. We interviewed three creative people. These three interviews, which I taped—without gap, I'll have you know—are my private treasure. We interviewed Jane Cooper, a poet whose first book of poems, *The Weather of Six Mornings,* won the Lamont Poetry Prize and whose second book,

Calling me from sleep, was published late in 1974; Grace Paley, who has written two fine books of short stories, *The Little Disturbances of Man* and her recent book, *Enormous Changes at the Last Minute;* and Joel Spiegelman, an exciting, internationally recognized modern composer.

The interviews, the personal documents, and the theories were my resources for dealing with paradox. So I listened again to the tapes, reread the autobiographical statements, and reviewed the theories. I hoped to find some thread to guide me out of what was beginning to appear like a hopeless morass. I wrote words on my pad like time, medium, discovery in order to try to capture the similarities and differences in the theories and in the personal statements. Then, one day, perhaps out of desperation, perhaps out of boredom, I decided to take that first word—*time*—seriously and to see where it led me.

I think I first wrote down the word time, because this is a dimension on which theorists differ. When Guilford asks how many uses can be thought of for bricks, he focuses on a task that takes minutes; when Freud and Jung write of artists and the work they make, the time span is in terms of days or months; Maslow speaks of the creative process in terms of a lifetime. When we spoke to artists, we became increasingly aware that the creations of works of art are episodes in a larger life that has to cope with all the other tasks and problems of life, a larger life that has been developing and changing and growing since birth.

So let us look at the creative process from the perspective of time by focusing on the creative episode which results in a product. Maslow may be saying something important when he speaks of a creative life without creative products, an open loving spontaneous life, but I would like to take a close look at the *creative episode in art,* that segment of time in a life when a work of art is made. Whether the processes that characterize the creative episode take place in contexts outside of the making of a work of art is also a creative question.

The boundary that marks the beginning of the creative episode can be identified; the episode begins with the intimation that the process has begun, with a hunch that there is a seed of thought that can be developed. Sometimes, the germ that starts the process is clear. Henry James describes such a beginning in his preface to *The Spoils of Poynton.* He speaks of eating Christmas dinner with some friends. A woman told of an incident about a mother and a son who cared about each other and who both were considered wonderful, exemplary people. But mother and son were suddenly "at daggers" over the disposition of the dead father's property. Here is how James described what happened as soon as he heard the story:

> I instantly became aware . . . of the prick of innoculation; the whole of the virus, being infused by that single touch . . . I "took" in fine "on the spot", to the rich bare little fact of the two related figures, embroiled perhaps all so sordidly; and for reasons of which I could most probably have given no decent account. Had I been asked why they were . . . "interesting", I fear I could have said nothing more to the point . . . than "Well, you'll see". By which of course I should have meant, "Well, I shall see". . . . That points, I think, to a large part of the very source of interest for the artist . . . that he alone has the *secret* of a particular case, he alone can measure the truth of the direction to be taken.[4]

Katherine Anne Porter speaks in one case of an idea starting inarticulately—simply the intuition that something is there to work on.

> Sometimes an idea starts completely inarticulately. You're not thinking in images or words or—well, it's exactly like a dark cloud moving in your head. You keep wondering what will come out of this and then it will dissolve itself into a set of—well, not images exactly, but really thoughts. You begin to think directly in words. Abstractly. Then the words transform themselves into images. By the time I write the story, my people are up and alive and walking around and taking things in their own hands.[5]

It is important to notice that the creative process begins with a sense of direction, with the hunch that there is something to go after. The hunch may come from an experience, from the play of divergent thinking, or from directed thinking about a problem. But something tugs, some yet inarticulate goal beckons; there is no creative process without a direction. Spontaneity without a direction emerging from it does not lead to creative work.

The creative episode begins with a sense of direction. How do you go after something that is not yet articulated? Part of the answer, I think, is that the artist *thinks through* his medium. The painter thinks in form and color; the poet thinks in images and words, the playwright thinks in characters and dialogue and events as they appear on stage. For example, an interviewer asked Faulkner how *The Sound and the Fury* began and grew.

> It began with a mental picture. . . . The picture was of the muddy seat of a little girl's drawers in a pear tree, where she could see through a window where her grandmother's funeral was taking place and report what was happening to her brothers on the ground below.

By the time I explained who they were and what they were doing and how her pants got muddy, I realized it would be impossible to get all of it into a short story, and that it would have to be a book. And then I realized the symbolism of the soiled pants and the image was replaced by one of the fatherless and motherless girl climbing down the rainpipe to escape from the only home she had, where she had never been offered love or affection or understanding.[6]

Faulkner began *The Sound and the Fury* with an image and he developed the novel by developing characters and events from the image. He thought directly in the fictional medium.

The artist—in fact, every thinker—needs such a medium, a vehicle for organizing and thinking about experience. And although some psychologists associate thought with logical operations and abstract verbal generalization, the artist, thinking in a medium, thinks differently.[7] He thinks forms, people talking, and images and rhythms. When the artist thinks in this way certain so-called logical distinctions disappear, for example, the distinction between intellect and emotion. In life we simultaneously grasp an experience and feel it emotionally; we understand that someone is trying to block us and we feel angry; we grasp that someone is helping us with no apparent benefit to himself and we feel gratitude. We see the grayness of the day as rain approaches and we feel the melancholy.[8] In a medium, an artist can simultaneously communicate event and feeling. This is one example, but I suspect that by thinking directly in a given medium, the artist can give form to complexities that are difficult to capture in other ways. Each medium has properties that make it easier to think in certain ways through it. For example, to think *time* is more difficult in the spatial arts than in writing or music.

In order to think through a medium, a person needs skill. I remember an incident Herbert Kohl wrote about. He was describing his work with pupils considered difficult to reach and his method was to get them to write. One little girl raised her hand and said something like, "I would like to write about my father if there is a word for him. But if there is no word for him, I don't want to."[9]

Learning a skill is again a process that takes time, a developmental process, and for artists it may be a lifelong process. In interviews, artists frequently speak of their struggles with the craft. For example, at one point Jane Cooper told us of "studying how to make time happen in the present."

Studying the medium, learning the craft is a part of the life of the creative artist which prepares her for the creative episode, but a conscious attempt to do tricky things with the medium to express an idea is probably doomed, because the artist does not dress a thought in some other form and then put it into the medium—she thinks through the medium. Grace Paley said, "For me to understand something, I have to put it in fictional terms." The ideas are thought in the flesh of character or event or shape or image or rhythm. In art, ideas are in flesh.

Thinking in the medium, clarifying and developing that original germ does not occur in an instant. Again, it is a process that takes time.[10] Partly this is because thinking in a medium is trying things out. An impulse from the ever changing flow of our stream of thought is made into a thing no longer ephemeral. It stands to face the artist. He can look at it or hear it and then say to himself, "That's it, that's what I was going after," or "That's not it—it has to be something more like this." Van Gogh wrote to a friend:

> When I have a model who is quiet and steady and with whom I am acquainted, then I draw repeatedly until there is one drawing that is different from the rest, which does not look like an ordinary study, but more typical and with feeling. All the same it was made under circumstances similar to those of the others, yet the latter have less feeling and life in them. . . . As to *The Little Winter Gardens*, for example, you said yourself they had so much feeling; all right, but that was not accidental—I drew them several times and there was no feeling in them. Then afterwards—after I had done the ones that were so stiff—came the others. How does it happen that I can express something of that kind? Because the thing has already taken form in my mind before I start on it. The first attempts are absolutely unbearable. I say this because I want you to know that if you see something worthwhile in what I am doing, it is not by accident but because of real intention and purpose.[11]

For Van Gogh, there was an intention, a direction which he could not put into words or put on canvas at first; but by working in the world of paint and canvas, the intention finally took shape. When Grace Paley talked about writing her stories she said, "I talk the people. I talk some of the people sixty times." And Hemingway wrote the last page of *A Farewell to Arms* thirty-nine times. An interviewer asked what the problem was. "Getting the words right."[12]

The medium, a kind of reality principle, shows us when we do not know what we think. A common experience in teaching is for students to tell me they have ideas but can't express them. And I tell them they do not know what the ideas are until they can express them in the world in some medium. We run into the barrier of the medium when trying to verbalize what we think we understand and then the words fail us. But when words fail we can locate the points where the thoughts, I should say the thoughts-in-the-words, are hazy. Then it is possible to investigate problems of which we were unaware.

A friend of mine, a composer, told me he dreamt the most marvelous melodies, but by morning they were forgotten. He resolved to keep music paper on his night table and write down the melody as soon as he awoke. That night, once again, he had a dream of a marvelous melody. He awoke and immediately wrote it down and then went back to sleep. The next morning, he looked at what he had written. My friend shook his head as he told the story. "Charlotte," he said, "it was *terrible*, in the light of day it was terrible."

The medium puts the clouds in our heads out in the world; it crystallizes them. They are perhaps awkward and foggy, but once objectified the creator can look, think, and build on them in a new way. The creative process then becomes an encounter between the creator and that which is being created.

So the creative process begins. First a hunch and a sense of direction develops and grows through thinking in the medium. If you are lucky, and Katherine Anne Porter, something forms and becomes a story. But if you are Joel Spiegelman,

> You never know when you start composing and when you think you are, you're not. You try and it doesn't go. You go away for a while and AHA, the problem, the notes you've been working with a long time—they begin to transform themselves.

Or Grace Paley. She told us that she writes the first paragraph of her stories out of pure language.

> It was the language that started me, made me think. . . . I haven't the vaguest idea what the story is, what page three is. . . . Then maybe in a couple months I write the next three pages and then I'm really stuck. . . . Suddenly I get this thing, these three to five pages which I really wrote before and I say "My God" and that's what the story is about because that's what my head has been forming.

These descriptions are reminiscent of a description of the art of thought put forward by Graham Wallas fifty years ago. He recognized thought as taking place in time and distinguished four stages: preparation, incubation, illumination, and verification. Preparation involves a thorough investigation of the problem. (He assumes that the problem first must be clear.) Incubation is a turning away from the problem consciously and hopefully—an illumination, a discovery emerges from what Grace Paley calls the compost heap of the mind. And then there is the workmanlike task of seeing whether the solution is in fact a solution (verification). (It's a dangerous thing to teach students Graham Wallas. A conversation that has taken place more than once in my office goes like this. "How's your paper coming?" "I'm still incubating." But never daunted I then ask—"Have you thoroughly prepared?" And if the answer is yes, my next question is, "Do you have a sense that you have a direction even if you don't yet know exactly what it is—because if you don't have this, the process hasn't really started and you should play with the material until it happens.") I do not know what goes on during incubation, but I suspect it is that initial sense of direction, if it is strong enough, that remains active, which is ready to rise again into consciousness if there is a hint that the mind can find a way to pursue it.[13] Joel Spiegelman, at one point, spoke of finding one key which permitted him a long extension and then he ran dry. "Then," he said, "I have to get far, far away . . . and then the magic of an idea . . . may come to you in the shape of a building or a skyline, all kinds of extra-musical sources, but you draw some kind of relation to the musical shape."

In this description, an important thing to note besides the account of incubation and illumination is that there is not a single moment of discovery that solves all the problems. Although some theoretical descriptions and some artists' accounts emphasize the moment of insight, the sudden falling into place of all the parts, I suspect that extended periods of work full of stops and starts punctuated by surprises large and small is more typical. Along the way, it is easy to despair. The idea-in-flesh as it faces the creator may be so far from his intuition of the goal. Other aspects of life which are not so difficult and so lonely may pull him away. The work may be aborted before what for me is the most marvelous, mysterious, and, so far, nameless part of the creative episode. Let me give it a name—the *period of total centration*.

It is the period for the writer when the characters take over, when the melodies flow without forcing, when the painting seems to paint itself. The artist is totally absorbed in the work. All the awkwardness that comes from watching ourselves at work, from the fear that what we are doing is no good, from careful critical selection is no longer a part of the flow of thought and action. The artist's head, his hands, his lips are totally directed by the forces that have been generated by the sense of direction and the ideas-in-flesh as he is working with them. All intellectual and emotional resources, all skills and experiences become part of the artist's reach and movement toward the eventual goal. This total centration is a particular kind of consciousness. This is not a drug state; in fact, I suspect that a sustained period of total centration might be almost impossible under drugs.

It is extremely difficult to talk about consciousness and its forms; psychologists gave up years ago and chose to study what was easier to make manifest. But let me try to point at what I am talking about. As we look at a person in the stream of life, we can think of experience as a constantly changing screen. Sometimes sense organs, thoughts, and actions—our cameras—are focused on particular objects in the world; sometimes what is on the screen is the result of scanning. At night, in sleep, the cameras are turned off and internal processes, not intentionally sought after or tied to moving about in the environment, are thrown up on the screen in dreams. While we are awake, the images are sometimes sharply focused, sometimes blurred. Sometimes the focus is on feelings.

As experience progresses from infancy to maturity, the structures of experience, the frameworks which organize the parts on the screen, become differentiated. We become aware of ourselves in relation to others, of a physical world that is separate from self and of a social world that self is separate from, but still dependent on and a part of. This framework of a self which is in the world, a self which acts and wants and needs, a self that is perceived and judged by others, a self which tries and might fail recurrently organizes much of the experience projected on the screen as well as the thoughts and actions that flow from that organization. During periods of total centration, self-in-the-world, as a way of organizing experience remains in the background. For extended periods, the organization, the flow and change, is determined by the object or the task on which attention is centered. Actions and thoughts interact directly with that which attention is centered on without being diffracted, narrowed, or redirected by other concerns. Total centration is not limited to the making of a work of art—the spectator who is completely lost in a play, the ball player whose mind and body, eyes, arms, torso are centered on the ball that is coming at him, the attentive student reaching to grasp what a teacher is explaining may be totally centered, so that self-consciousness no longer pulls attention away. These wonderful times have been described as moments of full spontaneity and freedom. But the freedom and spontaneity come from such total concentration on a task and *its* direction and *its* structure, that all resources are directed toward it. The person is freed of self-consciousness, of personal fears and hopes, and can respond fully and freely and spontaneously to whatever she is centered on.[14]

In the creative episode, when a period of total centration is reached, the developing work is the center. Only it is on the screen of experience, and the patterns of thought, action, and feeling can freely act on *it* and in terms of it without an intermediary framework which would change the pattern. To describe these periods—when what organizes and directs experience cannot be accounted for in terms of a conscious self acting in the world—psychologists and artists speak of primitive processes taking over. It is the personal unconscious, those repressed infantile wishes which now can emerge to act on the work, says Freud. It is the archetypical forms, those universal images that can finally organize the work, says Jung. Something like structure of personal emotional life and universal archetypal forms may indeed contribute to the development of the work, for at this point, no selective mechanism is preventing any important psychic pattern from being drawn into the work. But so too are those hard-won patterns of thought and skill, the intricacies grasped in perception, and those bits and pieces of work, awkward and awful as they seemed, which were early attempts to get at the something which impelled the artist. "A poem uses everything we know, the surprising things we notice, whatever we can't solve and keeps on growing, but it has to reach beyond autobiography if it is even to stay on the page," wrote Jane Cooper.[15]

During the period of total centration all the patterns of the mind are potentially active. There is a center toward which activity flows and I believe that center is neither the personal nor the collective unconscious; it is that growing object in the world, those developing ideas-in-flesh, developing in relation to that initial intuition which started the creative episode and the goal of articulate statement in the medium. This is the magnet that attracts and patterns all those resources which become available.

These periods are recalled as periods of incredible joy, even ecstasy. Thought and action are in harmony; interaction with the work becomes as smooth and flowing as a dance, and ideas seem to emerge out of nowhere. The work seems to create itself, because the creator's picture of himself as working does not obstruct the flow between himself and his work.

But reaching total centration does not mean that all problems are solved or that the work is finished. Sometimes the creative episode reaches a climactic conclusion in a period of centration. But more typically, these periods come and go in waves. If the work is long or complex, days and weeks are involved and in that time, the artist's attention is shared by other aspects of life. Centration achieved one day is lost the next. Aloneness valued one day because it is one of the conditions of centration becomes a horror of loneliness and emptiness the next. Artists do all sorts of tricks to try to lose themselves and get centered on the work. They play divergent thinking games, do Yoga or meditation, establish private rituals, order themselves to sit with their work a prescribed number of hours a day, go into psychoanalysis to get access to material they think may be preventing them from giving themselves to the work. This last way is a reminder that it is difficult for someone who is deeply frightened to achieve centration, because centration requires that no aspect of psychic structure be forbidden territory. This is what Jane Cooper meant when she spoke of "the necessary vulnerability that is involved in making decent poems."

The pull of the work must be strong enough to survive the frustrations of the early attempts which seem to mock the turning away from the work, the achievement, and then the loss of centration. What is the pull? Grace Paley tells what it is for her. "We were discussing one of the stories in which she said she was writing about a boy who was trying to be a 'good and creative' person. Someone asked whether she thought the words were synonymous. She said no, but that people who want to be good interest her very much."

> *Question*:   Then there's no morality that seems to underlie creative people.
>
> *Grace Paley*:   It's the morality of telling the truth. That has to be the prime and only thing. To be an artist is to have an absolute compulsion to tell the truth. Some people just want to be writers. That's different already. It's not the same thing at all.
>
> *Question*:   Did you want to be a writer?
>
> *Grace Paley*:   Yes, I did. I really wanted to be a writer. . . . I always did think I was a writer, and though I thought of myself as a writer, it was only when I hit that thing, which was not when I was young—it wasn't until I had developed this absolute compulsion to know the truth somehow, to deal with it, that I really considered that I became a writer dealing with it at all, or that I wrote decently.

We asked Jane Cooper how she knew when a poem was finished. "It's like a door clicking shut," she said. But then she added, "At a certain point you know that it's the best you can get it." And at that point the creative episode has reached its other boundary. From the initial sense of direction through the awkward first attempts in the medium which begin to form the impulse into a thing in the world, perhaps a turning away, through cycles of centration and failure, finally a work is made. Now the artist turns to the world and shares the truth he has embodied. This is another important period in the life of the artist. Like each of us, the artist is a social being who needs a place in the social world and a function in the social order, perhaps all the more because so much of his work is solitary. The act of showing the work is his affirmation of relatedness to human society.

Children do not produce mature works of art. But they can get the joy of having a sense of direction. They can get experiences which give them confidence that by their own thoughts and actions they can follow a direction to completion. They need encouragement and opportunity for learning skills. They need experiences both in thinking in a variety of media and in being exposed to excellent examples of such thinking. (Jane Cooper's mother used to read Shakespeare songs along with Mother Goose.) They need to discover that they can trust themselves to work alone. They need help in overcoming self-consciousness and fears of making fools of themselves if they submerge themselves in a task. They need models that exemplify the standard of truth.

Following the creative episode through time helps resolve the paradoxes with which I began. The creative process involves freedom and spontaneity. The creative process demands discipline and concentration, and a commitment to work. It involves the primitive and emotional, intelligence and thought; it calls upon fantasy and inventiveness, a willingness to deviate from what is; it demands honesty and a commitment to truth. It is an expression of self and it cannot take place without forgetting the self; it is a joy and a terror; it is its own reward; it requires encouragement and understanding from others. From the perspective of time, all of these enter into the creative process.

Notes

1. "A Special Type of Choice of Object Made by Men" (Contributions to the Psychology of Love, I) in *The Complete Psychological Works of Sigmund Freud*, trans. James Strachey, vol. 11 (London: Hogarth, 1957), p. 165.
2. *Toward a Psychology of Being* (New York: Van Nostrand, 1968), pp. 135–45.
3. In addition to these theories, the course also includes the works of Rudolf Arnheim, Solomon Asch, Max Wertheimer, Lawrence Kubie, Ernst Kris, Ernest Schachtel, Frank Barron, and Anne Roe.
4. Preface to *The Spoils of Poynton* in *The Creative Process*, ed. Brewster Ghiselin (New York: Mentor, 1955), p. 147.
5. Interview in *Writers at Work: The Paris Review Interviews, Second Series*, ed. G. Plimpton (New York: Viking, 1965), p. 154.
6. Interview in *Writers at Work: The Paris Review Interviews*, ed. Malcolm Cowley (New York: Viking, 1959), p. 130.
7. Arnheim has looked closely at the visual medium and the ways in which artists think in it. See his *Visual Thinking* (Berkeley: University of California Press, 1969) and his *Art and Visual Perception* (Berkeley: University of California Press, 1954).
8. I am indebted to Solomon Asch's analysis of emotion in *Social Psychology* (New York: Prentice-Hall, 1952).
9. "Children Writing: The Story of an Experiment," *New York Review of Books*, July 1966, p. 27.
10. Arnheim chronicles the progress of Picasso's thinking in the medium through time as he worked on the mural *Guernica*. See *Picasso's Guernica: The Genesis of a Painting* (Berkeley: University of California Press, 1962).
11. Letter to Anton Ridder Reppard. In Ghiselin, pp. 54–55.
12. Interview in Plimpton, p. 222.
13. The relevant experiments and theoretical ideas are summarized in Kurt Lewin, *A Dynamic Theory of Personality: Selected Papers* (New York: McGraw-Hill, 1935), ch. 8.
14. This account of total centration was stimulated and influenced by Max Wertheimer's account of centering on a problem in order to do "productive thinking." See his *Productive Thinking* (New York: Harper & Row, 1959), especially pp. 179–80.
15. *Maps and Windows* (New York: Collier, 1974), p. 47.

Paul Hernadi

THE ACTOR'S FACE AS THE
AUTHOR'S MASK
On the Paradox of Brechtian Staging

"POETRY IS THE SPONTANEOUS OVERFLOW OF POWERFUL FEELING," SAYS A
subdued but persistent voice in many of us. "It takes its origin from
emotion recollected in tranquillity," our critical intelligence replies.
Sooner or later a compromise emerges: "The emotion is contemplated
till, by a species of reaction, the tranquillity gradually disappears and
an emotion kindred to that which was before the object of contem-
plation, is gradually produced." After Freud and Jung, the New Critics, and the Structuralists, opinion will be couched in an idiom quite
different from Wordsworth's. But if we care to speculate about the
"mood" in which "successful composition generally begins and is
carried on," we are likely to agree with the main thrust of his
argument.[1]

It is doubtful whether the psychology of the actor's "successful
composition" of a stage figure can be described in the same spirit of
compromise. The writer has all the time he needs to "overflow,"
"recollect," "contemplate," and finally "produce" the aesthetic correl-
ative of his original emotion. But the actor must create his work—
not without preparation, to be sure—during an irrevocable sequence
of unique moments, in close interaction with other artists, and under
the very eyes of his audience (including the critics). Should he act
in a "spontaneous" way, affected by an "emotion kindred to" the
"powerful feeling" of the character he is portraying, or rather preserve his "tranquillity" so that he can affect the spectators through

carefully engineered expressions of a feigned emotion? In theory at least, no reconciliation seems possible between Horace's precept, "Feel grief if you would have me weep," and Diderot's paradox, "Complete lack of sensibility makes for sublime actors."[2]

In practice every great actor strikes a balance between the extremes of total identification with the part and total distance from it, and the kind of balance he strikes will be appropriate to his individual talent and the prevailing literary and theatrical tradition of his day. Around 1600, Shakespeare made Hamlet counsel the Players: "In the very torrent, tempest, and as I may say, whirlwind of your passion, you must acquire and beget a temperance that may give it smoothness" (III.ii). Around 1900, William Archer spelled out in fanciful but psychologically illuminating terms how Hamlet's advice might be followed. In a sense refuting the disciples of both Horace and Diderot, Archer ascribed to the actor a "dual"—or rather multiple—consciousness. In his *Masks or Faces?* (1888), the distinguished Scottish critic, playwright, and translator of Ibsen's works came to the following conclusion: "There are many 'brownies,' as Mr. Stevenson puts it, in the actor's brain, and one of them may be agonising with Othello, while another is criticising his every tone and gesture, a third restraining him from strangling Iago in good earnest, and a fourth wondering whether the play will be over in time to let him catch his last train."[3] This refutation of the two extreme theories is, to some extent, an unintended vindication of both: in order to "make us weep," Archer's actor should and should not "feel grief," should and should not "lack sensibility," at the same time.

Needless to say, Horace, Shakespeare, Diderot, and Archer were offering advice to the actors of their own times. Significant differences aside, most plays performed in the first century B.C. and the bulk of European drama between Shakespeare and Ibsen focused on lively interaction between human beings. The actor in a play of that nature could easily employ at least one "brownie" of his brain for the purpose of emotional identification with his part. Yet the situation was different between Horace (or rather Seneca) and Shakespeare. Particularly in the Middle Ages, the stage was largely a vehicle of religious celebration and didactic allegory. Any style of acting appropriate for the portrayal of Macbeth or even of his witches would have been inadequate to the task of impersonating Adam and Eve, Jesus Christ, Vice, Gluttony, or Good Deeds. Several trends of modern drama have likewise been moving away from those types of dialogue and characterization which Horace, Hamlet, Diderot, and

Archer seem to have had in mind. With Anton Chekhov and the soulful method of acting Konstantin Stanislavski developed before the First World War for the congenial staging of Ibsen's and Chekhov's plays, the theatrical portrayal of human beings in interaction with each other reached a point from which further progress had to be sought in completely different stylistic directions.[4]

One might say that 1916, when *A Portrait of the Artist as a Young Man* first appeared in print, was just about the last year for Joyce to make Stephen Dedalus declare with sufficient relevance to significant contemporary plays that the dramatist, "like the God of the creation, remains within or behind or beyond or above his handiwork, invisible, refined out of existence, paring his fingernails."[5] In the fourth scene of George Bernard Shaw's *Saint Joan* (1923), for example, the Earl of Warwick and Bishop Cauchon characterize the Maid as a dangerous proponent of Nationalism and Protestantism. Those terms, indeed the very concepts, were obviously unfamiliar to men of the early fifteenth century. As Shaw explains in the long Preface to the first printed edition of the play, he has opted for a "sacrifice of verisimilitude" in order to achieve "veracity" and represented Joan's feudal and clerical opponents as saying what they "actually would have said if they had known what they were really doing."[6]

Of course, good playwrights have always tended to prefer an effective story to accurate history and to adjust the available evidence to their preferred medium or message. But Shaw's *Saint Joan* and many other historical plays of the twentieth century deviate from the trodden paths of historical drama by virtue of the authors' refusal to justify the presentation of what they consider the actual truth in terms of factual plausibility. Recognizable details of local and temporal relevance abound in the first six scenes of *Saint Joan*. Yet conspicuous anachronisms of thought and language and, in the Epilogue, an exquisite flight of Shaw's dramatic imagination make our point of intellectual orientation keep shifting between what emerges as the author's stance and what we may construe as that of the historical figures. The required changes in our perspective indicate that some of Shaw's characters are neither mere projections of the authorial vision (that would make them caricatures or allegorical figures) nor ostensibly free verbal agents speaking what would strike us as the genuine language of their interpersonal action.[7]

What approach should actors and directors take to such a "split" character with his clearly divided allegiances to plot and theme, dramatic action and authorial vision? This question may well have occurred to a German *dramaturg*—one of several literary advisors contracted to Max Reinhardt's chain of theaters—as he attended the rehearsals for the 1924 Berlin production of *Saint Joan*. And since the ambitious young man by the name of Bertolt Brecht shared the Irish playwright's preference for the bird's-eye view of social and intellectual trends over a thoroughgoing psychological delineation of individual figures, he decided—or so it appears—to out-Shaw Shaw in two different ways. First, in his own plays written from this time on, he increasingly relied on spoken or sung choruses, monologues, asides, and other formal devices through which authorial vision may permeate the dramatic interaction of the characters. Second, in his theoretical and critical writings, he began to advocate a style of acting which perpetually suspends the spectator's illusion of witnessing a self-contained series of events so that the author's or the director's point of view might noticeably replace the perspective inherent to the represented action.

The assumption of Shaw's direct influence on Brecht's theory of distanced staging is corroborated by some pertinent dates. Before the first English and German productions of *Saint Joan* and the roughly simultaneous publication of the play with the substantial Preface (1924), Brecht wrote a biting review of Shaw's *Pygmalion* in 1920. Yet in July 1926, he published two acclamatory newspaper articles on Shaw; in the same month, Brecht was working on *Mann ist Mann*, his first play with formal devices for the breaking of dramatic illusion, and he gave an interview in which, for the first time on a public occasion, he rejected the actor's and the spectator's empathy (*Einfühlung*) with a dramatic character.[8]

The secondary issue of actual influence aside, two central tenets of Brecht's theory of staging are clearly related to ideas expressed in Shaw's Preface to *Saint Joan*. The first is that the actor should overtly superimpose his understanding of the character he is playing on the character's supposed understanding of himself: both Brecht and Shaw assumed that the dramatic characters, without such outside help, would not be "intelligible" to the audience. The second tenet is implied by the first and has to do with a tragicomic aspect of some works by both Shaw and Brecht. In the Preface to *Saint Joan*, Shaw called the burning of Joan a "pious murder," committed by "normally innocent people in the energy of their righteousness," and observed that "this contradiction at once brings an element of comedy into the tragedy: the angels may weep at the murder, but the gods laugh at the murderers."[9] In the age of Expressionism, the angels' emotional involvement with individual suffering was unlikely to be ignored on the German stage. Brecht, therefore, came to stress the gods' (and the Marxists') analytical detachment from it. The style of staging he now began to advocate reflected not only the assumption that the author had envisioned the vicissitudes of the characters from a point of view superior to their own; it also prescribed for the actors of serious plays an attitude closer to the clown's habitual detachment from his part than to the tragedian's feigned or sincere involvement with his. The generic tension expressed in the very concept of "serious play" (or in the Germanizing word for tragedy, *Trauerspiel*) was to be stressed by the actor's detached, play-ful, or at least frankly fictitious, presentation of a serious or even tragic character. Brecht trusted that the spectators, once accustomed to this style of staging, would not empathize with the plight of a character so presented; rather, they would give some hard rational thought to the question how his predicament could and should have been averted.[10]

It is clear but rarely mentioned in the pertinent discussions that most butts of comedy have always been presented in such a spirit of detachment. Even the villains of melodrama and tragedy engage the emotions in an adverse fashion; the actors and particularly the spectators tend to identify with Shakespeare's supposed scorn or hatred for Richard III and Iago, not with Richard's and Iago's self-love or the scorn and hatred of those characters for others. Thus Brecht's demand for distance is innovative mainly with regard to serious plays which, unless they are staged with detachment, would display tragic qualities and prompt us to identify with their central characters. There was, of course, a wholesome shift of emphasis in Brecht's views on this subject. In his sharply polemical statements around 1930, he rejected any kind of identification with dramatic figures.[11] Around 1950, Brecht still argued the primacy of detached observation in the theater of our "scientific age," but he now conceded that a moderate degree of empathy with the character is permissible both in the actor and the spectator.[12] As a result, the potentially tragic reality of human suffering could begin to receive in Brecht's and his disciples' Berlin productions almost as much stress as the potentially comic insight into its avoidability. To use Shaw's metaphors of the weeping angels and laughing gods, the author (and very detached, severe judge) of *Galileo* and *Mother Courage* may have come to realize that man's road to "divine" comprehension leads through "angelic" compassion. Or, as one might say in the earthier terms of a stage director, Brecht finally decided to give the spectators a vivid enough inside view of the characters whom they should ultimately contemplate from without—with critical detachment.[13]

From the late forties on, Brecht was thus applying something like William Archer's concept of the actor's dual consciousness to the audience; he now wished to manipulate the tension between different "brownies" of the spectator's brain. Archer had disputed Diderot's view that "the actor's tears come from his cerebrum" (rather than from his "heart")[14] and suggested, so to speak, that some tears may come from one place and others from the other. Yet both Diderot and Archer took it for granted that the actor's actual attitude, whether fully or partially distanced, should remain concealed from the spectator whose empathy with the character was to be aroused. In contrast, Brecht thought that the spectators should preserve most of their cool while watching heated characters and sultry situations presented to them by noticeably detached actors. Thus it might be argued that Brecht passed beyond Diderot and even beyond Archer in psychological sophistication since he demanded that the actor's attitude be revealed to the spectator.

It seems to me, however, that Brecht unwittingly[15] concurred with the rather naive opinion of Horace. After all, Brecht never ceased to insist that the theater's chief means of precluding the spectator's excessive empathy with a character is the conspicuous absence of complete emotional identification between the actor and his part. Thus Brecht tacitly assumed that the actor's attitude to the character is always imitated by the spectator who will "identify" with the detached actor just the same as he will identify with the actor playing his part with empathy. *Weep if you would have me weep*, said Horace to the actor. *Do not weep so that you can appear to be weeping and thus make me weep*, countered Diderot. *Do not weep so that you will not appear to be weeping and thus will not make me weep either*, runs the basic Brechtian doctrine. It can be restated in a positive form which is strikingly Horatian, *Keep your distance if you would have me keep mine;* or, to do better justice to the last phase of Brecht's development, *Keep your distance to the extent that you would have me keep mine.*

These formulas highlight some aspects of difference and similarity in the respective views of Horace, Diderot, and Brecht. Further reflection will reveal, however, that they correspond far too closely to Brecht's own understanding of his theory and practice of staging. In his "Short Organum for the Theater" (1949), Brecht described the ideal Brechtian performance in a memorable phrase: "the acting

Laughton does not disappear in the enacted Galileo." Although Brecht characterized this peculiar situation by saying that "the actor appears on stage in a dual form," John Willett's English translation of the words *in zweifacher Gestalt*, "in a double role," may better describe what actually happens: Brecht in effect requires the actor to play two parts, "the acting Laughton" (*den zeigenden Laughton*) as well as "the enacted Galileo" (*den gezeigten Galileo*).[16] Simultaneously or in an alternating fashion, the Brechtian actor must portray both the great scientist Galileo and the conscious (preferably also class-conscious) actor who shares Brecht's view that the great scientist, since he failed to stand up for his truth against the Church, was also a great social criminal. Clearly, the latter part, that of the distancing actor, must be "studied" in advance and "played" night after night with just as much skill and care as the former, the part of Galileo. After all, Charles Laughton, the private citizen and member of the acting profession, is not exactly the same person as "the acting Laughton"—the actor playing Galileo in a certain way, on a particular occasion. Without the actor's success in evoking a persuasive image of himself as the showman on a specific job, even his most sincere distance from the part will either fail to be communicated to the audience or else prevent the stage image of the character he plays from being constituted.

Remarkably enough, Brecht eschewed the full exploration of the question of role playing and especially the question of playing a double role. Was he too naive or too shrewd to embark on such an exploration? I suspect the latter. Why should Brecht, the second cousin of Good Soldier Schweik and the spiritual father of Azdak, have provided a theory which such spectators of his life as the Un-American Activities Committee or the East German authorities might apply to the practice of his own "living theater" with embarrassing results? Brecht and his East Berlin circle of friends and followers had especially good reason to repress any desire they might have had of probing into the possibility that, on the stage as well as in real life, one could appear to be a loyal party worker without actually being one. Besides, Brecht as the moving spirit of the Berliner Ensemble had little or no motivation to investigate whether his best disciples, the most convincing conveyers of the distancing, "scientific," "Marxian" attitude among the actors, were in fact the best disciples of Walter Ulbricht also. Thus Brecht's theory is quite "Horatian" in that it expects the audience of a Brechtian performance to see through only one of two layers of theatrical make-believe. The spectator's attention

is called to the fact that the distancing actor bears the features of
Galileo only as a "mask." Yet he should ignore the no less important
fact that the distancing actor's features—visible whenever the mask
of Galileo is dropped—are features of another mask, which may or
may not resemble the actor's real "face." In other words, Brecht
wants us to accept the actor's second mask at face value. But we need
not do so; and to the extent that a spectator retains his disbelief concerning the identity between the "distancing actor" and the actual
personality of the actor, he will also retain his own identity as the
actual spectator who only temporarily wears the mask of the "distanced spectator" assigned to him by a Brechtian playwright or
director.

For the purpose of clarifying the psychological implications of
Brecht's theory of staging, I shall typographically distinguish the
actual ACTOR and SPECTATOR from the "actor" and "spectator"—the
parts "played" by the former two in a Brechtian production.[17] The
actual ACTOR appears to identify with the "actor" and to keep considerable but not complete distance from the character; the ACTOR's
actual feelings remain unexplored. The "actor" who is played by the
ACTOR and is playing the character keeps his critical distance from
the character. The "spectator," deceived by the feigned identity between ACTOR and "actor," keeps his distance from the character and
thus identifies with the distancing "actor." Yet the SPECTATOR, who
realizes that the ACTOR and the "actor" are not identical, shares the
ACTOR's apparently mixed attitude toward the character and probably
evolves a similarly mixed attitude toward the one-sided "actor." The
SPECTATOR may in fact be said to "identify" with the ACTOR, that is,
with the way of thinking and feeling he attributes to the ACTOR on
the basis of the given performance. All this is, no doubt, complicated,
and a Brechtian production indeed presupposes sophisticated actors
and "mature audiences." But the psychological machinery involved
can forcefully enhance the aesthetic effect of certain plays. As Martin
Esslin noted, the Brechtian actor—our ACTOR—offers a most suggestive
"split image" of man—"impelled by his emotions, critically yet help-
lessly aware of their irrationality"—whenever he shows "the actions of
the character and simultaneously presents the critical reasoning that
might have stopped him from acting as he does."[18]

One great difficulty facing the Brechtian ACTOR as he plays his
double role is that usually the bulk of his entire text has been written
for the character "impelled by his emotions" and not for the "actor"
who, just like the author and the director, should be "aware of their

irrationality." It is mainly through gestures, including the gestures of his voice, that the "actor" can intrude the fictitious world in which the character he plays and the other characters exist. Yet Brecht liked to give his anti-heroes certain lines which in fact only the detached "actors" playing them could be expected to utter; Galileo's self-condemnation in the penultimate scene is a widely-known example. Along with other *Verfremdungseffekte*—dramaturgical and scenic devices helping the audience to keep its distance—those lines, properly spoken, will offer the spectator direct access to the author's vision which, in most other plays, is conveyed by a chorus, certain asides and monologues, or the entire work and *not* through conversations between the principal participants of the represented action.[19] To use the terms Shaw introduced in his Preface to *Saint Joan*, "verisimilitude" yields to "veracity" when Galileo as he may have appeared to himself and to his contemporaries is suddenly replaced by Galileo as Brecht wants the "actor" and the "spectator" to understand the historical figure in the light of the social consequences attributed to his recantation. Indeed, the Brechtian actor must no doubt identify with the author or the director at least as much as he identifies with "himself," the psychophysical substratum of the character he is playing. This means a shift in emotional commitment, not the absence of it.[20] Just as a class-conscious revolutionary or the loyal party worker must place the good of the community, usually determined by some "author" or "director" figure, above his own good, the Brechtian actor is expected to embrace a central interpretation of the "plot" or "story" (*Fabel*) rather than one participant's thoughts and feelings about it.[21] Once again, the friendly ghost of Horace hovers over Brecht's partisan stage: the greater the distance between the "actor" and the character, the greater the empathy (or something very close to empathy) between the "spectator" and the "actor" as well as between the "spectator" and the author or the director.

That the "author" implied by a literary work is not identical with the actual AUTHOR is a critical commonplace and should not require further elaboration. We should note, however, that the "implied author" of several plays by Shaw, Pirandello, Claudel, O'Neill, Wilder, Anouilh, and other modern playwrights including the Absurds makes himself more directly noticeable than the "author" implied by the typical play written between, approximately, 1600 and 1900. Consequently, some form of "Brechtian" staging—with or without the director's approval or even awareness of Brecht's theory—has been practiced in many congenial performances of contemporary plays during the last decades. And the radical use Peter Weiss recently made of the old device of "play-within-the-play" can be interpreted as an effort to write the psychology of distanced staging into the entire structure of a dramatic work.[22]

As the play's full title indicates, the very plot of *Marat/Sade* is *The Persecution and Assassination of Jean-Paul Marat as Performed by the Inmates of the Asylum of Charenton under the Direction of the Marquis de Sade*. With "as performed" Weiss has turned a Brechtian ideal, that the actor should not disappear in the character, into dramaturgical reality. The complacent director of the Charenton asylum and the other "spectators" of 1808 appearing on the stage see Marat and Charlotte Corday, the girl who stabs the sick revolutionary in the bathtub, only through the obviously "distanced" presentation of the respective characters by a paranoic and a somnolent, depressive woman patient. Yet Weiss keeps shifting our focus between his PLAY and de Sade's "play" within the PLAY. Thus the SPECTATORS will hardly suspend their disbelief concerning the reality of either action for any significant length of time. Rather, they will remain conscious of the fact that the "actors" and "spectators" of 1808 are played by ACTORS of their own day, twice removed from the re-presented assassination of 1793. Since de Sade is supposed to have written the "play" and to have assigned the part of Marat to a paranoic patient, his repudiation of Marat is no doubt repudiated by the negative image that the supposedly unbiased AUTHOR and DIRECTOR of the PLAY convey of him as a biased "author" and "director." But it is up to the SPECTATOR, of course, to choose between the AUTHOR's ostensibly radical message and the radical critique of any singleminded radicalism implied by the structure of the PLAY.

Peter Weiss may be just as devoted to the Communist cause as was Bertolt Brecht. But he lives in neutral, "distancing" Sweden rather than in East Germany under Stalin and during the first three years after Stalin's death. Perhaps it is due to this difference between the two writers' circumstances that it was reserved for Weiss' *Marat/Sade* to highlight the basic paradox of Brechtian staging. By doubling the triad AUTHOR-ACTOR-SPECTATOR within its structure and by letting the "author" (de Sade) assign specific parts to specific "actors," Weiss' play reveals that the distancing actor's "face" is one of the committed author's masks, whether or not it expresses the actual thoughts and feelings of the actor.

Notes

1. Cf. Wordsworth's Preface to the second edition (1800) of his and Coleridge's *Lyrical Ballads*.
2. "Si vis me flere, dolendum est/Primum ipsi tibi." Horace, "Ars Poetica" (Epistle to the Pisos), ll. 102f. Even though Horace speaks of the poet's art, the context of the words quoted supports the generally held view that he meant to give the same advice to actors. "C'est l'estrême sensibilité qui fait les acteurs médiocres; c'est la sensibilité médiocre qui fait la multitude des mauvais acteurs; et c'est le manque absolu de sensibilité qui prépare les acteurs sublimes." Denis Diderot, "Paradoxe sur le comédien," *Oeuvres complètes*, ed. J. Assészat, vol. 8 (Paris, 1875), p. 370.
3. Denis Diderot, *The Paradox of Acting*; and William Archer, *Masks or Faces?*, introd. Lee Strasberg (New York, 1957), p. 184.
4. Cf. Peter Szondi, *Theorie des modernen Dramas* (Frankfort, 1956).
5. James Joyce, *A Portrait of the Artist as a Young Man* (London, 1916), p. 252.
6. See the section titled "The Inevitable Flatteries of Tragedy" where Shaw insists that the stage make "its figures more intelligible to themselves than they would be in real life; for by no other means can they be made intelligible to the audience."
7. Cf. the section on "The Modes and Perspectives of Discourse" in my book *Beyond Genre: New Directions in Literary Classification* (Ithaca, N.Y., and London, 1972), pp. 156–70.
8. Cf. Bertolt Brecht, *Schriften zum Theater*, vol. 1 (Frankfort, 1963), pp. 35–37, 173–80; and John Willett, ed., *Brechton Theatre* (New York, 1964), pp. 10–17.
9. See the section titled "Tragedy, Not Melodrama."
10. Cf. esp. "Die Strassenszene: Grundmodell eines epischen Theaters" (1938 or 1940), first published in Brecht, *Versuche 10* (Berlin, 1950), and Willett, pp. 121–28.
11. Cf. esp. "Vergnügungstheater oder Lehrtheater?" in *Schriften zum Theater*, vol. 3 (Frankfort, 1963), p. 55; and Willett, p. 71.
12. Cf. "Das kleine Organon für das Theater" (1949) and especially the dialogues "Gespräch über die Nötigung zur Einfühlung" (1953) and "Einige Irrtümer über die Spielweise des Berliner Ensembles" (1955), published after Brecht's death under the heading "Die Dialektik auf dem Theater." *Schriften zum Theater*, vol. 7 (Frankfort, 1964), pp. 29f, 35f, 221–331; and Willett, pp. 190, 193, 270f.
13. From some of Brecht's posthumously published theoretical fragments, emotive empathy in a sense emerges as the *necessary* antithesis to rational distance in Brecht's new ideal of a "dialectical" rather than merely "epic" theater. Cf. esp. two of the"Nachträge zum kleinen Organon" and the section titled "Episches Theater" in Brecht's "Katzgraben-Notate," *Schriften zum Theater*, vol. 7, pp. 60 and 185f, translated in Willett, pp. 277f (appendix to Section 53) and 248f (under the heading "Emotions").
14. "Les larmes du comédien descendent de son cerveau; celles de l'homme sensible montent de son coeur." Diderot, *Oeuvres complètes*, p. 370.
15. Cf. *Schriften zum Theater*, vol. 7, pp. 261–63 and Willett, pp. 270f.
16. *Schriften zum Theater*, vol. 7, p. 36 and Willett, p. 194.

17. To elucidate the combination of identity and nonidentity between the "spectator" of a given theatrical performance as such and the actual personality of the SPECTATOR, I refer to Walker Gibson's witty essay, "Authors, Speakers, Readers, and Mock-Readers," *College English* 11 (1950): 265–69.

18. Martin Esslin, *Brecht: The Man and His Work* (1959), revised ed. (New York, 1971), pp. 262f.

19. See note 7, esp. pp. 158–60.

20. Cf. Brecht in conversation with Friedrich Wolf about "Formprobleme des Theaters aus neuem Inhalt" (1949), *Theaterarbeit: 6 Aufführungen des Berliner Ensembles* (Dresden, 1952), p. 254: "Die 'kritische Haltung,' in die [das epische Theater] sein Publikum zu bringen trachtet, kann ihm nicht leidenschaftlich genug sein." Willett translates: "The 'attitude of criticism' which [the epic theatre] tries to awaken in its audience, cannot be passionate enough for it" (p. 227).

21. Cf. esp. Section 65 of "Kleines Organon für das Theater." Small wonder that Brecht's theory of staging (as well as Aristotle's similar stress on plot rather than character [*Poetics*, ch. 6]) is more popular with playwrights and directors than with actors and actresses.

22. Short plays within plays such as Hamlet's "Mousetrap" for Claudius (III.ii) or the artisans' performance in *A Midsummer Night's Dream* (V.i) abound in dramatic literature. It is far less frequent to place a full-length play inside another play with the "author" and "spectators" of the former appearing on the stage of the latter. In *The Caucasian Chalk Circle* Brecht did so but kept the two actions completely separated; his "spectators," for example, never comment on the action of the play within the play. In German literature, only Ludwig Tieck's *Der gestiefelte Kater* (Puss in Boots, 1797) seems to anticipate *Marat/Sade*, and Tieck's play is a farcical comedy whereas Weiss makes us take the play with the play (and with the play within the play) very seriously indeed. Cf. also Lionel Abel, *Metatheatre: A New View of Dramatic Form* (New York, 1963).

E. Bond Johnson

SELF-CONSCIOUS USE OF NARRATIVE POINT OF VIEW

Controlling Intelligence and Narrating Consciousness in *The Good Soldier* and *Doctor Faustus*

SELF-CONSCIOUS USE OF NARRATIVE POINT OF VIEW OCCURS IN WORKS IN which the narrating consciousness is that of a writer concerned with compositional problems reflecting those of the controlling intelligence. By controlling intelligence I mean something close to what Booth has called "the implied author" or "the author's 'second self' " in *The Rhetoric of Fiction*,[1] and what Rubin has called "the authorial personality" in *The Teller in the Tale*.[2] "Controlling intelligence" signifies the author as he is shaping his fiction, but beyond that it signifies the logic of the successfully completed fiction in which the discernible patterning controls the reader's comprehension of the work. The controlling intelligence acts to establish a plateau of awareness to which the reader aspires in his experience of the work. "Narrating consciousness" signifies the mind through which the fiction is recounted to the reader.

In works which use narrative points of view self-consciously, there is a series of levels which may be diagrammed as follows:

controlling intelligence	plateau of awareness

reader	proceeding toward awareness
narrating consciousness	never completely aware

The narrating consciousness exists at a considerable remove from the plateau of awareness. The reader enters the work below the plateau of awareness, although he often has a greater awareness than the narrating consciousness from the opening sentence of the work. As the reader's experience of the work progresses, he begins to create within his mind an increasingly accurate perception of the reality of the novel by reacting to the inaccurate perception of the narrating consciousness. At the conclusion of his experience of the work, the reader has the possibility of achieving a state of awareness close to that established by the controlling intelligence.

The experience of works in which this process occurs might be graphed according to the model in the accompanying illustration.

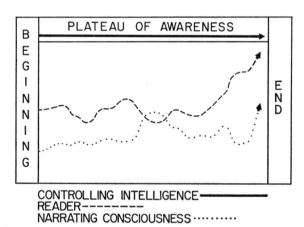

CONTROLLING INTELLIGENCE———
READER————
NARRATING CONSCIOUSNESS ·········

At points in the fiction, a reader's level of awareness may coincide with that of the narrating consciousness and may even descend below it briefly. As the story progresses, however, the reader's awareness will surpass that of the narrating consciousness and draw close to that of the controlling intelligence.

There are resemblances in the self-conscious use of narrative point of view in authors so diverse as Ford Madox Ford and Thomas Mann. John Dowell, the narrating consciousness in Ford's *The Good Soldier*, and Serenus Zeitblom, the narrating consciousness in Mann's *Doctor Faustus*, share similar doubts as to the efficacy of their narration. When they give voice to their intuitions of inadequacy, they often reveal essential structural principles of the novel. Furthermore, in commenting on the problems involved in writing what they wish to express, they permit the representation of an ambiguous and complex image of reality. I will consider several passages in these works which illustrate the effects that self-conscious use of narrative points of view can achieve.

At the opening of chapter two of part one of *The Good Soldier*, John Dowell rehearses the possibilities for relating the tale he has to tell and settles on a solution:

> I don't know how it is best to put this thing down—whether it would be better to try and tell it from this distance of time, as it reached me from the lips of Leonora, or from those of Edward himself.
> So I shall just imagine myself for a fortnight or so at one side of the fireplace of a country cottage, with a sympathetic soul opposite me.[3]

In this brief discussion of technical questions, the distance between the controlling intelligence and the narrating consciousness emerges. What Dowell has revealed in the passage, the reader has just witnessed in the previous chapter. Already his awareness is greater than that of the narrating consciousness. He has perceived, in the course of Dowell's musings, that the story is not being related from the viewpoint of Leonora or of Edward, but is being shaped through the consciousness of John Dowell. Dowell's vacillations between past and present in chapter one have made it clear that the tale is being told neither from the beginning nor from the distance of time, but as it presents itself to his distraught mind. The ironic distance between narrating consciousness and controlling intelligence has already begun to amplify the novel, making of it not only a tale of the difficulty of perceiving reality, but also a tale of one character's inability to comprehend the full import of his own narration.

John Dowell's extended apology for his narrative techniques at the opening of part four reveals more clearly the dimensions given the work by the ironic distance between narrating consciousness and controlling intelligence:

> I have, I am aware, told this story in a very rambling way so that it
> may be difficult for anyone to find his path through what may be a
> sort of maze. I cannot help it. I have stuck to my idea of being in a
> country cottage with a silent listener, hearing between the gusts of
> the wind and amidst the noises of the distant sea the story as it comes.
> And, when one discusses an affair—a long, sad affair—one goes back,
> one goes forward. One remembers points that one has forgotten and
> one explains them all the more minutely since one recognizes that one
> has forgotten to mention them in their proper places and that one
> may have given, by omitting them, a false impression. I console my-
> self with thinking that this is a real story and that, after all, real stories
> are probably told best in the way a person telling a story would tell
> them. They will then seem most real. (P. 183)

Coming at a point in the novel at which the structural pattern has
become apparent, this apology on the part of the narrating consciousness functions to reveal the design of the controlling intelligence.
Each inadequacy claimed by John Dowell is actually a key to the
narrative structure of *The Good Soldier*.

The story only seems to have been told in a rambling way. It is a
sort of maze; but a maze is, after all, a formally patterned series of
paths which lead to dead ends and which induce the reader to retrace his steps, taking him back over territory previously crossed and
gradually bringing him forward on the single true pathway through
the multiple possibilities. John Dowell's narration functions as a
labyrinth, constructed by the controlling intelligence of *The Good
Soldier*, through which the reader must find his way. The style of the
passage imitates a maze by defining "affair" with an appositive phrase
that goes backward to pick up the modifiers "long" and "sad," and
forward in the altered meaning which "affair" has when it recurs at
the end of the appositive phrase. Going backward and forward on a
larger scale constitutes the narrative structure of the work. The four
parts of the novel shuttle back and forth in time, each successive
one encompassing the time period of the previous part and expanding
its scope.

Part one, although it suggests the entire time span of the work,
focuses primarily on the period from the beginning of John Dowell's
acquaintanceship with Florence to the death of Maisie Maiden. Part
two narrates an earlier and a later portion of the events than part
one, revealing a segment of Florence's life previous to her engagement
and continuing to her death. Part three begins at a point after Edward's death when Leonora tells Dowell that he might have Nancy,
and reaches back in time to the history of Leonora's and Edward's

families and of the arrangement of their marriage. Part four corrects the image of Florence's behavior before her marriage and extends in time to the final image of John Dowell as the keeper of the deranged Nancy.

The reader experiences a constant shifting of his perception of the reality of the fictional world through Dowell's returning to situations he has described earlier. Not only is the description more minute, as Dowell professes; it also reveals new aspects of situations, and often considerably alters the import of certain events. Florence's strange behavior during Dowell's courtship at first seems the result of propriety. As the description of her behavior is continued in successive treatments of the episode, it turns out to have been the result of something quite different. An affair she had been having in Europe had been interrupted by her relatives, and she was actually weighing the possibility of escaping her family and deluding her husband-to-be in order to continue her affair. The reluctance of her relatives to consent to the marriage undergoes a shift in import from distrust and dislike of John Dowell, which it seems at first, to concern for him as the victim of Florence's scheming. The extent of her scheming becomes evident with the discovery of the degree to which her heart condition has been her own fabrication. The realization that she has committed suicide startles the reader almost as much as it has startled John Dowell: "How could I have known that, during all the years of our married life, that little brown flask had contained, not nitrate of amyl, but prussic acid? It was inconceivable" (p. 107).

Dowell apologizes for his forgetfulness, yet it is precisely the reordering of the narrative flow, obtainable through a forgetful narrating consciousness, which allows an event to make its impact more than once; the second impact derives from the new realization about a situation it brings. In chapter four of part one, the two couples pay a visit to a castle in which a document famous in the history of Protestantism is displayed. Florence says to Edward, "If it weren't for that piece of paper you'd be like the Irish or the Italians or the Poles, but particularly the Irish" (p. 44), and she touches Edward on the wrist. Leonora rushes from the room, and the explanation she gives to John Dowell is that she is an Irish Catholic. In chapter one of part four—surely the exact reversal of chapter and part numbers is an indication of the strict patterning of the book—Leonora explains the true import of the situation. She thought she had found a solution to the difficulties of her marriage: Maisie Maiden was to provide an outlet for Edward's passion which did not threaten Leonora. "And then—smack—it all went. It went to pieces at the moment when Florence laid her hand upon Edward's wrist. . . . Or, rather, it went when she noticed the look in Edward's eyes as he gazed back into Florence's. She knew that look" (p. 189). The reader not only perceives the true coloring of the situation, but also experiences again Dowell's inadequacies as a narrator and the way in which his inadequacies determine the structure of the novel.

Because of the liberty which John Dowell's forgetfulness allows in structuring the narrative sequence, incidents can receive their most detailed exposition at the point at which they will be most effective in revealing the significance of the story. The controlling intelligence of *The Good Soldier* develops the tale gradually toward a tragic denouement. The theme of tragedy enters on the first page with Dowell's insistence that this is the saddest story he has ever heard. What is stressed by the narrating consciousness, however, is the distance of the story from tragedy. In describing Florence's suicide, Dowell pauses in the narration to apologize: "It is all melodrama; but I can't help it" (p. 110). Later, in recounting Edward's financially disastrous affair with La Dolciquita in Monte Carlo, Dowell states again that the story is no tragedy: "There was no current to draw things along to a swift and inevitable end. There is about this story none of the elevation that accompanies tragedy; there is about it no nemesis, no destiny" (p. 164).

Toward the conclusion of his narration, Dowell begins to refer to the series of events he has described as tragedy, although he still does not claim for it swift inevitability or nemesis or destiny. "There was a great deal of imbecility about the closing scenes of the Ashburnham tragedy," he finally writes (p. 238). Even up to the closing scene, Dowell stresses the absence of any ultimate meaning to the story. He describes Nancy, with her great surface beauty and her mental void, in a way which makes her seem emblematic of his tale: "It is very extraordinary to see the perfect flush of health on her cheeks, to see the lustre of her coiled black hair, the poise of the head upon the neck, the grace of the white hands—and to think that it all means nothing—that it is a picture without a meaning" (p. 254).

Part of the meaning of the tale to the reader lies in its meaninglessness for Dowell, who fails to see the ultimate significance of the story he has related. Each of the major characters in *The Good Soldier* has experienced the dissolution of a personal reality and a resulting sense of the meaninglessness of existence. The narrative structure conveys to the reader a sense of the collapse of a common reality. Yet one character, Edward Ashburnham, manages to lend meaning to his personal world by acting in accordance with codes and convictions which have become untenable to his age. Edward Ashburnham's final heroic stature is perceived by John Dowell when he refers to the "Ashburnham tragedy," but Dowell does not fully comprehend the way in which Edward's suicide is the final moment of a tragedy.

On the level of the narrating consciousness, Edward's suicide is related at the end of the work because of Dowell's oversight. He prefaces his recounting of the scene in an offhand manner: "It suddenly occurs to me that I have forgotten to say how Edward met his death" (p. 255). On the level of the controlling intelligence, and of the reader who has reached a plateau of awareness, Edward's renunciation of Nancy and then his suicide, based on principles which have ceased to have any validity in the world in which he lives, give the tale the dimensions of tragedy.

John Dowell's apology for his haphazard narrative structure at the beginning of part four concludes with his justification that a random style of telling will approximate the experience of reality. It is true that *The Good Soldier* achieves in fiction a sense of the illusiveness of reality. However, the controlling intelligence, through its ironic distance from the narrating consciousness in the passage, educates the reader to the careful design creating the effect of reality behind Dowell's seemingly disordered account. What is not implied in the passage, and what the reader must go beyond any statement of John Dowell's to perceive, is the way in which the novel about the collapse of meaning in four lives conveys a sense of design and significance in the collapse itself.

The reader's experience of the novel involves a progression from the level of awareness of the narrating consciousness to that of the controlling intelligence. The narrating consciousness never perceives the subtle order in his disordered narration. However, when the reader achieves the awareness to which the controlling intelligence encourages him, he perceives a structure and meaning to a story which seemed to present only the dissolution of order and significance. Because the reader must recreate for himself the structure and meaning in his experience of the fiction, the final impression of *The Good Soldier* is of the possibility of discovering a significant reality in a world which seems to have lost its meaning.

Doctor Faustus is more ambitious than *The Good Soldier* in the reality it undertakes to present—including in its scope political and historical as well as social and personal dimensions—yet the reality of *Doctor Faustus* shares with that of *The Good Soldier* a similar complexity, and a similar means of transmitting its complexity to the reader's mind. Serenus Zeitblom has in common with John Dowell an earnest desire to voice his experience of reality combined with a realization of the difficulty of the task. As in *The Good Soldier*, the controlling intelligence brings the reader to an awareness of the complexity of the novel's reality partially through the inadequacy of the narrating consciousness to convey it.

In *Doctor Faustus*, Mann attempts to link the course of modern German history with the personal history of the composer Adrian Leverkühn through the use of the Faustus theme. The artist, isolated from his society and alienated from the Western tradition of music, attempts a breakthrough into a new artistic expressiveness by means of a diabolical heightening of his powers through disease. Adrian's actions in an intellectual realm have a bearing on Germany's actions in a political realm, possibly because they represent the withdrawal of the artist from the political arena, possibly because they suggest that the satanic pact which has been accepted by Adrian with responsibility in the intellectual realm has been sealed with abandon by Germany in the political sphere. The story of Adrian Leverkühn, with its implications of the ambiguous role the artist has played in his society, is filtered through the perception of Serenus Zeitblom, a traditional humanist who instructs classical languages. Adrian's childhood friend is qualified to recount his biography only by his love for the composer and by his intimate knowledge of the events of Adrian's life. The diabolical subject matter is entirely alien to Zeitblom's nature.

Serenus Zeitblom's professions of inadequacy are numerous and persistent, and they serve to accomplish precisely what Zeitblom is in doubt of being able to achieve—they present his subject matter with a high degree of artistic control. In the first chapter, for example, Zeitblom lets slip from his pen a reference to Adrian's pact with the devil. Then for the fourth time in four paragraphs he interrupts himself to comment on his narrative:

> Here I break off, chagrined by a sense of my artistic shortcomings and lack of self-control. Adrian himself could hardly—let us say in a symphony—have let such a theme appear so prematurely. At the most he would have allowed it to suggest itself afar off, in some subtly

disguised, almost imperceptible way. Yet to the reader the words which escaped me may seem but a dark, distrustable suggestion, and to me alone like a rushing in where angels fear to tread. For a man like me it is very hard, it affects him almost like wanton folly, to assume the attitude of a creative artist to a subject which is dear to him as life and burns him to express; I know not how to treat it with the artist's easy mastery.[4]

In the humorous consternation of the narrating consciousness, the profound misgivings of the controlling intelligence are expressed. How indeed is it possible to assume the standpoint of an artist, involved in compositional problems, in relation to the overwhelming subject matter of the collapse of a culture and a civilization? The self-conscious use of narrative points of view may not be an unequivocally successful solution to the dilemma of the writer, but it does at least allow for an expression of the problems involved in such an undertaking concomitant with the undertaking itself.

Consistently in *Doctor Faustus*, through the last line of the novel, there is an ironic reflection of the concern of the controlling intelligence in the consternation of the primary narrating consciousness which allows the communication of an unwieldy subject matter. Introducing the Faustus theme, with both artistic and political connotations, in a twentieth-century novel on Germany constitutes one of the major compositional difficulties of *Doctor Faustus*. Zeitblom's digression on compositional problems, his hasty retrenching and extended self-accusation for having allowed the theme to surface so early in his account of Adrian's life, solves the problem neatly. While the narrating consciousness is apologizing for having introduced the theme too early on, the controlling intelligence has managed to bring the theme effectively to the reader's attention, and has cajoled him into accepting it in a modern fiction.

In the three most crucial scenes involving the development of the Faustus theme, Mann has utilized a doubly self-conscious point of view by employing Adrian Leverkühn as an auxiliary narrating consciousness to Serenus Zeitblom. In a letter to Zeitblom, Adrian describes his visit to the bordello where he encounters for the first time the hetaera Esmeralda, whose disease will prepare his contact with the devil. Zeitblom introduces the letter to the reader and analyzes it thoroughly afterward, providing the viewpoint of his troubled and apprehensive narrating consciousness. Adrian's narration of the episode employs a style used earlier in the novel by a figure reminiscent of Luther and evokes a period at which the devil was much abroad in the minds of men. In both Adrian's and Zeitblom's accounts of the episode, there is an ironic interconnection between narrating consciousness and controlling intelligence, although the implications in each case are quite different. Adrian has consciously immersed himself in the language and the imagery of an earlier epoch, and has willingly delivered himself to an imaginative realm in which he can conjure forth Satan. Zeitblom has remained steadfast in his humanistic principles, even though he knows they are outmoded. That his is the primary narrating consciousness of *Doctor Faustus* reveals the trend of the controlling intelligence toward a humanistic conception of the world.

The controlling intelligence encourages a more ambiguous interpretation of Adrian's choice of styles than does the narrating consciousness of Zeitblom. Zeitblom points out that Adrian has chosen his style in the letter so that he may request a prayer from Zeitblom. That is, of course, only part of the reason he has opted to express himself in archaic Reformation language and figures of speech. The amplification and expansion of Adrian's style in his second appearance as a narrating consciousness, in the document which describes his satanic dialogue, demonstrate the power of the style to bring the devil into existence in the fiction. Adrian's choice of the language and imagery of the fifteenth and sixteenth centuries as his mode of expression is instrumental in the invocation of Satan. The controlling intelligence of *Doctor Faustus*, in making this function of Adrian's style apparent, brings into question the morality of his choice of style. Through the implication that Adrian's choice of style has been partially responsible for the emergence of the devil in his world, the undertaking of the novel itself, which moves in the imaginative realm chosen by Adrian, is brought into question.

The third extended presence of Adrian as a narrating consciousness occurs during the scene in which madness descends on him as he attempts to present his final work to a shocked and horrified audience. Adrian's work, "Dr. Fausti Weheklag," has grown out of his complete despair at the death of his nephew, Echo. For Adrian, the disease and death of the rare being who had claimed his love was the result of his own contact with diabolical forces. The work he has composed is intended to take back the expression of hope in Beethoven's Ninth Symphony. On the level of the controlling intelligence, the parallels with the optimism of Goethe's *Faust* and the despair of *Doctor Faustus* are clear: Mann's novel is to qualify the optimistic conclusion to Goethe's drama.

Adrian collapses in a volley of self-accusation and confession before he can complete the presentation of his work. It is at this point, when the devil's power is at its apex, that Zeitblom's style acts to vindicate Adrian's work, and ultimately to vindicate the novel itself. Zeitblom has described "Dr. Fausti Weheklag" immediately before the account of Adrian's collapse. In his humanistic prose, which has gained in force as the work has progressed, he describes the conclusion of the composition:

> Listen to the end, listen with me: one group of instruments after another retires, and what remains, as the work fades on the air, is the high G of a cello, the last word, the last fainting sound, slowly dying in a pianissimofermata. Then nothing more: silence, and night. But that tone which vibrates in the silence, which is no longer there, to which only the spirit hearkens, and which was the voice of mourning, is so no more. It changes its meaning; it abides as a light in the night.[5]

Zeitblom's style makes possible the emergence of hope from Adrian's expression of despair, and the impression of despair transformed into hope persists even through Adrian's lament in the following chapter.

On the level of the controlling intelligence, the description of the conclusion to "Dr. Fausti Weheklag" intimates an interpretation of the conclusion to Zeitblom's narration. In the Epilogue, Zeitblom describes his last visit to the physical form of Adrian in 1935 and his reception of the news of his death on 25 August 1940. The voices of the novel are silenced as those of Adrian's composition have been, and finally there remains only the voice of a lone man in prayer for Germany: "A lonely man folds his hands and speaks: 'God be merciful to thy poor soul, my friend, my Fatherland!'"[6] The unobtrusive mounting of Mann's name into the sentence signals to the reader the interconnection between controlling intelligence and narrating consciousness which allows a reflection of Mann's grief for Germany in Zeitblom's. The ironic utilization of a humanistic style ultimately allows Mann, through Zeitblom, to respond to the situation of Germany with a prayer for grace. Although the prayer itself is an expression of despair, as it lingers in the mind, the realization grows that in the very possibility of prayer there are the seeds of hope.

The utilization of two separate viewpoints in the two narrating consciousnesses of *Doctor Faustus* enables the work not only to create a fictional world of convincing perspective but also to imbue that world with a meaning which can be comprehended in terms of Western religion. In the process of arriving at the level of the controlling intelligence, the reader of *Doctor Faustus* may not come to a complete acceptance of the implications of the Faustus theme and its religious dimensions in the novel, and he may not accept the novel as the most valid interpretation of the reality of the Hitler epoch. He may, however, succeed in holding in balance contradictory aspects of the novel's reality, and that is a step toward comprehending what seems incomprehensible both in the novel and beyond.

The self-conscious use of narrative point of view in *The Good Soldier* and *Doctor Faustus* takes the reader from the position of being trapped within an individual perception of reality to the position of being endowed with a comprehensive awareness of the reality represented in each novel. Because of the narrative techniques they utilize, these novels are able to order and contain a convincing image of a modern reality, and to suggest that there is still a significant pattern in existence, however obscured it may be.

Perhaps the very process of arriving at an awareness of significant objective reality in art can lead to a renewed sense of significance in existence. In both works, that is the tantalizing possibility each controlling intelligence holds up beyond the unawareness of each narrating consciousness. It contributes to the dynamic of these works, and to their continuing fascination. They pose for the reader a task which is never entirely completed, and already in undertaking the task of constructing a meaning in the fiction there is comfort for the meaninglessness of individual existence in the contemporary world.

Notes

1. Wayne C. Booth, *The Rhetoric of Fiction* (Chicago: University of Chicago Press, 1961), p. 151. Booth elaborates on these terms in chapter six, in the discussion of distance between narrator and author. On pp. 158–59 he touches on the particular type of distance with which the present inquiry is concerned. Chapter twelve, on "Henry James and the Unreliable Narrator," is also concerned with related phenomena.
2. Louis D. Rubin, Jr., *The Teller in the Tale* (Seattle: University of Washington Press, 1967), p. 21.

3. Ford Madox Ford, *The Good Soldier: A Tale of Passion* (New York: Random House, 1955), p. 12. Pagination in the text will be from this edition.
4. Thomas Mann, *Doctor Faustus: The Life of the German Composer Adrian Leverkühn as Told by a Friend* (New York: Knopf, 1948), pp. 4–5.
5. Ibid., p. 491.
6. Ibid., p. 510.

Simon O. Lesser

MACBETH—DRAMA AND DREAM

WITH THE EXCEPTION OF HAMLET, AND PERHAPS KING LEAR, MORE MAY
have been written about *Macbeth* than any other play, yet some of
the most significant aspects of the drama have gone unremarked—or
noted too casually to provoke curiosity and analysis. Consider the
many loose ends and apparent inconsistencies in the play, for example. Lady Macbeth speaks of having "given suck," but Macbeth has
no son and no further reference is made to his wife's child, or children.
Although Macbeth sees apparitions even before the murder of Duncan and, in general, seems unsure of his course and plagued by guilt,
it is his strong-willed wife who breaks down first; though it is he who
feels that "all great Neptune's ocean" cannot wash Duncan's blood
from his hand and balks at returning the daggers, it is his wife who
returns them and belittles the deed. It is she who futilely tries, while
walking in her sleep, to rid her hands of the smell of blood. Or consider all that is made of the fact that Banquo has a son who may
become king and father to a line of kings. For a time Macbeth regards
Banquo and Fleance as the obstacles to the content he expected to
feel as king and he steeps himself more deeply in blood to have them
killed. Though Fleance escapes and the prospect that Banquo's descendants will rule is visualized during Macbeth's second visit to the
weird sisters, nothing further is made of this plot thread. It is Duncan's older son, Malcolm, who is to be crowned king as the tragedy
ends.

Even among the critics who show some awareness of *Macbeth*'s de-
fects, few conclude that the play is badly flawed. This is a more
remarkable tribute to the play than it may seem, for, as I shall try to

show, some of its strengths have also gone unremarked. Shakespeare does such a superb job of storytelling in *Macbeth* that we read it in an almost trancelike state and refuse to be distracted by this or that apparent flaw. To be sure, this is true to some extent of all of Shakespeare's plays and for that matter all competently written imaginative literature. Fiction is usually read with a willing suspension of disbelief, or to put Coleridge's insight into the language of our century, with a suspension of the vigilance normally exercised by the ego. But it is inadequate to regard Shakespeare's achievement in *Macbeth* as merely quantitative. Here as in some other cases a quantitative difference becomes qualitative—and of decisive importance. In most instances the extent and number of the departures from realism which occur in *Macbeth* would cause a reader to withdraw the trust he has provisionally granted the drama and to begin to read it detachedly and critically. Shakespeare does not permit this to happen. He induces a regression so deep that we read *Macbeth* as though it were an account of a dream.

More accurately, it is an account of a *series* of dreams, fantasies, and thoughts—a chain of mental speculations, mostly of the "What if . . . ?" kind. "What will happen if my valor comes to the attention of Duncan?" "What if he rewards me by making me one of the most powerful men in the land?" "What if he were to die and by some series of events I become king?"

It is remarkable that *Macbeth* can provide this sense of being privy to its hero's most secret thoughts and dreams, for drama is the most objective of all genres and may seem to have no devices save soliloquies and asides, which are somewhat awkward for taking a reader inside the mind, where thoughts and dreams are born. Shakespeare not only surmounts this difficulty with ease; he simultaneously accomplishes something which some might say is impossible in a drama: he tells his story largely from what today would be called the point of view of one of its characters. Macbeth's dreams are the basic subject of the play, and we see those dreams taking shape not only when he is on stage but often even when he is not. In scenes in which Macbeth plays a part, other characters—to say nothing of witches and apparitions—often talk and act as if they were enactments of Macbeth's dream-and-thought-fabric. More amazingly, when Macbeth is not physically present, other characters sometimes behave as if they were acting out his dreams. *Macbeth* may seem to be written in the same fashion as the other tragedies, but a close look reveals that it is not. Whole scenes, or crucial parts of scenes, are dramatized, not objectively (as they are, for example, in *Hamlet*, *King Lear*, and *Othello*) but *as Macbeth would imagine them*. Present or absent, he dominates almost the entire action. *Macbeth* is developed by what might be called, anachronistically, an objectified stream-of-consciousness technique.

Another important difference between *Macbeth* and Shakespeare's other plays, a formal one, is still less likely to be noted. To an astonishing extent *Macbeth* is written in the language of our dreams and daydreams, in what Freud calls the language of primary process thinking.[1] This is appropriate, but I am not sure it was deliberate. It would be my guess that Shakespeare let things well up from the unconscious to an exceptional degree while writing *Macbeth*, and that—allowing for the cuts, interpolations and loose ends, discontinuities and other changes believed to have been made by others— this is the main factor responsible for blemishes.

Whatever the genetic explanation may be, extensive use of primary process thinking in *Macbeth* contributes to an achievement of the highest order. It gives the play an organic quality it might otherwise lack. It lulls us into a state of relaxation in which we not only brush off inconsistencies, many of which, we sense, are only apparent or unimportant, but also understand the play much better and more easily than we would if we were more alert. It is largely responsible for our reading the play subliminally as a tissue of Macbeth's dreams, fantasies, and thoughts as well as an objective drama—this without becoming aware of the many violations of objectivity. Finally, it is responsible for the fact that we feel no need to choose between these two ways of apprehending the play. The shift back and forth between them is unconscious and effortless because the two ways of viewing the material of the play reinforce and enrich one another. At points the objective confirmation of some dream or desire is synergistic in its effect.

The claim that almost every scene of *Macbeth* can be experienced as a dream and an event dramatized, not objectively but from the hero's point of view, can be illustrated by glancing at the first three scenes. These fall into a pattern of increasing complexity. Other scenes will also be discussed, but the consideration of the opening three should show how almost any scene of the play can be understood simultaneously as dream and as event.

Perhaps Macbeth's second encounter with the weird sisters (IV. iii) is the scene which can most obviously be read as a dream. Until the appearance of Lennox at the end, the only characters besides Macbeth are witches, who are easy to see as embodiments of Macbeth's thoughts, and apparitions, whose claim to existential reality is more tenuous still. The fact that Macbeth does not even have to voice his questions to the apparitions confirms the impression that he has evoked them into being, and other characteristics of the scene help to establish its dreamlike quality.

Only a little less obviously, the first scene of the play is also a dream of Macbeth's, or a fragment of a dream: the witches are planning a meeting with him. What they will propose—that is, the exact nature of the desires stirring in Macbeth—is undefined; but the fact that the proposals are projected onto witches shows that they are felt to be evil. The "Fair is foul, and foul is fair" motif applies, not to those desires, but to Macbeth's battles, which are not only lost and won, but have evil as well as good effects.

It is not easy for a modern reader also to perceive the scene as objective. However, most Jacobean spectators evidently did not have this difficulty. They found it relatively easy to accept the existence of witches, perceived as embodiments of the evil in the world. As a corollary to this, they apparently found it no more difficult than the Greeks to think that such spirits would be concerned with mankind and individual people. The three witches in *Macbeth* are clearly concerned with the play's hero: this one touch suggests that the play is not wholly objective but often developed from Macbeth's point of view. Modern readers too, I believe—if not at the beginning at any rate by the time they are under the spell of the play—provisionally accept the existence of the witches as incarnations and agents of evil. This does not interfere with their perception of them as externalizations of the evil gestating in Macbeth.

The second scene is more easily read as objective; indeed, readers are seldom aware of having understood it in any other way. Unconsciously, the scene is read as a classic wish-fulfilling dream. Evidently Macbeth's desire to have his valor praised by everyone, and recognized and rewarded by the King, involves no conflict or self-reproach. In his dream, his exceptional bravery is not only brought to the attention of the King but singled out for special praise by the Captain. Duncan asks a question which couples his generals, but his only other interruption of the Captain's account is to praise Macbeth.

And the scene ends happily, as a wishful dream should, with Duncan dispatching Ross to inform Macbeth that he has been named thane of Cawdor—and praising him once again.

The very factors which make the scene so satisfying to read as a dream tilt the scene so far in Macbeth's favor that, if we were not already in a quasi-trancelike state, we would be dissatisfied with it. Evidently Banquo is also an able and courageous general. If we were more alert, the desire for both justice and formal symmetry would make us feel that he should be accorded more praise and that there should be some indication that he too will be rewarded. (So far as we are informed, he never is.)

Scene iii reads equally well as dream or as objective but actually Macbeth-dominated dramatization. The most obvious basis for apprehending the scene as a dream is the reappearance of the witches. This together with Macbeth's immediate reference to "foul and fair" may make us think of the scene as a continuation of the dream begun in scene i. Subliminally, we may also be struck by the close correspondence between the material in this scene and what Macbeth would be thinking at this very time.

We know that he is walking to see his sovereign and if, as I believe, we are by now inside his mind, we know that one of the things he is thinking about is how he will be rewarded for his valor and his victories. We even know what Macbeth has dreamed but perhaps momentarily forgotten, that one of his rewards has been decided upon. And we have no doubt that it is Macbeth's dream which is unfolding. The first part of the scene tells us that it is Macbeth the witches are awaiting. When he and Banquo appear, Banquo addresses them at length, but it is Macbeth they respond to. Not only the substance of what they say but the incantatory way they express themselves show that it is Macbeth they are thinking of—or projections of his thoughts.

Even Banquo may be part of Macbeth's dream fabric. If Macbeth were walking alone to see his sovereign and speculating about how he is to be rewarded, it would be natural for him to think of his fellow general. Banquo is a rival claimant for the recognition and honors for which Macbeth longs. Moreover, Macbeth fears Banquo. One of his fears is alluded to in the scene: Banquo has a son who may someday rule Scotland; Macbeth has no son. The second fear is not mentioned until III.i, an example of the extent to which the play follows primary process logic. (In other instances explanation also follows thought or act—or is not given at all.)

Much of I.iii revolves around two prophecies the witches make to Macbeth: they call him thane of Cawdor (this may be no more than an announcement), and promise him he will be king "hereafter." We may assume that both statements express wishes of Macbeth. No explanation of either wish is offered, and I will postpone discussion of speculations about the motives afforded by the play. What should be noted without delay is that the scene can also be read as a drama- tization of actual events; though here, perhaps to a greater extent than in scene ii, the occurrences are presented as Macbeth would imagine them. This is obviously true up to line 50. Banquo, begin- ning with his second speech, acquires substantiality. He alerts us to Macbeth's reactions to what the witches tell him, as he does later to Macbeth's reactions to what he learns from Ross and Angus. Banquo also induces the witches to notice him and prophecy to him. The prediction is interesting to Macbeth and Banquo, who does not hesi- tate to warn Macbeth of the dangers latent in the prophecy that Mac- beth will become king. Each general confirms the prediction made to the other, as though neither can quite believe what he has heard.

With the entrance of Ross and Angus the scene acquires additional substantiality. Here also, however, developments are dramatized from Macbeth's point of view and/or the focus is on him. The news the emissaries bring (I.iii.89–107) is all too obviously presented as Macbeth would imagine it. Although Banquo is present he is given neither praise nor a share in the King's bounty; indeed, he is utterly ignored. A critically alert reader would realize that this part of the scene would be embarrassing to all four participants. But being so completely under the spell of the play, the reader does not engage in reality testing. Shakespeare further protects the material by displac- ing our attention from the news Ross and Angus bring to its con- nection with the prophecies of the witches.

This scene illustrates Shakespeare's ability to induce the reader to slip back and forth between the two ways of apprehending the play. The first fifty lines of the scene are probably understood as being predominantly a part of Macbeth's dream-thought-fabric and, as mentioned, the Second Witch's speech, "All hail, Macbeth! Hail to Thee, Thane of Cawdor!"[2] is apprehended as an expression of his wish. In contrast, the King's emissaries seem to be real visitors from a real world. Ross's news that Duncan has actually named Macbeth Thane of Cawdor is such a startling coincidence that even Banquo is profoundly affected by it. To Macbeth the news is like a sign from fate. It seems to validate—and legitimatize—his most secret dreams, the whole pattern of desire of which becoming Thane of Cawdor is a part. It casts shadows beyond itself, appearing to sanction even the wish to become king. Macbeth's first words after Angus explains the fate of the previous thane tells us it has had this magical significance for him: "Glamis, and Thane of Cawdor:/The greatest is [to follow]."

The coincidence may make a modern reader think of a similar incident in a great nineteenth-century work of fiction—the apparently chance discovery by Raskolnikov that at precisely seven o'clock the next evening Lisaveta will be absent from her sister's apartment—a discovery that makes him feel he must go through with a murder which up to that point has seemed dreamlike and unreal. Shakespeare uses another conjunction of this sort in the very next scene of *Macbeth*. Duncan's decision to visit Inverness is interpreted by both Macbeth and Lady Macbeth as a sign that they should proceed with the terrible act they are contemplating. However, whereas it is a clear "go" signal to Lady Macbeth, it simultaneously imposes another constraint on her husband—and reminds him of all the other arguments telling him to abstain from the unjustified murder. But this attempt to strengthen his defenses is ineffectual. What he wants appears within easy reach and his scruples are overcome, or lost sight of, in a matter of minutes.

Shakespeare's double vision of almost every scene of *Macbeth* may have been inadvertent. Since he had two potential male heroes, he probably felt a need to emphasize Macbeth so that Banquo would simply be a foil to him, not a rival claimant for our interest. The emphasis was also necessary to induce audience identification with Macbeth.

The half-"real," half-dreamlike world Shakespeare conjures up in *Macbeth* is so enthralling that we feel no disposition to choose between alternatives, to decide on a single attitude toward the play, which would break its spell. It is helpful of course that Macbeth dominates both ways of perceiving the story, so that the gap between them is not great. Each kind of reality, or unreality, that of dreams, that of the actual, comes to suffuse the other. Thus we are not even taken aback when, in IV.i, Macbeth asks Lennox, "Saw you the weird sisters?" But we could wonder how Lennox even knows what Macbeth is talking about.

The deep suspension of disbelief with which we read helps to explain our refusal to pay much attention to other slips, gaps, inconsistencies, and the presentation of material in apparently illogical sequence. We do not question the primary process language and we tend to be uncritical even in thinking about the play after reading or viewing it. To accept I.iii as realistic would involve provisional belief either in witches or in the rare psychological occurrence of *folie à deux*. Few readers, or critics, seem troubled by such considerations.

The only casualties of our uncritical reading of the play are parts of it which do not admit of double vision and whose single strand of reference takes us away from Macbeth for what seems a considerable time. Parts of scenes which seem wholly objective—for example, II. iii up to the appearance of Macbeth—do not suffer, for they are swiftly traversed. Nor do objective, highly dramatic scenes which introduce appealing characters; the scene at Macduff's castle (IV.ii) will serve as an example. It is only when a scene is objective and takes us away from Macbeth for an extended period that our interest tends to flag. The scene in which Malcolm tests Macduff's loyalty (IV.iii) is perhaps the only good example. We may explain our dissatisfaction on some other basis, such as lack of realism, but its chief source, I believe, is our impatience to return to Macbeth.

Since *Macbeth* appears to have been written in a state of regression, it is not surprising that there are delayed explanations and numerous omissions. In particular, little attention is paid to motivation, even in Macbeth's case, despite the fact that we are often inside his mind. We are never told, for example, why Macbeth dreams of being named thane of Cawdor. Nor are we told why Macbeth wanted to be king. Some of the immediate determinants of the desire are fairly easy to surmise. From dreaming of being rewarded by the King to dreaming of becoming king is but a short and pleasant step. The skill and courage Macbeth displayed in the battles, which in a sense begin the tragedy, influence him in a more direct way. They may make him think of himself, probably with warrant, as preeminent on the fields of battle. Why not then preeminent during peacetime also? Almost certainly, Macbeth's victories bolster his sense of his own worth, make him feel that his countrymen in general will now esteem him more. This in turn makes the idea of higher station seem a realistic possibility. In a sense the criminal dreams which undo Macbeth are born of success. But as we shall see, that is not their ultimate source.

It is important to note that this first intimation that Macbeth will become king arouses fear rather than satisfaction. There could be no better evidence that the idea of murdering Duncan is already gestating in his mind. A little later he does face the need for this murder—only to be overcome by such fears that he falls into a trance in which he becomes oblivious to the presence of Banquo, Ross, and Angus. He shies away from the idea of killing Duncan with the wish that chance will crown him, but it seems that neither the reader nor Macbeth has any faith in this solution. Before his crime is named, Macbeth begins to suffer from guilt. The Crown is not golden even in anticipation, but mottled and tarnished.

The most strenuous objection to the way of reading *Macbeth* being developed here will come, I suspect, from those who believe that Lady Macbeth is a stronger character than her husband and maintain that she dominates him and the action of the early part of the play. Of course, she is not a stronger character or she would not collapse completely before her husband—and for that matter the play would not be called *Macbeth*. The failure to understand the nature of the interaction between Macbeth and his wife must stem in part from failure to read the work with sufficient care or to recall all we sensed as we read, in part from ignorance of ourselves and human nature generally—or temporary lack of access to what we know.

If we read the play carefully and have some experience of life and knowledge of ourself, it seems to me we can hardly fail to perceive that, far from Lady Macbeth dominating her husband, Macbeth skillfully enlists and uses his wife's help. In I.iv Macbeth encounters an apparently new obstacle to his desire with far less fear and am-bivalence than he showed in the preceding scene. At the same time, before we so much as meet Lady Macbeth, he diagnoses the weak-ness in himself which may make it impossible for him to attain his desire:

> The Prince of Cumberland! That is a step
> On which I must fall down, or else o'erleap,
> For in my way it lies. Stars, hide your fires;
> Let not light see my black and deep desires:
> The eye wink at the hand; yet let that be
> Which the eye fears, when it is done, to see.

(I.iv.48–53)

What Macbeth is hoping for is some way of outwitting conscience— or to use the language of twentieth-century depth psychology, the superego. His attempt to secure his wife's help is the most ingenious of the devices he employs, and her goading and participation reduce his guilt to the point where he can go through with the murder. Still, he is just barely able to do so; and after the first murder his efforts to circumvent or mollify his conscience are still less successful. To be sure, his superego does not stop him from murdering Duncan or others, but it does prevent him from deriving any satisfaction from the murders. Even this formulation is inadequate: as we have seen, Macbeth is tormented by guilt and anxiety before the murder of Duncan—even before the crime has assumed definite shape in his mind. At the time he plans the murder of Banquo and Fleance, he deliberately tries to harden himself in order to be impervious to the stings of conscience. Although he does in fact become harder and his sensibility dulls, this stratagem is no more successful than the others. He is guilt-ridden when he reluctantly enters the combat with Macduff which ends with his death. He goes to his grave without having achieved any satisfaction or even respite from self-reproach from his career of crime. Each murder augments his guilt, increases his self-condemnation, deepens his depression, and intensifies his fear of, and even desire for, punishment.

The fact that Macbeth has a severe superego must be stressed in order to correctly understand the play. Macduff and his other enemies talk of him as a devil, but they do not know him from the inside, as we do. Shakespeare does not want us to accept their judgment without important qualifications. I have no wish to extenuate, much less excuse, Macbeth's crimes, but he is a murderer of the Brutus or Raskolnikov kind, not the Richard III kind. The killing of the grooms perhaps excepted, he is never able to murder cold-bloodedly. He is never able to deceive himself by justifying his crimes.

Despite his inability to distort reality, it seems that his ego is crippled in some respects. It behaves like the ego of a person suffering from an obsession or compulsion. Otto Fenichel writes: "In all psychoneuroses the control of the ego has become relatively insufficient. . . . In compulsions and obsessions, the fact that the ego governs motility is not changed, but the ego does not feel free in using this governing power. It has to use it according to a strange command of a more powerful agency, contradicting its judgment. It is compelled to do or think, or to omit certain things; otherwise it feels menaced by terrible threats."[3] The hypothesis that Macbeth's ego is impaired in some such way as this helps to explain the anomaly of a man with a conscience like his being able to murder. The hypothesis also explains the feeling the play gives that the agonizing inner struggle

Macbeth undergoes is between id and superego, with practically no mediation by the ego. As a result of its weakness, he is victimized by both of the opposed and never reconciled parts of his psyche: he yields to his impulses but is lashed before, during, and after each surrender.

Macbeth realizes that he must do everything he can to deceive his conscience, and, immediately after expressing the vain wish to be blind to his own acts, he writes to his wife. Although sequence is not always a reliable guide in *Macbeth*, it does occasionally help in establishing causal connections. One does not have to examine Macbeth's letter searchingly to see that one of its aims is to induce his wife to persuade him to murder Duncan. If she persuades him, Macbeth believes he can claim that the idea comes from outside and he can deny his own responsibility. The ending of the letter is seductive in tone. It tries to recruit his wife not simply as a helper but as an accomplice in crime, and twice offers her an incentive for giving him her support. "This have I thought good to deliver thee, my dearest partner of greatness, that thou mightst not lose the dues of rejoicing, by being ignorant of what greatness is promised thee. Lay it to thy heart, and farewell" (I.v.11–15).

Macbeth wants to create the illusion that external forces are impelling him onward. The attempt to secure his wife's involvement is of a piece not only with his later use of hirelings to commit his crimes; it squares also with his tendency to externalize temptations, wishes, and fears in the forms of witches and apparitions.

The mechanism Macbeth hopes to take advantage of in enlisting the help of his wife must be older than marriage—as old as continuing close relationships of any kind between two people: a person communicates something to a confidant in order to provoke an anticipated and desired response.[4] Often a person wants encouragement to do something which he wants to do but which arouses so much conflict that it cannot be done without outside support—or support which appears to come from outside. Alternatively, help may be desired in resisting a course of action which is tempting, but which is perceived to be wrong and/or likely to lead to trouble.

Macbeth's situation and procedure fall into a common pattern. His desire to be king is so overpowering that he is *almost* willing to kill Duncan to attain his goal, though he recognizes he has no justification for such an act. He acquaints his masculine, aggressive, not overly-scrupulous wife with his dilemma on the assumption that she knows him well enough to identify his dominant wish and to give him just the kind of encouragement and active assistance he needs to gain it. (He is right about this, though it seems to me that Lady Macbeth never recognizes the basis of her husband's hesitancy as clearly as his speeches permit us to recognize it.) Whether his reasoning is conscious or, as is more likely, unconscious, Macbeth must feel that the letter is an important step in doing what he senses to be necessary—overcoming the inner resistances which keep him from killing Duncan. Meanwhile, the very act of sharing his tempting but frightening dream with his wife may somewhat reduce his guilt feelings.

Once aroused Lady Macbeth does such a vigorous job of persuasion we may forget that it was her husband who enlisted her support. The intensity of her desire that he become king may be a surprise to him and to Lady Macbeth herself. In the great invocation in I.v, which begins, "Come, you spirits/that tend on mortal thoughts, unsex me here . . ." she appears to be summoning strength from reserves never before tapped. There can be no questioning of Lady Macbeth's wifely devotion. She mobilizes all her strength to play the role she feels she must play to bring happiness to her husband and herself.

It is necessary to ask why Macbeth should want to kill Duncan, whom he cannot find fault with as man or king and who has been particularly gracious and generous toward him. Neither Macbeth nor, interestingly, Lady Macbeth ever makes an attempt to extenuate, much less justify, the murder. But if we did not feel that there was an adequate explanation for what Macbeth does, we would not have a high opinion of the tragedy.

Perhaps Macbeth is actuated by unconscious hostility. Some psychoanalytic interpretations of the drama have been based on this hypothesis: Macbeth is seen as a bad son acting out some unextirpated hatred for the father upon a surrogate. But apart from the fact that Macbeth at no point seems to be a son figure, unless the murder of Duncan itself admits of no alternative explanation, there is no trace of such hatred, either before or after the crime. When at the end of the superb after-the-murder scene with Lady Macbeth, he exclaims to the unknown person knocking at the gate, "Wake Duncan with thy knocking! I would thou couldst!" we have no doubt that he means it. There is more reason to suspect his public comment on Duncan's death in the next scene (II.iii.93–98), since he is here trying to make himself one with the others lamenting the murder, but I believe that, ironically, the occasion provides a welcome opportunity to say something he deeply feels; and his prognosis of his own situation is uncannily accurate.

What circumstances, what motive or motives, could drive a man like this to kill when there is no excuse for killing? As we have seen, it was success which crystallized and gave urgency to the desire to be king; and rewards stemming from success, such as being named thane of Cawdor and being visited by Duncan, seemed like signs from fate that he should act to attain his desire. But Lady Macbeth's reaction to her husband's letter—her lack of surprise as much as what she says—indicates that unrest and amorphous ambition antedate the action of the play.

Those feelings were born of failure, not success. Macbeth went through with an act for which he knew himself unqualified and killed a man he loved because he was an unhappy, discontented, even desperate man, who found life sterile and empty. And because he was desperate, he nurtured the absurd, groundless hope that being king would somehow change everything. When the play begins, Macbeth is already a thane of Scotland and a renowned general; but he is also middle-aged, childless, friendless, and loveless. Moreover, though an intelligent man, he is without any interests which might make his life seem meaningful.

The claim that Macbeth is loveless seems to be contradicted by his closeness to his wife during the early part of the play, but it is possible, even likely, that their partnership in crime brought them closer together than they had been for a long time, or perhaps ever before. The crime offered the vaguely defined but alluring promise of curing their discontents, of making their lives more fulfilling. During the planning of the murder of Duncan, as G. Wilson Knight points out, they are "in evil with" one another, just as Antony and Cleopatra are in love with one another. Even during this period of closeness, however, though Lady Macbeth is loyal and devoted to her husband and each of them is dependent to some extent on the other, there is no indication of passionate love, past or present, on either side. It is possible that Macbeth has had no children by his wife because he is impotent. His complaint about the "barren scepter" (III.i.62) the weird sisters have put in his grasp may include this second meaning. There are more definite indications that his marriage, like so many middle-aged marriages, has deteriorated into a kind of business partnership. Perhaps it had never been more than that.

If these speculations are correct, Macbeth is susceptible to the dream of becoming king because for a long time before the play opens he had been oppressed by a discontent so profound that he felt almost any change would be for the better. Perhaps Macbeth's willingness to court death was born of desperation, of a feeling that matters might as well be either better or worse. He fights Macduff with the same fury at the end of the play when he is not only desperate but hopeless. Interestingly, two of the murderers Macbeth enlists to kill Banquo and Fleance, the First Murderer in particular, express the very psychology I am describing as they accept their assignment:

> And I another
> So weary with disasters, tugged with fortune,
> That I would set [risk] my life on any chance,
> To mend it or be rid on't.
>
> (III.i.111–14)

Later there is firmer evidence that Macbeth was impelled to his first crime by discontent. He reminds his wife that the purpose of killing Duncan had been to gain their peace, but the statement, the most explicit the play offers, is embedded in a speech of such eloquence ("We have scorched the snake, not killed it . . .") that, bewitched by its beauty, we may not take in the plain sense of much that is said:

> better be with the dead,
> Whom we, to gain our peace, have sent to peace,
> Than on the torture of the mind to lie
> In restless ecstasy [frenzy].
>
> (III.ii.19–22)

The placement of the revelatory phrase, "to gain our peace," may also keep it from attracting the attention it deserves.

Just before Macbeth's entrance, his wife had soliloquized: "Nought's had, all's spent,/Where our desire is got without content." This too suggests that the hope for something like peace, a feeling of satisfaction and well-being, gave birth to the desire of Macbeth and his lady to become king and queen.

The still more famous "She should have died hereafter" passage (V.v.17–28) also may be evidence of this motive. The passage is usually viewed as a set piece, with no important relationship to the play as a whole, but I believe that the feelings of the emptiness, sterility, and meaninglessness of life it expresses are feelings Macbeth was trying to combat from the very beginning. To be sure,

now that his wife is dead and the mistakenness of his course is becoming more apparent with each new development, the feelings are
being reexperienced with greater poignancy.

Even with goading from his wife, Macbeth proceeds with the murder
of Duncan only with great difficulty. With the hysteric's facility for
converting thoughts and feelings into somatic or external terms, he
conjures up a dagger, and a little later sees it covered with gouts of
blood. Not only these hallucinations, but various things he says show
that he is already tormented by guilt: yet his crime is still "but fan-
tastical." In I.iii, once he began sensing what he would have to do to
become king, he took refuge in wishful thinking:

> If chance will have me King, why, chance may
> crown me,
> Without my stir.

Although he now realizes that this is a vain hope, he has not otherwise made much progress. He is still hoping that the "sure and firm-set
earth"—and by this I think he means the gods and destiny, not simply
the human beings at Inverness—will remain ignorant of his deeds.
Revelatory also is the phrase, "I go, and it is done." He glides over,
is unwilling to visualize, the murder itself.

What he tells his wife in II.ii makes it clear that during or immediately after the murder—here as elsewhere time indications are uncertain—his guilt deepened further. Even more significant is the way
his unconscious desire to be caught and punished discloses itself in
the very execution of his crime: he has forgotten to smear the grooms
with blood and to leave their daggers near them, and he has brought
the daggers to his own chamber. Now he is so overwhelmed by guilt
that he cannot return them and bloody the grooms. It is Lady Macbeth who undertakes these repugnant errands. His speeches when
he hears the knocking confirm the intensity of his guilt: he is continuing his self-punishment and clearly plans to punish himself
further.

Macbeth again receives desperately needed help from his wife after
the murder of Banquo. But after killing Duncan, Macbeth never
again *asks* for her help. It is important to observe what causes this
turnabout. His own inner feeling is the primary factor. He had un-

justifiably hoped that his wife's help would enable him not only to go through with a wanton murder, but to kill his King-benefactor-cousin-guest with little or no guilt. Instead he is flooded with guilt. His disappointment may make him realize that he has been unrealistic in his expectations and that his wife cannot give him the escape from self-reproach he had hoped for. After III.iv, he no longer gives her his full confidence, and the reader feels that some of his endearments are perfunctory. He thinks of her less and less thereafter. Once it is committed, the crime that was to bring them together and make their marriage more fulfilling isolates them further.

The banquet scene (III.iv), the last scene in which Macbeth speaks with his wife, or imagines himself doing so, may also be understood as a dream. Indeed, if we had not by this point abandoned reality testing we could scarcely accept it in any other way. It is hard to explain how the banquet guests could fail to note Macbeth's conversation with the First Murderer, harder still to explain how they could avoid overhearing the exchange between Macbeth and his wife, whose second speech to him (61–69) makes it plain that he is the murderer of Duncan.

We do not see Lady Macbeth again until the sleepwalking scene (V.i), and that is the last time we see her. In V.iii, the doctor gives Macbeth a report of her illness, and in the final speech of the play we learn that she may have killed herself. The sleepwalking scene does not seem to be part of Macbeth's dream fabric, but rather something which took place after he became so immersed in his anxieties that he seldom thought of his wife. It is possible, however, that, preoccupied as he was, he had become aware of his wife's disturbed and depressed state of mind and even of her sleepwalking. In that case Macbeth could have dreamt the sleepwalking scene to deal with the anxiety he felt about others learning of his wife's condition—and, what was more frightening still, learning of his crimes from what she said and did while in a somnambulistic state.

Although Macbeth has become separated from his wife, it seems to me that his responses to the news of her illness and the news of her death both show that he feels deep sympathy for her. His response to the account of the "thick-coming fancies/That keep her from her rest" is rich in feeling. It is obvious here (V.iii.39–54) and in the speech he makes when he learns of her death that some of the regret he expresses is for himself. He is in fact confusing his wife's situation and his own. Nothing could show more clearly that the tie with her is still not severed. To be sure, the second speech seems dry and impersonal, but its tone is a defense against feeling. Although Macbeth is controlled and detached, what he says expresses regret, and self-reproach, for such separation as has occurred between him and his wife, for the futility and meaninglessness of their crimes and their lives, and for her suffering and disappointment no less than for his own.

Certain parts of the group of scenes we have been considering—the Porter's soliloquy and exchange with Macduff and Lennox, and the exchange between Ross and the unnamed Old Man—do not seem to be products of Macbeth's mind. They lack resonance in consequence. Here and throughout the play the most intense scenes seem to be both parts of Macbeth's thought fabric and accounts of events. Their intensity derives in large part from the fact that they are apprehended in both ways.

Although Macbeth renounces the idea of using his wife a second time to deceive his superego, he tries to achieve the same end by different means. He never ceases to hope that, should he have to kill, he can find some way of doing so without being crushed by guilt.

In the final speech of the conversation with his wife which follows the planning of the murder of Banquo and Fleance, he invokes "seeling night" to "scarf up the tender eye of pitiful day." I think he is also expressing the wish that *he* may be blindfolded. Although the ambiguous "bond" he wants night to "cancel and tear to pieces" almost certainly refers to the prophecy that Banquo's sons will someday rule Scotland, it may also refer to *his* bond to his fellow general and to mankind.

Indirectly and obscurely Macbeth is expressing the old wish that he can be blind to his own acts and he reverts to it once more in III.iv.140–41. Nevertheless, it seems unlikely that he still has any real faith in this possibility. As we know, however, he has employed three murderers to get rid of Banquo and Fleance, and he appears to hope, in this way, to reduce or eliminate his own feeling of responsibility. He tries to prove his innocence to the Ghost of Banquo by claiming that he had not killed him. But the very fact that he conjures up the Ghost, whether in a hallucination or a dream, shows how ineffectual this new stratagem is in evading guilt.

In III.ii and again, more sharply, in III.iv, he expresses the wish that by deliberately hardening himself, by immersing himself more deeply in evil, he can make himself impervious to guilt:

> My strange and self-abuse
> Is the initiate fear that wants hard use.
> We are yet but young in deed.
>
> (III.iv.143–45)

At the time Macbeth makes this speech he is evidently already contemplating the murder of Macduff. By this point he has coarsened a great deal, and he coarsens further before our eyes in IV.i as a result of the rage and fear he feels when he learns that Macduff has fled to England. He again employs murderers, this time to do away with Macduff's family. But the combined effects of these mechanisms for hoodwinking the superego or becoming indifferent to its reproaches is nil. Whatever his actions may suggest, he never achieves cold-bloodedness and indifference to conscience. We learn this from Macbeth's first comment to Macduff on the battlefield before Dunsinane:

> Of all men else I have avoided thee.
> But get thee back! My soul is too much charged
> With blood of thine already.
>
> (V.viii.5–7)

Although against his will, Macbeth is a moral man to the very end of the tragedy, and this is his real problem: the source of his efforts to deceive conscience and keep himself in ignorance of his own deeds. Those efforts are foredoomed to failure. He is unable to keep any aspect of his behavior from awareness; he is compelled to perceive not merely his acts, but their wrongness and their consequences. From the time he subterraneously reaches the decision that murder is not too high a price to pay for being king (in the play seen as an action), his situation is probably hopeless. Certainly it is hopeless from the moment when, against the dictates of his own mind and heart, he goes through with the crime. He commits a murder for which he knows there is no excuse, and his punishment, whether "actual" or imagined, is Dantesque: he becomes a murderer.

His situation is irremediable and he knows it. The scorpions which have taken possession of his mind are an integral part of his punishment: he is plagued incessantly by self-reproach and the feeling that, to achieve a sense of security, he must murder again and again. The death he finally achieves is a release as much as a punishment. Two speeches in V.iii, 19–29 ("Seyton!—I am sick at heart . . .") and 39–45 ("Cure her of that . . ."), corroborate what the very tonelessness of the "She should have died hereafter" speech tells us more subtly: for some time he has been ready to welcome death.

Macbeth's feeling that he must do away with Banquo and Fleance may easily be perceived as another part of his dream fabric. His rivalry with Banquo and fear of him can be sensed in I.iii and is of course expressed explicitly in III.i. His fear of Banquo's descendants is unmistakable even in the earlier of these scenes and is heavily emphasized in lines 57–72 of the later scene. In dreams no less than in real life, even if he finally succeeded in killing Duncan and Banquo, he would continue to worry about the prophecy that Banquo's descendants would eventually rule Scotland.

Act IV, scene i, can be read like an account of an actual dream. Shakespeare had to be deeply inside the mind of Macbeth to write the scene; in addition to flowing like a dream and dealing with the worries which preoccupy Macbeth at this point, the scene expresses them in the logic and images Macbeth would fall into. If Macduff is not a friend, then he is an enemy. Thus the apparition of the Armed Head, which expresses his fear of Macduff.

We might suppose that at this point the dreamwork would attempt to provide reassurance against the warning. If so, the attempt is unsuccessful. It is ominous to begin with that Macbeth conjures up a Bloody Child. We know that as early as I.iii he feared the Crowned Child he is soon to see. The Bloody Child extends this fear to a still-to-be-born or just-born child; it must seem to Macbeth that he must fear all children, even those not yet conceived. At the same time the Bloody Child represents the retributive fears he has as a result of the murder of Banquo and the attempt to murder Fleance; and, equally, of the consequences of the "strange things" taking shape in his mind which crystallize at the end of the scene—the decision to kill Macduff's wife and children.

Nor do the words of the Bloody Child succeed in reassuring Macbeth. The way its promise is phrased—"none of woman born/shall harm Macbeth"—seems calculated to allow for loopholes. As we read, we notice this, if at all, only subliminally, but Macbeth's response shows clearly that his fear has not been quieted:

> Then live, Macduff: what need I fear of
> thee?
> But yet I'll make assurance double sure,
> And take a bond of fate. Thou shalt not live;
> That I may tell pale-hearted fear it lies,
> And sleep in spite of thunder.
>
> (IV.i.82–86)

The image of "a Child Crowned, with a tree in his hand" condenses Macbeth's deepest and most terrifying fears. From the beginning the realization that some other man's child would succeed him has galled him, making him aware of his childlessness and perhaps his impotence, and it has intensified his guilt by making his crimes seem selfish and futile. The tree the Child has in its hand is a fertility symbol, contrasting with Macbeth's "barren scepter." Inevitably, the apparition calls to mind the promise the witches have made to Banquo. He asks the apparition about this just before it disappears; and it paves the way for the heartbreaking image of the eight kings and Banquo—the "family tree" which the weird sisters show him immediately afterward. In an only slightly hidden way the apparition also voices Macbeth's growing fear of "conspirers." At some level he realizes that he is creating the coalition of forces which will ultimately destroy him.

We may become consciously aware of the hedged nature of the promise that Macbeth shall not be vanquished until "Great Birnam Wood to high Dunsinane Hill/Shall come against him." It is not until the play is analyzed that we are likely to realize how natural it is that Macbeth, a general used to sizing up terrain and developing strategies of attack and defense, should have thought of the trick which later occurs to Malcolm. The connection between the tree the child carries and fertility gives another implication to the moving wood, which later exposes the futility of Macbeth's hopes and leads to his death. Shakespeare wants us to feel that a sterile and death-oriented man like Macbeth cannot prevail for long against life-affirming forces.

Just as the news Ross and Angus brought after Macbeth's first encounter with the witches seems to confirm his hopes and justify the terrible act he is considering, so Lennox's news that Macduff has fled to England confirms his fears and is seized as an excuse to proceed with murders more wanton and useless still. I have had to scant the artistry of *Macbeth*. The formal symmetry of I.iii and IV.i is another example of how pervasive it is. The artistry is all the more remarkable if, as I suspect, *Macbeth* was written while Shakespeare was in a distraught state.

To a greater extent than any other drama I know, *Macbeth* is "written" in the language of what Freud calls primary process thinking, the language of the unconscious. This would perhaps be more apparent if the play were less concerned than it is with Macbeth's anxieties and fears. Primary process thinking is usually under the sway of the pleasure principle; its common function is to provide the hallucinatory gratification of desires. But there are anxiety dreams and fantasies as well as wish-fulfilling ones. Even when Macbeth seems preoccupied with his anxieties, numerous characteristics of primary process thinking are clearly in evidence.

If Shakespeare were less of an artist, gross content elements would make us aware of the extent to which primary process thinking prevails in *Macbeth*. Readers not only accept, but quickly begin to take for granted the strange world the play conjures up. In this world the prophecies of supernatural creatures and apparitions often correctly foreshadow and even seem to bring about events. Prophecies hinge upon such things as a wood moving or a person being invulnerable to someone born of a Caesarian operation, but not to someone born in the ordinary way. Our credulity is explained in part by our intuitive ability to understand primary process language—in particular, to perceive the subjective meaning of something apparently objective.

Other things besides unrealistic story elements suggest the extent to which *Macbeth* is written in the language of the unconscious. Like our fantasies and dreams the play is a rebus in which cause often follows effect and explanation often follows act. Equally significant is the almost complete disregard of time. Psychoanalysis has taught us that the idea of time does not exist in the unconscious. Similarly, in *Macbeth* there are practically no clues to the passage of time, though this plays an important part in the Holinshed account upon which Shakespeare drew. Not only have we no idea of how long a period of time the play covers; we seldom have a sure idea of how much time elapses between any two scenes. Such references to time as appear are often vague or careless. In the banquet scene Macbeth refers to charnel houses and graves sending "Those that we bury back," but in fact when he speaks there would not have been time to bury Banquo.

Perhaps more significant still is the extent to which a tendency to picture everything manifests itself in *Macbeth*. Wishes, fears, means, and guilt feelings (the bloody dagger, the Ghost of Banquo) are externalized, often personified, shown, and/or voiced. Figures of speech abound, pour out in such profusion that more than one metaphor seems mixed, more than one speech incoherent. As Cleanth

Brooks shows, however, the images and symbols which run through the play are (like many of our dreams) better organized than they appear to be.[5] Moreover, the more we penetrate the surface of the play, the more unified and understandable they become.

As we have seen, *Macbeth* can be read as a tissue of its protagonist's dreams, fantasies, and thoughts. Even when viewed as a dramatization of events, those events are often shown as they would be imagined by Macbeth: to some extent nearly every scene reflects his wishes or fears. Thus there is really little difference between the two ways of apprehending the play, and we feel no disposition to choose between them. Moreover, the play is written to an exceptional extent in the language of our dreams and fantasies. Although *Macbeth* has rivals in our century, for example, *Six Characters in Search of an Author*, it may remain the most subjective play ever written. We read it in a state of relaxation, in much the way we read fairy stories in childhood. However it is apprehended, we accept it primarily, I believe, as a dramatization of psychic reality.

Still, Shakespeare brings off the miracle of persuading us provisionally to accept *Macbeth* as an account of "real" events. A priori, nothing seems more improbable than the idea that a man with such an unrelenting conscience as Macbeth's would embark on a career of crime. Yet Shakespeare makes a play based upon such apparently irreconcilable plot elements believable. However understood, *Macbeth* is among other things one of the world's greatest cautionary tales. Even a person of probity and strong conscience might *dream* of committing an unjustified murder to obtain something desperately desired. Moreover, even such a person might find it impossible to relinquish the dream. Against his will he might find himself returning to it night and day, embellishing it, visualizing ways and means, imagining this or that vicissitude and contingency until, to his horror, a whole series of crimes had been thought through from beginning to end. As Shakespeare has shown, however, what would be uppermost in the mind of such a person is not the crimes or their rewards but the punishment to be endured. Again and again the dreamer would in effect be telling himself, "Only evil and suffering would come of this." The result, if not the purpose, of the dream-thought-fabric would be to pare down the temptation and emphasize its consequences, so that the feared impulse could be controlled. In most cases only the dreamer would profit from this, but when the dream fabric is embodied in a work of art readers and spectators share in the benefits.

Considered as a dramatization of actual occurrences, *Macbeth* is probably a still more effective cautionary tale. When events seem less contingent and more real, tragedy has its maximum impact on us—though the events are experienced vicariously. The vicarious gratification of impulses, which plague us no less than Macbeth, would make them less urgent and hence more amenable to control, especially if the gratification was apparently real. The emphasis, or overemphasis, on punishment would remind us of the terrible price the gratification entails and hence provide a constraint against yielding to desire.

It is of the utmost importance that Macbeth's first crime, which is the one that fathers all the others, is the murder of his sovereign, who is important in his own right and is the symbol of order in the state. Moreover, it is a murder he knows to be unjustified. No crime could better symbolize what might be called the sacred crimes, the violations of the primeval taboos upon which civilization rests. Nor could any crime better illustrate the strength and tenacity of our anarchistic desires. Many of those desires and the tendency to put the satisfaction of the desires above everything else go back to childhood, but neither the desires nor this tendency is ever completely relinquished; they may still be troublesome when we are grown-up. In our minds and hearts we have all experienced the temptation to which Macbeth was subjected, or temptations analogous to it, and at one time or another we have yielded to them, in thought if not in deed. The fact that *Macbeth* has this reference to a wide range of our most primitive desires and conflicts helps to explain its unshakable hold on the imagination of mankind.

Notes

1. Primary process thinking is largely in the service of the id, secondary process thinking in the service of the ego. It is easiest to understand the first mode of thinking by comparing it with the second, the kind of thinking dominant most of the time in maturity. Secondary process thinking is "ordinary, conscious

thinking." It is "primarily verbal" and it follows "the usual laws of syntax and logic."

In contrast, primary process thinking "is characteristic of those years of childhood when the ego is still immature." This helps to explain its characteristics. Since it is initially the mode of thought of the preverbal child, it makes relatively little use of verbal representation, often substituting "visual or other sense impressions" for words. It shows no concern with time and makes no use of "negatives, conditionals and other qualifying conjunctions." It permits opposites to replace one another and mutually contradictory ideas to "coexist peacefully." It makes frequent use of "representation by allusion or analogy . . ." and may employ "a part of an object, memory or idea . . . to stand for the whole, or vice versa. . . ." In addition to dominating our dreams and fantasies, primary process thinking plays a considerable though subordinate role in the thinking of adult life—in jokes and slang, for example, and also in such a highly esteemed activity as the creation of poetry. I have here mainly relied upon and often paraphrased Charles Brenner, *An Elementary Textbook of Psychoanalysis* (Garden City, N.Y.: Anchor Books, 1955). The quotations are also from this valuable book, pp. 52–55.

2. This and all other quotations from *Macbeth* are from the Signet Classic edition, ed. Sylvan Barnet (New York: New American Library, 1963).
3. *The Psychoanalytic Theory of Neurosis* (New York: Norton, 1945), p. 268.
4. For a wonderful example of this mechanism in contemporary fiction, see *To the Lighthouse*, "The Window," Ch. 7—the account of the way Mrs. Ramsey musters her energies to provide the sympathy and reassurance she senses her husband needs.
5. "The Naked Babe and the Cloak of Manliness," in *The Well Wrought Urn* (New York: Reynal and Hitchcock, 1947).

Jean Paris

THE MORTAL SIGN
Psychological Implication of Linguistic Elements in Literature

HYPOTHESIS

contrary to the intrinsic
coherence of thought
Pierre Klossowski

Given: *predictable*
    as well as: *dog*
and the accident that brings the two together. Or design. That
couples them? Ironically it is of the middle term, praised traditionally
as the position of moderation, that the monster is born: *predogtable.**

But why a monster? Because the missing element of all lexicons
belongs strictly to the unintelligible, while borrowing, as would a
creature of Bosch or Arcimboldo, its components from the natural
order, but above all, because, once born, it asserts its defiant nature,
posing a threat to normalcy.

---

* The author suggests the French "monster" *fourmidable*, engendered by
formidable and *fourmiant*. Tr.

PRECEDENTS

> When a writer prevents
> words from coming freely,
> he is sexless
> Henri Pichette

"Jakobson describes the examples of a word association test. If the verbal stimulus 'hut' is proposed, subjects' responses may be classed in one of two categories: substitution or prediction. If the response is 'cabin' or 'shanty', it belongs to the first category; if the subject answers 'has burned', his response belongs clearly to the second. 'Hut' may be replaced by 'cabin'; 'has burned' and 'the hut' constitute a syntactical unit. It functions as a predicate and thus establishes a link of contiguity. Suppose the word 'hut' is followed by 'is a poor little house'; in this case the response establishes both a relation of contiguity with the stimulus when seen syntactically and a substitutive relation when seen semantically."[1] Agreed. Yet it is strange that neither Jakobson nor Veron, who comments on the experiment, conceives a third category of responses, which would be based solely on assonance or homophony: *mut, slut, but(t), cud, thug, gut,* and so on, which would reject the prefabricated categories of "metaphor" and "metonomy."

The phenomenon, however, is by no means recent.

    1. Rabelais was not the first to realize that to brand *bedeaux* (sextons) as *veaux* (calves, i.e., stupid) he had only to call them *vedeaux*; similarly to brand *eveques* (bishops) as *potifs* (drunkards) and *putatifs* (lechers) the adjective *potatifs* would suffice.

    2. Lewis Carroll: "For instance, take the two words *fuming* and *furious.* Make up your mind that you will say both words if you have that rarest of gifts, a perfectly balanced mind, you will say *frumious.*"

"Supposing that when Pistol uttered the well-known words, 'under which king, Bezonian? Speak or die!' Justice Shallow had felt certain that it was either *William* or *Richard* . . . rather than die, he would have gasped out: Rilchiam!" [*The Hunting of the Snark*]

    3. Heinrich Heine: "I was seated next to Salomon Rothschild and he treated me as an equal—in a very *famillionaire* way."

    4. Thomas de Quincey recalls that old people, keen on *anecdotes* yet subject to *dotage*, sink naturally into *anecdotage.*

    5. Balzac mentions an *incalcuttable* fortune, because it was acquired in *Calcutta.*

    6. Freud quotes some of these hybrid words and provides others:

Cleopold, uniting the first names of a king and his mistress; *Orienter-preszug* combining *Orient-Express* and *Erpressung* (blackmail); Madame de *Maintenant* (now) for Madame *Maintenon; roux sot* (red fool) for *Rousseau;* alcoholidays, and so on.[2]

RULES OF THE GAME

> the spirit is lost whenever
> we neglect the technical
> procedures of expression.
>   Sigmund Freud

If some take pleasure in these discoveries, from what does the pleasure stem? Essentially from the regression that favors these puns. Why indeed would the absurd rejoice if its intrusion did not disturb the oppressive order of custom, if it did not replace the congealed logic of the adult world with the combinatory freedoms of childhood? "In what situation will the mind appear critically as a nonsense? Precisely when the mind adopts ways of thinking which the *unconscious* accepts, but which the conscious rejects, that is, when it makes use of faulty reasoning"[3] and abruptly returns to a verbal state prior to that separation of conscious and unconscious, in which the laws here violated had not yet solidified as social restraints.

  K. Fischer states that the pun "plays with the word, not as a word, but as a sound."[4] In other words, it brings us back to this "playful stage" anterior to the acquisition of meaning and to the corresponding repression of the signifier. Freud, thinking along similar lines, ascribes its euphoric power to three conditions. First, the pun is a reversion to the original unconscious (Humpty-Dumpty's fall, Alice's falling into the burrow, Finnegan's *pftjschute,* and so on), since the main dream mechanisms, displacement and condensation, govern this word splitting similarly. Second, the pun represents a gain of energy which accompanies certain transgressions: hostility, lewdness, obscenity, or cynicism. We succeed in "throwing off inhibitions," and in "liberating the illogical," in spite of grammar and the entire apparatus of repressive logic. Third, the pun is the principle of the least effort, supplanting intermediary explanations to bring us to the results. Although these three conditions are necessary, they are insufficient. And it is surprising that this "awakening of the infantile" was not apprehended by Freud in its destructive violence, as if the negation of language law were not equivalent to that of the parental law. Since no criterion exists at this level to distinguish their specific nature, puns are presented restrictively as a particular class of the "lapsus." According to Meringer and Meyer, they would fall into five categories:[5] (1) interversion—the *Milo of Venus*; (2) encroachment of one morpheme on another—*Brust* (breast) annexed by *schwer* (heavy) in the expression "It hung heavy upon my breast," changes to *Schwest*; (3) superfluous prolongation—"Join with me in a belch (*aufzustossen*)" instead of a "toast (*anstossen*) to the health of our chief"; (4) contamination—"He raises his head (*Kopf*)" and "He rears up on his hind legs (*Hinterbeine*)" coalescing into "He sat on his neck (*Hinterkopf*)"; (5) substitution—Stekel declaring to a female patient whom he believed to be suffering from Basedow's disease: "You are a goiter (*kropf*)" instead of "a head (*Kopf*) taller than your sister."[6]

This classification, both excessive and insufficient, is reduced by Wundt to three equally contestable categories: reproduction of a previous syllable or anticipation of a following one; incongruous intrusion of one sound in a series of different ones; and construction of words by association.[7] Freud finally selected this tripartite model, after having tried more "perplexing" models. From it he proposed his own division; (1) substitution of an error for the correct word. "In the case of the female genitalia, in spite of the temptations (*Versuchungen*) . . . I mean, in spite of the attempts (*Versuche*) . . ."; (2) statement of the opposite of what should have been said, for example, a certain President of Parliament, slightly confused, proclaims the session closed as he set about to open it; (3) incorrect assimilation of similar words as when a young man offers to accompany (*begleiten*) a female friend but is dying to transgress the law of courtesy (*beleidigen*), and fabricates unthinkingly *begleitdigen*. The hybrid words evidently belong in the last category. However, the price is a distortion that relegates their creation to the accidental. The gentleman, who was asked about his horse, whose illness not only made him sad (*traurig*) but also promised to last (*das dauert*) another month, and who stammered *das draut*, was not aware of his combining the two words that obsessed him. Synthesis occurs automatically and too quickly to foresee or to correct it. The very modality of this confusion permits Freud to categorize its instances: in the first, one verbal intention secretly alerts another; in the second, it "completely replaces" the other; and in the third, both create a composite foreign to the dictionary and hence divested of meaning. In any case, the fundamental requisite is that one of the conflicting intentions, and precisely the disturbing one, remain unconscious or at least repressed.[8] "The speaker has determined not to convert the idea into speech and then it happens that he makes a slip of the tongue; that is to say, the tendency which is debarred from expression asserts itself against his will."[9]

Formally (Saussure's *anagram* would provide a parallel example), let me indicate here an initial break in the linear order of the signifier, and perhaps we shall understand why the hybrid words, and why *Finnegans Wake* still receive so little attention from the linguists. If this "willful attempt to amalgamate incongruent linguistic patterns" ends, for those who at least have taken the trouble to hear about it, in nothing more than a "muddle," a "vexations result," an "abuse of language," "unintelligibility," a "nonsense," failing to reach a "coherent sequence," and therefore "not to be taken seriously,"[10] it is because this attempt deviates from the tacit postulate of their analyses. That is, as language is only justified by its finality (communication), its elements can only find their meaning and function in a code whose univocality reflects that of the subject. Thus the double path which in the classical diagram links the mouth of the speaker with the ear of the listener:

$$\text{source} \rightarrow \text{message} \rightarrow \text{signal} \rightarrow \text{message} \rightarrow \text{destination}$$

and vice versa, ideally implies these two heads to be transparent, a supposition tantamount to negation of the unconscious. It should come then as no surprise to note the insistence of metaphors that command even the structuralist vocabulary: spoken chain, concatenation, syntagmatic, axis, phonic series, morphemic sequence, thread of discourse, and so on. Nor do they contradict, through contamination by the written words, the multidimensional nature of spoken words. In fact, these metaphors do not refer at all to a phonological model—the network should be a much better image—but to a logical model, whose role is precisely to exclude ambiguity. It is this model that Descartes borrowed from mathematics: these "long chains of reasons," in which each term deduces itself from the others, but in a unilateral direction, respecting "their mutual affinity," all displaying their "intermediate rings" in "a continuous and uninterrupted movement of thought," so that "if we suppose the least omission, the chain is thus broken, and the entire certainty of the conclusion collapses." We have here a system where logic, syntax, and meaning are identical, where the "method" itself comes down to "the scrupulous observation of an order" oriented from the simple toward the complex, and where consciousness is required to survey without deviation all the degrees of the series one after the other. In this perspective, heeding several things at the same time, "in a single thought," would represent the cardinal sin, the chief characteristic of a "confused mind," a proliferation and ineffectual syncretism that the edifice of rationalism rose precisely to challenge.[11]

The ellipsis constituted by the hybrid word thus sets in motion a double destruction of the sign. On the one hand, it forces us to apprehend the linguistic sign no longer as a categorical entity to be defined once and for all, and committed to a fixed function, but rather as an ever provisional result of several dynamic processes. On the other hand, this ellipsis threatens the syntactic articulation of the sign by introducing in it gaps, uncertainties, short circuits, and deletions—discontinuities contradicting sequentiality, which is the very condition of intelligibility. In this perspective, its ambiguity even ceases to present itself as incompatible yet simultaneous elements; it is simply the status of the signifier that the ellipse denounces, the fact that it belongs simultaneously to the contradictory systems of the conscious and the unconscious, not to mention the numerous levels between them. It is perhaps this anticipation that finally led Freud to raise the acute question of semiological functioning.

Linguistic deviation can hardly be reduced to the meeting of the opposite intentions, since that operation would imply remaining within the rigidity of a formula such as Wundt's "free and spontaneous production of incoherent associations," because this incoherence itself eludes all possible definitions. Nor can one ascribe its origin to the suppression or suspension of the will. None of these approaches permits us to apprehend the problem that conditions them, that is, as Freud put it, ascertaining if "the disturbing element is to be found *inside* or *outside* the word."[12] Two eventualities do in effect present themselves: either the word ceases to behave normally according to its intrinsic functions, its constitution then coming into question, or this dysfunction is imposed on the word from elsewhere, by an agent whose origin could be only the unconscious. In the first case, the formal nature of the signifier, its phonological structure, should suffice to explain the errors and garbling that it causes, and its study will remain "purely linguistic." In the second case, uncertainty concerning the signified(s) will carry interrogation over into psychoanalysis, analogous with "this effort towards condensation that plays such an important role in the formation of dreams."[13]

The formalist hypothesis was to prevail initially. For Wundt, the spontaneity of the lapsus certainly betrayed a downfall of control; however, this negative disposition could never be a sufficient cause, for it does not facilitate understanding the mechanism of the lapsus nor, consequently, justification of specificity. The search must take place within the words themselves, in their relations of resemblance, attraction, implication, and proximity, a search for the positive reason behind their amalgamation. And this reason belongs only to their sonority: this so-called "free" creation of hybrids and ambiguities is in fact totally controlled "by the spoken word." Meringer postulates that "the various linguistic sounds possess different psychic values. The instant we innerve the first sound of a word, the first word of a sentence, the process of excitation moves on to the following sounds and words, and these simultaneous, concomitant innervations, infringing as they do upon one another, mutually imprint modifications and deformations." If the excitation of a sound bearing a greater psychic intensity precedes the less important process of innervation, or persists after it, thus disordering it either by anticipation or retroactively, it becomes imperative to ground the theory in the objective, even measurable properties of the words themselves. According to Meringer, the most highly laden phonemes are "the initial sound of the root syllable, the beginning of the word and the vowel or vowels on which the accent falls":[14] those are the splitting lines of the sentence, the points of departure for its aberrations.

Although he admits that the two components, phonetic chance and "psychic situation," operate simultaneously, are "equally indispensable," and melt into "one and the same process," Freud's interest lies practically only in the hypothesis of exteriority. The disturbing agent "has its source outside the discourse," in "unconscious" or in "partially repressed thought"; in any case, it is alien to the intention as well as to the manifest content of the statement. Hence Freud was gradually led to minimize the phenomenon's audio-verbal components, especially "the contact exerted by the sounds upon one another," as if he thought it was contradictory to elucidate both the phonological mechanisms and those influences "lying outside the verbal intention." But how would an "unconscious idea" have the power to alter a verb or a substantive, if it did not share an identical essence, that is, if the unconscious were not already language? The Freudian theory of the lapsus implies an imprecision, if not a contradiction, doubtlessly inherent in its subject, since the theory as well as the lapsus skip over the articulation that would cause problems. And this situation is not brought to light definitively until Lacan. By allowing a hiatus to exist between the intentional enunciation and the repressed force that modifies it, the Freudian theory required as a complement or a corrective, the recognition of this force as being linguistic: "this area stretches to include as much of the subject as is ruled by the laws of speech"; and thus "it is the whole structure of language that the psychoanalytical experience discovers in the unconscious."[15] By founding the subject himself on the symbolic order, by interpreting his acts, hence his errors, as "displacements of the signifier," Lacan's view reestablishes a homology between the discourse of the will and "the discourse of the Other," where the composite, whether fortuitous or not, finds a justification. "*It* speaks" and if "the same term proves upon examination to bear the truth and its concealment,"[16] then we do not find two "intentions" running head on in *Hinterkopf* or *das draut*, but rather a mixing process that permits us to specify its "morphemes"—their similarities as well as their divergences.

This bipolar structure that Freud assigned to the lapsus and extended to the pun, because it relies, in the last analysis, on a logic of representation, must unavoidably be altered. There is not, on the one hand, a lucid intention that would "dictate" rational speech, and, on the other, a hidden intention that would slyly upset the enunciation; the relation between them can be conceived only against the backdrop of a common language. Prior to whatever may express their split, consciousness and unconsciousness belong to a semiological system in which anomalies, hybrid words for example, attest to its functioning. From this point of view, if it is naive to consider the manifest text as a simple screen destined to conceal the truth of the latent text, the prejudice psychoanalysis urges us to renounce is that of the distinction between deeply hidden, true reality on the one hand, and misleading appearance, a surface directly assimilable, on the other; far from running up against an "outside" that would create a disturbance, linguistic space integrates not only the terms Freud isolated as heterogeneous, but also the very point of their junction: the subject himself.

Yet, in this perspective, a new question arises: how does one distinguish a witty remark from a simple lapsus? Commenting on the gaff of a woman according to whom a man needs only five erect limbs to look seductive, Freud wonders whether the statement is involuntary or deliberate: "All depends upon the intention, conscious or unconscious, with which the woman pronounced the phrase. As it turned out, her behavior excluded any conscious intention: and then it was not a *mot d'esprit*."[17] It should be apparent, however, how insufficient this criterion remains. What if the woman were a cunning comedian who made, like Ophelia, her "wantonness" her "ignorance"? How can an intention be judged from the outside? We arrive then at this paradox: although the lapsus would not rigorously be distinct from the pun, always letting the question of artifice hover suspiciously nearby, it is by openly displaying this artifice that the pun would distinguish itself from the lapsus. When Joyce spends seventeen years manipulating Celtic, Scandinavian, Latin, Slavic, and Saxon roots in order to contrive the very book of the composite, the result cannot be considered spontaneous, free, or fortuitous. But the system, once established, surpasses its own limits, engendering series of associations and interpretations the author was initially unable to foresee. Out of context, nothing separates such blunders as *Schwest* or *begleitdigen* from calculated inventions as *pensisolate* or *funferal*.

The decisive difference is not to be found in the content or form of these words: the signifier and the signified are ambiguous in both cases. The difference lies rather in the process of their production: the hybrid word stimulates the lapsus; it refers to the unconscious only by a resemblance it immediately strives to deny for its own profit. But for the hybrid word's true problematics, speculation must move beyond the analogy and come to the very field where the hybrid word operates—linguistics.

MEANING OF NON-SENSE
NON-SENSE OF MEANING

> a code or rather the blurring
> of a code that would be its most
> efficient negative
>
> Gilles Deleuze

Granted then: *predogtable*
Such a word is a threat, a seat of infection, a mirror where other words disintegrate. In vain has it been asserted that there is meaning only "where there is choice";[18] every statement, in order to be understood, requires the identification of one syntactic structure as

well as one morphemic structure, in other words, the identification of
its minimal units.[19] Now, it is precisely the identity of these components—and the very principle of their combination—that the hybrid word questions, for quite obviously it reverses the process
involved. Normal discourse splits into elements of first articulation
(*morphemes* or *monemes*), which have a double face (signifier/sig-
nified) and which, in turn, split into elements of second articulation
(phonemes) with a single face (signifier).[20] Simply stated, normal
discourse joins sounds devoid of meaning to form words carrying
meaning, and these words then form sentences and so on. On the
contrary, the hybrid word unites elements of the first articulation as
if they belonged to the second one; it takes their meaning as a point
of departure in constituting a mixture containing no meaning or,
what amounts to the same thing, an infinite number of meanings.
The distinctive function assumed by each level of language—the
semantic level, containing all the significant elements, and the phonological level, whose role it was to differentiate between them—becomes here, through the permutation imposed by the hybrid word,
impossible to make out.

In posing the question whether *persist* constitutes one morpheme
or two (since *per* is found in *pertain*, and *sist* in *consist, resist*, etc.),
Zellig Harris already outlined in a way the disintegration of the verb
itself.[21] Yet he did not go so far as to suspect malicious intentions from
the speaker. But if dubious words like *frumious* or *incalcuttable* turn
up in a discourse that requires the stability of its signs, how can the
suspicion be prevented from including all the rest? Suppose "normal"
words were "hybrid words" in disguise? Would not the appearance
of the norm bespeak more perversity than the deviations? Let us
leave aside the host of homophonies whose ambiguity is often dispelled by their context, for example, a *cross-eyed bear* or the *cross
I'd bear, a surf board* or *a serf bored*. But I say *pear* or *lichen*, and
the entire plant kingdom might become perplexity: who knows
if I am blending *pore* and *bear, peer* and *buyer*, or *light* and an *icon*,
or a *lie* in *Aachen*?

The absurdity of this threat is only instructive *a contrario*. It
reveals the domination that *meaning* exerts in the linguistic field, despite linguists' attempts to deny it. Thus, the "semi-sentences" studied by Katz, each constituting a grammatical twist, are understood
intuitively, but in terms of their correctly formed elements, or as
Paul Ziff has it, "by analogy with normal."[22] The subject spontaneously refers the aberration to an adjacent speech sequence in relation

to which he constructs the meaning of the one he just heard; so that to explain it within the perspective of a transformational grammar, it is necessary to light both the "comprehensive set" and its "transfer set" and its "transfer rules."[23]

This naivete is instructive: it points out the basic tendency to reduce the unknown to the familiar. Linguists themselves are no exception. The structuralists, from Bloomfield to Hjelmslev, but against Jakobson, incessantly insisted that meaning had to be expelled from language in order that the latter could reveal its formal mechanism. But everything indicates that meaning went out the front door only to reenter through the window. At all levels the occult presence of meaning governs in fact the locating of categories and functions. If, for instance, a grammar must distinguish "not only between proper nouns and common nouns, masculine and feminine nouns, but also between the animate and the inanimate, enumerable and unwieldy, concrete and abstract," and in the case of verbs, "between transitive and intransitive, and among the transitive verbs, between those that allow suppression of the object (*to eat*) and those that do not (*to admire, to fear*)," and so on,[24] it is difficult to imagine posing these differences without tacitly appealing to the order of the signified. It would be well and good to treat the opposition between animate and inanimate as "purely formal,"[25] but it is necessary to have learned before to distinguish between a seam and a seamstress. All relations dealing with selection are characterized ultimately by this sly, unavowable recourse to meaning.

Even our phonemic classification itself implies this "non-analyzed" semantic element. In order to differentiate between two almost identical sounds, the present expedient consists of replacing one by another in a given statement to see if comprehension is affected. But what does this signify, if not that the notion of phoneme, thus defined, remains dependent on the notion of meaning, of synonymy? Can we then be surprised by such confidence in the stable identity of signs, if the operations claiming the highest degree of autonomy vis-à-vis this identity are still based on what Quine denounces as "implicit semantics"?[26]

Once again, it is this identity, this stability, that is threatened by the hybrid word. As "disjunctive synthesis," the hybrid word is defined by an immediately demystifying role: it alone can shatter the imposture, the hypocrisy of other signifiers, their fictitious "unity," and their illusion of belonging to "the order of meaning." If its function is to give its own status as exemplary, that is, to insinuate that "normal" words merely conceal the cross-breeding that it exhibits, what parts of the lexicon would indeed escape contagion? Turn to any page of the *American Heritage Dictionary*, and it is impossible to find a term that does not fall prey to this mincing process. For example:

> *solidity*: so, sew, saw, sow, sol, soul, all, awl, owl, ode, sully, solid, id, lid, lea, lead, leader, idea, edit, audit, oddity, ditto . . .

And let us not even consider what possible meaning it may acquire, by analogy, in foreign languages, or the possibility of reading it backwards—*ytidilos*. These two mechanisms were employed by Joyce, in *Finnegans Wake*, to destroy every code and every sign.

We learn from Joyce's minute and laborious corrections, contractions, additions, permutations, and separations that if certain combinations prevail at the outset, degrees of lexicality exist within the hybrid word according to the possibilities offered by its components. Just how far, asks Katz, can a sequence deviate from grammaticality and still avoid non-sense? Just how far, asks Joyce, can the hybrid word be pushed without falling into insanity like Rabelaisian monsters? One must admit, as does Meringer, that certain phonemes, more pregnant than others, assure the stability of the word-mix itself, a compromise to which one is forced to consent at the risk of losing all power of analysis. In Joyce's notebooks, a grouping of paronyms has often as a starting point a single inductor, or "points of disjunction between which an entire network of synthesis is woven."[27] Around this "cluster of meaning," the technique consists of the progressive accumulation of as many elements as possible, then, in a more complicated form, the cluster's reabsorption in a system where it shall soon figure as no more than one of many kernels. Linguistically, the chief characteristic of *Finnegans Wake* is the introduction within the word itself of the recursivity that grammarians have admitted up to now only at the syntactic level. The number of dimensions, supposing it could be calculated, is of little import: two terms are sufficient, here, to specify a structure that will later function independently as the source of energy for a combinational process of which the author could state only the principle. At least two terms exist, their attraction depending exclusively on their common phonemes since it is not even required that they belong to the same code; the difference between them suddenly betrays their relation and reduces them both to nothingness within a third term. A handy recipe: the more the ingredients of the hybrid word are phonetically adjacent and semantically distanced, the more edible the end product.

RETINAL RIVALRY

Le *symbole* bafoué devient *diabole*
Michel Tounier

Thus the hybrid word appears as the source "of an alternative whose terms it forms as well. Each virtual part of such a word designates the meaning of the other, or expresses another which in turn designates it."[28] The following question now comes unavoidably to the fore: are these two parts to be perceived separately or together? For if, on the one hand, *dog* and *predictable* remain distinct one from the other, why indeed should they be joined? Would not this result in an oscillation between the two terms? This thinking serves certainly to obscure the problem, for if each period of the oscillation favors one of the two poles, how does the present synthesis differ from a simple juxtaposition? Yet, on the other hand, is it possible to unite these poles "in a single thought," to conceive of their duality in the very instant that abolishes it? This is at least desirable. "The hybrid word seen as a whole speaks its own meaning, and for this new reason is non-meaning. Indeed, the second law of normal nouns bearing meaning is that their meaning may not determine an alternative into which they themselves enter."[29] To judge from the word-mix, it seems, however, that one component, hence one meaning, springs forth only to condemn the twin components to evanescence: if *dog* comes to the fore, *predictable* is eclipsed, or vice versa, and simultaneously, the whole suffers a semantic reduction to one of its minima.

It appears that composite perception does not belong, in fact, to voluntary attention—otherwise neither the cinema nor simple vision would exist. If a psychological distinction is made between a strictly perceived image, it is because three types of activity—foveal, maculary, and peripheral—simultaneously place demands on the eye to form one process, and because visual perception calls on other senses: the fact that man distinguishes unknowingly between perceptual impressions that excite the retina and what he actually sees leads one to suppose that sensorial information originating elsewhere acts to correct the visual field.[30] The essential structure is thus antecedent to whatever consciousness of it may be obtained. Vision, for example, is stereoscopic only by virtue of a spontaneous mechanism whereby the brain must decide which eye is which; depth perception would otherwise become ambiguous. If one separates and inverts the two ocular images by means of a pseudoscope, the eyes will behave exactly like the components of the hybrid word: each rejects in turn the image that corresponds to it, but should normally correspond to the other, so that "parts of each image are successively combined and rejected in various ways" by a phenomenon known as *retinal rivalry*.[31]

The idea that perception is as unitary at the conscious level (meaning level) as it is plural at the sensorial level (level of receptivity) derives from the fact that selective successivity belongs to the former, while pure synchronicity marks the latter.[32] This touches on the very law of the organism.

But language also reveals this double mechanism whose "organization upon multiple superimposed levels" functions to the extent that it remains automatic and results only in the emission or reception of one piece of information. In the analytic process of reconstruction, phonemes group to form morphemes, and morphemes group to form sentences. However, for the speaker as for the auditor, this effort, having disappeared, is resumed in its final phase, as if this entirely unconscious process tended to repudiate itself in an intelligible signification.

And thus, the dilemma posed by the hybrid word renews itself continually, since among its terms, as among those of optical alternation, there is "no clue as to which of two alternative hypotheses is correct: the perceptual system entertains first one and then the other hypothesis, and never comes to a conclusion, for there is no best answer."[33] The reader, picturing himself in the situation of "a trial judge getting incompatible evidence from two witnesses and accepting both stories," cannot escape the paradox: "things that cannot possibly occur together," but that nevertheless do happen together, assert themselves in turn without being able to neutralize each other.

The other persists in the background as a shadow, as a negative counterpart, ironically reminding that meaning is derived from difference. When alternations accelerate, attention fixes little by little on a vertigo whereby the finally impeded necessity of meaning is balanced by the movement that brought it into being. And so, the hybrid word deconditions the act of reading in freeing it from the need to search for meaning or from the illusion of having found it. At this point, a new set of problems does arise: can attention grasp several concomitant terms? If so, what would be their numerical limit? Can attention function simultaneously? Can we perceive at the same time a whole and its parts? What would then be the perceptual mode of ambiguity? Can ambiguity even be apprehended in time without reducing it to alternation? Can pure relation be grasped without understanding its elements? And what about a meaning that illumines one of its possibilities only to cast the other into darkness? The hybrid word is simply a metaphor of thought.

THE GENERATIVE DISJUNCTION

Jewgreek is greekjew
_ James Joyce

Disjunction is then posed as the fundamental operation of consciousness—fundamental because consciousness is already a disjunction of the body. For this reason, any attempt to grasp its origin runs up against that which makes this origin unthinkable. This is to define in discourse and in art the principle of all works as problematic. In any case, if the hybrid word presents itself as both product and production, or rather, if it sets forth in its one form that of the very system that actualizes it, it suggests that a work of art is built accordingly upon the reiteration, at its various levels, of the disjunction out of which it arises and which all writing's efforts aim only to solve.[34] In this sense the status of the composite clearly requires a new critical approach; if "various modalities of any statement manifest the dispersion of the subject instead of referring to its unique synthesis or unifying function,"[35] then the problem is no longer to determine which convergencies create the illusion of some structure, but rather to retrace all transformations that lead to the textual surface.

One case will suffice to judge this attempt as a starting point for a generative theory of criticism. "You start a question, and it's like starting a stone. You sit quietly on the top of a hill and away the stone goes, starting others."[36] Phrased anecdotally, the supposition proposed by Robert Louis Stevenson equals a double affirmation. The narrative in which the supposition arises—here, Dr. Jekyll and Mr. Hyde—must be brought into being by a *question*, but far from solving the question, the narrative merely makes it worse since the question may be constituted in time only by setting more narrative series in motion. Which question? It is useless to search for it in the events that translate it. To do so is to make it disappear—just as Hyde "disappears" in Jekyll's body, and Jekyll will "disappear" in Hyde's corpse. The very reciprocity of its expressions assures the question a paradoxical status: both immanent and transcendent. The question is everywhere, presenting first a glimpse, and then slipping away. The walking stick broken in two after the murder, the constant battle between fog and lamps, and a narrative detail such as "all at once I saw two figures" (p. 293) manifest their absent presences no less than the tut-tut, bye-the-bye, little by little, right and wrong, balder and older, to and fro, unworthy and unhappy, serve and save, neither richer nor wiser, or duplications such as have you got it?, have you got it?, I saw what I saw, I heard what I heard scattered throughout the text.

At best these convergencies designate, albeit by their impossible prolongation, a blind, inaccessible, unnamable center to a disjunction. As Artaud put it, "the generic law of things is that one must divide to permit the creation of two, without two having been created by one, but having created itself" (p. 338). Accordingly, events such as Utterson's meeting Hyde and "the pair staring at each other pretty fixedly," or Utterson's searching in vain with the servant for Jekyll's corpse and "the two men looking at each other with a scare" reiterate at the plot level the fundamental scissiparity, as does the dream in which the monster is seen to "glide more stealthily through sleeping houses, or move the more swiftly and still the more swiftly, even to dizziness, through wider labyrinths of the lamplighted city" (p. 281), or the fire burning at the heart of the laboratory, diverging from the mirror "in a hundred repetitions along the glazed front of the presses" (p. 282).

This kariokinesis structurally calls up the theme of the split personality. But Stevenson will delay as long as possible before revealing this theme, as if to allow the narrative time to piece itself together according to its disjunctions. In confronting this text, as in the case of the hybrid word, the reader is urged either to abandon his demand of one meaning or to begin the book at the end. In fact, everything preceding the conclusion is simply artful suspense and the construction of hypotheses that cancel each other out to a delayed meaning that expectation alone valorizes as in Edgar Allen Poe or Raymond Roussel.

The fantastic atmosphere is hence magnified by the increasing density of contradictions as well as neutralized by the explanation that justifies in reverse its least elements. In this manner, proposing itself as a model for its own criticism, the entire work consists of the preparation, the final unfolding of its origin through an inversion which forces the reading of the text to split in two, and the beginning toward the conclusion and the conclusion toward the beginning. Thus these terms are deprived of the stable position they enjoy in literature, and the writing loses its immediate power to signify the terms.

The disjunction dissimulated at the narrative's origin and discovered at its conclusion can function concretely throughout the text only by substitutive series. For example, who speaks here? The absent, unnamed, invisible "author," starting questions from his hilltop, untouched by the grammatical fiction of the "I," which the book itself will attempt to explode, will be forced to actualize himself through Utterson, the lawyer; Richard Enfield; Doctor Lanyon; Poole, the butler; and finally the hero himself, confessing his double identity: Jekyll/Hyde.

In this group of characters, the first four appear obsessed by the fifth, by the mystery or the scandal that he incarnates, and from which they in principle should be exempt. However, far from being exempt, they seem to share with him, unknowingly, a double essence that sets them in opposition to each other. Thus, Utterson is pictured as an icy individual, "lean, long dusty, dreary," who never smiles, guards his words closely, and exhibits a stiffly formal manner—*but* who is found to be "somewhat lovable!" (p. 291). Admittedly, he is fond of wine *but* as a punishment drinks gin when alone; he adores the theater *but* has not seen a play in twenty years. His Sunday strolls with Enfield lead everyone to ask "what these two could see in each other, or what subject they could find in common," since "they said nothing" and "looked singularly dull," *but* for the two of them these Sunday outings appear "the chief jewel of each week" (p. 301) and they will go so far as to sacrifice business not to miss them. Lanyon, both friend and adversary of Jekyll, is contrasted to Utterson by his "hearty, healthy, dapper" geniality, "his boisterous and decided manner," and his "red-faced" complexion (p. 297). He is, nonetheless, another embodiment of contradiction. For example, he expresses his feelings in a "theatrical" way, *but* they do not cease to be "genuine." As for Jekyll, to the extent that he takes on the hidden disjunction witnessed in all the others, his description remains concise: a rather "large, well-made, smooth-faced man of fifty," *but* a sly gleam in his eyes upon occasion, *but* "every mark of capacity and kindness" (p. 294), *but* inhabited by a monster: Edward Hyde, the "pale and dwarfish" criminal who gives "an impression of deformity without any nameable malformation," a "murderous mixture of timidity and boldness," expressing himself in a "husky, whispering and somewhat broken voice," and so forth (p. 311).

This series of internal and external oppositions is contradicted by the series of names as if to destroy the negative by the positive and vice versa. *Utterson,* the direct emanation of the "author," is linked to him through filiation: *utter* (extreme) *son,* whose first clerk, named *Guest,* shares his secrets and reproduces this relation on a smaller scale. Utterson's role as a spokesman is confirmed when we later learn his Christian names: *Gabriel* and *John.* His cousin Enfield brings to mind *enfeoffed* and *in therefield,* translating his episodic nature and the authenticity of his involvement. *Lanyon,* through whom scandal first occurs, seems to be a contraction of *lane,* where many scenes take place, *anyone,* hence his mediocrity, and *lanyard,* a cord employed to fire a canon. The servant *Poole* suggests *poodle, poor, pool,* and so on. Last, *Jekyll* seems to combine *jackal* and *kill,* as if to point to the presence within of *Hyde.* Hyde rhymes with *glide* in Utterson's dream, is described as *hide*ous, and is pronounced like *hide,* a homophony that Stevenson exploits more than once: "If he be Mr. Hyde, I shall be Mr. Seek" (p. 311). "You have not been mad enough to hide this fellow?" (p. 283).

The same disjunction governs the scenery. The street behind Jekyll's house where Utterson and Enfield are seen strolling is located in a highly animated district, *but* "small" and "quiet" (p. 297), it stands in contrast to the dull and dingy neighborhood with its charming shops, enticing windows, well-polished copperwork, and repainted shutters. This "gaiety of note" is abruptly belied by a court leading to a "sinister," windowless, two-story building, showing "prolonged and sordid negligence" (p. 304). The night when the lawyer meets Hyde, his wanderings lead him to "a square of ancient, handsome houses," *but* which are "for the most part delayed from their high estate and let in flats" (p. 334). The night of Carew's murder is divided in two as is the weapon of the crime: fog billows over the city during the early morning hours, *but* in the evening not a single cloud is present and the alley-way is even "brilliantly lit by the full moon" (p. 315). We witness a similar succession and contrast when Utterson accompanies Poole in order to get to the bottom of the doctor's "disappearance." The wind sweeping through strangely deserted streets also makes for a clear sky, *but* returning, clouds hide the moon, it is "quite dark" (p. 315). Just as the setting and the characters metaphorically reflect each other through the breaking apart of their unity, we understand why Jekyll's house is described several times in great detail: it represents exactly the structure of its occupant. Purchased from a "surgeon," a man whose profession it is to convey disjunction even to the body, the house is divided into two main buildings: the vast, sumptuous living quarters, lit by lamps and a fire on the hearth, and facing onto the street front, and, separated by the damp court filled with twilight, the dark laboratory with grimy windows, itself divided into two floors: the amphitheater and the work room, connected by two stairways.

We see here that the smallest details, by their allusive or specular value, constitute reduced models, integrated into one another. Thus, Mr. Guest, an expert in graphology, comparing Mr. Hyde's letter with that of Dr. Jekyll, "laid the two sheets of paper alongside" (p. 320), exactly as the two individuals occupy proximate positions in time, and finds them to be of "a rather singular resemblance" (p. 350). Another image completes their articulation by adjoining the notion of containing/contained: the multiplication of envelopes. At the outset, one single envelope encloses Jekyll's will, according to which Hyde is the beneficiary. The two men inhabit together the same body; one seeks to exclude the other from it, however, in anticipation of his inheritance. Upon Lanyon's death, Utterson receives an envelope, which he hopes will provide him with the key to the mystery. It does indeed, but in a symbolic form: this envelope contains another, sealed as well, bearing the note "not to be opened till the death and disappearance of Dr. 'Henry Jekyll'" (p. 351), and Henry Jekyll's name appears in quotation marks, casting doubt on the will's integrity. This time Hyde's identity, exposed in the first document to the lawyer's disadvantage, fully assumes the hidden meaning that defines it: the accursed conceals himself in the letter in the envelope that was supposed to betray him, just as he conceals himself in clothes belonging to his "genitor" that are too large for him. Finally, similar to the Russian dolls, Utterson receives three envelopes once Jekyll/Hyde has/have disappeared. The first contains a new will in which the beneficiary, through a strange transfer, is now the lawyer himself. The second contains Jekyll's letter. And the third contains his written confession, which when joined with Lanyon's letter can be opened, since, in order to remain within the dualism to the very end, there are two narratives of two enemies that finally resolve the enigma.

It would be wrong to believe, however, that explanations will clear up the ambiguity of the whole affair, since the light cast on its origins calls up in fact two different systems: one political, presenting a critique of Victorian culture, and the other ontological, inspired by this very culture, as if beyond the grave discord were to continue forever between the doctor and the criminal. According to the first interpretation, disparity between the subjective and the collective constraint, "between a certain impatient gaiety of disposition" and the pressing need "to carry one's head high and wear a more than commonly grave countenance before the public" leads the young doctor to "conceal his pleasures." The hypocrisy of this attitude has been censured enough. Yet although Jekyll sees himself committed by the social norm "to a profound duplicity of life" (p. 351), he identifies with none of the conflict's terms, feeling himself to be no truer in a state of shame than in pursuit of knowledge. In concealing himself he cannot help but take on this virtue imposed on him as well as this vice fascinating him, both composing "man's dual nature," the "very root of religion, and one of the most plentiful springs of distress" (p. 352). In fact, Jekyll's discovery is less that of individual duplicity than of the contradiction of bourgeois ideology. His class forces him "in one direction only," toward enrichment, power, and prestige; but Christianity demonstrates that man "is not truly *one*, but truly *two*" (p. 352). The next step would then be the complete disjunction of its members. "If each, I told myself, could but be housed in separate identities" (p. 352), the angel could tend to his affairs and the devil to his.

If "the curse of mankind" (p. 353) is to persist in uniting these "polar twins," frustrating one in favor of the other, the problem is no longer which to choose, but rather how to dissociate them. Drugs have this power. But here we are no longer dealing with a political contestation, since dissociation, in preserving opposition, no longer tends to destroy the system opposing them; we confront an ontology of consciousness, with emphasis being placed no longer on the ethical, but on the structural.

In this respect, *Dr. Jekyll and Mr. Hyde* appears above all as the novel of the hybrid word—although it does not make any use of it. What Stevenson teaches about the person is paralleled by what Lewis Carroll teaches about the word: take *Richard* and *William* and make one man of them.

Each man is a hybrid and, in order to take meaning, recognizing inherent nonmeaning in the process, he must disjoin his own constituents. *Jekyllhyde* might be called *Rilchiam* or *Cleopold*; like them he remains unintelligible as long as he does not attack "the very fortress of identity" (p. 353). But once these two forces he dethrones inside,

once he enters into this bipartite life, each meaning will then be felt
as a painful limitation. This "miserable miracle" develops in four
phases in which the dialectic of the composite that we have attempted
to retrace is evident.

if 1 = Jekyll and 2 = Hyde, or if 1 = predictable and 2 = dog:

1) 1>2—read: proposition of the hybrid word,
1 represses 2   syncretism of its constituents:
                                       ambiguity

2) 1→1↔2:   disjunction of the two constituents
1 engenders 2 which alternates
with 1

3) 2>1:   each constituent attempts
2 attempts to eclipse 1   unsuccessfully to eclipse the
                                      other: *alternation, retinal rivalry*:

4) 1=2:   the two constituents equalize
1 and 2 mutually equalize,   and reform the dynamic ambiguity
here in death.   of nonmeaning.

First, the one, let us say the self, bears a potential two. "I am light,
would that I were darkness!" (*Zarathustra*). It may happen that the
two is accidentally freed as a gas explosion in one of the films taken
from the novel, but ordinarily the one represses the two; accordingly,
its language is ambiguous. Thus, Jekyll contains Hyde, as medicine
contains madness, in the two senses of the verb contain, a duality
already inscribed in his scientific research since he is simultaneously
the experimenter and the object. When he drinks the potion, he equal-
izes within himself the guinea pig and the researcher, at once separating them. One becomes two.

Second, the passage from one state to the other is lived and described as agony: "a grinding in the bones, deadly nausea, and a
horror of the spirit that cannot be exceeded at the hour of birth or
death" (p. 356). The one discovers that his two, although less sturdy
since he is less practiced in evil than one is in good, surpasses his
worst anticipation. This "fall" (repeating on a mythical level the evic-
tion of Abel by Cain, which itself repeats Adam's expulsion which
itself repeats Lucifer's downfall) is indicated by the inversion of the
alchemical phases. The *materia prima*, a metaphor for the spirit, is
supposed to undergo a series of transmutations, each signaled by a
color. The mixture begins with *black* (solution) and *more than black*
(putrification) and in the final *rubification* (powder of projection)
lead is transformed into *gold*. The mixture permitting Jekyll to be-

come Hyde and Hyde to become Jekyll again begins in a bright *red*, brought through boiling (volatile phase) to *violet*, then to a liquid *green* (dissolution) and ends finally in darkening the face of the drinker to a total *black*.

Structurally, the operation is identical to the one the interpreter imposes on the hybrid word in order to grasp its elements: the doctor dissolves within himself to form Jekyll and Hyde, as *frumious* forms *furious* and *fuming*. That which implicitly coexists in one develops into two elements, henceforth succeeding one another; that which was linked in a single moment is now rendered explicit in a temporal process. "I had now two characters as well as two appearances" (p. 361). Alternation replaces ambiguity.

Third, the two terms of the couple are incapable of arriving at complete autonomy without destroying the very thing that supports them. Disjunction is thus limited by the obligation placed on each part to bear its rival in mind: "my two natures had memory in common" (p. 356). On Jekyll's side, this obligation is manifested by a growing remorse inspired by Hyde's crimes; for Hyde, it consists of fear of the consequences that this very remorse might have: suicide, which would mean his own end. In a sense, the one always persists as the site of transformation: "the old Henry Jekyll, that incongruous compound of whose reformation and improvement I had already learned to despair" (p. 362). In disjunction, junction necessarily remains, otherwise the dialectic would become impossible.

Two possibilities confront Jekyll: to abandon Hyde to his murky depths and return to normal by choosing "the better half," or to opt definitively for him, that is, for "indifference" toward his initial condition. The disproportion of the advantage is obvious, reversing the terms of the Pascalian *pari:* in the first case, a permanent frustration of the desire that only Hyde can satisfy would have to be endured, whereas in the second, "Hyde would not even be conscious of all that he had lost" (p. 361). Thus the balance can only swing in favor of the latter: "I was slowly losing hold of my original and better self" (p. 368). To all appearances. The two breaks out of its dependence and reappears unforeseen and unsummoned.

Fourth, punishment appears then as merely the ethical translation of a specular symmetry: whereas in the beginning the one restrained the two, the two now works to suppress the one. "I still hated and feared the thought of the brute that slept within me" (p. 369), and all the more so because it is capable of waking up at any moment to take advantage of the smallest absence of its mentor. "If I slept, or even dozed for a moment in my chair, it was always as Hyde that I awakened" (p. 370). Accordingly the drug that Jekyll swallowed to bring the monster into existence must be consumed more and more frequently in order for him to be reborn himself. The rapid exhaustion of it serves simply, as does the contracting process in Balzac's *La Peau de chagrin*, to materialize the recession of a condemned man. Alternation simultaneously ceases to be governed by a lucid choice and, changing to compulsion, slyly returns its victim to a state of ambiguity. Henceforth split by "the hate that now divided them" as "equal on each side" (p. 370), Jekyll and Hyde can exhaust no longer the integrity of consciousness, but only the tension existing between them. The potion has become powerless to isolate them; their only remaining choice is to destroy each other, in other words, through a final disjunction, to become language. This narrative, for example, that has just been read and that should now be reread backwards.

[Translated from the French by Daniel A. Brewer]

Notes

1. Eliseo Verón, "L'analogique et le continu. Notes sur les codes non digitaux," *Communications*, no. 15 (1970): 53. Cf. also Roman Jakobson, *Essais de Linguistique générale* (Paris: Ed. de Minuit, 1963), pp. 62f.
2. Sigmund Freud, *Jokes and their Relations to the Unconscious* (1905) (New York: Norton, 1936).
3. Ibid.
4. K. Fischer, *Über den Witz* (1889), quoted by Freud, ibid.
5. *Versprechen und Verlesen* (1895), quoted by Freud, *The Psychopathology of Everyday Life* (1901), Standard Edition, vol. 6 (London: Hogarth, 1962), p. 62.
6. Ibid., pp. 81, 54, 55, 69.
7. *Völkerpsychologie* (1900), quoted by Freud, ibid., pp. 60–61, 81, 131–32.
8. "The suppression (Unterdrückung) of a previous intention to say something is the indispensable condition for the occurrence of a slip of the tongue." *A General Introduction to Psychoanalysis* (1920), trans. Joan Riviere (Garden City, N.Y.: Doubleday, 1952), p. 69.
9. Ibid., p. 68.
10. Joshua Whatmough, *Language: A Modern Synthesis* (New York: St. Martin's Press, 1956), pp. 64–65. This example among many others.
11. René Descartes, *Regulae ad directionem ingenii*, I, III, VI–XI, XIII, XVI: and *A Discourse on Method*, I and VI.

12. *The Psychopathology of Everyday Life*, pp. 60–61.
13. Ibid.
14. Ibid., p. 54.
15. Jacques Lacan, "La chose freudienne" and "L'Instance de la lettre," *Erits*, pp. 431, 495.
16. Serge Leclaire, *Psychanalyser* (Paris: Seuil, 1968), p. 53.
17. Freud, *The Psychopathology of Everyday Life*, p. 76.
18. John Lyons, *Chomsky* (Paris: Seghers, 1971).
19. Paul Ziff, "On Understanding Utterances," *The Structure of Language*, eds. J.A. Fodor and J.J. Katz (Englewood Cliffs, N.J.: Prentice-Hall, 1964).
20. Andre Martinet, *Elements of General Linguistics* (Chicago: University of Chicago Press, 1964).
21. Zellig Harris, "Distributional Structure," *The Structure of Language*.
22. Paul Ziff, quoted by J.J. Katz, "Semi-sentences," *The Structure of Language*.
23. Ibid.
24. Nicolas Ruwet, *Introduction à la Grammaire générative* (Paris: Plon, 1967), pp. 58–59.
25. Ibid.
26. Willard Quine, "The Problem of Meaning in Linguistics," *The Structure of Language*, p. 25. Cf. also *Work and Object* (Cambridge: M.I.T. Press, 1964).
27. Gilles Deleuze, *Logique du sens* (Paris: Ed. de Minuit, 1969).
28. Ibid.
29. Ibid.
30. Edward T. Hall, *The Hidden Dimension* (New York: Doubleday, 1966).
31. R.L. Gregory, *Eye and Brain: The Psychology of Seeing* (New York: World University Library, 1966), pp. 53–55.
32. Compare L.S. Penrose and R. Penrose on "impossible figure" in "Impossible Objects: A Special type of Illusion," *British Journal of Psychology*, no. 49 (1958). See also Bela Julasz' experiments on depth structuration in "Stereopsis and Binocular Rivalry of Contours," *Journal of the Optical Society of America* 53, no. 8 (1963); and "Texture and Visual Perception," *Scientific American* 22, no. 2 (1965).
33. Cf. Jean Paris, *Hamlet et Panurge* (Paris: Seuil, 1971); "La Machine à écrire," *La Critique generative, Change*, nos. 16–17, September 1973.
34. Michel Foucault, *L'Archéologie du Savoir* (Paris: Gallimard, 1969).
35. Robert Louis Stevenson, *The Novels and Tales*, vol. 7, *The Strange Case of Dr. Jekyll and Mr. Hyde* (New York: Scribner, 1897), p. 284. Pagination for subsequent quotations from *Dr. Jekyll and Mr. Hyde* will be from this edition and will be given in the text in parentheses.
36. Antonin Artaud, "Histoire entre la Groume et Dieu," *Fontaine*, 1948.

Robert R. Sears

EPISODIC AND CONTENT ANALYSIS OF
MARK TWAIN'S NOVELS
A Longitudinal Study of Separation Anxiety[1]

FICTION HAS BEEN WIDELY USED BY BOTH PSYCHOLOGISTS AND LITERARY critics as a source of data for understanding personality characteristics of authors. This is a legitimate use of fantasy materials for personality analysis, but the underlying assumptions should be made explicit. The fantasy expression of such motivational systems as aggression, dependency, sex, and anxiety may occur under three main circumstances. First, a strongly developed motivational system commonly has its many expressions not only in overt behavior but also in fantasy. For example, in five-year-old children there is a positive correlation of about .50 between aggressiveness as observed in a nursery school setting and the amount of aggressiveness shown in doll play fantasies. Second, lack of opportunity for overt and satisfying expression of a motive may lead to an increase in relevant fantasy. When a person is hungry but cannot get food, he tends to exhibit increased food-related free association or imagery. A third condition under which fantasy may express motives is that in which there is some internal inhibition to external expression in overt behavior. This is the circumstance dramatized in Freud's theory of dreaming, and widely observed clinically with respect to both sexual and aggressive motivation in inhibited adolescent males.

The simple occurrence of motive-connected imagery in a novelist's fantasies tells little about his personality structure or development. What little it does tell relates to the strength—or at least existence—of the motive at the time when the novel was being written. The quantitative variation in amount or intensity of imagery through the life cycle is more illuminating. The strength of most motives is in part a product of early childhood experience, but only in part. Its arousal by concurrent experiences in adulthood can also increase its strength, sometimes temporarily and sometimes permanently. Hence, a biographer must first examine the novelist's life history to see what conditions have existed for the formation of certain motivational systems. Then he must make a parallel study through the author's life cycle. By so doing, he can discover the excitatory and inhibitory conditions prevailing in the novelist's immediate environment at different times in his life. These conditions can then be related to changes in amount of fantasy-expressed motivation from one part of the life cycle to another. One ultimate aim of biography is to give an account of the development of motives and then show the relation of the subject's continuing behavior, both fantasy and other, to the conditions of arousal he experiences.

Several types of content analysis have been devised for quantifying the expression of motives, attitudes, and ideas in written materials. So far as motivational expression is concerned, a device that seems effective is that developed by David McClelland and his colleagues[2] for measuring achievement motivation imagery in Thematic Apperception Test picture stories. The brief stories told in response to an ambiguous picture can be scored for the simple presence or absence of any well-defined category of motivational expression.

In order to apply this type of content analysis, however, it is necessary to break up the continuous narrative flow of a novel into small segments that can be examined and scored separately. If a novel can be broken into 50 or 100 small units, then the percentage of these units that contains reference to some particular content category can be used as a score for that category. This score will represent the strength of that motive's expression in fantasy at the particular time in the author's life when the novel was being written. This is the procedure I have followed in studying Mark Twain's life cycle, but it must be stressed at the outset that such "analysis by counting" is relevant only to the use of the novels as data for biographical purposes and has no evident value for the critical study of novels as literature.

Something must be said about the process of episodic analysis by which the continuous narrative of a novel is separated into discrete units.[3] An episode is defined as a complete short story in its own right with thematic unity. Hence, each episode in a novel is psychologically equivalent to every other episode, and it is legitimate to count the percentage of episodes which display some particular content. The thematic unity of an episode is defined in terms of what the protagonists are doing, saying, thinking, or feeling. The unity of theme consists in the singleness of the actions. There are no universal objective characteristics associated with the change from one episode to another. Often the chief protagonists change, and sometimes the setting or the time of the action changes. Mainly, however, a change of theme is associated with a change in the purpose or the goal of the activity being performed by the chief protagonists. For example, in the first episode of *Tom Sawyer*, Aunt Polly is looking for Tom and finally catches him in the pantry stealing jam. While she gives him a reproving lecture, he steals an apple, and then distracts his aunt's attention by a ruse and dashes out the door. His aunt reacts to this with a final soliloquy on how hard it is to bring up a boy. That is the end of the episode. The next one has to do with an altogether different kind of action in which Tom is attacking his younger brother Sid. Each of these little episodes can be read as a small story in its own right.

This episodic analysis is not always easy, but for many novels it can be done with fairly good reliability. My colleague Deborah Lapidus and I performed an episodic analysis on thirteen novels, seven of them by Mark Twain and the others by Hemingway, Hesse, and Steinbeck. We worked independently, marking the exact point of termination of each episode. We were able to agree on the exact word in 68% to 77% of the cases. With another colleague, Christine Cozzens, similar reliability was obtained with three other of Mark Twain's novels.

There were two kinds of disagreement. We found that a couple of simple rules reduced them considerably. The first type of disagreement we have called *transitional*. Between any two themes there is often a sentence or brief paragraph that carries the reader from one theme to the next. A substantial number of our disagreements occurred because one of us marked the end of an episode at the beginning of the transitional sentence and the other marked it at the end. We made a rule that the transitional passage always belongs with the next episode rather than the previous one. If these transitional errors are disregarded, the reliabilities were substantially better, ranging from 81% to 92% agreement. This is a satisfactory level of reliability for permitting a single coder to make an episodic analysis of a novel.

The other kind of disagreement is one which we have called *segmental*. Sometimes one coder will break a particular passage into two episodes while the other coder sees unity to the whole passage and counts it as one episode. We have found no satisfactory way to reduce this source of disagreement other than to follow the rule of trying to keep the episodes as brief as possible without violating thematic unity. In general we have found more disagreements in our content analysis with long episodes than with short ones.

Books differ in length, of course, but the use of episodic analysis brings them to a common scale. The average length of episodes differs from one writer to another and even within the writings of one author. Among Mark Twain's novels, *Tom Sawyer* has the briefest episodes, eighty-one of them averaging about 800 words each. *The Connecticut Yankee in King Arthur's Court* is almost twice as long but has only five more episodes. They average about 1,350 words each.

An additional advantage from the use of episodes is perhaps greater in the case of Mark Twain than of most other writers. Mark Twain had a habit of writing a novel in stints, that is, in sections. For example, *Tom Sawyer* was half written in the early summer of 1874, and then the author put it away in a drawer until the following summer, when he finished it. Similarly, *Huckleberry Finn* was written in four different stints spread over several years. *Joan of Arc* and *The Chronicle of Young Satan* were likewise written in stints at known times. In all but a couple of instances in these five books, the end of a writing stint corresponded with the end of an episode. Not so with chapters. Hence, using episodes as units, it is possible to specify exactly *what* fantasy expressions were produced *when* in the author's life cycle.

Now let me turn to a particular aspect of Mark Twain's personality —his fear of the loss of love. Separation anxiety was both a deep and a salient part of his motivational pattern. He revealed it in many of his letters to his wife when he was absent on lecture trips, and it is even more tellingly displayed in his writings. The content analysis of nine of his novels, which were written between 1868 and 1900, shows, however, that this fear was not a simple persistent personality trait, but fluctuated greatly in its intensity from time to time during this thirty-two-year segment of his life cycle. What can be found out about him by putting together his fantasies and the externally documented facts of his life?

First consider the novels. Different parts of them were written at different times; 18 sets of episodes are available, 599 of them altogether, covering this thirty-two-year period. Each episode was scored as showing the presence or absence of more than forty categories, but I will report only one here—a category labeled *loss of love* and defined as "an expression of anguish at separation; mourning, grief, fear of losing love object; homesickness; withdrawal or withholding of love; both direct and empathic suffering, e.g. by lovers or parent-child." Our initial independent coding reliability was approximately 80% agreement, but the final data were obtained by a discussion of all of the disagreements, and hence quite accurate as measures of the extent to which the fear of the loss of love was expressed in Mark Twain's fantasies through these three decades of his life from age thirty-three to sixty-five.

The percentage scores can be charted sequentially for the eighteen periods during which he was writing the pieces of these novels. What stands out vividly are three great peaks of expressive intensity of *loss of love* imagery. The vast majority of instances involve a mother-child or husband-wife relationship. I can recall no instance in which such anxiety is expressed in a theme involving a father and son. The three peaks occur in 1874, 1880, and from late 1897 to 1900. These three samples are the first summer's work on *Tom Sawyer,* the second stint of *Huckleberry Finn,* and the entirety of *The Chronicle of Young Satan* (better known to the reading public in its edited form as *The Mysterious Stranger*). The adjacent parts of *Tom* and *Huck, Captain Stormfield's Visit to Heaven,* Mark Twain's parts of *Gilded Age,* and all of *The Prince and the Pauper, Connecticut Yankee, Joan of Arc,* and *Puddn'head Wilson* contained barely more than half as much separation or loss fantasy, on the average, as did the three peak parts.[4]

How can Mark Twain's seeming prepossession with these emotions be accounted for? And how account for the extreme variations in expression? An answer to the first question is found by looking to his childhood; an answer to the second is found in a search among the events of his adulthood when he was doing the writing.[5]

There are substantial reasons for believing that Mark Twain's childhood was one which would create a great deal of separation anxiety and fear of the loss of love. First, his birth was premature. During the first few years of life, prematures commonly show extreme sensitivity to emotional reactions, to sounds, and to colors, as Mary Shirley has shown.[6] Irritability and attention seeking were both prominent in her large group of prematures. Second, his mother was very warm and affectionate but also quite tart and irascible. Her marriage was loveless, her household was demanding, and she had six children. Finally, Mark Twain was the fifth of these six children, the lowest in the pecking order for maternal attention. These conditions seem appropriate for inducing high attachment to the mother through intermittent reinforcement, and high anxiety because of the intermittence.

Given a high potential apprehensiveness over loss and separation, a child will attempt to cope with his fears in one way or another. Some children become overdependent and constantly seek love from the loved object. Others tend to decontextualize, that is, they avoid situations and objects which arouse the anxiety. Mark Twain seems to have chosen the latter initially. He left home permanently in early adolescence, writing regularly but maintaining distance between himself and his mother. He seems to have avoided other emotional attachments with women also, and there is no record of any significant love affair until he was thirty-four years old. He then fell in love with Olivia Langdon and married her in 1870, a year and a half later. Marriage put an end to the decontextualization and thereafter any threats to his love relationship would have to be met directly. New copings and new expressions could be expected.

It is in connection with his marriage that his fantasy expressions of loss of love seem most relevant. Olivia Clemens was of much higher social class than Mark Twain. She subscribed to conventional morality and a belief in all the proprieties. Mark Twain was a rough diamond from the West. She tried to make him over. It is evident from the nature of her letters to him and his to her that she held high standards for him and used the giving of contingent love as one method of control. In effect, she played the role in the adult Mark Twain's life that Aunt Polly played in Tom Sawyer's life.

Now, what happened during the first years of their marriage? Not only was she faced with making over this new husband but she promptly had three children. The first, born within less than a year, was a weakling boy who died eighteen months later; the next two were girls, one born in 1872 and the other in 1874. It was in 1874, during the three months surrounding the baby's birth, that separation anxiety imagery reached its first peak point in Mark Twain's writing (*Tom Sawyer*, stint 1). After the birth of this child, there was a continuing reduction of separation anxiety as expressed in the novels. The crisis seemed to be over.

Then, suddenly, in the second writing stint of *Huckleberry Finn*, there was a recurrence. Six years had passed. Life had been eventful for the Clemenses, with fame and success for Mark Twain and massive entertaining and a busy but happy family life for his wife. The present and future both looked good. In fact, however, Mrs. Clemens became unexpectedly and unwantedly pregnant again. This became evident during the winter of 1879–80, and the baby Jean was born the following July. It was in that two- or three-month period immediately after Mrs. Clemens' pregnancy was discovered that Mark Twain drew out his four-year-old manuscript and added the tremendously aggressive and anxiety-ridden section that constituted the feud episodes in *Huckleberry Finn.* To my literary colleagues I make no apology for interpreting this part of *Huckleberry Finn* as primarily a reflection of the author's feelings. It has no preparation in the story, no relation to any other theme in it, and no connection with anything that happens later. Indeed, had the book been printed without chapters seventeen and eighteen no reader would have known the difference.

I suggest the hypothesis that Mark Twain was a highly apprehensive man who responded to the birth of his children as significant threats to his relationship to his wife. There is one rather pathetic letter which his biographer, Paine, reproduced that deserves attention.[7] It was written a month after the birth of Jean in 1880. In it Mark Twain laments the birth of the child and says, in effect, that he has now become low man on the totem pole in the family and has even been displaced by the cats. It is both an angry and a sad letter, but it is fully expressive. There is no indication of internal conflict or inhibition.

Both of these exacerbations of loss anxiety might properly be called regressions. They seem to have been reactivations of the fear of the loss of love under conditions of external frustrations—the birth of children—that threatened to (and possibly did) separate the writer from his wife. And remember that his wife had many of the same symbolic stimulus values as his mother.

The final explosion of loss-of-love anxiety may also be called regressive in part, but there was a reality quality to the stimulus situation that cannot be ignored. In 1894 Mark Twain went bankrupt through his publishing business. In 1896 his oldest daughter died suddenly, and in 1899 his youngest daughter was diagnosed as having epilepsy. Soon after he faced the recognition that his wife's heart trouble would no longer permit him to have more than a few minutes a day with her. During this tragic period Mark Twain wrote *A Chronicle of Young Satan.* In this final story, written between 1897 and 1900, the expression of loss of love—that is, separation anxiety—reaches its highest point. In the section written last, the score is 60%, that is, that proportion of the episodes contained such imagery. The stimulus conditions were appropriate for a regressive return to old emotional habits, but even a last-born, full-term, nonapprehensive child who experienced a period of diminished strength, health, and capability might have been expected to react to these realistic losses with some added prepossession in his fantasy.

Now, let me return to the three sources of fantasy expression that I mentioned at the beginning. I suggest that Mark Twain had a high potential for responding with anxiety to the threat of the loss of love, and that this was a product of his prematurity and child rearing. I suggest, too, that the increased expressions in fantasy at certain times in his life were reactions to stimulus conditions that served to reactivate earlier childhood anxieties. These conditions ranged from the only partially realistic stimulus of discovering his wife to be pregnant to the truly damaging experiences of losing his money, two daughters, and his terribly-much-depended-upon wife. From the standpoint of his life chances, then, Mark Twain began life as a high-risk child. In spite of his genius, he was a man who suffered deeply—and displayed it unwittingly in his novels—from the beginning to the end of his remarkable literary career.

Notes

1. The substance of this paper was presented to a meeting of the International Congress of Applied Psychology in Montreal, 29 July 1974.
2. D.C. McClelland, J.W. Atkinson, R.A. Clark, and E.L. Lowell, *The Achievement Motive* (New York: Appleton-Century-Crofts, 1953).
3. A technical report on the method, the reliability of coding, and ground rules for improving it, has been published elsewhere. See R.R. Sears and D. Lapidus, "Episodic analysis of novels," *Journal of Psychology* 85 (1973): 267–76.
4. A more detailed report of these findings is being prepared in collaboration with Deborah Lapidus, who participated in development of the episodic and content analyses of the novels, and Christine Cozzens, who helped in the elaboration of the system to permit its use for scoring Mark Twain's letters.
5. For the events of Mark Twain's childhood I have relied primarily on Albert

Bigelow Paine's *Mark Twain: A Biography* (New York: Harpers, 1912). For the later events in his life, Paine's work is fundamental, but Mark Twain's own letters have provided much additional material. See D. Wecter, ed., *The Love Letters of Mark Twain* (New York: Harpers, 1949); A.B. Paine, ed., *Mark Twain's Letters* (Harpers, 1917); H.N. Smith and W.M. Gibson, eds., *Mark Twain-Howells Letters* (Cambridge: Harvard University Press, 1960); and D. Wecter, ed., *Mark Twain to Mrs. Fairbanks*, Huntington Library, 1949.

6. M. Shirley, "A Behavior Syndrome Characterizing Prematurely-born Children," *Child Development* 10 (1939): 115–28.

7. Paine, *Mark Twain*, pp. 682–83.

Harry Slochower

CONTEMPORARY PSYCHOANALYTIC THEORIES ON CREATIVITY IN THE ARTS

IN HIS LAST PUBLICATION, DIMENSIONS, ETC.,[1] AND JUST BEFORE HE COM-
mitted suicide, the poet John Berryman wrote:

> I dont think I will sing
> anymore just now;
> Or ever. I must start
> to sit with a blind brow
> Above an empty heart.

Our time of wars, undeclared and genocidal, of moon-raising technical "successes," which bring with them air-water poisonings and
electric "blackouts," induces a compulsive craving "to forget" by use
of alcohol and drugs. And above it all hovers the threat of "Mensch-
heitsdämmerung" by nuclear warfare. Can we hope for creativity
when there is a sense that we may be approaching the end of our
days, if not by design, then by accident?

George Steiner spells out some of the forces working against creativity in our time.[2] He focuses on our "ennui," a climate of psychic
entropy, in which energies are channeled into gray routine motions,
alternating with exasperated febrile explosions. In a time of gas ovens
and napalm fires, the flowers of evil proliferate.

This temper of apathy makes itself felt in Peter Weiss' drama *The
Investigation* (*Die Ermittlung*), an account of the Auschwitz trials
that were held between 1963 and 1965.[3] What emerges from this
"Oratorio in 11 Cantos" is the spiritlessness of the accusers, even as
they are now free to speak. They recite the story of the endless recurrence of torture and killing in a monotone. To them, the abnormal
seems normal, the bizarre commonplace. Their lives had become

at once monotonous sameness and agonized restlessness. Like the
figures in Dante's *Inferno*, they experience the hellish futility of
changeless repetition. To them, too, the door of the future was being
shut.[4]

This nonhuman condition in part accounts for the impoverishment of contemporary culture and creativity in the arts. It also bears
on the abstract quality of our psychoanalytic approaches to creativity
by contributing to methodological pitfalls: the continued (though
less blatant) employment of genetic reductionism; content-analysis;
and, above all, the resultant failure to examine style and imagery.
And all this reflects the neglect of the epigenetic factor, namely, the
economic and social pressures. These issues will be discussed in terms
of significant figures in the modern debate carried on in psychoanalytic theories of creativity.

Much psychoanalytic examination still uses the genetic strategy
and explains an art work primarily in terms of the author's biography
with emphasis on the pathographic background—the id and its de-
rivatives. A variation of the genetic pitfall is the examination of characters in art as though they were living people. One example of this
approach is the paper by J. Barchillon and J. Kove entitled "Huckleberry Finn: A Psychoanalytical Study."[5] The authors argue that
characters in fiction can be understood analytically, as if the works
in which they appear were the stories of real people. This view slights
the crucial fact that the artist re-constructs the disparate data gathered from observation of a living person and gives this data symbolic
import.[6] In divesting art of its transcending nature, this approach also
ignores its creativity.

Clinical practice indicates that people do not really "know" themselves and what is happening to them. It is through their dreams,
screen memories, and slips that they reveal themselves, even as they
tend to fictionalize their lives through them.[7] Commenting on the
approach used by Barchillon and Kovel, John E. Gedo writes:

> By treating their characters "as if they were real people," we surrender
> the opportunity to make a real psychoanalytic contribution to litera-
> ture which would require explanation of the specific meaning of each
> author's particular use of the same material within the context of the
> linguistic and literary culture of his time . . . an analysis of this kind
> is no contribution either to psychoanalysis as a science or to literature.[8]

In addition to the distortion created by genetic explanation, there is
Ernst Kris' observation that the psychology of artistic style is unwritten. It is still unwritten. Indeed, some critics even think that this task

goes beyond the bounds of psychoanalytic investigation. This attitude is often carried over into writing about art. With some exceptions (Kris, Reik, Eissler, Kohut, Sterba, Gedo, Greenacre, Niederland, Kanzer), their abstract formulations read as if they were about something other than poetry, drama, and the novel.

Art externalizes. And externalization, in Ella Sharpe's word, is "restorative." Art objectifies its "truth" by presenting the particular dense material embodiment of its subject.[9] And this is revealed through an imagistic and metaphoric style.[10] It is these concrete and immanent qualities which differentiate an art work from a forensic essay or brief. It is this "how" by which the artist magically evokes those *feelings and affects* that distinguish its meaning from a philosophical, religious, sociological, or metapsychological argument. And the point I am making is that, where analysis does not investigate style, it bypasses the crucial elements in an artist's creativity. In this connection, Jaroslav Havelka observes:

> A creative act necessarily embodies a condition of style in its developmental process before it reaches its absolute formal expression. Consequently, the terms "creative expression" and "stylistic formulation" are equivalent. . . . Symbol, imagination and style were shown in an active interaction forming the indispensable background in which the creative expression developed.[11]

Freud once wrote that psychoanalysis must "lay down its arms before the artistic genius and the problem of artistic technique." This one-time statement is often used to rationalize the failure to examine the importance of style and technique.

Freud's own style was on such a high literary level that he was awarded the Goethe prize, in part for his superior use of the German language, and he himself remarked that he was astonished to find that some of his case presentations read like short stories. This aspect of Freud's contribution has recently been examined in Walter Schonau's book on the literary elements of Freud's style.[12] His study indicates that Freud's objective was not only to teach, but also to persuade and move.[13]

In *The Interpretation of Dreams*, Freud pointed to the need for analyzing form in dreams; he asked: "What *formal* characteristics of the method of representation in dreams signify in relation to the thoughts underlying them."[14] And, in the 1912 Postscript to the second edition of his *Jensen's Gradiva*, he wrote: "We need to examine the methods and processes by which [the artist] has converted this material into a work of art."

That the artist can transform his pathology by the composition of his work is indicated by Freud in his *Leonardo*. Even here, where he focuses on the artist's narcissism, Freud notes that in his figures, "Leonardo denied the unhappiness of his erotic life and has triumphed over it in his art."[15] In this connection, Paul Ricoeur comments that works of art "are not simply projections of the artist's conflicts, but the sketch of their solution . . . the work of art . . . is a prospective symbol of [the artist's] personal synthesis and of man's future, rather than a regressive symbol of his unresolved conflicts."[16] Similarly, Heinz Hartmann, in *Ego Psychology and the Problem of Adaptation*, notes that "the process of artistic creation is the prototype of synthetic solution . . . such a tendency toward 'order' is inherent in every work of art, even when its content or intent represents 'disorder.' "[17] This is in line with Freud's statement in his *Autobiography* that art is not "asocial" or narcissistic.

A variation of the approach that does not take style into account is the restriction to content analysis. Here, the writer's "point of view" tends to be equated with the plot and the story line. This misses the writer's latent "sympathy" as artist for the writers; aesthetic is found in his "how"—his cadences, rhythm, imagery, and so on, which point to the "what."[18] For example, Aeschylus, Sophocles, and Euripides dealt with essentially the same heroes and plots; style and technique differentiate the "meanings" of their dramas. Greatness can also be distinguished by technique and style. Compare Shakespeare's *Hamlet* with inferior treatments of the Hamlet story.

K.R. Eissler addresses himself directly to this problem. To begin with, like Theodore Reik before him, he suggests by his own writing something of the language of beauty. In his *Talent and Genius: The Fictitious Case of Tausk Contra Freud*,[19] he writes that here Freud himself made a contribution. He refers to a letter Freud wrote when he was seventeen years old which he characterizes as beautiful in a "bewitching way," and Eissler comments:

> In reading this letter, one becomes convinced that it was the linguistic function that was the carrier of Freud's genius. . . . A psychological explication of Freud's genius will, I think, have to center in his language. His power to observe, to judge, to draw inferences—indispensable as these were to the greatness of his work—nevertheless, in my opinion, have to take a secondary place to the genius of his language.

In "Formulations Regarding the Two Principles in Mental Functioning" and in *A General Introduction to Psychoanalysis* (Lecture 23), Freud states that "with his special gifts [the artist] moulds his phantasies into a new kind of reality." He does this by his unique ability "to elaborate his day-dreams, so that they lose their personal note."[20] Lionel Trilling once stated that the artist's return to reality takes place after he has finished his work. But I think that the artist's return transpires in the course of his work to the extent that by structuring his material, he establishes the condition for communicating with his audience.

Psychoanalytic criticism has not sufficiently responded to Ehrenzweig's urging that it is necessary to examine art forms and styles, along with the social background.[21]

To summarize: neglect of style constitutes the failure to distinguish between a psychic and an aesthetic object. To understand a work of art—in the sense of Wilhelm Dilthey's concept of "Verstehen"—the critic needs to use a style which is in tune with the tone and rhythm of the subject matter he is dealing with. In the case of art, the examination of style is primary.[22] Ego psychology is especially equipped to make a contribution in this area. The most dramatically new approach of recent psychoanalytic examination of creativity is the emphasis on the productive function of psychopathology. Freud had spoken pessimistically of the inescapable "discontent" of modern man living amidst the stresses and anxieties of "civilized morality." Would critics in our day *use* such pathology with the hope that it can be transcended and assimilated? Thus, George Steiner, following R.D. Laing, speculates that personal existence can be restored to "a full pitch of reality by the cultivation of the pathological." Madness, even death, he writes, "are preferable to the interminable Sunday and suet of a bourgeois life-form."[23]

Among contemporary psychoanalysts, K.R. Eissler has written most extensively on this theme. And the unique contribution in his major studies,[24] especially in his book on Goethe, is the view that psychopathology is one of the necessary conditions for creativity, especially in the case of a genius. In his Goethe book, Eissler argues that "one of the preconditions for the creation of great art is a tendency—even a strong tendency—toward psychosis (probably of the schizophrenic variety) which is mastered or diverted by (automorphic) countermechanisms that transform this tendency toward psychosis into the molding of an artistic product" (pp. 1375, 1097).

However, in *Talent and Genius*, Eissler grants that we "do not yet know why superb creativity so often has its roots in seeming psychopathology" (pp. 252, 280, 310). At any rate, the genius is profoundly and inevitably dissatisfied with the world as it is. He disturbs the peace of the world for which he must pay the price of suffering. Eissler cites Goethe's confession that he, who was thought to be "fortune's favorite," had experienced hardly four weeks of real well-being.

Although the genius must be strong enough to endure the severest conflicts, he needs them as a *vis a tergo* "in order to be incited over and over again to renewed accomplishments."[25] In Goethe, we have an example of a "healthy disease" (Carus' designation), of a "constructive or organizing disease" (pp. xxxi, 1353, xxxiii).

Heinz Kohut seems to take an analogous position in "Concepts and Theories of Psychoanalysis."[26] Here a structural model, which allows for the interaction of nonpathological functions, is based on findings derived from dreams and psychopathology. In this model, the unconscious activities are in broad contact with the preconscious, forming a continuum from the depths to the surface. In such a dialectic framework, both the dynamic continuum and the dynamic discontinuity are operative in the creative process. Thus, in the creative personality, a single mental apparatus contains symbols of widely differing degrees of neutralization.

The question has been raised whether Eissler's theory applies to creativity in the social-cultural field. On the one hand, we find that our mythopoeic classics—from *The Book of Job* to Thomas Mann's epic of *Joseph and his Brothers*—arose in periods when the time was out of joint. Their characters become heroic precisely by their violations of basic taboos. They mature and become culture heroes only after they have suffered.[27] To be sure, the extent to which the social-economic malaise makes for enforced "coordination," as in totalitarian regimes, creativity is driven into the catacombs.

Philip Weissman's stand on the relationship between psychopathology and creativity is nearly identical with Eissler's.[28] Weissman's distinctive contribution is the emphasis he places on transitional objects in creativity.[29]

In her distinguished essays on creativity,[30] Phyllis Greenacre makes no attempt to explain the phenomenon of genius, since it is a "gift of the Gods" and is "already laid down at birth" (p. 469). She does not restrict creativity to any one field ("Play in Relation to Creative Imagination," 1959). Also, she sees no marked difference between the work of a genius and that of a gifted person.

In deviation from Eissler, Kleinschmidt, and others, Greenacre regards the later stages of libidinal and ego development as more crucial than the pre-oedipal. Still, although she finds no "intrinsic connection between talent and neurosis," she grants that psychopathology has a function in the creative artist different from that in noncreative persons.

Greenacre's central position is that a gifted person possesses a heightened sensitivity and responsiveness and that in the lives of markedly creative people, there occur "splits in the self-representation, going over into even a split in the sense of identity." The child of potential genius, she writes, is "inevitably a lonely child . . . a child who senses his own difference, feels isolated and inferior thereby."

However, Greenacre modifies this view by holding that the artist has the ability to shift and expand his cathexis from primary processes toward a "collective love affair" with the world; that this love affair is *not narcissistic* but partakes "more of an object relationship" or "collective alternates" (ultimately cosmic, emotional conceptions), which are modifications of transitional objects. This becomes possible partly through the social matrix of the artistic process, "the delivery into an externalized and communicable form of an economically organized piece of the artist's interaction with the world around him."

A limitation of Greenacre's work is that in her analysis of writers (Swift and so on), little attempt is made to show how they transformed their pathologies by their styles, forms, and techniques. Yet her work as a whole is both inspired and patient, a carefully detailed contribution to the complexities of the creative process.

In a recent address (unpublished) before The Association for Applied Psychoanalysis, William Niederland submitted that, instead of a single process, we should consider varying processes in creativity. He also differentiates between the creativity of a scientist and that of an artist, not only in respect to content and goal, but also its dynamics and structure.

Referring to Kris' bi-phasic formulation—the "inspirational" and the "elaborative"—Niederland stated that, in his study of Schliemann, he was led to distinguish various phases or subphases of the creative process. Kris' "inspiration" tends to focus on the so-called "flash" or "spell" that fascinates by its occasionally spectacular and meteor-like emergence, "while the more 'silent' features, such as incubation, latent and preliminary stages, remain more or less unattended."

Niederland shows the function of bodily defect in the creative process—how a bodily "stigma" can stimulate attempts at restitution and be converted into a "mark of excellence." Similarly, being "different" can give rise to birth or rebirth fantasies. Such instances display the phenomenon of regression in the service of ego restitution. In summary, Niederland's position is that Kris' inspirational phase is a culmination. Niederland's thesis is richly documented in his authoritative study of Schliemann and in a number of other studies.[31]

Among Heinz Kohut's distinguished contributions is his perceptive and sharp critique of psychoanalytic reductionism.[32] In his more recent work on narcissism, Kohut evinces an affinity with Eissler's thesis that inspiration is not regressive but is "the highest form of progression."[33] He argues that the artist does not eliminate narcissism but transforms it. Greenacre's "collective alternates" and her formulation of the artist's "love affair" with the world are really "an indication of a narcissistic experience of the world (an expanded self which includes the world) rather than a manifestation of a 'love affair' within an unqualified context of object love." The art work itself is invested with "transitional and narcissistic libido." Thus, narcissism is the Adriadne-thread in the creative process, which develops toward "a cosmic narcissism—the work of an autonomous ego."

Kohut develops this theory systematically in his recent *The Analysis of the Self*. In it, he applies his theory to clinical practice: "Scientific and artistic activities . . . constitute transformations of the analysand's formerly archaic narcissism. . . . Broadly speaking, the narcissistic cathexes of the artist tend to be less neutralized than those of the creative man of science." In the case of artistic creativity, there takes place "a redeployment of the very narcissistic cathexes that had formerly driven him to dangerous voyeuristic activities."[34]

Anton Ehrenzweig's special concern is with *creative perception*—vision and hearing—which he relates to the aesthetic experience of style and form. He urges that the examination of perception is the primary task in the approach to art;[35] it transcends the oedipal, requiring a multidisciplinary approach. To be sure, in his Kleinian persuasion, Ehrenzweig points to the depressive feelings in the creative process, which are seen as reparative defenses against punishment for aggressive impulses. Following this line of thought, Ehrenzweig regards anxiety as an ineluctable element in the creative process and argues that "creative surrender induces a potential loss of ego boundaries."[36] But Ehrenzweig also leans toward the view that the creative process develops toward a better *Gestalt*. In his book *The Hidden Order of Art*, Ehrenzweig introduces the term "poemagogic imagery."[37] It refers to unfocused vision with which, he believes, the creative quest begins and is the root of symbol formation. But, in the truly creative person, unfocused vision develops toward the conscious perception of the Gestalt.[38]

Mark Kanzer traces the motives, inspirations, and fantasies that bridge the personal and the public import of an artist's work. His broad range includes the derivation from legend and literature that led to Sophocles' *Oedipus Rex*.[39] In "The Figure in the Carpet," Kanzer examines Henry James' own self-analytic insights.[40] Mention should also be made of his recent papers. In "Sigmund and Alexander Freud on the Acropolis," Kanzer suggests that Freud was tempted to commit suicide by leaping off the Acropolis (also to kill his sibling rival Alexander). This is followed by Freud's self-punitive confession to Rolland and to his reading public.

In his papers on Victor Tausk,[41] Kanzer argues that Tausk's creative fantasy was introspective, self-analytic, and prophetic. Tausk was a pioneer analyst who also possessed superior literary gifts. In Tausk's drama *Twilight* (the writing of which helped him during a crisis) and in his brilliant paper on "The Influencing Machine," the role of creativity is compared with dreams, oracular inspirations, and conversions. These have the stamp of superego-dictated self-destruction turned back from the paranoid wish to destroy Freud in analysis. Tausk's suicide had the quality of a rebirth-fantasy.

Of recent studies on the creative process, Jaroslav Havelka's book is perhaps the most penetrating and comprehensive.[42] Some of Havelka's theses are examined in other works. But what distinguishes Havelka's book is its discussion of the implications of metapsychological principles for artistic style, and his conceptions of myth, the "double," and the tragic.

In contrast to Eissler, whose work he does not mention, Havelka sees no necessary link between creativity and neurosis. Havelka is critical of those who dwell on the disorganization of the artist's mental health, because in his view this tends to undervalue the formal and symbolic powers by which the artist produces his work. Havelka argues that we need to shift the emphasis from the artist's pathology to his successful struggle against creative barrenness.[43] Hence, he urges that we go beyond Freud's clinical studies, which necessarily drew on pathological data, and examine his metapsychology, which contains suggestions on "the development of imagination, symbolic articulation, style, and expressive intentionality" (p. 5). In that way the theory of art as substitute satisfaction and Freud's —to be sure reluctant—notion that art is an aid in "adjustment" to existing social conditions is transcended. This, Havelka adds, has become "a curse" in the examination of "the noble strategy of genius" (p. 6).

Among Havelka's distinctive points is that "a creatively disposed mind utilizes some of the repressed emotions *before* the defensive measures harden into a neurotic symptom. . . . What is essential for a creative tendency . . . [is] the capacity to acquire *new* emotional units against which the repressive functions *fail* to exert any control" (pp. 36–37).

Perhaps Havelka's most original contribution is his discussion of the connection between the creative process, the "double," the myth, and the tragic. Creativity makes contact between the oedipally determined personality and the suprapersonal by incorporating values from the environment. And if these are transformations of father-figure images, they will take on mythic significance. The mythical, Havelka concludes, is "one of the most basic aspects of man's creative intentionality" (p. 223).

Mythical consciousness finds "its *unlimited gratification in a mythical 'double.'* There emerges during this transformation a new psychic experience of 'liberation' from the limits of the human condition." Through the symbolic substitution of "the double," the ego can experience "omnipotence." The created hero (substituting for the ego) participates in this omnipotence, even if he must be sacrificed. Through this radical temptation to vie with the gods, tragedy is born (pp. 219, 221).

In the creative act (through the mythical function and the ego's mental ally, his "double") the tragic hero is born. For even in this act, the hero knows that his attempt is futile.

> The mythical mentality is the most tragic extension of a creative act, expressing in vain man's aspiration for omnipotent immortality. . . . The creative mind experiences an image of its fullest extension, beyond the limits of the reality principle, even if the gain carries along a tragic tension of the goal never being *actually attainable* [but]. . . . is intentionally "illusory" in the anticipation of an understanding of its own destiny.[44]

Although mythical intentionality is creative, it "carries along one of the purest elements of tragic mental tension of purposeful self-deception which forms one quality of the creative expression transcending man's limitation, even if it transcends through a tragic 'illusion' " (pp. 223–25).

In examining recent psychoanalytic literature on creativity, I was impressed by the increasing refinement in the use of ego psychology.

But only a few critics try to show the connection between creativity and its social-historical condition, even insofar as such examination falls into the orbit of ego psychology. Most references are fugitive and hesitant.[45] The artist's personal pathological "environment" is scrutinized, but the pathology of his social milieu is skirted.

To begin with, Freud himself was quite aware of the impact of social forces on culture. This appears not only in his "Why War" (1933), but also in the context of his psychoanalytic observation in which he referred to social determinants as "Ananke" and "Lebensnot." In an address to the Psychoanalytic Society ("Lines of Advance in Psychoanalytic Therapy" [1919]), Freud spoke of the "sleeping conscious of society," and in *Civilization and its Discontents* (1930), he wrote that neurotics were made by society.

Following Hanns Sachs, Ernst Kris stated: "Wherever artistic creation takes place, the idea of a public exists, though the artist may attribute this role only to one real or imaginary person . . . the acknowledgment by response, however, is essential to confirm [the artists'] own belief in their work and to restore the very balance which the creative process may have disturbed."[46] The artist who merely "expresses" himself without caring whether he communicates, creates relative failures (what Eissler calls "symptomatic productions"). And when commercially profitable, art is impoverished and stunted.[47]

One of the most outspoken proponents for the inclusion of the social vector in creativity is Gunter Ammon.[48] Ammon's central contention is that ego development and creativity grow out of a communication between the individual and the social group and that, therefore, creativity depends on a "facilitating environment" (Winnicott's term). As an ego function, creativity depends on an ego identity that develops in a dialogue with the surrounding group.

Ammon's view is that in the creative condition, we have a special form of ego and identity diffusion and that the creative potential develops in the period of prelatency. The steps toward forming one's identity arise in the preoedipal symbiotic development. These steps are retarded or furthered through the mother and the surrounding social grouping.

For Ammon, creative work is not a "regression in the service of the ego," but a change in the ego itself and in its environment. Ammon calls the ego-state in the creative act "a tertiary thinking process."[49] It is not only an intrapsychic phenomenon, but it develops in a creative climate of the group and the social situation. He concludes: "Creativity cannot be considered under the category of pathological distortion, but only under the category of ego and group identity."[50]

The creative imagination for some is an expression of revolutionary futurism. In *Freud and Philosophy*, Paul Ricoeur writes:

> For Freud, art is the non-obsessional, non-neurotic form of substitute satisfaction: the charm of esthetic creation does not stem from the return of the repressed. . . . If Michaelangelo's *Moses*, Sophocles' *Oedipus Rex*, and Shakespeare's *Hamlet* are creations, they are so in proportion as they are not mere projections of the artist's conflicts, but also the sketch of their solution. . . . thus works of art tend to be *prospective symbols* [my emphasis] of one's personal synthesis and of man's future.[51]

Here, Ricoeur touches on the transcendent—and in this sense revolutionary—character of the artistic imagination, raising it to the mythopoeic level, in that it links "the present of a current impression, the past of infancy, and the future of a situation to be realized."[52]

Among contemporary Marxists, Ernst Bloch locates such revolutionary futurism in the category of Hope, eloquently developed in his seminal major work, *The Principle of Hope.* "Every great work of art," Bloch writes, "above and beyond its manifest content, is carried out . . . in the light of the content of a future which has not yet come into being, and indeed of some ultimate revolution as yet unknown." For Bloch, man has the capacity to "dream ahead" (*Traum nach Vorwärts*).[53] Similarly, the Marxist Max Raphael states: "art is an ever renewed creative act . . . [it] holds man's [creative] powers in a crystalline suspension from which it can again be transformed into living energies."[54]

Freud implicitly pays tribute to this power of the human mind, as expressed in dreams, myths, and poetry—even as they are based on the objective world of familial and social reality. In Freud's thinking, creative art is the sensitive vehicle that leads not only to the understanding, but also to the imaginative reshaping of the human condition.[55]

Notes

Abbreviations

Amer. Im.	*American Imago*
Int. J. Psy.	*International Journal of Psychoanalysis*
J. Amer. Psy. Ass.	*Journal of the American Psychoanalytic Association*
Psy. Quar.	*Psychoanalytic Quarterly*
Psy. St. Soc.	*Psychoanalytic Study of Society*

1. John Berryman, *Delusions, Etc.* (New York, New Haven, n.d.)
2. George Steiner, *In Bluebeard's Castle* (New Haven, 1971).
3. Peter Weiss, *Die Ermittlung* (Frankfurt A.M., 1965).
4. See my article "Peter Weiss' *The Investigation*," *Jewish Currents*, September 1966.
5. *J. Amer. Psy. Ass.* 14 (1966): 775.
6. Anton Ehrenzweig, "The Undifferentiated Matrix of Artistic Imagination," *Psy. St. Soc.*, vol. 3. In a discussion of Heinrich von Kleist, Freud observed that in stressing Kleist's abnormal components, one says almost nothing of his creativity as a writer. In *Minutes of the Vienna Psychoanalytic Society*, vol. 1, p. 78.
7. Thus, when patients bring us their art work, we treat it as "dream" material. In the sense that the therapist realigns and interprets the data patients bring, he too is creative. See Heinz Kohut's *The Analysis of the Self* (New York, 1971), pp. 318ff.
8. John Gedo, "The Psychoanalyst and the Literary Hero: An Introduction," *Contemporary Psychiatry*, vol. 2, no. 2 (March 1970).
9. In this sense, Ransom calls art "The World's Body," and Heidegger speaks of the language of art as "apophantic."
10. For Freud, drives also appear to us in pictorial images in what he calls "Vorstellungsrepräsentenz . . . den Trieb repräsentierende Vorstellung" (the representational presentation). See Paul Ricoeur, *De l'interpretation: Essay sur Freud* (Paris, 1965), pp. 120–50.
11. *The Nature of the Creative Process* (The Hague, 1968), pp. 105–8.
12. *Sigmund Freud's Prosa: Literarische Elemente seines Stils* (Stuttgart, 1968).
13. In *Civilisation and its Discontents*, Freud wrote: "Happiness in life is sought first and foremost in enjoyment of beauty." Standard Edition, vol. 13, p. 24.
14. Standard Edition, vol. 4, pt. 1 (London, 1962), p. 328.
15. William G. Niederland, "Freud's Literary Style: Some Observations," *Amer. Im.* 28 (1971). Cf. R.F. Sterba, in "The Psychoanalyst in a World of Change" (*Psy. Quar.* 37, 1969), calls attention to Freud's humanistic background and training. See also Leonard Shengold's "The Metaphor of the Journey in 'The Interpretation of Dreams,'" *Amer. Im.* 23 (1966).
16. Quoted by Paul Ricoeur in his *Freud and Philosophy* (New Haven, 1970), pp. 174, 175. Ricoeur notes that in his *Leonardo*, Freud differentiates sublimation from inhibition and obsession, and that in "On Narcissism," he opposes sublimation to repression.
17. Ibid., p. 175.
18. The point is analogous to the understanding of a patient's dream. Here too,

we gain deeper insight into its meaning by concentrating on the patient's affect and imagery rather than on "the story" of the dream.

19. Kurt R. Eissler, *Talent and Genius. The Fictitious Case of Tausk contra Freud* (New York, 1971).

20. Standard Edition, vol. 12, p. 217.

21. *The Psychoanalysis of Artistic Vision and Hearing* (New York, 1953). Ehrenzweig's focus is on creative perception. In "Laughter as an Expressive Process," Kris refers to form and shape as ego function. Even when he discusses the psychotic artist Messerschmidt, he dwells on the *formal* characteristics of his series of busts. Kris also holds that where an analysis of form is neglected, we are limiting ourselves to the artist's psychopathology.

22. Otto Rank pointed out that the German word "Dichter" (poet) is connected with the verb "verdichten" (to condense). In the case of the more corporeal arts, the dance, painting, sculpture, and architecture, abstract analyses are especially impoverishing.

23. *In Bluebeard's Castle*, pp. 21, 17.

24. K.R. Eissler, *Leonardo da Vinci* (New York, 1961); *Goethe 1777–1786*, 2 vols. (Detroit, 1963) (unless otherwise indicated, quotations are from this study); *Discourse on Hamlet and 'Hamlet'* (New York, 1971); *Talent and Genius*.

25. *Talent and Genius*, p. 289. Eissler notes that Freud's contributions were greatest during the time when he was suffering maximal frustration, and that Freud succeeded in interpreting the Irma dream in 1895, upon hearing that his father was suffering from a fatal disease.

26. Written with Philip F.D. Seitz, published in *Concepts of Psychoanalysis* (Chicago, 1963).

27. This point is developed in my *Mythopoesis* (Detroit, 1970).

28. Philip Weissman, "Theoretical Considerations of Ego Regression and Ego Functions in Creativity," *Psy. Quar.* 36 (1968): 37–51, esp. 48, 49. Cf. "Panel on Creativity" (in the *Int. J. Psy.* 53, pt. 1, [1972]) by Leon Grinberg and Richard Sterba; also, David Beres' "The Contribution of Psychoanalysis to the Biography of the Artist," *Int. J. Psy.* 11 (1959): 26–37. Edith Jacobson holds that "favorable" vicissitudes of oral development account for the intensive and "devouring" interest of the creative person. See *The Self and the Object World* (New York, 1964).

29. "The Artist and his Objects," *Int. J. Psy.* 52 (1971): 401–6. Cf. D.W. Winnicott, "Transitional Objects and Transitional Phenomena," *Int. J. Psy.* 32 (1953). See also Weissman's earlier, somewhat popular statement in his book *Creativity in the Theater* (New York, London, 1965).

30. They are now available in her collected papers, *Emotional Growth*, 2 vols. (New York, 1971). These papers appeared in various psychoanalytic journals from 1955 to 1966. Page numbers refer to this publication.

31. William G. Niederland, "An Analytical Inquiry into the Life and Work of Heinrich Schliemann," in *Drives, Affect, Behavior*, vol. 2 (New York, 1965). "Clinical Aspects of Creativity," *Amer. Im.* 24 (Spring–Summer 1967). "Psychoanalytic Profile of a Creative Mind" in *Psychotherapy and Psychosomatics* (Basel, 1967), pp. 200–19. "Conrad Ferdinand Meyer—eine tiefenpsychologische Studie," *Carolinum*, Göttingen, 1968/69.

32. "Beyond the Bounds of the Basic Rule," *J. Amer. Psy. Ass.* 8 (1960). Kohut believes that psychoanalytic writings on art can (should?) themselves be artistic productions. He cites the Beethoven book by the Sterbas and Greenacre's essays, especially the one on Carroll, as examples.

33. "Forms and Transformations of Narcissisms," *J. Amer. Psy. Ass.* 14 (1966): 243–73.

34. New York, 1971, p. 318. Cf. Gilbert J. Rose, "Narcissistic Fusion States and Creativity" in *The Unconscious Today: Essays in Honor of Max Schur*, ed. Mark Kanzer (New York, 1971), pp. 495, 305. Kohut notes that after Freud had accomplished his great creative task, he "was able to dispense with the illusionary sense of Fliess' greatness and thus with the narcissistic relationship in contradistinction to a resolution of transference by insight," "Beyond the Bounds," p. 317.

35. *The Psychoanalysis of Artistic Vision and Hearing* (New York, 1953). Professor Meyer Schapiro has long urged psychoanalysts to examine Ehrenzweig's work.

36. "The Creative Surrender," *Amer. Im.* 14 (1957): 195–210.

37. *The Hidden Order of Art: A Study in the Psychology of Artistic Imagination* (Berkeley and Los Angeles, 1967). See also Max Wertheimer, *Productive Thinking* (New York, 1945) and Rudolph Arnheim, *Toward a Psychology of Art* (Berkeley and Los Angeles, 1967), pp. 292–301. For a discussion of Ehrenzweig's position, see Mark Kanzer's excellent review article "Contemporary Psychoanalytic Views of Aesthetics," *J. Amer. Psy. Ass.* 5 (1957): 516–19.

38. "On Interpreting the Oedipus Plays," *Psy. St. Soc.* 3 (1966): 6–38.

39. *Amer. Im.* 17 (1960).

40. *Amer. Im.* 26 (1960).

41. "Victor Tausk: The Creativity and Suicide of a Psychoanalyst," *Psy. Quar.*, 1972; "Victor Tausk: Analyst and Dramatic Critic," *Amer. Im.* 30 (1973).

42. *The Nature of the Creative Process: A Psychological Study* (The Hague, 1968). Since this important book has, thus far, received little recognition in the United States, I am quoting from it at some length.

43. Cf. Lionel Trilling's point that creative liberation results *despite* the neurosis in the artist's life (*Kenyon Review*, 1940).

44. Cf. Mircea Eliade, *Birth and Rebirth* (New York, 1958).

45. In the panel on "Creativity," (*Int. J. Psy.* 53, pt. 1 [1972], p. 28), Charles Kligerman noted that "sociocultural factors must also play a crucial role."

46. *Psychoanalytic Explorations in Art* (New York, 1952), pp. 60–62.

47. In *Ego Psychology and the Problem of Adaptation* (1958), Heinz Hartmann has noted the need of the artist for an adaptational function in his environment. For some illustrations of the social effect on modern literature, see Harry Slochower, "Symbolism and the Creative Process of Art," *Amer. Im.* 22 (1965).

48. "Kreativitaet und Ich-Entwicklung in der Gruppe," *Dynamische Psychiatrie*, vol. 4, no. 13 (1971).

49. Modern society, Ammon notes, does not suppress instinctual needs, but channels them toward narrowing the areas of conflict-free development. But the creative process is marked "by a diminishing of defense mechanisms against instincts within a protective milieu." Thus creativity is not an aspect of the vicissitudes of instincts, "but a part of the ego-destiny," ibid., p. 134.

50. Cf. Silvano Arieti (*The Intrapsychic Self* [New York, 1967], p. 239), who proposes the term "tertiary process" to designate the combination of the primary with the secondary process" mechanism in the creative process.

51. Pp. 163, 521. Ricoeur sees a function continuity between what he calls "the oneiric" (dreams and day-dreams) and creativity in that both can be located on the same symbolic scale. "That is why Freud is justified in moving from one to the other as he does in *Creative Writers and Daydreams*" (p. 520). In surrealism, the poetic tends to revert to the oneiric.

52. P. 166. For an analogous view, see the schema of Three Acts in my *Mythopoesis*. To be sure, in my study, the Third Act is followed by the Epilogue

in which the tragic conflict is reenacted, but, I hope, on a higher plane.

53. Cf. Frederic Jameson in *Marxism and Form* (Princeton, N.J., 1971), p. 149. See also the following: Maynard Solomon, *Marxism and Art* (New York, 1972); Harry Slochower, "Introduction: Ernst Bloch," *Judaism*, vol. 21, no. 1 (1972).
54. Max Raphael, *The Demands of Art* (Princeton, N.J., 1967), p. xi.
55. Herbert Marcuse, *Counterrevolution and Revolt* (Boston, 1972). Marcuse sees truth as lying "in the beauty, tenderness and passion of the victims."

METACRITICAL SURVEYS

Anne Clancier

FRENCH LITERARY CRITICISM
AND PSYCHOLOGY

FRENCH LITERARY CRITICISM SINCE SAINTE-BEUVE HAS BEEN INTERESTED
in the psychology of the writer and has occasionally looked to psychology for enlightenment. But psychologists in the nineteenth century and at the beginning of the twentieth were scarcely preoccupied
with aesthetic research.

Freud was the first to take a lively interest in art, and to seek in
literary and plastic works a field of study that could illustrate his
discoveries and furnish him with models for the theoretical elaboration of his clinical observations. Thus he borrowed from Sophocles
the model of the Oedipus complex, which he considered to be the
fundamental unconscious structuring element of the human psyche.
The doctrine of the unconscious places notions of intentionality and
symbolic expression at the center of unconscious psychic life, and
substitutes a psychological vision of neuroses and deliria for organi-
cist theories.

This theory and the method of dream interpretation inevitably
brought about a reworking of the principles of literary criticism. A
new comprehension of symbols, based on the study of certain manifestations of mental life—lapsus, neuroses, deliria, dreams—induced
literary critics to revise their methods.

Once it is admitted that both dream images and a writer's language carry several meanings, literary criticism can no longer neglect

the fact that in literature there is a latent meaning contained in the manifest meaning. This leads to a metacriticism.

In France, Albert Thibaudet, in an article entitled "Psychanalyse et critique" ["Psychoanalysis and Criticism"] in *Nouvelle Revue Française* in 1921, signaled the existence of a psychoanalytical criticism. The first work devoted to *La Psychanalyse de l'art* [*The Psychoanalysis of Art*] was that of Charles Baudouin, of Geneva, published in Paris in 1929. Between 1920 and 1940, two works of literary psychoanalysis appeared: *L'Echec de Baudelaire* [*The Failure of Baudelaire*] by René Laforgue (1931) and, in 1933, *Edgar Poe* by Marie Bonaparte. Later, from 1943 to 1960, the aesthetic works of Gaston Bachelard, his inquiries into the imagination and poetic creation gave birth to thematic criticism. Jean Delay's work on *La jeunesse d'André Gide* [*The Youth of André Gide*] in 1957 gave a new start to psychobiography. And the research of Charles Mauron stretched from 1936 to 1966. (His first work, *Mallarmé l'Obscur* [*Mallarmé the Obscure*], appeared in 1941.) This research permitted the author to elaborate an original method of psychoanalytical criticism that he called psychocriticism.

Elaborated by psychoanalysts, professors, and critics, an anthropological criticism was born several years ago and, though it cannot be precisely classified, has given rise to works of great interest.

The structuralist theories, born of linguistic models, have been extended to the study of the social sciences and literary works. Thus we see on the one hand, in the wake of Jacques Lacan, psychoanalysts using linguistic notions in their studies of applied psychoanalysis and, on the other hand, literary critics undertaking structural analyses of texts and taking for their own account certain psychoanalytical concepts.

A classification is necessary to account for the different lines of force by which psychoanalysis has penetrated literary criticism. The five groups we have just described seem to cover the field of a literary criticism which borrows concepts largely from psychoanalysis. Numerous authors, however, without claiming to perform psychoanalytical criticism, have evidently been influenced by the theories of Freud or Jung. Others, on the contrary, have used the term psychoanalysis, but have changed its meaning and applied it to psychological theories that have nothing to do with the theses of Freud. This is the case of Jean-Paul Sartre and his existential psychoanalysis. These authors will be mentioned briefly in the discussion of psychological literary criticism.

PSYCHOBIOGRAPHY

Dominique Fernandez' term *"psychobiography"* is defined by him as "the study of the interaction between the man and the work, and of their unity grasped in its unconscious motivations."[1] Fernandez is currently the theoretician of psychobiography. In an *Introduction to Psychobiography*,[2] he shows the ambition of this method, which strives to fill the gaps of classical biography and literary criticism. Literary criticism often neglects the importance for creation of childhood events and unconscious sources. The fundamental principle of psychobiography is that "everything has a meaning in the life of a man." The life of the body, psychic life, intellectual life "correspond to one and the same continuity." He stresses the difficulty of the method: it should not be a literal transposition of the biography into the work, it should not assimilate the work to material given by a subject under psychoanalysis, and, finally, the documents relative to the childhood of the author being studied are not always available. For Fernandez, childhood is essential in the determination of the vocation of the artist, as well as the content and form of his work. "The works, and no less than the works, the man . . . are posterior constructions, erected to serve as a refuge, to avert, to exorcise a childhood situation that has not been completely surmounted."

Fernandez has illustrated his method in an important work on the Italian author Cesare Pavese.[3] Fernandez is influenced by Jean Delay and Gaston Bachelard. He devotes chapters to the study of the imagination of elements in Pavese, and he practices an "horizontal analysis" of texts, a study of a work in its entirety and all of its details; and a "vertical analysis," a superposition of all texts relative to the same subject and comparisons of the variations on this theme. The thematic analysis of Pavese is centered about the themes of flight, affronting, and solitude. Fernandez also studies the writer's style.

In an essay entitled *L'Arbre jusqu' aux racines, psychanalyse et creation* [*The Tree Down to Its Roots: Psychoanalysis and Creation*],[4] he devotes three studies to Michelangelo, Mozart, and Proust. These analyses show the primordial importance of infantile conflict in each type of artistic activity.

Fernandez' method seems difficult to apply because of its eclecticism. The result, positive in works by this author, is due to the intuitions and sympathies of the critic for the work and the author under consideration. Fernandez is conscious of the danger of subjectivity from which, he stresses, one cannot escape, insofar as an affective relation is established between the psychobiographer and the chosen author.

Charles Baudouin, in *Psychanalyse de l'art* [*The Psychoanalysis of Art*],[5] has studied parallels between certain poems and the lives of their authors; but it is in *La Psychanalyse de Victor Hugo* [*The Psychoanalysis of Victor Hugo*][6] that he retraces and analyzes the principal themes in the poet's works, interpreting them by bringing together the themes and the author's childhood and life. He has also brooded over the style of Victor Hugo and has shown, for example, that the importance of antitheses in this author is probably tied to unconscious conflicts and strong ambivalent feelings. Charles Baudouin's works reveal one of the most current preoccupations of psychoanalytical critics, namely, whether the study of the author's unconscious permits us to understand the writer's style.

René Laforgue, in *L'Echec de Baudelaire* [*The Failure of Baudelaire*],[7] uses the works of the poet to illuminate his failure neurosis.

Marie Bonaparte was the first to publish a work devoted to the parallel study of a writer and his work: *Edgar Poe*.[8] The author stresses the relationship between the dream mechanisms described by Freud and those of literary creation. It is on the basis of the study of displacement, condensation, and dramatization that Marie Bonaparte searches for the latent, unconscious content contained in the manifest content of the work.

Jean Delay modernizes the tradition of Sainte-Beuve by basing himself on those works of Freud that relate to the importance of the first years of life. In a work entitled *La jeunesse d'André Gide* [*The Youth of André Gide*],[9] he tries to find the root of the creative personality in the writer's childhood. Gide himself knew Freud's works and often stressed the importance of childhood in the genesis of the literary vocation; he thought that a weakness, an illness, a torment could bring about "an individual protest of which the work would be the expression in more or less symbolic forms."

Psychobiography studies parallels between childhood and adolescence and their corresponding psychic evolution; the stages of literary creation which appear to correspond to the history of the individual; and finally, the transposition or refraction by the finished work of these initial givens. Thus Jean Delay evokes the heredity of André Gide, the conscious and unconscious images of the father and mother, and ends with the years of apprenticeship which are of capital importance in the life of a writer, since it is in the course of these that the author's first fictional *doubles*, or characters, are formed.

THEMATIC CRITICISM

The philosopher Gaston Bachelard (1884–1962) originated thematic criticism, one of the great currents of contemporary criticism. Paradoxically, however, this author never claimed to be a literary critic. In his work on the epistemology and the phenomenology of the image, he always strove to distinguish between reason and reverie, and between science and poetry, to prevent the dream from contaminating the science and reason from hindering the appearance of poetic images.

Gaston Bachelard did not codify the principles of a literary criticism. His fundamental contribution is a method of reading, a philosophy of language and literary creation by which he was led to an encounter with psychoanalysis. This epistemological encounter is analyzed in *La formation de l'esprit scientifique (Contribution à une psychanalyse de la connaissance objective)* [*The Formation of the Scientific Spirit (Contributions to a Psychoanalysis of Objective Knowledge)*] published in 1938. *La psychanalyse du feu* [*The Psychoanalysis of Fire*], published in the same year, is a chapter from an earlier work. By adopting Freudian principles in these two books, Bachelard proposes to use psychoanalytical reflection for the study both of scientific knowledge, still impregnated with unconscious reveries, and the study of mythical and literary creations.

His attitude toward psychoanalysis is, however, ambiguous. Without ceasing to use the vocabulary of Freud and Jung, and psychoanalytical theses, Bachelard, in pursuing his work on the elements (water, air, and earth) emphasizes more and more the dangers of an overly mechanized psychoanalysis of literary works. Psychoanalysis, according to Bachelard, always tries to find the reality underneath the image and yet, more profoundly, this reality is defined as a social or interpersonal reality. For him, on the contrary, the image is its reality —there is an autonomy of the imaginary. Bachelard criticizes psychoanalysis for its sociosexual conceptualism, but he continues to use psychoanalytical vocabulary. Thus he often qualifies his discipline as "material psychoanalysis." Sometimes, also, he adopts, and does not flinch at transforming, part of the vocabulary of Jungian psychology, notably the notion of the noncausal archetype.

In his last works, *La poétique de l'espace* [*The Poetics of Space*] (1957), *La poétique de la rêverie* [*The Poetics of Reverie*] (1961), and *La flamme d'une chandle* [*The Flame of a Candle*] (1961), he criticizes the conception which, according to him, psychoanalysis has of language, opposing to it the phenomenological method. He also passes over in silence the law of the elements articulated in *Water and Dreams*. The acausalism of the image is ever more central in his conception. Although the psychoanalyst, according to him, always claims to understand an image, to attach it to a psychological context, for Bachelard "the poetic image escapes causality," which explains, he feels, the communicability of poetic images and their reverberation in the reader. Thus he diverges, in this sphere, from the psychoanalysts who believe that literary works move the reader by evoking unconscious conflicts. Thus Bachelard arrives at an antipsychologism. His works ought to be considered, according to François Pire, as "prolegomena to a future metaphysics of the imagination."[10]

Two errors should be avoided in this study: thematic criticism is not a unified field; and it is not derived exclusively from Bachelard. Yet, it does use certain of Bachelard's themes. Georges Poulet analyzes literary themes through the writer's grasp of time or space. He rejects the notion of the unconscious and does not adhere to Bachelard's work except from that time when "it found a *cogito* based on the poetics of space and reverie."[11]

Other critics emphasize the rapport of the poet with the world by studying the complex *thematic structure* of the poet's universe. Among these are Jean Starobinski, Jean-Pierre Richard, Jean-Paul Weber, Michel Guiomar, Michel Mansuy, and Jean Burgos.

Jean Starobinski, whose dual background as professor of literature and as psychiatrist has given him a profound knowledge of Freud, has not neglected the Freudian contribution to the domain of literary criticism. With him, it is never a question of the intellectual application of a theory but rather, of a lively grasp of the author. Thus, the analyses that Jean Starobinski has done of Corneille, Racine, Rousseau, and Stendhal allow us a profound grasp of the problematics of vision [*le regard*]—fascination, captivation, and narcissism. They give us both a psychoanalytical and literary vision of scopophilia. "To see," he writes "opens all of space to desire. . . . We know how sad the covetous glance can be. Seeing is a dangerous act. It is the passion of

Lyncée, but Bluebeard's wives die of it. Mythologies and legends are singularly unanimous on this point. Orpheus, Narcissus, Oedipus, Psyche, and Medusa teach us that by wanting to expand the range of its vision, the soul gives itself up to blindness and night."[12]

Jean-Pierre Richard acknowledges the influence of Bachelard. His profound identification with authors allows him to feel and describe what the psychoanalysts call the object relation of the author, that is, the relation which the author has established with internal or external objects. In his study of the creation of form in Flaubert,[13] Jean-Pierre Richard stresses the importance of the oral (avidity, voracity, themes of nourishment) in the works and the correspondence of the writer. Emma Bovary does not manage to set up a suitable relationship with objects and dies because of it. Flaubert, suffering from the same ailment, tries to find the distance that would allow him to survive.

Jean-Paul Weber is the theoretician of a *monothematism*. For him, "the totality of the creative act can be understood as an infinite modulation of a single theme."[14] Three postulates ground his method: the reality of the unconscious, the importance of childhood, and the representation by a single symbol of a "past reality" which the subject is not aware of. He thus comes close to psychoanalysis yet resolutely moves away from it by rejecting sexuality (Freud) and archetypes (Jung). In his studies, Weber retains as essential the obsessional theme of the clock in Vigny, the tower of rats in Hugo, and drowning in Valéry. Michel Guiomar appeals both to Bachelard and to Weber, and refers at times to psychoanalysis.

Michel Mansuy can be situated in the tradition of Bachelard, to whom he has devoted an essay. If Bachelard has described the imagination of matter, Michel Mansuy centers his research on a "specific imagination of life," which he defines as follows: "It is a tendency in us to evoke—more or less voluntarily—and to project on our interior screen aspects of the surrounding world which correspond to the life we lead, the life that we wish to have and which we dread."[15]

Jean Burgos, who devotes a major portion of his research to the work of Guillaume Apollinaire, introduces personal points of view into the perspective of Bachelard. In his *La thématique d'Apollinaire, lapidaire, herbier, bestiaire* [*Thematics of Apollinaire, Lapidary, Herbal, Bestiary*],[16] he tries to "capture at their source" these themes in order to follow their metamorphoses, to grasp the creative dynamism of the poet in his work.

PSYCHOCRITICISM

Charles Mauron (Saint-Rémy-de-Provence, 1899–1966) created a new literary criticism based on the discoveries of Freud and on the postulate of the existence of the unconscious that he called psychocriticism. It is a literary theory and a method of application.

According to the author, three variables are at the origin of artistic or literary creation: the social milieu; the personality of the creator; and language. The second of these variables, personality, contains a conscious and an unconscious part; the unconscious is Mauron's field of research. He has often stated that psychocriticism is a partial criticism and that it does not pretend to give a total explanation of the work from a privileged point of view. Mauron, in applying himself to the discovery of traces of the author's unconscious in texts, sets himself the final goal of increasing "our understanding of literary works and their genesis."[17]

After having discovered, in 1938, certain networks of obsessional associations comparable to dreams in the poetry of Mallarmé, Mauron formulated an approach to texts that would be the equivalent of the method of free association for a subject undergoing psychoanalytical treatment. His method is made up of four successive operations: First, the superposition of several texts by an author by means of a process comparable to that of Galton's photographs "causes a network of associations or groups of images, obsessional and probably involuntary, to appear." This method differs from a comparison because it aims at locating common elements rather than differences. Second, these obsessional networks constitute structural traits which will delineate mythical figures and dramatic situations. The search for these structures through the work of a writer ends up in a display of the "personal myth" of the author. Third, the personal myth and its variations are considered as "expressions of the unconscious personality and its evolution."[17] Fourth, the final step refers to the biography of the author in order to control the acquired results.

If we take as an example the analyses carried out by Mauron on the works of Baudelaire, we see that the superposition of certain texts— "Un hémisphère dans une chevelure," "La chevelure," "Les vocations," "La belle Dorothée"—allowed him to show the following grouping: hair [chevelure], elasticity, a heavy weight drawing the head backward; constraint, encumbered gait. Then, superposing other texts—the dream of Baudelaire, which he relates in a letter to Asselineau (13 March 1856); "L'Albatross"; "Le cygne"; "La Malabaraise"—he finds the same network, the encumbered gait undergoing an accentuation and being linked to a new element: a grotesque exhibition. The affect that is linked with these networks varies, going from a happy motion toward men, from the search for a contact, to the affect of shame and then anguish in the face of defilement, of a dangerous and degrading contact. The constellations thus traced have been named *obsessional metaphors* by Mauron.

The affects tied to these groupings of images may, in the texts of Baudelaire, be designated as a desire for exhibition followed by shame, or, in psychoanalytical terms, the masochistic desire for aggression by others. This analysis permits an unexpected rapprochement with other texts in which the aggression comes either from a burden ("Chacun sa chimère") or from a third party ("Le mauvais vitrier") and this allows us to discern a relationship with "Une mort héroïque." Here, the burden has disappeared and we find two of the elements of the group: the play-actor who makes an exhibition of himself, and the aggressor-prince.

Through these superpositions, Mauron was able to trace "an interlacing of latent relationships," which would not otherwise be revealed. These associations are bound by an archaic mode of thought; Baudelaire certainly did not consciously connect the beautiful Dorothea and the albatross with the evil glazier.

Mauron discovered that the verbal associations were reinforced by "a network of figures" that will constitute the mythical figures; to show them more clearly, it is necessary to compare various networks. Only then are we able to catch a glimpse of the author's personal myth.

The mythical figures do not coincide exactly with the characters of the texts, which belong to the manifest subject of the work. The traits common to characters who are very different on the surface allow us to trace, in filigree, the mythical figures. The latter are, in Baudelaire, defined as "bearers of chimeras," characterized by a psychological evolution in two stages: they direct themselves toward a goal by exposing themselves to view, to contact. But, in a second stage, the walking becomes difficult; they feel ridiculous or degraded, and contact with others becomes dangerous.

Abstract words such as prostitution, dissipation, or concentration, which are tied to the conscious preoccupations of the poet, correspond in a profound way to unconscious, affective conflicts.

Mauron is in agreement with the works of Crépet and Blin, but he also shows the unconscious conflict which underlies and structures the process of creation. There exists in Baudelaire, beneath a desire for happy communion with others, a conflict between two forces—a passive tendency, of which the prostitute and the artist are symbolic, and an active tendency. Out of this conflict arises a dramatic situation among the characters who represent this antagonism. According to the interrelationships established between the two groups, an equilibrium of the personality emerges that can vary according to the situation. Mauron states that if the author has a fairly clear consciousness of a part of his personality, he does not evidently know the unconscious side.

In pursuing the superposition of works, Mauron discovers another series of characters—the figures of cats which are, little by little, transmuted into figures of princes. This is the line of "princely cats" who love languor, rest, and solitude. At an unconscious level, the first group undoubtedly corresponds to fixation on the mother and the second group to an identification with the paternal character. The child, in his development, identifies in turn with each of his parents, with the unconscious paternal and maternal imagos which must evidently be found in a more or less occult manner in the works of a creator.

Mauron thus manages to catch a glimpse of Baudelaire's personal myth which could briefly be articulated as follows: "She ceases to serve me and to charm me, me her prince, and, become a heavy chimera, she drags me along to our prostitution."[18] The myth of Baudelaire thus appears to us in the relationships between the figure of the prostitute and that of the prince. If the dramatic situations between these figures are ordered as they present themselves from work to work, it will be possible to decipher, in the texts, the unconscious phantasm.

The personal myth is a phantasm that constantly applies pressure upon the consciousness of the writer while he writes. This could be defined as a metaphorization of the unconscious psyche. It is, according to Mauron, "an a-priori category of the imagination."

We cannot establish the personal myth of a writer until after we have studied the entire works, for only an exhaustive study allows us to discern the permanent phantasm and its possible transformations throughout the evolution of the work and life of the author.

As an example, here is the formulation given by Mauron to the myths he has traced in several authors: the myth of Mallarmé may be defined as "I sit up, solitary, in anguish, for my dead sister is behind this partition: she will appear, a musician." E.M. Forster's myth is that a "superior being will go in search of his inferior brother in a more instinctive world, through a social complex whose resistance they break together."[18]

Charles Mauron declares his method to be empirical. It has enabled him, starting from texts, to make discoveries that have led him to take an interest in the mechanisms of creation. Having discerned a "filigree psychic structure beneath the work," he has studied the events in a writer's life that would account for the origin of this structure. He has asked himself how the writer is born from the man. It is important that the author has decided to become an artist even though this often poses considerable risks and sacrifices for him.

Mauron's fundamental idea is the distinction between the social and the creative ego, which begins to develop at puberty. At puberty, everyone develops an abundance of energy. The adolescent tries to master it, either by channeling it into various social activities or by using a part of this energy to create works.

The social ego of an artist includes all the functions that are not creative activity. The author establishes unconscious relationships with the works around him and then, when he in turn becomes a creator, he establishes a particular relationship with his own works. The creative ego then develops new functions. (Mauron utilizes Ernst Kris' concept of "oscillating function.") When the process is finished, the artist has acquired his own structure. The creative ego and the social ego retain in common a past and an energy. The unconscious phantasm common to both egos will be manifested in both social and creative activity.

Mauron tried to determine the respective roles of personal and social factors in the formation of the creative ego. The foundation of the ideo-affective structuring that underlies the personal myth of the author dates from the first months of life. It would thus be the individual who would have priority over the social even though the social might already intervene, for example through the traditional modes of child-weaning. Social factors are more important in later stages. The role of the successive identifications of the writers with elders he admires has an influence on the creation of the work and on the formation of style. It is only when a creator can detach himself from these influences and find his original style that cultural contributions have been integrated by the unconscious personality.

The relationships between the creative ego and the social ego in a writer may be harmonious, but in certain cases there is conflict. Often one of the activities is inhibited, sometimes even both, according to variations in the course of the creator's life. We can thus find an explanation for the years of silence in Racine. The painter Van Gogh renounced what he calls the "true life," that is, the activities of the social ego (marriage, social career), in order to throw himself into the true spiritual adventure which for him was creation. In Rimbaud, the social ego becomes afraid and represses the artist. Baudelaire's social ego establishes a masochistic relationship with the world and the creative ego stays free—at least up to the last years of the poet's life when the social ego exercises a masochistic hold over the creative ego.

Mauron devoted his first research to works of lyrical poetry: Mallarmé, Baudelaire, Nerval, Valéry. He studied the epics of Mistral. (The Provençal language used by this poet was Mauron's native tongue.) In the field of the novel, he took an interest in the works of the Abbé Prévost, E.M. Forster, and Victor Hugo. Finally, a number of dramatic authors attracted his attention—Racine, whose entire work he studied, Corneille, and Molière.

The study of Molière led Mauron to a psychocriticism of the comic genre.[19] He stumbled upon a difficulty: since Molière took over characters and typical situations used since antiquity, how was it possible, in this case, to find what was linked to the author's unconscious? This led Mauron to consider the problem of laughter. The study of a literary genre does not separate out the unconscious structures of a personality but, rather, searches for imaginative schemes. At the end of his work, Mauron shows that comedy is founded in the unconscious "on a fantasy of triumph, itself born of the inversion of a dream of anguish." Thus the classical theme of the young man playing hoaxes on an old man is an inversion of the situation of tragic myths. The theme of the rebellious son chastised is "inverted by the mechanism which transforms melancholy into mania." The problem of sources is here taken up by psychocriticism. This method could be used to decide disputes over the authorship of a work.

One can say of psychocriticism that it is a literary criticism, scholarly, partial, and nonreductive. It is literary because its research is based essentially on texts; it is scholarly because its point of departure is the theories of Freud and some of his disciples, and its empirical method relates to the experimental method of Claude Bernard; it is partial because it confines itself to seeking the structure of the unconscious phantasm underlying the work; it is nonreductive because Mauron attributes an architectural value to the personal myth—he compares it to a crypt hidden under a Romanesque church. He has, elsewhere, sketched out a theory of man's creative liberty and the value of art[20] in which art is the highest manifestation of human thought.

If psychocriticism appears to us to be a productive method, capable of giving a new reading of works, its practice comes up against a snag. The other methods of literary criticism require knowledge and intelligence; psychocriticism also demands that the critic be attuned to his own unconscious. The method of superposition, like psychoanalytical treatment, implies a resonance of the unconscious of the critic in relation to that of the author through the text. This hardly seems possible without an actual psychoanalytical experiment having been performed by the critic. This experiment is not always possible or desirable. This, it seems to me, limits the practice of psychocriticism and explains the relative dearth of published works. But psychocritical studies have been published by some authors in addition to Mauron: Albert Chesneau, Anne Clancier, and Marcelle Marini.

ANTHROPOLOGICAL CRITICISM

Janine Chasseguet-Smirgel, preoccupied with problems of artistic creation, proposes, in her work *Pour une psychanalyse de l'art et de la créativité* [*For a Psychoanalysis of Art and Creativity*],[21] a method of psychoanalytical interpretation of the work of art that disregards data extrinsic to the work and allows an approach not only to the content of the work but also to its form, showing their indissoluble interrelation. At the center of her studies is the concept of "object-relation," which she understands in the broadest sense. It includes the idea of a personal "life style," which leads us to think that the unconscious content of the work is finally integrated into the writing, into the style. This contributes to the illumination of the relationship between form and content. In this perspective, the author studies the scenario and film of Alain Resnais and Alain Robbe-Grillet—*Last Year at Marienbad*.

Gérard Mandel has defined the framework, the method, and the goals of a new discipline which he called socio-psychoanalysis. His method is partially based on the analysis of literary works. In *La révolte contre le père, une introduction à la sociopsychanalyse* [*The Revolt Against the Father: An Introduction to Socio-Psychoanaly-*

sis],[22] he studies three literary texts: *The Future Eve* by Villiers de l'Isle Adam, Thomas Mann's *Mario and the Magician*, and Hermann Hesse's *Magister Ludi*. He also studies a political text—Adolf Hitler's *Mein Kampf*; a philosophical text—*Words and Things*, by Michel Foucault. He considers these texts "not in relation to their authors, as is usually the case, but as a reflection of unconscious conflicts of the collective soul in a given age."

Francis Pasche, in his work *A partir de Freud* [*Since Freud*],[23] examines the meaning of psychoanalysis. What are its ends, its scope, its limits? Some of his analyses have literature for their object. In *La metapsychologie balzacienne* [*The Metapsychology of Balzac*],[24] Pasche discovers in Balzac's works a psychological theory close to that of Freudian metapsychology, a conception of human psychism at once topical and economic. Studying certain characters—Raphaël de Valentin (*La peau de chagrin*) and Louis Lambert—Pasche shows that Balzac had conceptions of death and illness analogous to those of Freud. In *Death and Madness in the Works of Balzac*,[24] Pasche completes his study and stresses that almost all of the important characters in *La Comédie Humaine* suffer a psychogenetic death: suicide or psychosomatic illness. The problems of creation and of sublimation are also treated in Balzac's works.

Marthe Robert, translator of Goethe, Kleist, Nietzsche, and Kafka, is the author of several essays on literature which contain psychoanalytical views. In *L'ancien et le nouveau de Don Quichotte à Franz Kafka* [*The Old and the New from Don Quixote to Franz Kafka*],[25] she sketches a new conception of literary relation based on a parallel study of Cervantes' *Don Quixote* and Kafka's *The Castle*. In another work entitled *Sur le papier* [*On Paper*][26] she deepens the study of *Don Quixote* in which she sees the prototype of a literary genre that blends fiction and a philosophy of creation. Her conception of novelistic creation is close to that of Freud, who saw the beginnings of literary creation in the games of children and in reverie. Marthe Robert attaches a fundamental importance to the *"familial novel"* that all children create. The child, in order to escape his conflicts with his parents, to mask the rancor that he may harbor toward them, and at the same time to restore to them all their power, imagines himself the son of great personalities, kings, or fabulous heroes. The adult forgets this phantasm, but the "professional novelist . . . prolongs and varies infinitely the mythomaniacal themes by which the child gives free rein to his love and aggressive desire." In doing this he really refers to a "generality" which his work, by its very origin, takes into account. Marthe Robert thinks that by acting in this manner, the novelist is an agent of communication, for he reveals the truths experienced by everyone and then forgotten because of repression. She worries about the future of literature because of the denunciation of fiction offered by certain contemporary literary schools. According to her, to suppress fiction would be the death of the novel, for the principal psychological function of novelistic creation consists in fortifying an illusion that is useful for the psychological equilibrium of both novelist and reader.

In her latest work, *Roman des origines et origines du roman* [*Novel of Origins and Origins of the Novel*],[27] Robert performs a psychological study of the novelist. Novelists are classified in two categories—romantics and realists. In the psychological scheme, the romantic writer is the "orphan" [enfant trouvé] who denies the paternity of his begetter and wants to return to a lost paradise that is preoedipal. The realistic novelist, on the other hand, is a "bastard" in revolt against the father, affronting him and thus accepting the Oedipal conflict and reality. Robert puts Cervantes, Jean-Paul, Novalis, and Melville into the first category, and Hugo, Balzac, Dickens, and Proust into the second.

Marc Soriano, in his cultural anthropology, studies folklore, sociology, and psychoanalysis in order to illuminate certain literary problems. *The Tales of Perrault* have seemed to him particularly fit for this study; for they come out of a popular tradition and the texts have been taken up again by a writer. He has devoted two works to these tales—*Les centes de Perrault, culture savante et tradition populaire* [*The Tales of Perrault: Learned Culture and Popular Tradition*],[28] and *Le dossier Perrault* [*The Perrault Dossier*].[29]

At first, Soriano wanted to clarify the problem of the supernatural in literature. It seemed to him strange to find both scientific concepts and superstitions in a single consciousness. The coexistence, in every person, of rational thought and magical thought, seemed to him to deserve explanation. Having chosen the tales of Perrault for his study, he realized that the analytical methods employed thus far had neither uncovered the question of magical thought and the supernatural nor clarified the psychological problems these tales pose. He uses various procedures to clarify these problems, but I will consider only the use of psychoanalysis. Psychoanalysis helped him resolve the enigma which had preoccupied exegetists of these tales for centuries.

Alain Costes, in his work *Albert Camus ou la parole manquante* [*Albert Camus or the Missing Word*],[30] which he resolutely declares to be a psychoanalytical study, shows the important axes of the writer's thought and offers a stimulating reading of the works. He refuses to make a choice between the alternatives of biographical and textual analysis. He uses both to follow Camus' intellectual progress and tries to find the unconscious infrastructures. Starting with the study of the maternal and the paternal imagos, traceable in the works and in the biography, Costes hypothesizes concerning the bases of creativity and sublimation. He thinks the maternal imago is a main source of Camus' creativity. The maternal imago is important both as inspiration and as lost object. He stresses Camus' difficulties in mourning, the frequency of depression, and assigns a saving function to literary creation.

The works of Didier Anzieu, Jean Gillibert, and Marcel Moré must be mentioned. Moré stresses the importance of childhood in his books on Jules Verne. Gilbert Durand, in his studies on the imaginary, refers primarily to the works of the Swiss psychologist Piaget and to those of C.G. Jung. Gilberte Aigrisse, in *La psychanalyse de Paul Valéry* [*The Psychoanalysis of Paul Valéry*],[31] claims to use the method of Charles Baudouin. Guy Michaud, though concerned with the analytical psychology of Jung and the psychoanalysis of Freud, sets himself the task of applying characteriology to literature. This characteriology, coming out of the typology of Lecène and broadened by the morphopsychological studies of Louis Corman, allows him to deepen the study of psychological types and creation myths in literary works.

STRUCTURALIST CRITICISM

The influence of linguistics on the social sciences in the last several years has been considerable. Some psychoanalysts, such as Jacques Lacan, have tried to reconcile a structuralist conception of the human psyche with Freudian psychology. Lacan often refers to literature, and in *The Seminar on the Stolen Letter*[32] he takes a text by Edgar Poe as a model for the functioning of the unconscious. Certain psychoanalysts cite him as a source and have published works on aesthetics and literature; others attempt to reconcile the notion of structure with the dynamic and economical points of view of Freudian theory. (Such

is the case of André Green.) As for literary critics, some have introduced concepts borrowed from psychoanalysis into their structural
analyses.

The philosopher Jacques Derrida's study, "Freud and the Science
of Writing"[33] seems to me an excellent introduction to these works.
André Green, in his work *Un oeil en trop* [*One Eye Too Many*],[34]
studies the negative side of the Oedipus complex (matricide in tragedy). In a prologue on the psychoanalytical reading of the tragedians,
he states the conditions of a psychoanalytical literary criticism. He
then studies in turn classical tragedy, where he comes upon matricide
in Aeschylus' *Oresteia*; Elizabethan tragedy, in which Shakespeare's
Othello provides the theme of the husband's murder of his wife; and
finally French classical tragedy where the murder of a daughter by
her father is the subject of Racine's *Iphigénie en Aulide*. In an epilogue, the author examines the relationships between the myth of
Oedipus and the truth which he hides and shows at the same time.

In the prologue, Green stresses the strange link that exists between
theater and psychoanalysis; the theater is, according to him, "the best
incarnation of that *other* stage which is the unconscious." A theatrical performance is closer to a phantasm than to a dream, for the role
of secondary elaboration is more important to it.

In studying the relationships between texts and performances, André Green examines Aristotle's theories about the theater and then
those of Antonin Artaud. For Green, there is a theater "according to
Freud." In his three studies on tragedy, Green studies the negative
side of the Oedipus complex, which ends in the murder of the object
of desire, and he stresses the inversion of the complex by the death
impulse.

The epilogue concludes with a praising of Hölderlin's text on the
tragedy of Oedipus (from which he borrows the title of his book).*
He states that the Oedipus complex "is caught between the annihila-
tion of all speech that leaves the field clear for the language of the
body, and the multiple meanings of the signifier [*significant*] which
destroys Oedipus. The superfluous eye is that which condemns man
to interpretation. . . . There is always too much to interpret about
parental relationships. There is always one eye too many, that of the
spectator who is not admitted to observe the scene."

Jean Laplanche in his work *Hölderlin et la question du père* [*Hölderlin and the Question of the Father*],[35] studies in parallel the work

---

* "King Oedipus has, perhaps, one eye too many."

of the poet and his evolution toward madness and acknowledges the methodological schemes of three authors—Jean Hyppolite, Jean Delay, and Jacques Lacan. He thinks the poet's psychosis is due to the fact that "the father as promoter of the Law, the *Name-of-the-Father*, was never admitted into the system of the *subject's* significations, never found its place in the chain of *signifiers* that constitute his unconscious." This localized absence of symbolization is at the source of psychosis. Through poetic creation, the poet raises the question of the father.

O. Mannoni in his *Clefs pour l'Imaginaire ou l'autre scène* [*Keys to the Imaginary or the Other Stage*][36] has assembled twenty essays of which a certain number are devoted to literature and the theater. Nerval, Baudelaire, Mallarmé, Proust, Henry James, Salinger, and Boris Vian have attracted his attention.

J.-B. Pontalis in *Après Freud* [*After Freud*][37] has gathered, among others, essays on Flaubert, Michel Leiris, and Henry James. The study of Michel Leiris is particularly interesting because he attempts to use a psychoanalytical method in his works. It seems that he tries always to pursue the unconscious into all of its detours, and, in *L'Age de l'homme, Fourbis, Biffures,* he shows traces of a constant dialectic among the ego, death, and the double.

Guy Rosolato, author of *Essais sur le symbolique* [*Essays on the Symbolic*],[38] is the theoretician of a psychoanalytical aesthetic that centers about the study of the creative mental function. His theory rests essentially on the "Metaphoro-metonymic oscillation" on the level of language in which he situates the dynamism of the work, its efficacy, both on the level of the author and of the reader. The works of Catherine Backès-Clément, J.-L. Baudry, Jacques Caïn, and Serge Leclaire should also be mentioned.

Roland Barthes, in a theoretical work—*Critique et vérité* [*Criticism and Truth*][39]—has shown himself as the defender of new criticism. In a pamphlet entitled *Nouvelle critique ou nouvelle imposture* [*New Criticism or New Imposture*],[40] Raymond Picard had attacked three new types of criticism—psychoanalytical criticism (Mauron), structuralist criticism (Barthes), and sociological criticism (Goldmann). Barthes responds to this criticism and shows that a new theory of literature is being born. He brings together structuralist and psychoanalytical criticism, which have in common the fact that they study the transformation of symbols, but he reproaches psychoanalysis for wanting to "reduce the symbol."

In his essay on Racine, Barthes uses psychoanalytical language to define the Racinian man. He stresses the constant presence, virtual or real, of the father in Racinian tragedies and also stresses the role of blood which "holds an imminent place in Racinian metaphysics" and would be "an expanded substitute for the father." Barthes stresses the relationships of the double and of possession which unite certain characters as a psychoanalyst might.

René Girard, in his work *Mensonge romantique et vérité romanesque* [*Romantic Lie and Novelistic Truth*],[41] shows an interest in psychoanalysis out of which he takes certain concepts. Thus he studies the structure of the Oedipal triangle in the novel. His research is primarily oriented toward the problematics of the desiring subject, the desired object, and the role played by the introduction of a third term which may be either a rival or a model. Girard designates this model the *mediator of desire*.

PSYCHOLOGICAL CRITICISM

Some literary critics, without pretending to use psychoanalysis, have alluded to that discipline. For instance, Marcel Raymond, of Geneva, noted the influence that psychoanalysis had on such literary movements as Dadaism and Surrealism. Some of his analyses indicate an acute sense of the psychology of the creator.

R.M. Albérès, in his study on Saint-Exupéry,[42] is one of the first to have attempted to show obsessional themes in a work: themes of the desert, of the sterile world of minerals. He relates this obsession to the author's unconscious. Albérès also analyzes the novelist's oscillation between the desire for contact with men and a fear of this contact that makes him regress to a petrified universe. He feels that for Saint-Exupéry, literary creation was a victory over anxiety.

I can still cite numerous authors who sometimes referred to psychoanalysis or did analyses obviously influenced by it. Among these are Georges Blin, Georges-Emmanuel Clancier, Gaetan Picon, and Claude Vigée.

Jean-Paul Sartre uses the expression "existential psychoanalysis."[43] However, he takes exception to Freudian psychoanalysis and denies the existence of the unconscious, which he considers to be an abstract postulate. He thus uses the word "psychoanalysis" but changes its meaning. Existential psychoanalysis is a philosophical conception which "seeks to determine the original choice of a subject." According to Sartre, man makes an "original choice" consciously and freely. Thus Baudelaire chose to be a writer and to be persecuted. We could compare his conception to that of Mauron who feels, also, that a writer chooses to be a writer by virtue of a creative liberty, but, in opposition to Sartre, he thinks that this liberty can be impeded by unconscious conflicts and that if Baudelaire wanted to be a poet, he nevertheless did not choose unhappiness; neurosis, invading the social ego of the writer, made his fate a tragic one.

In the tradition of Jean-Paul Sartre, we could cite works such as those of Serge Doubrovsky, Francis Jeanson, Bernard Pingaud, and Jean Pouillon, who nevertheless introduced personal points of view. Pingaud agrees with the psychoanalytical conceptions of Michel de M'Uzan on literary creation.[44] An affirmation made by Bernard Pingaud in an essay on Freud[45] concludes my study of psychoanalytical literary criticism: We can no longer, he says, "after Freud, think or even read as before."

[Translated from the French by Norbert Linden]

Notes

1. In "Incidences de la psychanalyse," *Nouvelle Revue de Psychanalyse*, no. 1, 1970, Gallimard, Paris.
2. Ibid.
3. *L'Echec de Pavese* (Paris: Grasset, 1967).
4. Paris: Grasset, 1972.
5. Paris: Librairie Felix Alcan, 1929.
6. Edited by Mont Blanc. New edition and with a preface by Pierre Albouy, Armand Colin, Paris, 1972.
7. Paris: Denoël et Steele, 1931.
8. 2 vols., Paris, 1933.
9. 2 vols., Paris: Gallimard, 1957.
10. *De l'imagination poétique dans l'oeuvre de Gaston Bachelard* (Paris: J. Corti, 1967).
11. *Les chemins actuels de la critique: Faits et thèmes* (Paris: Plon, 1966).
12. *L'oeil vivant* (Paris: Gallimard, 1967).
13. In *Les chemins actuels de la critique: Faits et thèmes* (Paris: Plon, 1972).
14. *Neócritique et paléocritique ou contre Picard* (Paris: J-J. Pauvert, 1966).

15. *Etudes sur l'imagination de la vie* (Paris: J. Corti, 1970).
16. In *Guillaume Apollinaire*, no. 8, *La revue des Lettres Modernes*, nos. 217–22, Paris, 1969.
17. *Des métaphores obsédantes au mythe personnel. Introduction a la psychocritique* (Paris: J. Corti, 1963).
18. "La psychocritique et sa méthode," *Orbis Litterarum. Revue Internationale d'études littéraires*, Copenhagen, 1958.
19. *Psychocritique du genre comique* (Paris: J. Corti, 1964).
20. *La liberté créatrice*. Text not published, information related by Madame Charles Mauron.
21. Paris: Payot, 1971.
22. Paris: Payot, 1968.
23. Paris: Payot, 1969.
24. In *Entretiens sur l'art et la psychanalyse* (Paris La Haye: Mouton, 1968).
25. Paris: Grasset, 1963.
26. Paris: Grasset, 1967.
27. Paris: Grasset, 1972.
28. Paris: Gallimard, 1968.
29. Paris: Hachette, 1972.
30. Paris: Payot, 1973.
31. Paris: Edition Universitaires, 1964.
32. Lacan, Jacques. *Ecrits* (Paris: Le Seuil, 1965).
33. *L'Ecriture et la différence* (Paris: Le Seuil, 1967).
34. Paris: Editions de Minuit, 1969.
35. Paris: Presses Universitaires, 1961.
36. Paris: Le Seuil, 1969.
37. Paris: Gallimard, 1965.
38. Paris: Gallimard, 1969.
39. Paris: Le Seuil, 1966.
40. Paris: J-J. Pauvert, 1965.
41. Paris: Grasset, 1961.
42. *Saint-Exupéry*, La nouvelle édition (Paris, 1946).
43. *L'Etre et le Néant* (Paris: Gallimard, 1955).
44. "Apercus sur le processus de'la création littéraire," *Revue Française de Psychanalyse*, no. 1 (1965).
45. *La pesta* in *L'Arc*, no. 34, *Freud*, Aix-en-Provence, 1968.

Select Bibliography

Abraham, Karl. *Oeuvres complètes.* Vol. 1. Paris: Payot, 1965.

Anzieu, Didier. "Le discours de l'absessionel dans les romans de Robbe-Grillet." *Les Temps Modernes.* October 1965.

———. "Le corps et le code dans les contes de J-L. Borges." In *Nouvelle Revue de Psychanalyse.* No. 3. Lieux du corps, Gallimard, 1971.

Bachelard, Georges. *La formation de l'esprit scientifique: Contribution a une psychanalyse de la connaissance objective.* Paris: Vrin, 1938.

———. *La psychanalyse du feu.* Paris: N.R.F., 1938, and Gallimard, Collection Idees, 1965.

———. *Lautréamont.* Paris: J. Corti, 1939. New supplemented edition, Paris: J. Corti, 1951.

———. *La philosophie du non: Essai d'une philosophie du nouvel esprit scientifique.* Paris: Presses Universitaires de France, 1940.

———. *L'eau et les rêves: Essai sur l'imagination de la matière.* Paris: J. Corti, 1943.

———. *L'air et les songes: Essai sur l'imagination du mouvement.* Paris: J. Corti, 1944.

———. *La terre et les rêveries de la volonté: Essai sur l'imagination des forces.* Paris: J. Corti, 1948.

———. *La terre et les rêveries du repos: Essai sur les images de l'intimité.* Paris: J. Corti, 1948.

———. *La poétique de l'espace.* Paris: Presses Universitaires de France, 1957.

———. *La poétique de la rêverie.* Paris: Presses Universitaires de France, 1960.

———. *La flamme d'une chandelle.* Paris: Presses Universitaires de France, 1961.

Backes, Catherine. "Lacan ou le porte-parole." *Critique.* February 1968.

Barthes, Roland. *Sur Racine*. Paris: Le Seuil, 1965.

Berge, A., Clancier, A., Ricoeur, P., Rubinstein L-H. *L'Art et la Psychanalyse*. Colloque du Centre Culturel International de Cerisy-la-Salle 1962. Paris-La Haye: Editions Mouton, 1968.

Blin, Georges. "Préface à Stendhal." *Armance*. Paris: Editions de la revue Fontaine, 1946.

————. "Critique et mouvement," *Nouvelle Revue Française*, June 1967.

Cain, Jacques. *Le fantasme sadique et la réalité*. Center at Aix of Studies and Research of the Eighteenth Century. Le Marquis de Sade. Paris: Armand Colin.

————. "Le masochisme chez Masoch." *Bulletin de l'Association Psychanalytique de France*. No. 4, 1968.

Chesneau, Albert. "Essai de psychocritique de Louis-Ferdinand Céline." *Archives des lettres modernes*. No. 129. Paris: Minard, 1971.

Clancier, Anne. "Le manuel du parfait analyse, Les Fleurs bleues de Raymond Queneau." *L'Arc*. No. 28. Raymond Queneau. Aix-en-Provence, 1966.

————. *Le hasard objectif, L'inquiétante étrangeté*, Interventions au Colloque de Cerisy-la-Salle sur le surréalisme, 1966. In *Le surréalisme*, conversations directed by Ferdinand Alquié. Paris-The Hague: Mouton, 1968.

————. "La psychocritique." In *Circe*. No. 1. Methodologie de l'imaginaire, directed by Jean Burgos. Paris: Les Lettres Modernes, 1969.

————. *Psychanalyse et critique litteraire*. Toulouse: Editions Privat, 1973.

————. "Guillaume Apollinaire, etude psychocritique." In *Guillaume Apollinaire*. No. 11, sous la direction de Michel Decaudin. Paris: Les Lettres Modernes, 1973.

Clancier, Georges-Emmanuel. "Psychanalyse et litterature." In *La poesie et ses environs*. Paris: Gallimard, 1973.

Doubrovsky, Serge. *Corneille et la dialectique du héros*. Paris: Gallimard, 1963. New edition 1968.

Ferenczi, Sandor. *Oeuvres complètes*. Paris: Payot, 1968.

Freud, Sigmund. *Collected Works*. Standard Edition, 24 vols. London: Hogarth Press, 1953–68.

————. *Un souvenir d'enfance de Léonard de Vinci*. Paris: Gallimard, 1927.

————. *Essais de psychanalyse appliquée*. Paris: Gallimard, 1933.

Girard, René. *La violence et le sacré*. Paris: Grasset, 1972.

Guiomar, Michel. *Principes d'une esthétique de la mort.* Paris: J. Corti, 1967.

———. *Inconscient et Imaginaire dans le Grand Meaulnes.* Paris: J. Corti, 1964.

Jones, Ernest. *Hamlet et Oedipe.* French translation. Paris: Gallimard, 1967. Preface by Jean Starobinski.

Luquet, Pierre. "Art et Fantasmes." *Revue Française de Psychanalyse.* Vol. 28, no. 4 (1964).

———. "Ouvertures sur l'artiste et le psychanalyste: La fonction esthétique du Moi."

———. *Revue Française de Psychanalyse.* Vol. 27, no. 6 (1963).

Mannoni, O. "Poesie et psychanalyse." In *La Psychanalyse.* No. 3, 1957.

Marini, Marcelle. *Ricochets de lecture, la fantasmatique des "Diaboliques."* In *Littérature.* No. 10. *Fonctionnements textuels.* Paris: Larousse, May 1973.

Mauron, Charles. *Poems of Mallarmé.* Translated by R. Fry, with commentaries by Charles Mauron. London: Chatto and Windus, 1936.

———. *Mallarmé l'Obscur.* Paris: Denoël, 1941. Reedited, Paris: J. Corti, 1968.

———. "Mallarmé et le Tao." *Cahiers du Sud,* No. 246, 1942. Reedited with l'Introduction à la Psychanalyse de Mallarmé, 1968.

———. "Nerval et la Psychocritique," *Cahiers du Sud,* No. 293, 1949. (This text written after l'Introduction à la Psychanalyze de Mallarmé, i.e., in autumn 1948.)

———. *Introduction à la psychanalyse de Mallarmé.* Neuchâtel-Paris: La Baconnière, 1950. Reedited in 1968 with an appendix.

———. *Poems of Mallarmé.* Reedited with revised and supplemented comments. New York: New Directions, 1951.

———. *Estudi Mistralem, étude psychocritique* (Prix Mistral). Saint-Rémy-de-Provence, 1959.

———. *Jung et la psychocritique.* Paris: Le Disque vert, 1953.

———. "Notes sur la structure de l'inconscient chez Vincent Van Gogh," *Psyché.* Nos. 75–78. 1953.

———. "La vierge qui fuit." In *Mélanges Mistraliens.* Paris: Presses universitaires de France, 1955.

———. *Psychologie littéraire de Mistral.* Bull. de l'Association des Amis de Lourmarin, 1956.

———. *L'Inconscient dans l'oeuvre et la vie de Racine.* Yearbook of the Department of the Humanities of Aix, Gap. Ophyrs, 1957. Re-edited by J. Corti.

―――. "La personnalité affective de Baudelaire." *Orbis litterarum. Revue internationale d'etudes litteraires.* Vol. 12, fasc. 3-4, 1957.

―――. *Le vocabulaire affectif de Mireio.* (Remarks at the first International Congress of Language and Literature of the Midi of France, 1955). Actes et Mémoires du Ier Congrès International de langue et littérature du Midi de la France, Avignon, 1957.

―――. *Frédéric Mistral, Mireio.* Chant VIII. Lecture of Mireio, Saint-Remy-de-Provence, edited by the G.E.P., 1958.

―――. *Van Gogh au seuil de la Provence.* Arles, February to October 1888. Published by the City Hall of Arles, 1959.

―――. *Le vocabulaire affectif de Mistral.* Remarks of the eleventh International Congress of Language and Literature of the South of France. Center of Studies of the Provence of the Department of Humanities of Aix-en-Provence, 1961.

―――. *Mistral et Baudelaire.* Congress of Civilisation and Culture of the Provence, 1957. Published by the Institut méditerranéen du Palais du Roure, Avignon, 1961.

―――. *Introduction to the Psychoanalysis of Mallarmé.* American translation revised and supplemented with a preface and an appendix. Berkeley: University of California Press, 1963.

―――. *Des métaphores obsédantes au mythe personnel. Introduction à la psychocritique* (Baudelaire, Nerval, Mallarmé, Valéry, Corneille, Molière). Paris: J. Corti, 1963.

―――. *Psychocritique du genre comique.* Paris: J. Corti, 1964.

―――. *Mallarmé par lui-même.* Paris: Edited by Seuil, 1964.

―――. *Manon Lescaut et le mélange des genres.* In Actes du Colloque sur l'Abbé Prévost, December 1963. Published by the Yearbook of the Department of Humanities, Gap, Ophrys et Aix-en-Provence, 1965.

―――. *Le Dernier Baudelaire.* Paris: J. Corti, 1966.

―――. *Dalle metafore ossessive al Mito Personale.* Translated by M. Picchi. Milan: Il Saggiatori, 1966.

―――. *Les personnages de Victor Hugo, étude psychocritique.* Vol. 2 of the chronological edition of the works of Victor Hugo. Paris: Club Français du Livre, 1967.

―――. "En marge du dernier Baudelaire: le rire baudelairien," *Europe.* April/May 1967.

―――. *Premières recherches sur la structure inconsciente des Fleurs du Mal.* Minutes of the Colloquium in Nice on Baudelaire, 25–27 May 1967.

———. *Phèdre, la situation dramatique.* Paris: J. Corti, 1968.

———. *Théâtre de Jean Giraudoux.* Paris: J. Corti, 1971.

———. *Les origines d'un mythe personnel chez l'écrivain.* In *Critique sociologique et critique psychanalytique.* Colloquium organized by the Institut de Sociologie, the Free University of Brussels, and l'Ecole pratique des Hautes Etudes of Paris, with the support of UNESCO, December 1965.

Mauron, Claude. *Le Jeu de la Feuillée, étude psychocritique.* Paris: J. Corti, 1973.

Mendel, Gerard. *Psychanalyse et Paralittérature.* In *Entretiens sur la paralittérature,* directed by Noël Armand. Paris: Plon, 1970.

Michaud, Guy. *Message poétique du symbolisme.* Paris: Librairie Nizet, 1966.

———. *Le visage intérieur.* Paris: Klingsieck. [in preparation]

Moré, Marcel. *Le très curieux Jules Verne.* Paris: Gallimard, 1960.

Picon, Gaëtan. *L'usage de la lecture.* 3 Vols. Paris: Mercure de France, 1961/63.

Pingaud, Bernard. "L'oeuvre et l'analyste." *Les Temps Modernes.* No. 233, 1965.

Poulet, Georges. *Etudes sur le temps humain.* 4 Vols. Paris: Plon, 1950–69.

Rank, Otto. *Don Juan et le double, études psychanalytiques.* Denoël et Steele, new edition, Paris: Payot, 1973.

Raymond, Marcel. *De Baudelaire au surréalisme.* Paris: J. Corti, 1940.

Richard, Jean-Pierre. *Littérature et sensation.* Paris: Le Seuil, 1954.

Sartre, Jean-Paul. *Baudelaire.* Preceded by a note by Michel Leiris. Paris: Gallimard, 1963.

Starobinski, Jean. "Ironie et mélancolie: La princesse Brambilla de Hoffman." *Critique.* No. 228, May 1966.

Vigee, Claude. *Les artistes de la faim: Essais.* Calmann-Levy, 1960.

———. *Révolte et Louanges: Essais sur la poésie moderne.* Paris: J. Corti, 1962.

Weber, Jean-Paul. *Domaines thématiques.* Paris: Gallimard, 1963.

———. *Genèse de l'oeuvre poétique.* Paris: Gallimard, 1960.

Peter Dettmering

THE DEVELOPMENT OF STUDIES
IN CREATIVITY IN THE
GERMAN LANGUAGE AREA

A SURVEY OF THE ALMOST THREE DECADES SINCE THE END OF THE SECOND World War with regard to the present topic reveals two successive movements. One movement, characterized by the names of the psychiatrists Wilhelm Lange-Eichbaum, Ernst Kretschmer, and Theodor Spoerri, reached its peak at the beginning of the 1950s, when so-called classic or academic psychiatry still dominated the psychiatric scene. The second school emerged at the beginning of the 1970s, when the psychoanalysts Johannes Cremerius and Alexander Mitscherlich published representative anthologies of psychopathographic studies that initiated a resurgence of psychoanalytic studies on art and creativity. Since that time many similar volumes have been written, indicating that the monopoly in this line of research is no longer held by psychiatrists and psychoanalysts but has passed to literary criticism and sociology. I will attempt to retrace the separate steps of this development.

Wilhelm Lange-Eichbaum's *Genie, Irrsinn und Ruhm* [Genius, Madness, and Fame],[1] first published in 1927, continued through numerous revisions to exert a powerful influence on postwar generations. The distinguishing trait in Lange-Eichbaum's method was his search for psychiatrically determined, value-free linkages among the three elements named in the title of his work. His efforts immediately captured creative imaginations. In 1929 the poet Gottfried Benn wrote an essay, "Zum Genieproblem" [On the Problem of Genius],[2] in which he further refined Lange-Eichbaum's theses. "Genius is a specific manifestation of pure degeneracy, releasing creativity." "Because of the degeneracy—its demonic fascination, its enigmatic features—the collective completes the transformation into genius." He further notes: "There emerges before our eyes a countering syndrome of the ideality of the social and medical norm; as a singular case within the scientific-aseptic-technological world, a countervalue becomes defined and absorbs the full spectrum, from pleasure to subservience, from idolatry to horror." "The concept of biogenetivity (Lange-Eichbaum) comes into being even as we watch; not only do we see it personified in the natural shape of the bearer of genius, but also—stranger still—we see it worshiped, encouraged, and courted by the social group, the cultural community. As opposed to Harvey's system of circulation [of the blood], it seeks out this other circulatory system, composed of psychopathy and negative variations; parallel with health, and at the expense of health, it constructs a modern mythology out of intoxication and decline and calls it genius." Benn summarizes this paradoxical phenomenon by an extreme image: "Over here the bums, the alcoholics, the poorhouse crowd, the freaks, the tuberculars, the sick horde; and over there Westminster Abbey, the Pantheon, and Valhalla, the temples where their busts are displayed." There is no better way to demonstrate the fascination that must at one time have radiated from Lange-Eichbaum's theories than through this essay by Gottfried Benn.

But the essay also shows where the particular danger of such an approach lies. Although it offers the advantage of recognizing the common element in the depth effect of artistic, religious, and sociopolitical phenomena (the "impressive" or "numinous," to use Lange-Eichbaum's terminology), it also results in the relaxation of ethical-moral values, replacing them with a disinterested spectrum of psychological-aesthetic values. It requires only a slight distortion of the social balance for the worship of "bionegativity" to turn into the determination to destroy it as unworthy of life. Gottfried Benn exemplified this danger in his own person. Only four years after the essay quoted above, he became a (temporary) follower of fascism and its theories of systematic breeding and thus took the step from "pleasure" to "subservience," from "idolatry" to "horror." A seemingly archaic ambivalence can be detected lurking behind the overt indifference toward moral issues. It is the same ambivalence that can be found in even as committed an anti-fascist as Thomas Mann, though on a much more conscious level. At that level Mann could afford, at least for the length of one essay, to understand "Brother Hitler"[3] as a self-alienated artist who had strayed into politics.

Lange-Eichbaum, however, entrusted the continuation of his enterprise to a "student," who in his last revision (1967) routinely cited the National Socialist notables as relevant, whereas Gottfried Benn is characterized as "a broken man and a nay-sayer." Is this Lange-Eichbaum's fault? The least we can say is that the present edition of his work has degenerated into a compendium of petit-bourgeois narrow-mindedness.

The same disinterestedness that adapted to the role of observer of endogenous (or sociopolitical) processes also marked other aspects of German psychiatry—far beyond the limits of the Second World War. As late as the end of the 1950s a renowned professor of psychiatry was able to demonstrate to a rapt audience the pointlessness of resistance against Hitler: "It is useless to want to interfere with endogenous processes. . . . One must let them run their course." Such instances explain the basic mistrust we bring to a mentality like that of Lange-Eichbaum (considered as a symptom).

And mistrust seems to me still the indicated response when Ernst Kretschmer, in his book *Geniale Menschen* [Men of Genius], assigns the late Rilke to the "most advanced psychic danger zone" where one "cannot dwell for long without cracking."[4] It is true that all his life Rilke dwelled with the possibility that he might lose his mind and took corresponding testamentary precautions. But the pathograph who defends the view that psychosis, and with it total psychic collapse, were imminent for Rilke need not deal with a creative product that originates in the "most advanced psychic danger zone." Is it only coincidence that when Kretschmer attempts to document his thesis of Rilke's potential psychosis, he speaks about the late Rilke but quotes exclusively from the (early) *Book of Hours?*

In all justice it must be noted that this danger of pathographic misunderstanding is not limited to psychiatrists; psychoanalysts also succumb to it. Our objection is therefore directed quite generally to any form of pathographic hubris that measures all unusual intellectual or artistic phenomena by the yardstick of Hölderlin's madness or Goethe's seven-year rhythms. For this mentality (with which German psychiatry is perhaps more deeply afflicted than it knows) nothing really new can occur; everything is reduced to the "endogenous," "biological," "constitutional." Conflicts between the individual and his environment, which psychoanalysis attempts to interpret as the result and repetition of early discrepancies in the life of the child, have always been the expression of a primary disharmony, of a constitution not structured according to the rules which project its tension onto the environment. "Have you ever stopped to think," Kretschmer asked the audience to whom he first read his *Geniale Menschen,* "why the man of genius often works his life through so laboriously, as if through an infinite thorny thicket, why he goes unrecognized by his teachers, rejected by his parents, ridiculed and ignored by his peers, why time and again he has a falling out with his party, why time and again, as if by malignant fate, the most attractive prospects are blocked, why his life is passed in care, anger, bitterness, and melancholy?" (p. 15). The answer is clear: the cause lies within "the man of genius" himself. With this, however, the stress of such an approach is placed exclusively on the disharmony, and the autonomous achievement that has resulted from the clash of "genius" and environment remains ignored as such.

With reservation, it must be noted that, even with the method practiced by Kretschmer, it is possible to contemplate a more careful, cautious procedure. The Swiss psychiatrist Theodor Spoerri, who was strongly influenced by Kretschmer, in his 1954 study of the poet Georg Trakl[5] moved toward an approach that concedes to the poetic work a self-contained, autonomous significance. This publication is clearly affected by interest in, if not love for, Trakl's poetry; many of its sections come close to being literary criticism. It is true that the study sets out to verify the hypothesis that Trakl was suffering from a schizophrenic psychosis (possibly complicated by incest with his sister and involving suicide). But parallel to this pathographic strain runs another, of equal weight: a professional concern with the singularity of the work of art. One could almost say that the pathographic questions serve only as the pretext for dealing with the artist and his product, all the while including psychiatric-psychological points of view (incorporating even the suggestion that the term "pathography" be replaced with "anthropography," p. 9).

This intent becomes particularly evident if we compare Spoerri's study of Trakl with a work published two years earlier that examines the Feuerbachs;[6] this family of genius produced, one after another, a noted jurist, a noted philosopher, and a noted painter. Inspired and with an introduction by Ernst Kretschmer, the work describes various generations of one family and proves the point that "old, highly bred families of talent are among the most common preconditions for genius" and that the talented genius appears with the greatest probability "when the family begins to degenerate." "When, following generations of proficiency, the decline sets in—commercial failure, suicide, criminality—then the hour of genius has also struck" (Gottfried Benn).

In summary: the psychiatrically oriented school found its limitation in its tendency toward relativizing ethical-moral values and in the fact that it was rooted in the bourgeois cult of genius. But before turning to the second, the psychoanalytically influenced, school of psychological approaches to literature, I must mention Carl G. Jung, who, taking his departure from psychoanalysis, represents a unique position. His paper "Das Phänomen des Geistes in Kunst und Wissenschaft" [The Phenomenon of the Spirit in Art and Science][7] has been included in the framework of his collected writings. More important than his studies on individual writers and works—such as Picasso and James Joyce's *Ulysses*—was his essay "Psychologie und Dichtung" [Psychology and Literature] which, though it appeared in 1930, was reprinted among the collected works in 1950 and therefore properly belongs among the works under discussion.

In this essay Jung distinguishes "primary visions"—writings that vouchsafe visionary images of the collective unconscious—and all other literature, which is psychological-empirical (that is, corresponding to our human experiences). He illustrates this difference with the two parts of Goethe's *Faust*. His distinction has an immediate appeal; it seems highly plausible, something in the nature of a serendipitous discovery; and the warning that psychoanalytic analysis can lead "away from the psychology of the work of art into the personal psychology of the artist" deserves to be taken seriously.

Nevertheless, critical objections arise. For example, what about works in which "psychological" and "visionary" creativity exist side by side or overlapping on various levels? Is there not a danger that the common element in both forms of creativity (which must exist at least in Goethe's psyche) will be overlooked? Is it not possible that the term "primary vision" will become a label for all those works which arouse an impression of the "visionary" for one reason or another but whose accessibility as far as psychological analysis is concerned was never adequately examined? Thus Jung includes among the visionary works H. Rider Haggard's *She*, whose psychological interpretation still remains to be undertaken before a decision can be made as to its membership in Jung's category of the visionary. In the final analysis, Jung's method results in the elimination of psychology as a method of literary criticism, for according to Jung, psychological-empirical literature effectively explicates itself and thus does not require the work of a psychologist; and visionary literature aims at a transcendent moment, vouchsafes a glimpse of "other worlds," "prehistoric origins of the human soul," in the face of which the psychologist is equally out of place.

It is clear, however, that Jung convincingly represented the point of view that the depth-psychological interpreter of a literary work may on occasion stand in the way of his own understanding of the work by granting too much importance to matters of pathographic interest. Unless we are completely mistaken, this corrective—whether due to Jung or emerging spontaneously within psychoanalysis—has been effectively at work during the last few decades.

Two principal tasks confronted the newly revived discipline of psychoanalysis after the war in its application to biography, art, and literature: the realignment with tradition, such as was exemplified before 1933 in contemporary publications (such as the periodical *Imago*), and correspondence to the situation of such psychoanalytic studies in art and creativity as are represented, for example, by Eissler, Kohut, Greenacre, and Kris. Both purposes were important, but they were difficult to combine. It is in keeping with this difficulty that both the books mentioned at the beginning of this paper, which initiated the renaissance in the early 1970s, more or less unequivocally addressed themselves to one or another of these tasks. *Neurose und Genialität: Psychoanalytische Biographien* [Neurosis and Genius: Psychoanalytic Biographies][8] primarily served the realignment with tradition; its domain was the "classical" study (or study along classical patterns) of the driving fate of a historical personality—an artist or a political figure. The fact that there was a heavy stress on the political (the volume contains Freud's study of Wilson and Erikson's study of Hitler, and Cremerius himself contributed a paper on Philip II of Spain) assured the book of relevance. As far as methodology goes, however, at least as expressed in its title, it remained dedicated to the older view of genius.

One of the substantial merits of *Psycho-Pathographien I* [Psycho-Pathographies],[9] which was published the following year, in 1972, under the editorship of Alexander Mitscherlich, is that it broke with the concept of genius shaped by the middle-class value system. "The best result that could grow out of the book to hand," states the foreword, "would be for the reader to be able to diminish the distance between the idealized figure of the artist and himself. Given a certain amount of empathy, he approaches closer to creative ability to the extent that he can overcome idealization. For idealization is, after all, a great resistance against creative invention, against the creative upheaval which the idealist would like to reject, leaving the artist uniquely burdened with it (as in fact was characteristic for a middle-class understanding of art)." Thus the emphasis, in accordance with Mitscherlich's intention, is displaced from a concept of genius that hinders our self-development to the potential creativity in all of us: a transformation that attempts to realize the democratic postulate in an area where, in spite of countless political encroachments, the idea of the "nobility of the spirit" (Thomas Mann) had remained preeminent for a very long time. It was in this sense that Thornton Wilder, in the Paulskirche in Frankfurt in 1957,[10] spoke of the "new dignified status" that man had attained under the sign of democracy.

The polarization of the historical and the clarifying-progressive trend seem indeed to determine the new phase of creativity studies. Without a doubt the generously conceived project on which Johannes Cremerius is presently working with the critic Bernd Urban, which proposes to deal with the acceptance of psychoanalysis among German-language writers, belongs on the side of historical reconstruction. Further, Urban is also the editor of the anthology *Psychoanalyse und Literaturwissenschaft* [Psychoanalysis and Literary Criticism] (1973),[11] which contains a number of classical psychoanalytical papers by Otto Rank, Hanns Sachs, and Theodor Reik, and which further furnishes proof that as early as 1930 there was an attempt on the part of German literature to come to terms with psychoanalysis. Today it is instructive to see the grotesque distortions to which psychoanalysis was forced to submit under the pressure of political-ideological trends; the attempt was made to deprive it of precisely those stimuli that were useful to literary studies of the period while overlooking its clarifying rational tendency. If we can rely on the impression made by advance sections of the work in progress by Cremerius and Urban, the situation of literary criticism was not very different.

The Germanist Hermann Pongs, for example, whose 1930 essay "Psychoanalyse und Dichtung" [Psychoanalysis and Literature] is included in Urban's collection of relevant essays, is anxious "to secure the ground of literature against the burrowing of psychoanalysis." In the search for a counterweight to analytical undermining he hit on the concept of "anagogics," which is incorporated in the figure of the mother, just as analysis is embodied in the father figure. In Dostoievsky's *Brothers Karamazov*, Pongs saw the mother image as the great anagogic principle balancing the father image in the life of the sons. Although it is true that in the history of psychoanalysis the father figure at first occupied the center of attention and that similar interest was turned on the mother figure only as a second step, this stress on the mother image in Pongs is, nevertheless, clearly reactionary. Is it possible that today's attempts—with reversed signs—to tie psychoanalysis to Marxism, sociology, and the like, will one day, in retrospect seem similarly grotesque? In any case, it is instructive to see what becomes of psychoanalysis when one is determined at any cost to reconcile it with the reigning ideologies.

"Psychoanalysis and Literary Criticism" is related to numerous similarly titled publications whose editors or authors are without exception critics. It might be said that this serves to introduce a new phase in the relationship of psychoanalysis and criticism; that a lack of interest or even hostility had turned into a concern with psychoanalysis and its inherent possibilities. Nevertheless, the fundamental questions raised by the interdisciplinary approach are still largely unresolved. Will literary analysis content itself with adopting the historical or methodological attitude, or does it plan on taking charge of the psychoanalytic interpretation of literary texts as well? Is an acquaintance with the most important psychoanalytic writings sufficient to this purpose, or are there still further requirements? Is interdisciplinary cooperation developing between psychoanalysis and literary criticism, such as already exists in the fields of education and general medicine?

Such a team-like solution of the problem is outlined in the collection *Psychologie in der Literaturwissenschaft: Viertes Amherster Kolloquium zur modernen deutschen Literatur 1970* [Psychology in Literary Studies].[12] It is based on the fourth Amherst Colloquium in Modern German Literature, which brought together a number of United States scholars, most of them German-speaking, including the psychoanalyst Frederick M. Wyatt and the critics Heinz Politzer and Lawrence Ryan. "Did Oedipus have an Oedipus complex?" was the title of Politzer's paper, which tersely pointed to the semantic irritation caused by the fact that, since Freud's day, "Oedipus" carries a dual meaning: protagonist of an outstanding drama and a quasi-technical term used to identify a psychological set of circumstances. Perhaps this contradiction is in fact unreconcilable; but an open dialogue, such as the one held at Amherst, must be the first step in any eventual resolution of the linguistic confusion. Further to the point may be K.R. Eissler's opinion to the effect that Freud did not apply the (clinically observed) "Oedipus complex" to literature in a secondary way, as it were, but that his familiarity with *Oedipus Rex* and *Hamlet* was from the outset an integral component of the psychoanalytic discovery process.[13] It is probably only later, after subsequent analytic writers had come to apply analytic thinking to literature, that the public consciousness assimilated and rigidified the contradictory impression.

There remain a number of other publications that document a new situation in creativity studies, by no means limited to psychoanalytic statements of the problem. The volume *Literaturpsychologie* [Literary Psychology],[14] by Norbert Groeben, is intended as a "working base" for teachers, students, and researchers. In dealing with all previously explored aspects of psychological researches on personality and interpretation of works, Groeben stresses the fact that there is such a thing as empirically determined, nonneurotic creativity; wherever neurosis and creativity have appeared in tandem, creativity was not a consequence of the disorder but a force prevailing against it. The old formula of genius and madness, neurosis and genius, with its demonic overtones, thus loses significance by gaining a new content; in Groeben's words, it is no longer proper "to localize the aesthetically new and contextually different . . . as 'somehow' incomprehensible, beyond any possibility of exploration." It follows that literary studies must to the largest possible extent use interpretation in the language of reason to make the work accessible to scholarly theoretical comprehension.

A further important publication is *Literaturwissenschaft und Psychoanalyse: Eine Einführung* [Literary Criticism and Psychoanalysis: An Introduction][15] by the Germanist Peter von Matt. It consists of the transcript of a series of lectures given at the University of Zurich as an introduction to the psychoanalytic method in literary studies. The psychoanalytic method appears here thoroughly assimilated; for example, on Heinrich von Kleist's *Prince of Homburg* Matt states: "Our subconscious very clearly recognizes how Kleist's suicide relates to the prince's capitulation before the father figure of the Elector; that not the least fascination of the *Prince of Homburg* lies in the fact that Kleist shot himself shortly thereafter and thus furnished an interpretation of the work that does not emerge from the usual readings" (p. 49).*

I want to go beyond the German-speaking area and direct attention to two native German psychoanalysts now resident in the United States. Their attempts to give new clarity and system to the relationship of psychoanalysis and literature by structuring new categories have had a far-reaching influence. "Kinds are the very life of art," said Henry James, which can here be applied to the discipline in question. Thus Eissler, departing from Henry Collins, distinguished between "exopoetic" and "endopoetic" modes of interpretation, whereby the former approaches the work of art "from the outside" (that is, by referring to biographic and other facts), whereas the second method keeps to the limits set by the work (p. 459). No less significant seems the proposal by Heinz Kohut to distinguish among psychoanalytic pathography, depth biography, and psychoanalytic studies of creativity.[17] Although pathography is primarily concerned "to clarify a chapter of psychoanalytic psychopathology" (p. 583), both the other categories aim at employing psychoanalytic means for the greatest possible clarification and understanding of the object of inquiry. If we add a final category—not mentioned by Kohut—of psychoanalytic interpretation of literature, which deals both with a single work and with a writer's total output from a particular aspect, the result is a spectrum that surpasses the possibilities of classical psychoanalysis in its capabilities for variation. To indicate something of this potential multiplicity—in the face of the old reproach about the monotony of psychoanalytic interpretation—was one of my goals in compiling this survey.

---

*I hope shortly to publish an interpretation of the *Prince of Homburg* and other works by Kleist in line with my previous essays on the writings of Thomas Mann, Rainer Maria Rilke, Heimito von Doderer, and others.[16]

Notes

1. Sixth ed., rev. by W. Kurth (Munich: Reinhardt-Verlag, 1967).
2. In *Gesammelte Werke*, vol. 3 (Wiesbaden: Limes Verlag, 1968).
3. In *Politische Schriften und Reden*, vol. 3 (Frankfurt: Fischer-Bücherei, 1968).
4. Berlin, Göttingen, Heidelberg: Springer Verlag, 1958, p. 218.
5. *Georg Trakl: Strukturen in Persönlichkeit und Werk. Eine psychiatrisch-anthropographische Untersuchung* (Berne: Francke-Verlag, 1954).
6. *Genie und Krankheit: Eine psychopathologische Untersuchung der Familie Feuerbach* (Basel and New York: Karger, 1952).
7. In *Gesammelte Werke*, vol. 15 (Olten and Freiburg: Walter-Verlag, 1971).
8. Johannes Cremerius, ed. (Frankfurt: S. Fischer, 1971).
9. Frankfurt: Suhrkamp-Verlag, 1972.
10. *Kultur in einer Demokratie. Vortrag anlässlich der Verleihung des Friedenspreises des deutschen Buchhandels* (Frankfurt: Fischer-Verlag, 1957).
11. Tübingen: Niemeyer-Verlag, 1973.
12. W. Paulsen, ed. (Heidelberg: Lothar Stiehm Verlag, 1971).
13. *Discourse on Hamlet and "Hamlet": A Psychoanalytic Inquiry* (New York: International University Press, 1971), p. 467.
14. Stuttgart: Kohlhammer, 1972, p. 51.
15. Freiburg: Rombach paperback, 1972.
16. Peter Dettmering, *Dichtung und Psychoanalyse: Thomas Mann, Rainer Maria Rilke, Richard Wagner* (Munich: Nymphenburger Verlagshandlung, 1969); *Trennungsangst und Zwillingsphantasie; Neue Aufsätze zum Thema "Dichtung und Psychoanalyse"* (forthcoming).
17. "Beyond the Bounds of the Basic Rule," *Journal of the American Psychoanalytic Association* 8 (1960): 3.

Melvin Goldstein

LA VERITA NON E STATA
ANCORA INVENTATA
Anglo-American Literary Criticism and Psychology

THE STRENGTH OF THE PSYCHOANALYTIC APPROACH TO LITERATURE LIES in its ability to make us aware of why we think of literary characters as living people.[1] At the same time, a weakness of this approach is its tendency to ignore "art" by reducing it to a clinical example of a type, or a projection test for the reader. The relationship between psychoanalysis and literary criticism has been the subject of numerous articles studying the possibility of expanding the strengths and delineating the weaknesses of such a marriage.[2]

The development of psychoanalysis, whose purpose is to cure psychoneurotics, and the application of it to characters in literature who appear psychoneurotic indicates a decision to find, through a psychoanalytic study of literary and dramatic characters, some of the reasons for our own feelings, thoughts, and behaviors. Psychoanalysis has stated without equivocation the ancient proposition that "every person is all persons" if only we will be flexible and courageous enough to examine all aspects of our personalities. But even the most courageous person defends against unacceptable fantasies; all of us have an unconscious, repressed part of ourselves we simply will not or cannot face. Psychoanalysis uncovers these terrifying repressions by penetrating defenses; this the analyst does through a study of the analysand's language. The psychoanalytic critic studies the language of a writer, or of the character created by that writer, to discover what is beneath the surface of description and speech and to determine what is being defended against. To get at these "hidden patterns" is to elucidate for the audience some of the psychological reasons for people's responses to experience.

Psychoanalytic and existential thinking about mental processes and human behavior differ significantly in that existentialism concentrates on the present rather than on the past and it denies the existence of the unconscious, making consciousness a willful as opposed to a predetermined dynamic. Both as a therapy and as a form of literary criticism, psychoanalysis is a psychological study of language.[3] Existentialism sees itself not as a science, but as a philosophy; it does not have a specialized vocabulary like psychoanalysis.[4] It is important to remember that existentialists like Kierkegaard, Marcel, Maritain, Tillich, Berdyaev, and Buber were and are religious thinkers, and that the nonreligious existentialists like Sartre, Camus, and de Beauvoir do not represent the entire school of existential thought. Like psychoanalysis, phenomenology has a specialized vocabulary, but unlike psychoanalysis it is unhappy to be bound to language at all. Phenomenologists have an unhealthy contempt for the tools they must use. Also, a greater antagonism exists between phenomenologists themselves, in and out of print, than between members of any group of psychoanalysts or existentialists I know. That is, phenomenology attempts to objectively describe intuitively apprehended phenomena. How intuitively apprehended subjective experience can be *objectively* described by a subject is a dilemma without solution.

The descriptive philosophy of experience called phenomenology was pioneered by Franz Brentano, but it became a method through the work of Edmund Husserl (1859–1938).[5] In wrestling with the question of how people get to know and what they get to know,[6] Husserl developed a philosophy of human consciousness as the basis, not of the world, but of the meaning of the world. Consciousness and world are inextricably woven together. Setting aside all presuppositions, Husserl determined, through phenomenological reduction, how the world is given to human consciousness. Consciousness is *intentional*, that is, directed toward an object in the world, and the object does not exist or does not reveal itself until it is an object for consciousness. Further, in following through with his idea of reduction, Husserl makes the intentional act of consciousness itself an object for consciousness; the result of this is to reveal that consciousness is the source of meaning in the world.

Psychoanalysis, existentialism, and phenomenology were created and developed by psychologists and metapsychologists, observers of human behavior and students of the mind. Freud, Sartre, and

Merleau-Ponty were, or are, men of language and literature; Freud sought verification for his clinical theories in Greek, Jewish, and European literature; Sartre, a man of literary accomplishment, exhibits his theories in the characters of his literary works; Gabriel Marcel wrote plays; Jean Wahl wrote poetry; Merleau-Ponty analyzed Simone de Beauvoir's *L'Invitée* and André Malraux's *Voice of Silence*. All these figures worked or are working simultaneously in intellectual history and literature. And all are concerned with time as it both traps and frees the mind. Psychoanalysis is always aware of the past (which depressives concentrate on), of the present (the focus of hysterics), of the future (the compulsive element of obsessives), and a need to integrate the three; existentialism and phenomenology are always in danger of too great a concentration on the present. This is especially true of existentialism, which often works hard to deny that history determines choice. Phenomenology concentrates on the present in terms of a personal sense of time, but when put in perspective it sees this time moving from the future back to the past in order to make the present meaningful. Psychoanalysis, with its model of the "sick" person, builds a system of "cures," the goal of which is the perfectability of a person. Existentialism reacts to this with its view of people as "healthy" and a person as "many" personae responding to a "sick" world. And phenomenology presupposes a healthy mind and healthy body capable of metamotivation, of going beyond the already accomplished self and describing how this may be done. All three fields center on the acceptance of the idea that man is the most valuable and most worthwhile of creatures. Psychoanalysis, existentialism, phenomenology, with their mutual interests in mind, behavior, language, literature, and time, all meet on common ground: people in their infinite variety need to discover the ways and means to become all that they are capable of becoming.

Neo-Freudians redefined and expanded psychoanalytic concepts to include additional theories of development (Adler, Erikson, Maslow), additional views of the individual in the family situation (Horney, Sullivan, Laing), additional contexts in which the individual functions, the social and the political (Fromm), and then back again to studies of earliest stages (Klein, Hartmann, Rapaport, Spitz, Fraiberg). Among the influential extensions of the classical psychoanalytical school is psychology. This development comes from a study of the genetic approach (the need to understand all antecedents of the present to understand the present), the dynamic approach (a person's behavior is understandable once the interplay of all the forces in his mind is understood), and the economic approach (understanding people in terms of psychic energies—quantitative). Following from these, ego psychology led to the development of the adaptational approach emphasizing the role of the ego (Hartmann divided the concept into ego and self: ego as a psychic system distinct from other aspects of the personality; and self, in opposition to the "other" or object) both as an integrator of normal and pathological mental and behavior processes and as a concentrator on the internal and external environments of a person. Ego psychology explains the need of the individual to be open to various psychological and social forces in order to tolerate fluctuations of the sense of self, and self in relation to others. This last sentence is my understanding of Ernst Kris' now familiar statement, "regression in the service of the ego." Whereas descents into the murky unconscious terrify the general public, artists are able to swim about in the depths of their fantasies, including those of uncontrolled hells, and to rise to the surface, bringing these thoughts to consciousness for use in their art. In this way, artists have stronger and "healthier" egos, are less neurotic because they are less repressed, and therefore are able to create more out of their self.[7]

Jung, as a disciple of Freud, moved psychoanalysis out of Vienna, Europe, and Western Civilization in general, and put it into all cultures for all times. Using clinical and literary experiences, Jung elaborated on myth, legend, and ritual, and the ways in which these beliefs and rites are universal, in some form, to all cultures. The concentration in Jung was on the work and not, as in Freud, primarily on the artist. (But in certain brilliant cases, "The Theme of the Three Caskets," Freud's concentration is very much on the literature.) If, for Freud, the artist and neurosis were aligned in the work, for Jung, such an alignment was an indication of an inferior work. That is, "personal idiosyncrasies" made the work something less than a work of art. For Jung, the poet's individuality is subordinated to the collective will. "It is not Goethe who creates *Faust*, but *Faust* who creates Goethe." Therefore the great work of art must be objective and impersonal: It expresses something to which people respond in a state of *"participation mystique"* at "that level of experience at which it is man who lives, and not the individual." There is a bit of charming irony in reading the poet's "own work outgrows him as a child its mother."[8] Concentration on the importance of the "mother" has been nothing short of explosive in recent psychological literary criticism. Two schools of thought on "mother" have arisen. The first may be said to be represented by Erich Neumann and the second by Joseph Rheingold.[9] Neumann's studies are in the Jungian tradition, which places concept of mother in a complex of mythical traditions. Rheingold's concept of mother centers about the object-relationship between mother and child. Neumann's work seems to grow naturally out of Jung's, and Rheingold's out of Freud's. Both are indebted to Freud's concept of woman as life giver, nurturer, and bearer of death ("Caskets").

Our acceptance of ourselves as mortals who may die at any moment, and our dread of loneliness and isolation (constant reminders of that end of life we call death) make it impossible for us to be comfortable, at least without illusions.

Or is it possible? Yes, say the existential and humanistic psychologists. We can be authentic; we can accept our existential anxiety, act, make choices, and be responsible for what happens to us. This does not mean that we have total control or want to have total control over what is happening to us. What it does mean is that if we choose not to act and not to choose, we take responsibility for such a choice. But this group of humanists lays claim to the idea that the nature of being is such that love is an essential part of our natures. The American humanistic psychological movement sees man as the creature most to be valued, and his welfare is of major concern to its views of the world. This "third force" or "third revolution," as it has been called, disavows scientific detachment and a scientific philosophy of man. Humanistic psychology values meaning more than procedure, has no interest in a quest for abstract truth, and seeks human rather than nonhuman validation. What we experience and our feelings about that experience are valid and true for us. Humanistic psychology does not fear a loss of the intellect. It is a reaction against an overintellectualized world. Laing reminds us that giving up feelings for intellectualization is the carting off of emotion to a nightmare world.

Wolfgang Köhler says, "Never, I believe, shall we be able to solve any problems of ultimate principle until we go back to the sources of our concepts, in other words, until we use the phenomenological method, the qualitative analysis of experience, [which] requires a radical devaluation of the notion of thinking." And this begins with a stripping away of "dangerous words" to get at some particular realm of "intrinsic requiredness." Köhler declares he would give up some knowledge of universal propositions about man for a great deal of knowledge about a single concept such as "ought to be." One result of such a stance is in a forty-five-page analysis by Fritz Heider of the dynamic concepts of the terms "can" and "will."[10] The assumptions of language, which is the enemy more than language itself, have been examined, and their phenomenological nature reduced to such a point that their essential nature has been exposed. The irony here is that Köhler's goal, the desire to increase an appreciation of human beings, a goal similar to that of the existential and humanistic psychologists, leads to an overintellectualized description of behavior. Language is reduced to its essential components, but humans are not appreciated more. They are themselves reduced and seen as slaves of the world of facts about them with their need to accept communal agreement as truth.[11]

The resultant schools of thought sometimes connected with phenomenology, structuralism, and formalism are similar to linguistics; that is, despite Köhler's "case against science," they tend to become scientific. Linguists, as Angus McIntosh writes, work with the sentence as the primary unit of analysis. But "quite often . . . the impact of an entire work may be enormous, yet word by word . . . sentence by sentence, there may be nothing very unusual or arresting. . . . Any approach . . . which looks at anything less than the whole text as the ultimate unit has very little to contribute."[12] The study of language and linguistic study are not the same thing. In a course of study in psycholinguistics with Aron Carton (City University of New York) this distinction became apparent; and the case for such a distinction is well made by Julius Laffal.[13] However, Carton's discussions of such figures as Roman Jakobson revealed the usefulness of psycholinguistics in studies of literature. But structuralism, which stems from Gestalt psychology and has branched out into the fields of anthropology, generative grammar, mathematics, philosophy, physics, and biology, has opened up numerous ways of seeking for micro and macro structural aggregates (sometimes opposed to one another) within a piece of literature.[14] Put another way, structuralism finds its full and conscious scientific expression in formalism, which looks at a work of art as a combination of artistic techniques. The work's content, meaning, and reality are all put aside for a view of the intrinsic structure of the work. The structure is alive; it has an autonomy all its own. (This bears striking resemblance to what the "Epoche" or setting of reality inside parentheses does for Husserl's phenomenology.) If anything, the content (Hamlet's madness) makes it possible for Shakespeare to use many sources and to tie them all together.[15] This kind of structuralism and formalism, in moving away from interpretation, moves away from the psychology of literature as a sharing of human experience to a specialized appreciation of the artist at work with his tools and not his product. And even this common bond of a concentration on the artist is divided into a series of divergent views which, when drawn, become as calligraphic as a series of forks along splintered roads.

Psychoanalysis has generated the greatest variety of psychological literary criticisms. Classic psychological theory continues to prove itself infinitely expandable and incorporative. Theories as old and as varied as those regarding the death wish, psychosomatic medicine, and defense mechanisms become, in the hands of astute critics such as M.D. Faber, Marjorie Nicolson, and Ruth Tiefenbrun, new ways of viewing suicide in the Greeks, Pope's poetry as expressive of his physical disabilities, and Franz Kafka's short stories.[16] Under the guidance of talented anthologizers, initiation rites in primitive societies and theories of the abnormal personality and of psychopathology become equally new ways of beginning to understand unusual situations and the bizarre, sometimes grotesque people who find themselves in these situations.[17]

Neo-Freudians apply ego theory to Prometheus, cognitive psychology to Virginia Woolf, theories of the generation gap to *King Lear*, object-relationship theory to mothers and children, and a women's liberation idea, vagina envy, to Cinderella, as do Ned Marcus, Harvena Richter, Kurt Schlesinger, M.D. Faber once again, and Beryl Sandford. The results, though fine, are not always appreciated. For instance, six critics respond to Beryl Sandford, a British psychoanalyst. She is treated gently by two women respondents and told by four male respondents that her scholarship is shoddy, her logic fallacious, her knowledge inadequate, and her standing as a psychoanalyst questionable. I think Dr. Sandford was trying something new and, though serious about the matter, was also enjoying her exploration of it. Perhaps this latter fact that she was not taking herself entirely seriously was responsible for the criticism.[18]

Mythic approaches to literature seem to me best when informed by psychoanalysis. Nancy Topping Bazin's *Virginia Woolf and the Androgynous Vision* is reductive in its application of the bisexual and/or hermaphroditic view of people as a myth critic might see the issue when compared with Carolyn Heilbrun's *Toward a Recognition of Androgyny*; here a psychoanalytic view of history informs the author's view of Queen Elizabeth and Queen Victoria in such a way as to give the idea of bisexuality a dimension not to be found in Bazin's work. Nor is Bazin as penetrating in her study of Virginia Woolf as Jean Love, whose *Worlds in Consciousness: Mythopoetic Thought in the Novels of Virginia Woolf* works out of theories of cognitive psychology, Neumann's views of consciousness (deriving as they do from the analytical psychology of Jung and from the earlier Freud), and a broad vision of how myth becomes poetry. Leslie Fiedler's *The Stranger in Shakespeare* has the kind of boldness of thought that excites the reader's mind, at first, but when studied more carefully becomes thinner, whereas Harry Slochower's *Mythopoesis: Mythic Patterns in the Literary Classics* bears repeated readings. A trained psychoanalyst and a student of mythology for half a century, Slochower brings to the reader an unsurpassed combination of psychoanalytic insight with a knowledge of mythology, Marxism, and history. In encouraging me in my studies of cannibalism in *Death in Venice* and of Mother Russia as the heroine of *Brothers Karamozov*, Slochower always left me with a sense of the proud depths of the creative work. His studies, from the start, have been what we now call psychohistory.[19]

This leads to a discussion of the two most active schools of psychological criticism of literature: psychohistory and dynamics of literary response. Psychohistorians try to present an overall view of the elements outside a work and relate them to the elements within a work; those interested in the dynamics of literary response try to understand a work by understanding the heart and mind of the reader. They desire to penetrate to the innermost core of both work and reader. In a manner of speaking, the psychohistorians are the inheritors of Freud, from *Totem and Taboo* to *Civilization and its Discontents*, as well as of Jung and his idea that if a work is sufficiently great it reflects all things to all people. Those interested in the psychological response of the audience to a work are in a tradition that goes back to Plato and Plotinus through Ficino, and up to contemporary psychological and artistic studies of perception and its relations to the brain and heart. Freud studied audience response to Sophocles' *Oedipus Rex*. And Jung, for whom the artistic disposition involves "an overweight of collective psychic life as against the personal" (psychohistory), also wrote, in his article "On the Relation of Analytical Psychology to Poetic Art" (1928), that there is a special emotional significance possessed by certain poems related to the awakening of primordial images or unconscious archetypes within the reader's mind. "The creative process," writes Jung, "in so far as we are able to follow it at all, consists in an unconscious animation of the archetype. . . . The secret of effective art [is a] shaping of the primordial image . . . a translation into the language of the present which makes it possible for every man to find again the deepest springs of life which would otherwise be closed to him."[20] Thus, psychohistorians amplify Freud's culture theories, and experimenters of audience response amplify Jung's theories.

From a psychohistorical point of view, Robert Coles, Bronson Feldman, and Erik Erikson illustrate what can be done in an article on a man's "imperial dreams" and in a book-length study. Coles' eleven-page note on Maisie Ward's book about Pen Browning applies the psychoanalytic notion of "discipline" to what went wrong in the life of a very talented young man who was the product of two of Victorian England's most famous literary people, Robert and Elizabeth Browning. Feldman brings to bear a knowledge of "dreams" and sets them in the framework of the Victorian England in which an ambitious Jewish politician, as a "foreigner," had to work to become "successful." Erikson's early study of Martin Luther (the outline of which I believe John Osborne applied to his play *Luther*) as well as his later and now famous study of Ghandi are exemplary works of the psychohistorian. The value and the attraction of the psychohistorical approach is expressed in a special review of Erikson's work on Gandhi by Alan Roland, "Psychoanalysis and History: A Quest for Integration."[21]

The desirability and the necessity for such an approach is expressed in a personal communication to me by Richard W. Noland: "I think psychological criticism has yet to explore the uses of existential-phenomenological psychology and also, for all the lip service paid to it, ego psychology. I don't really know what else to say about those last two areas except to say that if we are to have a non-reductive, comprehensive psycho-historical literary criticism (which is what I now think of as the goal) then these two areas seem to be of great importance."[22]

Some of those interested in the psychological responses of the audience to literature are Katherine Stockholder, Susan Elliott, David Bleich, and Norman Holland. I have wondered, when another person and I agree that we see the same color blue, whether we are seeing only an approximation but, actually, not in fact the same color. This parallels my awareness of the differences in responses to literature, and my interest in determining what people are saying when they agree to liking a piece of literature. The more I expressed my literary evaluation of a work the more I became conscious that I was expressing, as well, my own values, stages of development, and reasons for my tastes. With this awareness I became more and more able to accept student, as well as professional literary responses different from my own. I also realized why some of us need to put down a book after reading ten, fifty, or a hundred pages. At least three alternatives present themselves: we are sufficiently free to allow unconscious material to be brought to the surface without endangering our equilibrium, and so we may read on and on; or we are so defensive against what is being presented that we read entirely untouched by what is psychodynamically being transmitted; or we stop reading after only a few pages. Between the ages of twenty and twenty-five I found Shakespeare's comedies dull, boring, and out of tune with contemporary psychological interests in literature. When I began to admit to myself that the comedies appeared to me bizarre, even grotesque, because they made me feel uncomfortable I decided to investigate the reasons for this response. It is not until almost twenty years later, with what I regard as sufficient training in psychoanalysis and existential-phenomenological theory, that I find myself able to investigate *A Midsummer Night's Dream* and to view the play as a series of identity crises created by a society working against a person's development toward autonomy and authenticity, a problem similar to the one I was going through in those painful twenties.[23]

Although the span of years is somewhat larger in David Bleich's "The Determination of Literary Value," and the responses a bit different, the opposition between readers in 1928 and readers in 1966 is similar to my personal differences in response to Shakespeare's comedies. Bleich says that the obviousness and sentimentality of psychoanalytic criticism in the late twenties have recently been exchanged for an appreciation of its complexity and its urgent needs. One way of putting the matter is to say that the tiresome finger pointing to the threat to our manhood, our latent homosexuality, Bleich says, is now so manifestly apparent that the "boom" of homosexuality on the social scene makes such a matter more acceptable when it is discovered, once again, on a latent level in literature. "Whatever the contemporary standard of judgment is, however, a 'good' poem can now be said to be one which does not call for defensive action from its readers, does not ask for ego-help from its audience, gives us, as it were, a psychically tolerable experience, wish *and* defense." From a psychocritical standpoint, the concept of "form as a psychological defense" becomes a way to determine the value of a literary work.[24]

Susan Elliott's book-in-the-making entitled "Fantasy Beneath Play: A Study of Affective Responses to Harold Pinter's *The Birthday Party, The Caretaker* and *The Homecoming*" is an effort to illuminate the psychological dynamics of the Pinter experience by first discussing the puzzlement expressed by many reviewers and critics of Pinter's work, and the intellectual defenses of their subjective responses. She analyzes the "play activities" Pinter engages his audience in, and, finally, confronts Pinter's "game" plays through her own free associations as well as intellectual responses; these serve as a guide to understanding how the critical interpretation and evaluation of these plays relate to the emotional experience of them.[25]

The most accomplished psychological critic using psychoanalytic theory is Norman Holland. All twenty of the American psychological critics to whom I wrote listed his *Dynamics of Literary Response* (1968) with the most important contributions to the field. For me it is the most significant contribution to psychological criticism since Ernst Kris' *Psychoanalytic Explorations in Art* (1952), and it supersedes the still valuable *Fiction and the Unconscious* (1957) of Simon O. Lesser. It is helpful and necessary to sketch out the progress of Holland's work.[26]

Holland was led to Freud's theory of jokes when teaching a course in "The Comic Sensibility," many years ago. Freud examined literary works in detail as aesthetically formed and unified texts; and for Holland, Freud showed how this purely literary (or subliterary) experience worked in terms of larger explanatory principles that applied to other areas of human behavior as well (dreams, slips of the tongue, or symptoms). Out of a desire to discover what had been done by applying psychoanalytic theory to literature in general, Holland surveyed what had been said about the life and works of the author psychoanalytic critics turn to most often, and this became *Psychoanalysis and Shakespeare* (1966). Holland noted some astonishing correspondences between psychoanalytic experience and Shakespearean and other literary works, but he also observed that little psychoanalytic theory was being applied, and that within a limited framework. Unprovable statements about the author were preferred to statements about the living, actually present mind of the reader. Literary characters were being studied like photographic copies of living people, a naive view of realism few literary critics would accept. Within psychoanalysis, some symbolic decoding was being applied: the literary work was treated as a congress of phalluses, vaginas, and anuses, with lip service to aesthetic beauties but no real analysis of them or treatment of intellectual themes. Of the developmental stages, only the oedipal was applied to literature— as a result, the psychoanalytic critic talked only about narrative or dramatic works which had father or mother figures. These procedures had given psychoanalytic criticism a reputation which, Holland fears, it has not overcome even today. Nevertheless, there were enough insights coming from this school to warrant further explorations.

Holland says he was lucky at this juncture of his life to be able to train at the Boston Psychoanalytic Institute. There he learned of other aspects of psychoanalytic theory and experience not being applied to literature, notably those strategies for warding off anxiety and coping with inner and outer reality. Holland calls those strategies defenses (instead of "defensive and adaptive strategies"). They appear in literature as what is usually called form, both in the large sense of the selection and structuring of parts and more specificially as rhymes, alliteration, stanza patterns, and so on. He found that psychoanalytic psychology could be used to discuss lyric poems and even nonfiction prose, not just dramatic or narrative versions of the oedipus complex. He also learned more about the preoedipal stages, those desires and fantasies that have to do not with oedipal triangles but one-to-one relationships or just one's own body. These, it turned out, played the key role in lyric poetry and other literature that did not tell a potentially oedipal story. Even in narrative and dramatic works rich with father and mother figures, these preoedipal fantasies served as deeper, more pervasive versions of oedipal material, as they do in real people.

Thus Holland learned that responses to literature involve a transformation of drives, impulses, and fantasies back and forth from the most primitive strata of psychic life to the highest by means of forms acting like defenses. With this model, the social, intellectual, or moral themes found in literature can be understood as the highest level of this dynamic and continuing process of transformation. The feeling of being "absorbed" or "taken out of oneself" when engrossed in literature is understandable: processes of transformation meld with the exterior work so that a difference between "in here" and "out there" is no longer perceived. In short, drawing on other psychoanalytic concepts besides symbolism and the oedipus complex, notably defenses and the preoedipal stages, led to a complex model of literature-as-transformation; this facilitated explaining a number of literary phenomena such as meaning, realism, the relation of the author's personality to his work, the role of embedded myths, and the criteria behind evaluation. Holland explores this model and its application in *The Dynamics of Literary Response.*

He then went on to test this model, which he had derived fundamentally from a combination of psychoanalytic experience with introspection. He has just completed *5 Readers Reading*, the result of those tests. Essentially, *Dynamics* has stood up exceedingly well, requiring one point of additional emphasis: psychological processes, like fantasies or defenses, do not happen in books, Holland insists, but in books as they are absorbed by people. Thus, one sees the five readers who are the subjects of this new book recreate the original literary creation in terms of their own character structures, building their own processes of transformation (as in *Dynamics*) out of materials given them in the work of art. Specifically, this book develops four principles governing the interaction of the reader with what he reads, but these four separate principles are themselves simply four different ways of accenting one more general and basic principle. Each reader has a continuing but changing personality structure, which can be described as an "identity theme." In reading, he filters the literary work through his characteristic defenses, that is, the defensive aspect of his identity theme, to ward off anxiety. He then transforms the literary materials he has taken in according to his characteristic modes of satisfaction, that is, the pleasure-seeking aspect of his identity theme; finally, he consolidates and integrates the whole experience according to his characteristic aesthetic, intellectual, or moral concerns. This basic principle, recreating identity out of the materials of experience, applies not only to reading, but to human interaction with an external reality, human or nonhuman. For example, in *Poems in Persons* (1973), a shorter and more literary book, Holland is able to show how this one basic principle governs teaching, criticism, theatergoing, and the very action of creation itself. Conversely, the same principle seems to apply not only to interactions of people but to interactions by an entity that has a style such as an institution, a culture, or a nation.

Thus, the study of the phenomenon of reading may pay back to psychoanalysis the insight it has borrowed, giving as interest the intrapsychic model of classical psychoanalysis to an interpsychic psychology. The psychohistorian, the object-relations theorist, the social psychologist, anyone concerned with the interactions of groups and individuals may find, in reading, the basic principles that govern the human activities which matter to him.

This summary of a long and prominent career is a survey of psychoanalytic critics' concerns in literature from its inception to the present. This is not to say that Holland has the final word, however well and inclusive is his work. For instance, Katherine Stockholder, in a challenging paper, takes issue with what she sees as Holland's attitudes toward literature and life. Holland, she writes, "seems to hold a more cynical or despairing stance even than Freud from whom he draws his model of man, seeming to believe even less than he in the possibility of man using awareness to make fruitful his irrational unconscious, and implying that conscious awareness must function to obscure what really goes on in man in order that daily business be done." Stockholder believes that " 'serious' literature" will also provide "either a model of how . . . phantasy could be in fact satisfied within historical and social circumstances, or a warning against the destructive effects of seeking to satisfy that phantasy in the external world." In short, she argues that a work of art "figures forth a means of sublimation whereby the passionate energy contained in . . . repressed phantasies may be made available for the task of world building. The final satisfaction is as much from a sense of that possibility as from the primal satisfaction itself, and the satisfaction in positive sublimation brings us back to the ordinary sense of meaning in literature, and to value systems, i.e., systems of ideals having to do with making discriminations about useful and destructive modes of fulfilling phantasy requirements." I am not certain how much of this Holland (and Bleich) would agree with, but the disagreement challenges us to further thought and growth.[27]

For instance, Karl Kroeber, an admirer of Holland, has done a study of fictional structure in Jane Austen, Charlotte Brontë, and George Eliot, using a variety of analytic techniques, but primarily he uses the computer. Despite Kroeber's modesty, his is a sophisticated use of the computer; the results of his investigations open up avenues for the study of style through comparisons and contrasts of linguistic patterns. Kroeber says Eliot's "figurative language becomes increasingly complicated (and meaningful) because it increasingly forces us to respond to likenesses within differences and differences within likenesses simultaneously," and his elaboration of the increased complexity of the metaphors in Eliot's work is extremely informative. In still another chapter ("Narrative and Dialogue: Large and Small Structures"), Kroeber shows the relation between narrative and dialogue to be a particularly useful focal point for stylistic analyses, though he is aware of the "special problems" inherent in an analysis of dialogue sentences. His self-evaluations are not representative of the successes of his studies. He has given hope to the linguists, who have never gotten beyond the sentence as a unit of reference and examination. He suggests a "systematic method" of study, concentrating, through a structural approach, "on patterns of relations which make fictional structures cohere." He declares the desperate need for the humanities of a "development of subdisciplines which will render humanistic studies cumulatively effective."[28]

Notes

Abbreviations

Coll. Engl.	*College English*
Int. J. Psy.	*International Journal of Psychoanalysis*
Lit. and Psychol.	*Literature and Psychology*
Psy. For.	*Psychoanalytic Forum*
Psy. Rev.	*Psychoanalytic Review*
Psy. Quar.	*Psychoanalytic Quarterly*

1. I have not encumbered the text with numerous names and titles. General statements are supported with selective references. In addition, for the convenience of the reader, there is a selected bibliography divided into categories. Disagreement is inevitable about how works are to be classified. I ask the reader's indulgence if I have overlooked any significant articles, books, facts, or developments. Such omission is due to my ignorance and I shall be pleased to receive from readers any matter that will add to my knowledge.

The adage "La Verita Non E Stata Ancora Inventata" ("The Truth Has Yet To Be Invented") is inscribed in Italian on a belt buckle given to me by my friend and former colleague, Christopher Joseph Rogers (University of Toledo), who is in the process of becoming a psychoanalytic-existential-phenomenological-mythopoetic critic.

I sent a questionnaire to ten prominent British literary critics, ten British publishers, and twenty American literary critics, in which I asked them to list for me the most significant current psychological studies of literature, and to let me know of their most recent investigations. The questionnaire yielded some interesting results. From my British correspondents Kenneth Muir and Frank Kermode came the most representative responses. Muir has written only one relevant article, "Freudian Interpretations of Shakespeare," in the *Proceedings of the Leeds Philosophical and Literary Society* (1952), which I have found impossible to get hold of. Muir suggests that many books on literary criticism deal directly or indirectly with psychological problems, but the implication is that they are not truly psychological studies. Muir does mention an American critic, Simon O. Lesser, and his *Fiction and the Un-*

conscious (New York: Random House, 1957), whose work is clearly psychological. But Muir says this work is "not in fact particularly good." All twenty of my American respondents listed Lesser's book as among the most important contributions to the psychological study of literature. Frank Kermode's letter sums up the British critical viewpoint in this way: "I'm not very well qualified to answer your question—D.W. Harding is our best psychologist-critic and his essays are collected. The most intelligent Freudians are the late Adrian Stokes and Richard Wollheim, but Stokes was interested in art, and Wollheim is a philosopher. *As you know, psychoanalysis has never won much favour with English critics* [italics mine] except Auden and in some degree Empson. (See the 'Alice' essay in *Some Versions of Pastoral.*)"

Why psychoanalysis or approaches to literary criticism other than the literary-historical has never had much vogue with British critics is a subject for study all by itself. A quotation by Auden (whom Kermode mentions) from a recent review on Housman may be pertinent for this essay: "I am pretty sure that in his sexual tastes he was an anal passive. Ancient Greece and Rome were both pederastic cultures in which the adult passive homosexual was regarded as comic and contemptible." This is an unnecessary and unwise conjecture in an otherwise fine review. See W.H. Auden, "Books: 'A Worcestershire Lad,'" *The New Yorker* (19 February 1972). Kermode's self-effacing response does not take away what is to his credit, an appreciation of imaginative psychological criticism. Kermode was responsible for Leslie Fiedler's sojourn at the University College, London, during which time Fiedler delivered a series of lectures recently published as *The Stranger in Shakespeare* (New York: Stein and Day, 1972). Kermode's review of the Fiedler book and his setting this book off against a fine and very traditional study of the Bard by Reuben Brower, *Hero and Saint* (New York: Oxford University Press, 1972) indicate his appreciation of the new and the vital, as well as his desire to keep certain species of criticism from extinction, despite their self-annihilating tendencies.

2. The following three articles are concerned primarily with psychoanalysis and fiction studies. Hiag Akmakjian, "Psychoanalysis and the Future of Literary Criticism," *Psy. Rev.* 49 (1962): 3–28; Melvin Askew, "Psychoanalysis and Literary Criticism," *Psy. Rev.* 51 (1964): 43–50; and Philip Withim, "The Psychodynamics of Literature," *Psy. Rev.* 56 (1969–70): 565–85. For a similar essay on nonfiction, see Norman N. Holland, "Prose and Minds: A Psychoanalytic Approach to Non-Fiction," *The Art of Victorian Prose,* ed. George Levine and William Madden (New York: Oxford University Press, 1968), pp. 314–37. On the relationship between the artist (the writer of fiction) and psychoanalysis, see Herman Hesse, "Artist and Psychoanalyst," *Psy. Rev.* 50 (1963): 5–10, as well as remarks by Hesse and Jung in their letters, pp. 15–16; cf. p. 13, n. 1. Hesse denies a Jungian analysis helped him at all; he pays his respects to a limited Freudian analysis, as one might call it, and expresses his reservations about continuing his analysis.

3. In saying this I have in mind the following: Ernst Cassirer, *Language and Myth* (New York: Harper, 1946); Sandor Ferenczi, "On Obscene Words" (1911); and "Stages in the Development of the Sense of Reality" (1913) in *The Selected Papers of Sandor Ferenczi,* vol. 1 (New York: Basic Books, 1950); and Sigmund Freud's early "Project for a Scientific Psychology" (1895) in *The Origins of Psychoanalysis* (New York: Basic Books, 1954), as well as his "Formulations on the Two Principles of Mental Functioning" (1911), vol. 12, Standard Edition (London: Hogarth, 1951); Jean Piaget, *The Language and Thought of the Child* (New York: Harcourt Brace,

1926). These are summarized by Julius Laffal in "Language and the Structure of Experience," *Pathological and Normal Language* (New York: Atherto Press, 1965), pp. 97–124.

4. See Gordon E. Bigelow, "A Primer of Existentialism," *Coll. Eng.* (December 1961): 171–78, and William W. Spanos, *A Casebook of Existentialism* (New York: Crowell, 1966) for a good introduction to existentialism.

5. The following four paragraphs are made up of my own view of the subject, a paraphrase of Richard James Calhoun, "Existentialism, Phenomenology, and Literary Theory," *South Atlantic Bulletin* 28 (1963): 4–8, and two suggestions taken from Cyrena Norman Pondrom, "Kafka and Phenomenology: Josef K's Search for Information," *Wisconsin Studies in Contemporary Literature* 8 (1967): 78–95.

6. None of the six dictionaries of literary terms in my possession lists the term "phenomenology." Therefore, for students of literature in general, it seems likely that no definition of the term is readily available, despite numerous essays on the term available now for years. See, for example, "What is Phenomenology?," *Phenomenology: The Philosophy of Edmund Husserl and Its Interpretation,* ed. Joseph J. Kockelmans (New York: Doubleday Anchor, 1967), pp. 24–36, and Pierre Thevanaz, *What is Phenomenology?* (Chicago: Quadrangle Books, 1962).

7. See Louis Fraiberg, "New Views of Art and the Creative Process in Psychoanalytic Ego Psychology," *Lit. and Psychol.* 11 (1961): 45–55. See also *Encyclopedia of Psychoanalysis,* ed. Ludwig Eidelberg (New York: Free Press, 1968); although Eidelberg has been criticized for having authored too many of the entries, his and the others seem to me to be as helpful and useful as any of their competitors in the field.

8. Paul C. Obler, "Psychology and Literary Criticism: A Summary and Critique," *Lit. and Psychol.* 8 (1958): 50–59. George Michael Evica is doing exciting studies along these lines. One of his essays begins: "Genre studies have traditionally dealt with historical, stylistic, thematic, and attitudinal similarities and differences in oral and written literature. *These generic distinctions* in both folk art and written literature *are ultimately the consequences of symbolic transformations in human sacred consciousness*" ("Sacred Consciousness and Literary Genre"). I hope his manuscripts will soon be in print.

9. Erich Neumann, *The Great Mother,* Bollingen Series (Princeton: Princeton University Press, 1973), and Joseph C. Rheingold, *The Mother Anxiety and Death* (Boston: Little, Brown, 1967).

10. "The Naive Analysis of Action," *The Psychology of Interpersonal Relations* (New York: Wiley, 1958, 1959), pp. 79–124.

11. Wolfgang Köhler, "An Analysis of Requiredness," *The Place of Value in a World of Facts* (New York: Meridian, 1959), pp. 63–101; see also pp. vii, 26, 32ff. (These chapters were originally presented at Harvard as lectures in 1934, and subsequently published in 1938 by the Liveright Publishing Corporation.)

12. "Saying," *Review of English Literature* 6 (1965): 9–20, quoted in Karl Kroeber, *Styles in Fictional Structure: The Art of Jane Austen, Charlotte Brontë, George Eliot* (Princeton: Princeton University Press, 1971), p. 205.
    The new *Journal of Literary Semantics* (The Language Centre, The University of Kent at Canterbury, Kent, England) aims "to concentrate the endeavours of theoretical linguists upon those texts traditionally classed as 'literary,' in the belief that such texts are a central, not a peripheral concern of linguistics."

13. "Psycholinguistics and the Psychology of Language," *Journal of General Psychology* 69 (1964): 51–64.

14. Jean Piaget, *Structuralism*, trans. Chaniah Maschler (New York: Harper & Row, 1970).
15. Jameson, p. ii.
16. Of Faber's works on suicide, I like best "Suicide and the 'Ajax' of Sophocles," *Psy. Rev.* 54 (1967): 49–60; Marjorie Nicolson and G.S. Rousseau, "*This Long Disease, My Life*": Alexander Pope and the Sciences (Princeton: Princeton University Press, 1969); Ruth Teifenbrun, *Moment of Torment: An Interpretation of Franz Kafka's Short Stories* (Carbondale: Southern Illinois University Press, 1973).
17. *The Rite of Becoming: Stories and Studies of Adolescence*, eds. Arthur and Hilda Waldhorn (Cleveland: World, 1966); *The Abnormal Personality Through Literature*, eds. Alan A. Stone and Sue Smart Stone (Englewood Cliffs, N.J.: Prentice-Hall, 1966); *Psychopathology and Literature*, ed. Leslie Y. Rabkin (San Francisco: Chandler, 1966).
18. Ned N. Marcus, "Prometheus Reconsidered: Sublimation and Vicissitudes of the Symbolic Ego," *Psy. Rev.* 54 (1967): 83–106; Harvena Richter, *Virginia Woolf: The Inward Voyage* (Princeton: Princeton University Press, 1970); Kurt Schlesinger, "Thoughts on *King Lear* and the Current Generation Gap," *Psy. For.* (one of the few journals not afraid of controversial views of literature nor does it fear scraps between critics). Beryl Sandford, "Cinderella," *Psy. For.* 2 (1972): 127–44. Despite the impressive body of studies of ego theory and psychoanalytic literary criticism, which has benefited from these theories, Rollo May believes that "the compartmentalization of the personality into ego, superego, and id is an important part of the reason why the problem of will has remained insoluble within the orthodox psychoanalytic tradition." See his *Love and Will* (New York: Norton, 1969), p. 199.
19. Nancy Topping Bazin, *Virginia Woolf and the Androgynous Vision* (New Brunswick, N.J.: Rutgers University Press, 1972); Carolyn Heilbrun, *Toward a Recognition of Androgyny* (New York: Knopf, 1972); Jean Love, *Worlds in Consciousness: Mythopoetic Thought in the Novels of Virginia Woolf* (Berkeley: University of California Press, 1970); Leslie Fiedler, *The Stranger in Shakespeare* (New York: Stein and Day, 1972); Harry Slochower, *Mythopoesis: Mythic Patterns in the Literary Classics* (Detroit: Wayne State University Press, 1970).
20. "On the Relation of Analytical Psychology to Poetic Art," *Contributions to Analytical Psychology* (1928), and "Psychology and Literature," *Modern Man in Search of a Soul* (New York, 1933), pp. 193–94, quoted in Obler, "Psychology and Literary Criticism," p. 55.
21. "Introduction," in Maisie Ward's *The Tragic Comedy of Pen Browning* (New York: Sheed & Ward, 1972), pp. xi–xxii; Feldman Bronson, "The Imperial Dreams of Disraeli," *Psy. Rev.* 53 (1966–67): 607–41; Erik Erikson, *Gandhi's Truth* (New York: Norton, 1969) and *Young Man Luther* (New York: Norton, 1958); Alan Roland, "Psychoanalysis and History: A Quest for Integration," *Psy. Rev.* 58 (1971–72): 631–40 (Special Review of Erik Erikson's *Gandhi's Truth*).
22. Personal communication from the University of Massachusetts, Amherst, 22 January 1973.
23. Melvin Goldstein, "Identity Crises in a Midsummer's Nightmare: Comedy as Terror in Disguise," *Psy. Rev.* 60, no. 2 (1973):169–204.
24. "The Determination of Literary Value," *Lit. and Psychol.* 17 (1967): 19–50.
25. Susan Elliot, "Fantasy Beneath Play." Work in Progress.
26. The following four paragraphs are essentially an abstract of a "prefatory stocktaking" that Norman Holland was kind enough to send me in a letter, 28 March 1973. I hope my version of his "stocktaking" does him justice.

Holland's concentration on audience response I see as part of the movement to dethrone the author, the director, and the actors of a play and to substitute the audience for all three. Such splendid off-Broadway plays like *Dionysius '69*, in which the audience directed the actions of each performance, took the liberty of changing the script as they saw fit, and went so far as to replace actors, made every performance a creative venture.

27. "Fictions, Phantasies and 'Reality': A Reevaluation," unpublished manuscript.
28. *Styles in Fictional Structure: The Art of Jane Austen, Charlotte Brontë and George Eliot* (Princeton: Princeton University Press, 1971), pp. 99, 169, 181. The Bibliographical Appendix is very helpful, and I think the evaluations of the many works mentioned throughout pages 199–208 are quite correct. However, Kroeber seems to wrestle too much when, for example, he uses terms like subconscious, unconscious, and preconscious in other than a specialized way and then tries to clarify them (p. 151).

Bibliography

AMERICAN PSYCHOLOGICAL
THEORIES OF ART

Arnheim, Rudolf. *Art and Visual Perception: A Psychology of the Creative Eye*. Berkeley: University of California Press, 1971.

———. *Toward a Psychology of Art*. Berkeley: University of California Press, 1972.

Balakian, Anna. *André Breton: Magus of Surrealism*. New York: Oxford University Press, 1971.

Chipp, Herschel B., ed. *Theories of Modern Art: A Source Book by Artists and Critics*. Berkeley: University of California Press, 1969.

Dewey, John. *Art as Experience*. New York: Capricorn Books, 1934.

Ehrenzweig, Anton. *The Hidden Order of Art*. Berkeley: University of California Press, 1971.

———. *The Psycho-Analysis of Artistic Vision and Hearing*. New York: George Braziller, 1965.

Kepes, Gyorgy, ed. *The Visual Arts Today*. Middletown, Conn.: Wesleyan University Press, 1966.

Klee, Paul. *Notebooks of Paul Klee*. Vol. 1, *The Thinking Eye*. New York: Wittenborn, 1961.

———. *Notebooks of Paul Klee*. Vol. 2, *The Nature of Nature*. New York: Wittenborn, 1972.

Kris, Ernst. *Psychoanalytic Explorations in Art*. New York: Schocken Books, 1952.

Protter, Eric, ed. *Painters on Painting*. New York: Grosset & Dunlap, 1971.

Stokes, Adrian. "Form in Art: A Psychoanalytic Interpretation." *Journal of Aesthetics and Art Criticism* 18 (1960): 193–203.

———. *Painting of the Inner World*. New York: Barnes & Noble, 1963.

Waelder, Robert. *Psychoanalytic Avenues to Art*. New York: International Universities Press, 1965.

Whittlesey, E.S. *Symbols and Legends in Western Art*. New York: Charles Scribner's Sons, 1972.

Wollheim, Richard. *Art and Its Objects: An Introduction to Aesthetics*. New York: Harper & Row, 1971.

LITERARY BIOGRAPHY AND PSYCHOLOGY

Bell, Quentin. *Virginia Woolf*. New York: Harcourt Brace Jovanovich, 1972.

Dembo, L.S., and Pondrom, Cyrena, eds. *The Contemporary Writer*. Madison: University of Wisconsin Press, 1972.

Edel, Leon. *Henry James*. 4 Vols. New York: Lippincott, 1969.

Meyer, Bernard C. *Joseph Conrad: A Psychoanalytic Biography*. Princeton: Princeton University Press, 1967.

BRITISH THEORY OF ART

Harding, Denys Wyatt. *Experience into Words*. London: Chatto, 1963.

———. *Social Psychology and Individual Values*. London: Hutchison, 1966.

Kermode, Frank. *Sense of an Ending: Studies in the Theory of Fiction*. New York: Oxford University Press, 1967.

Read, Herbert. *Art and Alienation: The Role of the Artist in Society*. New York: Viking, 1967.

———. *Icon and Idea: The Emotion of Art in the Development of Human Consciousness*. Cambridge: Harvard University Press, 1965.

Stokes, Adrian. *Invitation to Art*. New York: Barnes & Noble, 1966.

———. *Greek Culture and the Ego: A Psychoanalytic Survey of an Aspect of Greek Civilization and of Art*. New York: Barnes & Noble, 1958.

———. *Michelangelo: A Study in the Nature of Art*. New York: Barnes & Noble, 1955.

————. *Quattro Cento: A Different Conception of the Italian Renaissance.* New York: Schocken Books, 1968.

————. *Reflections on the Nude.* New York: Barnes & Noble, 1967.

————. *Stones of Rimini.* New York: Barnes & Noble, 1969.

————.*Three Essays on the Painting of Our Time.* New York: Barnes & Noble, 1961.

BRITISH LITERARY CRITICISM FROM PSYCHOLOGICAL PERSPECTIVES

Bateson, F.W. *Essays in Critical Dissent.* Totowa, N.J.: Rowman and Littlefield, 1972.

Bodkin, Maud. *Archetypal Patterns in Poetry.* London: Oxford University Press, 1934.

Empson, William. *Seven Types of Ambiguity.* 3rd ed. Toronto: Longmans, 1955.

————. *Some Versions of Pastoral.* Norfolk, Conn.: New Directions, 1950.

Kermode, Frank. *Puzzles and Epiphanies.* New York: Chilmark, 1963.

————. *Shakespeare, Spenser, Donne Renaissance Essays.* New York: Viking Press, 1971.

Lucas, Frank L. *Literature and Psychology.* Ann Arbor: University of Michigan Press, 1957.

Read, Herbert. *Wordsworth.* New York: Hillary, 1949.

EXISTENTIAL-HUMANISTIC PSYCHOLOGIES—LITERATURE

Clendenning, John. "Hemingway's Gods, Dead and Alive." *Texas Studies in Literature and Language* 3 (1962): 459–63.

May, Rollo. "The Meaning of the Oedipus Myth." In *Guilt, Man and Society.* Edited by Roger Smith. New York: Doubleday, 1971.

Sowder, William J. "Colonel Thomas Sutpen as Existentialist Hero." *American Literature* 33 (1962): 485–99.

Van Kaam, Adrian. "The Impact of Existential Phenomenology on the Psychological Literature of Western Europe." *Review of Existential Psychology and Psychiatry* 1 (1961): 63–83.

GENERAL–LITERATURE

Bloom, Edward, ed. *Shakespeare 1564–1964*. Providence: Brown University Press, 1964.

Leech, Clifford, and Margeson, J.M.R., eds. *Shakespeare 1971: Proceedings of the World Shakespeare Congress*. Toronto: University of Toronto Press, 1972.

Peckham, Morse. *Man's Race for Chaos: Biology, Behavior and the Arts*. Philadelphia: Chilton Book Company, 1965.

Pierce, Robert. *Shakespeare's History Plays: The Family and the State*. Columbus: Ohio State University Press, 1971.

Rabkin, Norman. *Shakespeare and the Common Understanding*. New York: Free Press, 1967.

Soellner, Rolf. *Shakespeare's Patterns of Self-Knowledge*. Columbus: Ohio State University Press, 1972.

Wallerstein, Ruth. *Studies in Seventeenth Century Poetic*. Madison: University of Wisconsin Press, 1950.

Wilson, Edmund: *Wound and the Bow: Seven Studies in Literature*. New York: Oxford University Press, 1947.

METACRITICISM–LITERATURE

Calderwood, James. *Shakespearean Metadrama*. Minneapolis: University of Minnesota Press, 1971.

Spitzer, Leo. "The 'Ode on a Grecian Urn' Or Content vs. Metagrammar." In *Essays on English and American Literature*. Princeton: Princeton University Press, 1962.

MYTH–THEORY

Brody, Alan. *The English Mummers and Their Plays*. Philadelphia: University of Pennslvania Press, 1970.

Burke, Kenneth. "The Thinking of the Body: Comments on the Imagery of Catharsis in Literature." *Psy. Rev.* 50 (1963): 375–418.

Campbell, Joseph. *Hero with a Thousand Faces*. New York: Pantheon Books, 1949.

Deutsch, Helen. *A Psychoanalytic Study of the Myth of Dionysus and Apollo*. New York: International Universities Press, 1969.

Evica, George Michael. "Sacred Consciousness and Literary Genre." Work in progress.

————. "Times Arrow and the World's Order." *ETC.* 20 (1963): 421–37.

Frye, Northrup. *Anatomy of Criticism.* Princeton: Princeton University Press, 1957.

Kirk, G.S. *Myth: Its Meaning and Function in Ancient and Other Cultures.* Berkeley: University of California Press, 1970.

Levi-Strauss, Claude. *The Raw and the Cooked: Introduction to a Science of Mythology.* New York: Harper & Row, 1964.

Neumann, Erich. *The Archetypal World of Henry Moore.* Bollingen Series. New York: Pantheon Books, 1959.

————. *Art and the Creative Unconscious.* Princeton: Princeton University Press, 1971.

————. *The Great Mother.* Princeton: Princeton University Press, 1972.

————. *The Origins and History of Consciousness.* Princeton: Princeton University Press, 1972.

Platt, Rhoda. "The Myth and Reality of the 'Matriarch': A Case Report in Family Therapy." *Psy. Rev.* 57 (1970): 203–23.

Slater, Philip. *The Glory of Hera.* Boston: Beacon Press, 1968.

MYTH–LITERATURE

Bazin, Nancy Topping. *Virginia Woolf and the Androgynous Vision.* New Brunswick: Rutgers University Press, 1972.

Brower, Reuben. *Hero and Saint: Shakespeare and the Graeco-Roman Heroic Tradition.* New York: Oxford University Press, 1971.

Eisenstein, Samuel. "Literature and Myth." *Coll. Engl.* 29 (1968): 369–73.

Fiedler, Leslie A. *The Stranger in Shakespeare.* New York: Stein and Day, 1972. (Reviewed by Frank Kermode in *New York Times Book Review,* 10 December 1972.)

Finestone, Oliver Evans Harry, ed. *The World of the Short Story: Archetypes in Action.* New York: Knopf, 1971.

Fletcher, Angus. *Allegory: The Theory of the Symbolic Mode.* Ithaca: Cornell University Press, 1964.

Foulke, Robert, and Smith, Paul, eds. *An Anatomy of Literature.* New York: Harcourt Brace Jovanovich, 1972.

Hassan, Ihab. *The Dismemberment of Orpheus*. New York: Oxford University Press, 1971.

Heidel, Alexander. *The Gilgamesh Epic and Old Testament Parallels*. Chicago: University of Chicago Press, 1946.

Heibrun, Carolyn. *Toward a Recognition of Androgyny*. New York: Knopf, 1972.

Herbert, Edward T. "Myth and Archetype in *Julius Caesar*." *Psy. Rev.*, 57 (1970): 303–14.

Jung, Carl G. *Collected Works of Jung*. Bollingen Series. Princeton: Princeton University Press.

Love, Jean. *Worlds in Consciousness: Mythopoetic Thought in the Novels of Virginia Woolf*. Berkeley: University of California Press, 1970.

Moseley, Edwin. *Pseudonyms of Christ in the Modern Novel: Motifs and Methods*. Pittsburgh: University of Pittsburgh Press, 1963.

Neumann, Erich. *Amor and Psyche: The Psychic Development of the Feminine*. Bollingen Series. Princeton: Princeton University Press, 1956.

Slochower, Harry. *Mythopoesis: Mythic Patterns in the Literary Classics*. Detroit: Wayne State University Press, 1970.

———. *Thomas Mann's Joseph Story: An Interpretation*. New York: Knopf, 1938.

———. *Three Ways of Modern Man*. London: Lawrence, 1937.

Slote, Bernice, ed. *Myth and Symbol*. Lincoln: University of Nebraska Press, 1963.

Vickerey, John B., ed. *Myth and Literature*. Lincoln: University of Nebraska Press, 1966.

Waldhorn, Arthur, and Waldhorn, Hilda, eds. *The Rite of Becoming: Stories and Studies of Adolescence*. Cleveland: World Publishing, 1966.

RELEVANT PERIODICALS

American Imago; Existential Psychiatry; Hartford Studies in Literature; Int. J. Psy.; Lit. and Psychol.; Modern Fiction Studies; Paunch; Philosophy and Phenomenological Research; Psy. For.; Psy. Rev.; Psy. Quar.; Review of Existential Psychology and Psychiatry.

PHENOMENOLOGICAL LITERARY CRITICISM

Anderson, Peter S. "Shakespeare's *Caesar*: The Language of Sacrifice." *Comparative Drama* 3 (1969): 3–25. Responded to by R.J. Kaufmann and Clifford J. Ronan in "Shakespeare's Julius Caesar: An Apollonian and Comparative Reading." *Comparative Drama* 4 (1970): 18–51.

Bachelard, Gaston. *The Poetics of Space*. Boston: Beacon Press, 1969.

Bleich, David. "Emotional Origins of Literary Meaning." *Coll. Engl.* 30 (1969): 30–40.

————. "More's *Utopia*: Confessional Modes." *American Imago* 28 (1971): 24–52.

————. "Psychological Bases of Learning from Literature." *Coll. Engl.* (1971): 32–46.

————. "The Determination of Literary Value." *Lit. and Psychol.* 17 (1967): 19–30.

Brodtkorb, Paul, Jr. *Ishmael's White World: A Phenomenological Reading of Moby Dick*. New Haven: Yale University Press, 1965.

Calhoun, Richard James. "Existentialism, Phenomenology, and Literary Criticism." *South Atlantic Bulletin* 28 (1963): 4–8.

Charney, Maurice. *How to Read Shakespeare*. New York: McGraw-Hill, 1971.

Elliott, Susan. "Fantasy Beneath Play: Uncovering Affective Responses to Harold Pinter's *The Birthday Party*, *The Caretaker*, and *The Homecoming*." Work in progress.

Hartman, Geoffrey. *Beyond Formalism*. New Haven: Yale University Press, 1970.

————. *Unmediated Vision*. New Haven: Yale University Press, 1954.

————. *Wordsworth's Poetry 1787–1814*. New Haven: Yale University Press, 1972.

Leiter, Louis. "A Problem in Analysis: Franz Kafka's *A Country Doctor*." *Journal of Aesthetics and Art Criticism* 16 (1958): 337–47.

McEwen, Fred B. "Phenomenology in Literary Criticism." *Lock Haven Review* 10 (1968): 47–55.

Pondrom, Cyrena Norman. "Kafka and Phenomenology: Josef K's Search for Information." *Wisconsin Studies in Contemporary Literature* 8 (1967): 78–95.

Ricoeur, Paul. *The Symbolism of Evil*. Boston: Beacon Press, 1967.

Stockholder, Katherine. "Fiction, Phantasies and 'Reality': A Reevaluation." Unpublished manuscript.

Warner, John. "The Epistemological Quest in Pinter's *The Homecoming.*" *Contemporary Literature* 11 (1970): 340–43.

PSYCHOANALYSIS–THEORY

Akmakjian, Hiag. "Psychoanalysis and the Future of Literary Criticism." *Psychoanalysis and the Psychoanalytic Review* 49 (1962): 3–28.

Alexander, Franz. *Psychosomatic Medicine.* New York: Norton, 1950.

Allen, Gay W. *Encyclopaedia Britannica.* "Metaphor."

Anderson, C.C. "The Latest Metaphor on Psychology." *The Dalhousie Review* 38 (1958): 176–87.

——. "The Psychology of Metaphor." *Journal of Genetic Psychology* 105 (1964): 53–73.

Askew, Melvin. "Psychoanalysis and Literary Criticism." *Psy. Rev.* 51 (1964): 43–50.

Baym, Max I. "Brief Statement Concerning the Present State of the Study of Metaphor." *Langue et Litterature* (1961): 375–76.

Bush, Marshall. "The Problem of Form in the Psychoanalytic Theory of Art." *Psy. Rev.* 54 (1967): 5–35.

Deutsch, Helen. *Neuroses and Character Types.* New York: International Universities Press, 1965.

Eidelberg, Ludwig, ed. *Encyclopedia of Psychoanalysis.* New York: Free Press, 1968.

Fenichel, Otto. *The Psychoanalytic Theory of Neurosis.* New York: Norton, 1945.

Selected Papers of Sandor Ferenczi. Vol. 1. New York: Basic Books, 1950.

Flugel, J.C. *The Psycho-Analytic Study of the Family.* London: Hogarth, 1957.

Fraiberg, Louis. *Psychoanalysis and American Literary Criticism.* Detroit: Wayne State University Press, 1960.

Freeman, Thomas. *A Psychoanalytic Study of the Psychoses.* New York: International Universities Press, 1973.

Freud, Sigmund. *Complete Psychological Works.* 24 Vols. Standard Edition. London: Hogarth, 1951.

Grinstein, Alexander. *The Index of Psychoanalytic Writings.* New York: International Universities Press, 1956–66.

Holland, Norman N. "Freud and the Poet's Eye." *Lit. and Psychol.* 11 (1961): 36–45.

Kaplan, Donald. "Classical Psychoanalysis: Policies, Values, and the Future." *Psy. Rev.* 53 (1966): 99–111.

Levenson, Edgar. "The Fallacy of Understanding." *Psychotherapy and Social Science Review.* 30 October 1972, pp. 2–4.

Mack, John E. *Nightmares and Human Conflict.* Boston: Little, Brown, 1970.

Mitscherlich, Alexander. *Society Without the Father.* New York: Harcourt, Brace & World, 1963.

Moses, Paul J. *The Voice of Neurosis.* New York: Guine & Stratton, 1954.

Muncie, Wendell. "The Psychopathology of Metaphor." *Archives of Neurology and Psychiatry* 37 (1937): 796–804.

Peterfreund, Emanuel, in collaboration with Jacob T. Schwartz. *Information, Systems, and Psychoanalysis: An Evolutionary Biological Approach to Psychoanalytic Theory.* New York: International Universities Press, 1971.

Robertiello, Richard C. "A More Positive View of Perversions." *Psy. Rev.* 58 (1971): 467–71.

Schoenfeld, C.G. "Three Fallacious Attacks upon Psychoanalysis." *Psychoanalysis and Psychoanalytic Review* 49 (1962): 35–37.

PSYCHOANALYSIS–LITERATURE

Edel, Leon. *The Modern Psychological Novel.* New York: Grosset & Dunlap, 1964.

Faber, M.D. "Suicide and the 'Ajax' of Sophocles." *Psy. Rev.* 54 (1967): 49–60.

————. *Suicide and Greek Tragedy.* New York: Sphinx Press, 1970.

Grinstein, Alexander. *On Sigmund Freud's Dreams.* Detroit: Wayne State University Press, 1968.

Hesse, Hermann. "Artist and Psychoanalysis." *Psy. Rev.* 50 (1963): 5–10, 15–16.

Jones, Ernst. *Hamlet and Oedipus.* New York: Mentor, 1954.

Kiell, Norman, ed. *Psychoanalysis, Psychology and Literature.* Madison: University of Wisconsin Press, 1963.

Lesser, Simon O. *Fiction and the Unconscious.* New York: Random House, 1957.

Malin, Irving, ed. *Psychoanalysis and American Fiction*. New York: Dutton, 1965.

Manheim, Leonard, and Manheim, Eleanor, eds. *Hidden Patterns*. New York: Macmillan, 1966.

Rabkin, Leslie, ed. *Psychopathology and Literature*. San Francisco: Chandler, 1966.

Rogers, Robert. *A Psychoanalytic Study of the Double in Literature*. Detroit: Wayne State University Press, 1970.

Schwartz, Murray. "Between Fantasy and Imagination: A Psychological Exploration of *Cymbeline*." In *Psychoanalysis and Literary Process*. Edited by Frederick Chews. Cambridge, Mass.: Winthrop Publishers, 1970.

Tiefenbrun, Ruth. *Moment of Torment: An Interpretation of Franz Kafka's Short Stories*. Carbondale: Southern Illinois University Press, 1973.

Withim, Philip. "The Psychodynamics of Literature." *Psy. Rev.* 56 (1969–70): 565–85.

PSYCHOANALYSIS–NEO-FREUDIAN–THEORY

Efron, Arthur. "Philosophy, Criticism, and the Body." *Paunch*. Nos. 36 and 37 (1973): 72–162.

Erikson, Erik H. *Childhood and Society*. 2nd ed. New York: Norton, 1963.

Fairbairn, W.R.D. *An Object-Relations Theory of the Personality*. New York: Basic Books, 1954.

Fraiberg, Louis. "New Views of Art and the Creative Process in Psychoanalytic Ego Psychology." *Lit. and Psychol.* 11 (1961): 45–55.

Gelernt, Jules. Review of *The Dynamics of Literary Response*, in *Lit. and Psychol.* 20 (1970): 129–34.

Goldstein, Melvin. "Identity Crises in a Midsummer's Nightmare: Comedy as Terror in Disguise." *Psy. Rev.* 60, no. 2 (1973):169–204.

Green, Bernard A. "The Therapeutic Stance: An Eriksonian Approach to Diagnosis and Technique." *Psy. Rev.* 59 (1972): 73–88.

Greenacre, Phyllis. *Emotional Growth: Psychoanalytic Studies of the Gifted and a Variety of Other Individuals*. 2 Vols. New York: International Universities Press, 1971.

Holland, Norman N. *The Dynamics of Literary Response*. New York: Oxford University Press, 1968.

Jules Nydes Memorial Conference: Mothering and Psychoanalytic Concepts. 6 essays. *Psy. Rev.* 60 (1973): 1–70.

Lacan, Jacques. *The Language of the Self: The Function of Language in Psychoanalysis.* Translated with notes and commentary by Anthony Wilden. Baltimore: The Johns Hopkins University Press, 1968.

Manheim, Leonard. "Newer Dimensions in Psychoanalytic Criticism." *Peabody Journal of Education.* October 1972, pp. 29–34.

Marcuse, Herbert. *Eros and Civilization.* Boston: Beacon Press, 1955.

McDevitt, John, and Settlage, Calvin, eds. *Separation—Individuation.* New York: International Universities Press, 1971.

Munroe, Ruth L. *Schools of Psychoanalytic Thought.* New York: Holt, Rinehart and Winston, 1967.

Obler, Paul C. "Psychology and Literary Criticism: A Summary and Critique." *Lit. and Psychol.* 8 (1958): 50–59.

Peterfreund, Emanuel, in collaboration with Jacob T. Schwartz. *Information, Systems, and Psychoanalysis.* New York: International Universities Press, 1971.

Rapoport, David, ed. *Organization and Pathology of Thought.* New York: Columbia University Press, 1965.

Rieff, Philip. *Freud: The Mind of the Moralist.* New York: Doubleday, 1961.

———. *Triumph of the Therapeutic: Uses of Faith After Freud.* New York: Harper & Row, 1968.

Shapiro, David. *Neurotic Styles.* New York: Basic Books, 1965.

Spiegel, John P. "Campus Disorders: A Transactional Approach." *Psy. Rev.* 57 (1970): 472–504.

Spranger, Otto. "Some Remarks on Erik H. Erikson's 'Reality and Actuality.'" *Psy. Rev.* 54 (1967): 77–82.

Wilden, Anthony. "Libido as Language." *Psychology Today.* May 1972.

Winnicott, D.W. *The Maturational Processes and the Facilitating Environment.* New York: International Universities Press, 1965.

———. "Therapeutic Consultations in Child Psychiatry." *Psychotherapy and Social Science Review.* 26 November 1971, pp. 3–5.

PSYCHOANALYSIS—NEO-FREUDIAN—LITERATURE

Crews, Frederick, ed. *Psychoanalysis and Literary Process.* Cambridge, Mass.: Winthrop Publishers, 1970.

Faber, M.D. *The Design Within: Psychoanalytic Approaches to Shakespeare.* New York: Science House, 1970.

Handke, Peter. *Kasper and Other Plays*. Translated by Michael Roloff. New York: Farrar, Straus and Giroux, 1969.

Holland, Norman N. "Prose and Minds: A Psychoanalytic Approach to Non-Fiction." In *The Art of Victorian Prose*. Edited by George Levine and William Madden. New York: Oxford University Press, 1968.

Huss, Roy. "Adler, Oedipus and the Tyranny of Weakness." *Psy. Rev.* 60 (1973): 277–96.

Kris, Ernst. *Psychoanalytic Explorations in Art*. New York: International Universities Press, 1952.

Marcus, Ned N. "Prometheus Reconsidered: Sublimation and Vicissitudes of the Symbolic Ego." *Psy. Rev.* 54 (1967): 83–106.

Neumarkt, Paul. "Chamisso's Peter Schlemihl." *Lit. and Psychol.* 17 (1967): 120–28.

Richter, Harvena. *Virginia Woolf: The Inward Voyage*. Princeton: Princeton University Press, 1970.

Sandford, Beryl. "Cinderella." *Psy. For.* 2 (Summer 1972): 127–44.

Schlesinger, Kurt. "Thoughts on *King Lear* and the Current Generation Gap." *Psy. For.* 4 (1972): 63–99.

PSYCHOANALYSIS–NEW DIMENSIONS IN LITERATURE

Hartford Studies in Literature. Three issues in one volume. Festschrift in honor of Leonard Manheim, 1973: Wayne Burns, "In Death They Were Not Divided: The Moral Magnificence of Unmoral Passion in *Wuthering Heights*"; Helen Corsa, " 'The Cross-Grainedness of Men': The Rev. Josiah Crawley—Trollope's Study of a Paranoid Personality"; Louis Fraiberg, "Poe's Intimations of Mortality"; Michael Steig, "Psychological Realism and Fantasy in Jane Austen: *Emma* and *Mansfield Park*."

Rabkin, Leslie Y., ed. *Psychopathology and Literature*. San Francisco: Chandler, 1966.

Stone, Alan, and Stone, Sue Smart, eds. *The Abnormal Personality Through Literature*. Englewood Cliffs, N.J.: Prentice-Hall, 1966.

PSYCHOANALYSIS–NEW DIMENSIONS OF THEORY

"All Men Are Bisexual." *Forum* 1 (1972): 38–41.

Halleck, Seymour. "A Psychiatrist Looks At the Use of Abnormality." *Reflections* 7 (1972): 65–74.

Hartford Studies in Literature. Three issues in one volume. Festschrift in honor of Leonard Manheim, 1973: M.D. Faber, "Analytic Prolegomena to the Study of Western Tragedy"; Robert Rogers, "A Gathering of Roses—An Essay on the Limits of Context"; William Wasserstrom, "Abandoned in Providence."

Price, Richard H. *Abnormal Behavior.* New York: Holt, Rinehart and Winston, 1972.

Szasz, Thomas S. *The Myth of Mental Illness.* New York: Dell, 1961.

PSYCHOANALYSIS—PSYCHOHISTORY—THEORY

Brody, Benjamin. "The Conventional Elite." *Psychotherapy and Social Science Review.* 17 September 1971, pp. 22–25.

Coles, Robert. "Shrinking History—Part One." *The New York Review of Books.* 22 February, 1973.

Dowling, Joseph A. "Psychoanalysis and History." *Psy. Rev.* 59 (1972): 433–50.

Hargrove, Erwin C. *Presidential Leadership: Personality and Political Style.* London: Macmillan, 1966.

Hofling, Charles K. Book review of "The Psychoanalytic Interpretation of History." *Psy. Rev.* 59 (1972): 149–50.

Langer, William J. "The Next Assignment." In *Psychoanalysis and History.* Edited by Bruce Mazlish. New York: Grosset & Dunlap, 1971.

"Living History in Psychoanalysis." *Science News.* 16 December 1972, pp. 389–90.

Roland, Alan. "Psychoanalysis and History: A Quest for Integration." *Psy. Rev.* 58 (1971–72): 631–40. (Review of Erik Erikson's *Gandhi's Truth.*)

Wolman, Benjamin B. *The Psychoanalytic Interpretation of History.* New York: Basic Books, 1971.

PSYCHOANALYSIS—PSYCHOHISTORY—LITERATURE

Brown, Norman O. *Life Against Death: The Psychoanalytic Meaning in History.* Middletown, Conn.: Wesleyan University Press, 1959.

Erikson, Erik. *Gandhi's Truth.* New York: Norton, 1969.

———. *Young Man Luther.* New York: Norton, 1958.

Feldman, Bronson. "The Imperial Dreams of Disraeli." *Psy. Rev.* 53 (1966–67): 609–41.

Hassan, Ihab. *Radical Innocence: Studies in the Contemporary American Novel.* New York: Harper & Row, 1961.

Kaplan, Donald. "Sugar and Spice Revisited." *Psychotherapy and Social Science Review.* 28 April 1971. (Review of Kate Millet's *Sexual Politics.*)

Nicolson, Marjorie, and G.S. Rousseau. *"This Long Disease, My Life": Alexander Pope and the Sciences.* Princeton: Princeton University Press, 1969.

PSYCHOANALYSIS–PROJECTIVE TESTS–LITERATURE

Leedy, Jack J. *Poetry Therapy.* Philadelphia: Lippincott, 1969.

SOCIAL PSYCHOLOGY AND LITERARY CRITICISM

Asch, Solomon. *Social Psychology.* Englewood Cliffs, N.J.: Prentice-Hall, 1952.

Fernandez, R., ed. *Social Psychology Through Literature.* New York: Wiley, 1972.

Friedenberg, Edgar A. *The Vanishing Adolescent.* Boston: Beacon Press, 1959.

———. *Art of Loving: An Enquiry into the Nature of Love.* New York: Harper & Row, 1956.

Fromm, Erich. *The Crisis of Psychoanalysis.* Greenwich, Conn.: Fawcett, 1970.

———. *Man for Himself: An Inquiry into the Psychology of Ethics.* New York: Holt, Rinehart and Winston, 1947.

———. *Sane Society.* New York: Holt, Rinehart and Winston, 1955.

Grana, Cesar. *Fact and Symbol: Essays in the Sociology of Art and Literature.* New York: Oxford University Press, 1971.

"Roles in Society and in Psychotherapy: Three Essays." *Psy. Rev.* 58 (1971–72): 497–552.

Wilson, Edmund. *To the Finland Station: A Study in the Writing and Acting of History.* New York: Doubleday, 1953.

STRUCTURALISM—THEORY

Akoun, Andre, et al. "The Father of Structural Anthropology Takes a Misanthropic View of Lawless Humanism." *Psychology Today*, May 1972.

Arlow, J., and Brenner, C. *Psychoanalytic Concepts and the Structural Theory*. New York: International Universities Press, 1964.

Barnett, Joseph. "A Structural Analysis of Theories in Psychoanalysis." *Psy. Rev.* 53 (1966): 85–98.

Bush, Marshall. "The Problem of Form in the Psychoanalytic Theory of Art." *Psy. Rev.* 54 (1967): 5–35.

Friedman, Lawrence. Special book review. "Structure and Psychotherapy. *Psy. Rev.* 59 (1972–73): 539–48. (A review of Jean Piaget's *Structuralism*.)

Lawall, Sarah. *The Critics of Consciousness: Existential Structures of Literature*. Cambridge: Harvard University Press, 1968.

Levenson, Edgar A. "The Fallacy of Understanding." *Psychotherapy and Social Science Review*. 30 October 1972, pp. 2–5.

Levi-Strauss, Claude. *Structural Anthropology*. New York: Basic Books, 1963.

———. *Tristes Tropiques*. Translated by John Russell. (English title: *A World on the Wane*.) New York: Criterion, 1962.

Piaget, Jean. *Structuralism*. Translated and edited by Chaninah Maschler. New York: Harper & Row, 1971.

Schechner, Richard. "Incest and Culture: A Reflection on Claude Levi-Strauss." *Psy. Rev.* 58 (1971–72): 563–72.

STRUCTURALISM—LITERATURE

Anderson, Peter S. "Shakespeare's *Caesar*: The Language of Sacrifice." *Comparative Drama* 3 (1969): 3–26.

———. "The Fragile World of Lear." *Comparative Drama* 5 (1971–72): 269–82.

Bleich, David. "Artistic Form as Defensive Adaptation: Henry James and 'The Golden Bowl.'" *Psy. Rev.* 58 (1972): 223–44.

Miller, J. Hillis. *Charles Dickens: The World of His Novels*. Indianapolis: Indiana University Press, 1969.

LIST OF CONTRIBUTORS

ARNHEIM, RUDOLF

Born: July 15, 1904, in Berlin, Germany.

Education: University of Berlin, Ph.D. in Psychology, 1928.

Present Position: Professor of the Psychology of Art, Department of Visual and Environmental Studies, Harvard University.

Books: *Radio: An Art of Sound.* London, 1936; *Art and Visual Perception.* Berkeley, 1954; *Film as Art.* Berkeley, 1957; *The Genesis of a Painting: Picasso's Guernica.* Berkeley, 1962; *Towards a Psychology of Art.* Berkeley, 1966; *Visual Thinking.* Berkeley, 1969; *Entropy and Art.* Berkeley, 1971.

Editor: 1933–1938, Associate Editor of Publications, International Institute for Educational Film (League of Nations), Rome, Italy.

BAIRD, JAMES

Born: November 2, 1910, in Jellico, Tennessee.

Education: University of Tennessee, B.A., 1931, M.A., 1935. Columbia, M.A., 1945. Yale, M.A., 1942, Ph.D., 1947.

Present Position: Professor of English at the Connecticut College.

Books: *Ishmael: A Study of the Symbolic Mode in Primitivism.* Baltimore, 1956; *The Dome and the Rock: Structure in the Poetry of Wallace Stevens.* Baltimore, 1968.

Editor: Associate Editor of *American Literary Masters.* New York, 1965.

CLANCIER, ANNE

Education: Doctor of Medicine in Neuro-Psychiatry.

Present Positions: Medical consultant, Institute Claparede a Neuilly; Assistant lecturer at the Faculty of Arts, Sciences, and Humanities of Paris X—Nanterre.

Books: *Parents Without Fault*, with Roland Jaccard. Paris, 1972; *Psychoanalysis and Literary Criticism*. Toulouse, 1973.

DETTMERING, PETER
Born: May 25, 1933, in Oldenburg/O., Germany.
Education: Hamburg, medicine. Universitätsnervenklinik Tübingen, 1962–1968.
Present Positions: Psychiatrist in West Berlin; Lecturer at the Freie Universität Berlin.
Book: *Dichtung und Psychoanalyse*. München, 1969.

DOYLE, CHARLOTTE LACKNER
Born: 1937, in Vienna, Austria.
Education: Temple University, B.A. University of Michigan, M.A., 1961, Ph.D., 1965.
Present Position: Professor of Psychology, Sarah Lawrence College, Bronxville, New York.
Books: Co-author with W.J. McKeachie, *Psychology*, 1966; *Psychology: The Short Course*, 1972; *Psicologia*, 1973.

GOLDSTEIN, MELVIN
Born: May 31, 1926, in New York City, New York.
Education: Long Island University, B.A., 1949. Columbia University, M.A., 1950. University of Wisconsin, Ph.D., 1958.
Present Positions: Professor of English, University of Hartford; Psychotherapist and psychological examiner, Community Psychiatry Clinic, Middletown, Connecticut.
Editor: Associate Editor, *Hartford Studies in Literature: An Interdisciplinary Journal*, 1968–; *Hartford Studies in Literature: Festschrift in Honor of Leonard Manheim: Metapsychological Literary Criticism, Its Theories and Literature*, 1973.

HERNADI, PAUL
Born: November 9, 1936, in Budapest, Hungary.
Education: University of Vienna, Ph.D., 1963. Yale University, Ph.D., 1967.

Present Position: Associate Professor of German and Comparative Literature at the University of Rochester.

Book: *Beyond Genre: New Directions in Literary Classification.* Ithaca and London, 1972.

JOHNSON, E. BOND, III

Born: May 19, 1940, in Birmingham, Alabama.

Education: Washington and Lee University, B.A., 1962. University of California, Berkeley, M.A., 1966, Ph.D., 1971.

Present Position: Assistant Professor of Germanic Languages and Comparative Literature at University of California, Los Angeles.

LERNER, LAURENCE

Born: 1925.

Education: Capetown, B.A., 1944, M.A., 1945. Cambridge, B.A., 1949.

Present Position: Professor of English at the University of Sussex.

Books: *English Literature: An Introduction for Students Abroad.* London, 1954; *The Englishmen.* London, 1959; *Domestic Interior* (poems). London, 1959; *The Truest Poetry.* London, 1960; *The Directions of Memory.* London, 1963; *The Truthtellers: Jane Austen, George Eliot, D.H. Lawrence.* New York, 1967; *A Free Man: A Novel.* London, 1968; *Selves* (poems). London, 1969; *The Uses of Nostalgia; Studies in Pastoral Poetry.* New York, 1972.

Editor: With John Holmstrom, *George Eliot and her Readers. A Selection of Contemporary Reviews.* New York, 1966; *Shakespeare's Comedies: An Anthology of Modern Criticism.* Harmondsworth, 1967; with John Holmstrom, *Thomas Hardy and his Readers. A Selection of Contemporary Reviews.* New York, 1968.

LESSER, SIMON O.

Born: April 16, 1908, in Henderson, Kentucky.

Education: B.A. University of Chicago. Graduate work at the University of Chicago, Kenyon School of English, Columbia University, Chicago Psychoanalytic Institute, Washington School of Psychiatry, New York Psychoanalytic Institute.

Present Position: Professor of English at the University of Massachusetts.

Books: Co-author with George A. Works, *Rural America Today—Its Schools and Community Life.* Chicago, 1942; *Fiction and the Unconscious.* Boston, 1957, New York, 1962.

PARIS, JEAN

Born: 1921, in Paris, France.

Education: Sorbonne, Licence-ès-Lettres. Diplome d'Etudes Supérieur de Philosphie, 1948. University of Besançon, Doctorat d'Etat, 1971.

Present Positions: Head of the Department of Documentation in Aesthetics and Arts at the National Scientific Research Center in Paris; Professor at the Johns Hopkins University.

Books: *Hamlet*. Paris, 1953; *Shakespeare*. Paris, 1954, New York, 1960; *Goethe Dramaturge*. Paris, 1956; *James Joyce*. Paris, 1956; *Anthologie de la Poésie Nouvelle*. Monaco, 1956; *L'Espace et le Regard*. Paris, 1965; *Rabelais au Futur*. Paris, 1970; *Hamlet et Panurge*. Paris, 1971; *Miroirs Sommeil Soleil Espaces*. Paris, 1973.

Translator: Kentfield, Calvin. *Le Voyage de l'Alchimiste*, Paris, 1959; Behan, Brendan. *Un Otage*. Paris, 1962; O'Neill, Eugene. *Le Marchand de Glace Est Passé*. Paris, 1965.

PECKHAM, MORSE

Born: August 17, 1914, in Yonkers, New York.

Education: University of Rochester, B.A. Princeton, Ph.D.

Present Position: Distinguished Professor of English and Comparative Literature at the University of South Carolina.

Books: *Humanistic Education for Business Executives*. Philadelphia, 1960; co-author with Seymour Chatman. *Word, Meaning, Poem*. New York, 1961; *Beyond the Tragic Vision*. New York, 1962; *Man's Rage for Chaos*. Philadelphia, 1965; *Art and Pornography*. New York, 1969; *Victorian Revolutionaries*. New York, 1970; *The Triumph of Romanticism*. Columbia, South Carolina, 1970.

Editor: *Charles Darwin's "The Origin of Species," A Variorum Text*. Philadelphia, 1959; *Romanticism, The Culture of the 19th Century*. New York, 1965; *Swinburne's Poems and Ballads and Atalanta in Calydon*. Indianapolis, 1970. Editorial Board, Ohio Edition of the *Complete Works of Robert Browning*. Editor of *Paracelsus, Pippa Passes, The Return of the Druses, Luria, Men and Women*.

SEARS, ROBERT R.

Born: August 31, 1908, in Palo Alto, California.

Education: Stanford, A.B., 1929. Yale, Ph.D., 1932. Harvard, M.A. (hon.), 1950.

Present Position: Professor of Psychology, David Starr Jordan Professor of Social Sciences in Psychology, Stanford University.

Books: *Frustration and Aggression* (with others). New Haven, Conn., 1939; *Survey of Objective Studies of Psychoanalytic Concepts*. Social Science Research Council, 1943, Bulletin 51; *Patterns of Child Rearing* (with others), Evanston, Illinois, 1957; *Identification and Child Rearing* (with others), Palo Alto, California, 1965.

Editor: *Child Research Monographs*, State University of Iowa, 1942–45; *Monographs of the Society for Research in Child Development*, 1970–75; Consulting Editor at various times for *Genetic Psychology Monographs, Contemporary Psychology, Psychologia, British Journal of Clinical and Social Psychology*.

SLOCHOWER, HARRY

Born: 1900, in Austria.

Education: Columbia University, Ph.D., 1928.

Present Position: Faculty, The New School.

Books: *Richard Dehmel. Der Mensch und der Denker*. Dresden, 1928; *Three Ways of Modern Man*. New York, 1937; *Thomas Mann's Joseph Story. An Interpretation*. New York, 1938; *No Voice is Wholly Lost. Writers and Thinkers in War and Peace*. New York and London, 1945; *Mythopoesis. Mythic Patterns in the Literary Classics*. Detroit, 1970.

Editor: *American Imago*.

STAROBINSKI, JEAN

Born: November 17, 1920, in Geneva, Switzerland.

Education: Geneva, Licencié ès lettres classiques, 1942, Diplôme fédéral de médecine, 1951, Doctorat ès lettres, 1958. Lausanne, Doctorat en médecine, 1960.

Present Position: Professor at the University of Geneva.

Books: *Montesquieu*. Paris, 1953; *J.J. Rousseau: la transparence et l'obstacle*. Paris, 1957, 1971; *L'oeil vivant*. Paris, 1961; *L'invention de la liberté*. Geneva, 1964; *La relation critique*. Paris, 1970; *Portrait de l'artiste en Saltimbaugre*. Geneva, 1970; *Les mots son les mots*. Paris, 1971.

Translator: Kafka, Franz. *La colonie penitentiaire*. Fribourg and Paris, 1965.

INDEX OF NAMES